AF519676

STATE, LABOUR AND DEVELOPMENT
AN INDIAN PERSPECTIVE

STATE, LABOUR AND DEVELOPMENT

AN INDIAN PERSPECTIVE

Editors
K. K. BAGCHI
N. GOPE

ABHIJEET PUBLICATIONS
DELHI 110 094

ABHIJEET PUBLICATIONS
2/46 Tukhmeerpur Extension
Delhi 110094
Phones: 011-22960492, 65698474
e-mail: abhijeetpublication@gmail.com
abhijeet_singh1@indiatimes.com

STATE, LABOUR AND DEVELOPMENT: AN INDIAN PERSPECTIVE

First Published **2017**

Second Published 2019

ISBN 978-81-89886-36-3

Rs. 1050/-

[All rights reserved. No part of this publication may be reproduced, copied, stored in a retrieval system, transmitted or used in any form or by any means, whether electronic, mechanical, photocopying, recording or otherwise, without the prior permission from the author or publisher, except for brief quotations in critical articles or reviews.]

PRINTED IN INDIA

Published by J.K. Singh fo Abhijeet Publications, Delhi 110094, Lasertypeset by Gaurav Graphics, Delhi and Printed as Himanshu Printers, Delhi.

PREFACE & ACKNOWLEDGEMENTS

The present volume is a collection of papers contributed by dedicated researchers in the field of labour, market and economics. First and foremost we express our heartfelt gratitude to all of them for their unhesitating response to make their valuable contribution for the book. We, however, apologize for the inadvertent little delay in editing and publication of the book. We also acknowledge with thanks the permission given by Dr. R. P. Mamgain, Managing Editor of the *Indian Journal of Labour Economics* for reproducing the paper by Professor Errol D'Souza published in its Volume, 48, No. 4, 2005. While editing the book we have received a lot of encouragement from the contributors, well-wishers as well as from the publisher. We are grateful to all of them. We are especially thankful to Mr. Jitendra Kumar Singh, the efficient steward of Abhijeet Publications and his staff at the press for bringing out this volume in time. Last but not the least, we express out gratitude to our parents, children and wives for providing us with their ungrudging moral support to undertake and complete the work.

K.K. Bagchi

N. Gope

PREFACE & ACKNOWLEDGEMENTS

The present volume is a collection of papers contributed by dedicated researchers in the field of labour market and economics. First and foremost we express our heartfelt gratitude to all of them for their unhesitating response to make their valuable contribution for the book. We, however, apologize for the inadvertent little delay in editing and publication of the book. We also acknowledge with thanks the permission given by Dr. R. K. Mamgain, Managing Editor of the *Indian Journal of Labour Economics* for reproducing the paper by Professor Errol D'Souza published in its Volume 48, No. 4, 2005. While editing the book we have received a lot of encouragement from the contributions, well-wishers as well as from the publisher. We are grateful to all of them. We are especially thankful to Mr. Jitendra Kumar Singh, the efficient steward of Abhijeet Publications and his staff at the press for bringing out this volume in time. Last but not the least, we express our gratitude to our parents, children and wives for providing us with their unfaltering moral support to undertake and complete the work.

K. K. Bagchi
N. Gope

CONTENTS

INTRODUCTION

K.K. Bagchi & N. Gope

Labour is an indispensable factor of production. But the degree of indispensability varies from one type of production to another. Role and remuneration of labour will therefore depend upon labour content in production and the possibility of substitution of labour with other factors. As is obvious, in a production process with considerably high labour content or when at the extreme 'labour is itself the end product', labour's role and remuneration will be high compared to a situation where labour is 'primarily an instrument, an incidental requisite for the attainment of the final product' (Baumol, 1967). Thus the degree of labour content in production is one of the determinants of remuneration of labour.

Another determinant of remuneration of labour is its productivity. With rising productivity wages of labour increase either proportionately or less than that. Productivity differentials cause wage differentials. One of the determinants of productivity is the incentive provided to the labour. There is a two-way causal relationship between incentive and productivity. Incentives actuate labour to improve productivity and improved productivity encourages employers to provide more incentives to labour. Incentives to labour may be provided not only in the form of better wages but also in the form of improved work environment, better housing, security of employment and different forms of social security.

But what is at stake in the current globalised scenario of

the labour market is the security of employment. Now 'flexibility' is the buzzword for the labour market. Employers often adopt 'hire and fire' policy. Employees are encouraged to make 'golden handshake'. Government, like private employers, is also resorting to the policy of 'Voluntary Retirement Scheme (VRS)' in order to trim down the size of personnel to lessen the staff burden to the minimum level possible. Casualisation and feminisation of workforce is the order of the day. Contraction of employment in the organized sector is rampant and the expanding size of the informal/ unorganised sector is the harsh reality. There is almost complete absence of any social security available to workers in the unorganised sector. However, the Indian Government is going to introduce some modicum of social security for workers engaged in the unorganized sector. The condition of agricultural labourers is also not improving much due to agrarian distress and several other reasons (Bagchi and Gope, 2005; Bagchi, 2006; Bagchi and Ghosh, 2007).

Right to strike is almost at the point of extinction as is evident from recent spell of events (ISLE, IHD, 2004). Other rights and privileges are also gradually denied to the labour. In the present context of liberalization, privatization and globalisation, labour as a factor of production appears to be in great difficulty as the state is gradually withdrawing itself in providing relief to the labourers. Labour is now largely at the mercy of the employers. Under the situation, informed researchers apprehend that perhaps there is going to be an end to labour movement (Hassan, 2000; Yates, 2001; Ghosh, 2003; Reddy, 2003; Varman and Chakrabarti, 2003; Gapasin, Fernando E. and Michael D. Yates, 2005).

The above perspective of the world of work in India has been beautifully narrated by eminent scholars working in the area (Mishra, 2001; Chandrasekhar and Ghosh, 2002; Patnaik, 2003; Bagchi, 2004; Roychoudhuri, 2004;). It has been rightly held that the forces unleashed by technology, liberalization and globalisation have adversely affected the rights of workers and their bargaining power vis-à-vis employers. On the other hand, there is ascendancy of managerial rights. It is said that while the trade unions have weakened, the militancy of employers is on the rise (Sharma, 1997; Ratnam, 2001). The more important reasons are said to be confinement of unionization mainly to the organized sector, shrinking of the employment in the organised sector, privatization, downsizing and resort to contingent and flexible categories of workers etc. among others (Sharma, 2005). The weakening of the worker's bargaining power and rise in the militancy of employers are also captured by the significant increase in the incidence of lockouts and a decline in the incidence of strikes. It is also evidenced by the fact that the average duration of lockouts is considerably higher, roughly 2.5 times than those of strikes (Datt, 2003).

The position of the Indian State concerning rights of labour in the era of economic reforms has been aptly described by Sharma. According to him: 'The shift in ideology of the state from welfarism to the neo-liberal values of market that call for labour flexibility is pushing such reforms through legislative, executive and judicial action. Unable to initiate legislative action because of the constraint of parliamentary democracy, the state has resorted to executive action and judicial activism for reinterpreting legal rights of labour in the light of the prevalent values. The Parliament has so far not been able to liberalise labour legislation to a significant extent despite the recommendations of the Second National Commission on Labour' (Sharma, 2005).

According to Jha the world of labour has been affected, in a variety of adverse ways during the period of globalisation (Jha, 2005). He says that in the current phase of the ascendancy of neo-liberal policy regime, the state seems determined to throw out of the window whatever progressive labour laws the country has had, so as to finally legitimize their violations and non-enforcement; the ultimate objective is none else but to disarm the working class movement completely. He adds that, the increase in the hostility of the organs of the state towards labour is intimately and organically linked to the logic of globalisation. Commenting on the current Indian scenario he says that different kinds of rights of workers such as the right to organize, right to collective bargaining, right to form trade unions, right to strike etc. are being scuttled at the work place, with the indirect or direct support from the state, and the use of physical repression by the state apparatus, to achieve such ends, has tended to increase in the recent years.

Thus from the current attitude of the State towards labour it appears that whatever growth and development takes place in the economy, labourers are likely to be deprived of their legitimate share both due to the exploitative nature of capitalists and apathetic behaviour of the state. There is, therefore, no alternative to the labourers but to remain alert and united in the situation to get their equitable share of the economy's growth and development. There is a definite symbiotic relationship between labour and development. Both are complementary to each other. Whatever development takes place it should be humane. It should have a human face. The State, therefore, with its mighty power should ensure that whatever higher level of growth and development takes place with the use of huge capital and sophisticated technology, it becomes pro-labour and poverty and inequality reducing.

The papers included in this volume written by learned researchers have aptly portrayed the declining condition of labour rights in the current Indian scenario. The scholars have also suggested remedies for solving the problems of labour under globalisation. Three papers have made a comparison of Indian perspective with other countries like Japan, the USA, Australia, Indonesia and Nepal. The experiences of the problems of labour under globalisation and their solutions in these countries may be of lesson for the Indian Government and labour. In what follows we have summarized the theme of each of the paper in order to enable one to have a quick idea about the essence of the papers.

Misra in his paper 'State, Market and Labour' has beautifully portrayed the relationship between state, market and labour. According to him, proper functioning of a market needs the support and at times, the guidance of other institutions, especially that of the state. Conversely, the state cannot do without the market. He has made a comprehensive coverage of the duties of the state with respect to people in general and labour in particular.

Venkateswarlu in his paper has made an attempt to trace out the evolution of labour movement in a global perspective. He has brought out the pre-conditions for the labour movement and state's responses in England that was once the workshop of the world. He has also analysed the labour movement and state's role at global level and finally examined the relevance of the thesis of 'end of labour' and 'end of labour movement'.

Mukherjee and Majumder in their paper look at likely impact of state interventions into labour policies in India that are directed towards ensuring both job security and income security. According to the scholars, the laws serve the organized workers primarily while large masses of unorganized workers are without any security. To escape legislations, employers have substituted labour by capital, hired casual workers, and set up ancillary units. Consequently, output elasticity of employment has consistently declined and there is marked casualisation of workforce. Legislations have thus institutionalized and perpetuated labour market dualism. The authors, therefore, suggest that reforms are necessary but should be implemented in a careful and phased manner to avoid deteriorating conditions in both the sectors in the name of uniformity.

Alamar and Murali look at labour market flexibility in their paper. According to the authors right to work will disappear with the advent of labour market flexibility. They suggest that the government should address the livelihood concerns of the workers and think of them while taking major policy decisions. The government should give primacy to the removal of the unemployment and 'right to work' to be recognised as a basic human right and a new model of GDP growth and employment be developed to provide, firstly 'work for all' and then 'decent work for all'. In the present globalised scenario, training and retraining needs are continuous since the sectoral composition will constantly undergo changes under new innovative technologies. It should also chalk out a completely new approach to blend growth and employment generation.

Hariharan's paper tries to examine how the wage is

determined in the public sector in India. The paper concludes that the total emoluments paid to the public sector employees even though recorded a remarkable growth in current prices, it maintains its share around two per cent of the GNP. Further as a proportion of the total government revenue, it has not showed much variation and indeed, the proportion is declining marginally. The author suggests that the government may maintain this stage, if increase is not desirable. However, the author says that the increase in per capita emoluments needs to be linked with productivity. Further, the wage policy of the government should see that the benefit of increased real wage should be provided not only to the employees of public and organized sector, but also to the workers of unorganized sectors. Moreover, a strict control over inflation will check the rise in prices and in turn the rise in consumer price index and thereby reduce the commitment of the government to spend more to pay dearness allowances to the public sector employees.

Errol D'Souza's paper shows that if free contracting between workers and firms is allowed, in efficiency wage set up both firms and workers can behave opportunistically requiring third-party enforcement of employment protection legislation. The author observes that in labour markets both firms and workers are susceptible to opportunism and verifying breach of contract is difficult. A meaningful way to get workers to invest in a job and employers to honour contracts is to legislate employment protection. The author observes that the difficult task is to ensure that employment protection does not become protectionist and enemy of economic progress. Finally the author concludes: 'It is premature to conclude that anti-retrenchment laws are inefficient and end up hurting workers'.

Adhikary and Majumder's paper examines the growth of factor productivities (both partial and total) and performance of 16 major industry groups in West Bengal aggregated at the 2-digit level of classification for the period 1981-99 on the basis of industry level ASI data. By analyzing growth patterns of value added the paper shows that industries having relatively higher labour intensity picked up while those having relatively higher capital intensity suffered during post-1991 era. According to the study, employment and wage share exhibit falling trends but capital intensity shows a rising trend even during pre-reform years. The authors observe that economic reforms cannot be held responsible for falling total factor productivity, employment and wage share in the state manufacturing. They guess that strong liberalization of 1991 might have been unfavourable to efficiency of factor use and pace of automation.

Nath in his paper has firstly focused on the changing nature of state corresponding to the changes in capitalism as an economic system. Secondly, he has brought out the relation between state and labour in India in a globalised scenario. Finally, he has examined the consequences of globalisation on the working class due to the ongoing changes.

Perry's paper compares the apparent rise of neo-liberal labour market reforms in India, Indonesia, the United States and Australia during recent decades. It is noted that all the economies under review have undergone major labour market reforms, though the exact nature of the reforms has varied quite considerably for each of the countries. Work stoppages in each of the economies have also generally declined in more recent years for all of the economies, though the extent and timing of the decline has varied quite considerably, especially for Indonesia. On the basis of empirical evidence, the author holds the view that neo-liberal labour market reforms have contributed to a decline in labour dispute numbers, though other factors have also contributed the decline in stoppages, including declining inflation, changing labour market conditions and declining union density.

Misra's paper has analysed the key policies in Japan in the last few years under structural adjustment to reduce the degree of unemployment of labour and derive some lessons for India. According to the author the ideas contained in the paper seem to be relevant and a useful guide for designing the effective strategy for employment adjustment in a country like India even though India's social and cultural features of a heterogeneous society might not be identical with those in countries like Japan.

Katuwal in his paper has made an attempt to appraise some major provisions of labour laws in Nepal relating to issues of labour rights and standards. With an objective of evaluating the effectiveness of the laws to protect labour rights, maintain industrial peace and productivity improvement, this paper analyses these provisions in the light of the findings of some major researches. By analysis, this paper concludes that though the labour laws have made a lot of provisions to protect the varieties of labour rights, it is found ineffective to implement these provisions uniformly in the country, leaving scope for amendments and revisions.

Upadhyay's paper, on the basis of illustrations from India's north eastern states, attempts to argue that in situations of prolonged ethnic conflicts, the space to articulate the demands of labour gets narrowed down. As migration, resulting partly from the process of development itself creates and sharpens insecurities and competitions among ethnic communities, any organized attempt to secure the rights of the workers becomes extremely difficult, and the working poor become vulnerable to various forms of violence by state and non-state forces. The migrant workers and particularly those considered to be illegal and unwanted, suffer the most.

Nirmala Kumari has focused on different kinds of social security systems for the old aged people. According to her, though nearly 85 per cent of the total workforce is in the unorganized sector with no little of formal old age income security, the issue of old age security is gaining importance and it is now high on the public policy agenda. In response to the growing changes in the age composition and faster ageing, the central and state governments in India have for past few years been engaged in drawing a set of policy initiatives to help the older persons. Besides, there have been commitments by the governments at various national and international fora to assimilate the growing number of aged people in the process of development.

Kamble's paper examines the issue of social security for the unemployed in India in the era of globalisation. After discussing the causes and current scenario of unemployment in India he concludes that along with the provision of social security measures, provision of maximum amount of employment will really help to maximize the welfare of the unemployed.

Anupama's paper takes Bhatinda city of Punjab as a case to study the economic conditions of the domestic workers. She has collected a mixed sample of all categories of domestic workers for the analysis. In her field survey based study she has investigated into the working conditions, average earnings, job security and social security of the domestic workers, who are virtually unorganized. She has reached the conclusion that the domestic workers are poor and vulnerable. They neither earn adequate income nor do they obtain any social security benefits due to absence of definite employer-employee relationship. Further, they do not have the power to fight discrimination and victimization for protecting their rights to minimal standard of living. She therefore suggests that there should be honest efforts to improve the working conditions of the domestic workers through collective and public action, by means of appropriate legislation by lobbying or by self-organisation.

Madhavi has analysed the problem of home based bidi workers, especially that of women workers in Telengana region of Andhra Pradesh. According to her the legislation itself was never really designed to protect home workers in a comprehensive way. Most of the benefits of legislation is meant for the workers who work in factories. Therefore, the author suggests that since about 90 percent of beedi workers are women home workers they should be given adequate protection especially in a backward region like Telengana where lacs are employed in the industry.

The paper by Nanavati focuses on the social sector expenditure scenario at state level and correlates this to the employment characteristics of the states. By using secondary data she has attempted to identify the potential areas where State activism is revealed. According to the author, though the relationship between government expenditure on economic sector and economic development is well documented, the same is not true between expenditure on social sector and its consequent impact on the process of economic and human development. For a detailed state level analysis, the paper concentrates on three states, Gujarat, Kerala and Maharashtra. The paper concludes that the overall public expenditure scenario is not sustainable in all the three states except Gujarat.

Across the states, Kerala is the most active in social sector in general and 'labour' in particular, Gujarat the least. The author observes that since employment structure of the three states in terms of activity status, rural urban break up, public versus other business types is diverse, therefore, it call for appropriate State activism.

Giri and Das in their paper have examined the role of State in Orissa in the unorganized sector, focusing upon the unorganized labour. The paper concludes that although unorganized labour constitutes 95 per cent of the total labour force of 14.8 million in the state, the government's attitude to the issues of the unorganized labour has been lukewarm. A weak trade union movement in the state, apathy of the bureaucrats in general to the issues concerning unorganized labour, inadequate media coverage on the problems in the unorganized sector, and lack of efforts by the NGOs to educate the labour about their rights are some of the factors that perpetuate the misery of the unorganized labour in the state. It is suggested that the government in Orissa would do well to draw a few lessons from the Kerala experience with regard to the state's role in unorganized sector.

Goel and Goyal's paper has made a study of the objectives and outcomes of the Child Labour (Prohibition and Regulation) Act, 1986. Through a detailed study of the Act and review of contemporary research works they have shown that it suffers from many drawbacks. According to them this Act is selective in its application. It prohibits employment of children only in certain processes and occupations. These occupations and processes are ostensibly hazardous in nature. But in reality there are some other occupations and processes that may appear to be apparently harmless but undertaking them may be full of risks. After citing some examples of some occupations and processes which are hazardous but not covered by the law, they suggest that if the scope of the Act is extended to all types of occupations and processes and also to the child labour working in the households the problem could be solved to a great extent.

Chakrabarti and Varman in their paper have made an attempt to capture the process and consequences of institutionalisation of payment of minimum wages in a public sector academic institution. The authors say that the case signifies that progressive labour policies are imperative to ensure fair wages to the contingent work force. And yet only having a formal policy is not enough under the offensive of present neo-liberal order given the political reality at the ground level. According to the authors the civil society must also intervene at the grassroots and be committed for a long haul. And even then, any tangible change will come only if middle class action is combined with a vibrant working class movement. The authors finally concludes that only if economic struggles are combined with political movements will they reach anywhere, where it can potentially give meaning to a progressive policy framework.

Toor, Chahal and Kingra's paper has examined the employment scenario in the state of Punjab on the one hand and the role of government policies on the other. The paper concludes that an well organized and integrated farming system with crops and other labour intensive enterprises like dairy, poultry, vegetable, fruits, mushrooms, etc. can significantly increase the income and employment of farm families particularly small and marginal farmers having surplus family labour. The authors suggest that as agriculture and livestock remained major contributors in state GDP, emphasis should be given to the proper development of this sector in the coming years to sustain the growth of the state GDP. The introduction of these enterprises is not possible without the proper guidance and help from the government sector. The role of the state lies in creating proper infrastructure and a set of policies conducive for employment generation.

Reddy's paper has explored the effective labour management relations in Singareni Collieries Company Ltd. (SCCL), a public sector giant. He has shown that the case of SCCL is a turn-around story of a colliery. Paradoxically all those forces and factors that led to the sickness of the unit transformed it into a success story. It demonstrates the vitality of maintaining cordial relations between the labour and management in setting aside a situation of mutual acrimony and distrust into an atmosphere of partnering and caring. According to the author, this example can be picked up by other organizations passing through similar phases and try to emulate its practices to tide over tough times.

References

Bagchi, A.K. (2004), 'Nanny State for Capital and Social Darwinism for the Workers', *The Indian Journal of Labour Economics*, Vol. 47, No. 1.

Bagchi, K.K. (2006), 'Rural Development and Socio-Economic Change Among Agricultural Workers in India' in Prasad, R.R. and G. Rajanikanth (eds), *Rural Development and Social Change*, National Institute of Rural Development, Hyderabad.

Bagchi, K.K. and Ghosh, B.K. (2007), 'Development with Human Face in Indian Agriculture: Challenges and Opportunities Under Globalization', paper presented at the 6th *Development Convention at the Madras Institute of Development Studies, Chennai* on February 22-24, 2007.

Bagchi, K.K. and Gope, N. (2005), 'Working and Living Condition of Agricultural Labourers in India – Role of the State in their Betterment', paper presented at the 47th *Annual Conference of the Indian Society of Labour Economics*, at Jawaharlal Nehru University, New Delhi in November 2005.

Baumol, W.J. (1967), 'The Macroeconomics of Unbalanced Growth', *American Economic Review*, 57, June, p.416.

Chandrasekhar, C.P. and Ghosh, Jayati (2002), *The Market that Failed: A Decade of Neoliberal Economic Reforms in India*, Leftword, Delhi.

Datt, Ruddar (2003), *Lockouts in India*, Indian Society of Labour Economics and Institute for Human Development, New Delhi.

Gapasin, Fernando E. and Michael D. Yates (2005), 'Labor Movements: Is There Hope?, *Monthly Review*, Vol. 57, No. 2, June.

Ghosh, Jayati (2003), 'Changes in the World of Work', *The Indian Journal of Labour Economics*, Vol. 46, No. 4.

Hassan, Khalil (2000), 'The Future of the Labour Left', *Monthly Review*, Vol. 52, No. 3, July/August.

ISLE and IHD (2004), *Workers and the Right to Strike: A Report on Four Consultations*, Indian Society of Labour Economics and Institute for Human Development, New Delhi.

Jha, Praveen (2005), 'State's Growing Intolerance Towards Labour in India: A Note Based on Some Recent Developments', *The Indian Journal of Labour Economics*, Vol. 48, No. 4.

Mishra, L. (2001), 'Can Globalisation and Labour Rights Coexist?', *The Indian Journal of Labour Economics*, Vol. 44, No. 1.

Patnaik, Prabhat (2003), 'The Judiciary and the Empowerment of People', *Braja Mohan Sharma Memorial Lecture*.

Ratnam, C. S. Venkata (2001), *Globalisation and Labour-Management Relations: Dynamics of Change*, Sage Response Books, New Dehi.

Reddy, D. Narasimha (2003), 'Changing World Economic Order and World of Workers: New Trends in Organising Labour', *The Indian Journal of Labour Economics*, Vol.46, No.2, April-June.

Roychowdhury, Supriya (2004), 'Globalisation and Labour', *Economic and Political Weekly*, January 3.

Sharma, Alakh N. (2004), *Economic Reforms and Labour: Evidences from Micro-Level*, Institute of Economic Growth, Delhi (Mimeo).

Sharma, Alakh N. (2005), 'Globalisation, Labour Markets, Employment and Poverty: Emerging Perspectives in India', *The Indian Economic Journal*, Vol. 53, N0. 1, April-June.

Varman, Rahul and Manali Chakrabarti (2003), 'Workers Struggles in Times of Globalisation: A Critique of Trade Unions in Historical Perspective', *The Indian Journal of Labour Economics*, Vol. 46, No. 4, October-December.

Yates, Michael (2001), 'The 'New' Economy and the Labour Movement', *Monthly Review*, Vol. 52, No. 11, April.

1

STATE, MARKET AND LABOUR

L. Mishra

I

'X' is a freed bonded labourer living in Simra village 18 Kms from Daltonganj, headquarters of Palamau district. He along with 50 families of bonded labourers was deemed to have been rehabilitated after their release from bondage in 1975-76. About a decade later (4.12.82 to be precise) they stand socially ostracized and economically isolated. Their children cannot go to school located in the main bastee. Their cattle and goats cannot go for grazing in the nearby village forest, as they have to pass through the paddy fields of the landlords. 'X' has been completely maimed and mutilated by a merciless assault from his erstwhile landlord. When he goes all the way to Daltonganj hospital he is refused treatment, as he cannot meet the earthly demands of the treating physician.

II

On 22nd June 1996 in village Barkikarao in Sadar police station in Bhojpur district in Bihar 22 landless agricultural labourers belonging to the Scheduled Caste community are gunned down. Their only offence is that they raised a demand for payment of minimum wage notified by the State government. Even women, girls and infants were not spared.

A similar act of wanton cruelty was committed a few years later on 25th January 1999 in another village called

Shankarbigha in Jahanabad district of Bihar when 21 members of the SC community were gunned down for repeating the same demand for minimum agricultural wages.

III

It was the night of 2nd December 1984. Unknown to the residents of JP Nagar, a slum adjacent to the Union Carbide Corporation Pesticide factory in Bhopal, a large quantity of water had entered one of the storage tanks of the factory through leaking valves and corroded pipes. The tank contained 60 tones of methyl isocyanate (MIC). The water, which entered the tank, triggered a runaway chemical reaction which in turn resulted in discharge of 40 tons of lethal combination of MIC, hydrogen cyanide, mono methylamine and carbon monoxide, engulfing a sleeping town of one million people. Over 2500 workers were instantly killed by the deadly poisonous gas while several others who ran for life and survived were maimed, crippled and deformed for life. There was no advance warning to the effect that the technology used in the plant had the hidden potential to cause such a ghastly tragedy.

IV

Years later on 27th September 1995 it had been raining incessantly. The river Damodar that passes through New Kenda Colliery of Dhanbad was in spate and had caused a breach of the embankment. Floodwater started gushing into the colliery inundating it and trapping all the seventy six miners inside which meant a certain death for all of them. The tragedy is reminiscent of the one that had struck the Chasnala mine in the same mining belt in 1975 pushing over 300 miners into a watery grave. A simple system of communication signaling timely warning to the unsuspecting miners and to the outside world could have prevented this great human tragedy.

V

Over 10,000 workers who have been interrogated by me in

early 1984 (as a socio-legal investigating Commissioner of the Supreme Court) have migrated from the desert districts of Rajasthan, dry and drought-prone eastern Uttar Pradesh, parts of Madhya Pradesh and Chattisgarh and working in the stone quarries and crushers of Faridabad under despicable conditions of human misery and suffering. Venal middlemen approach these workers, mostly landless agricultural labourers, pay them some nominal advance and recruit them by alluring them with promises of an urban paradise. No sooner do they land at the worksite than all these promises are belied and they are subjected to ruthless exploitation. They are engaged in series of operations for long hours without any spread over such as removal of over burden, making of working phase, drilling and blasting which involve use of explosives and fuse wire. Being basically illiterate, unskilled and unaware of the scientific techniques of storage and handling of explosives they suffer injuries which are often fatal. These accidents are never reported. They see before them the grisly spectre of death every moment of their pathetic existence. Their anguish does not reach the outside world; they have no outlet to ventilate and redress their misery and suffering.

VI

I have narrated five incidents. Of these, two relate to agricultural workers, one to industrial workers and two to mining/quarry workers. Regardless of their classification the lives of workers have been affected by the immensity of a tragedy, which is not of their own making. The central message is loud and clear which may be summed up in the following words:

- Human life is treated with utter contempt, callousness and insensitivity.
- There is no risk sharing and communication with a view to pre-empting crises and disasters in an industrial plant, mining or any other enterprise.
- Demand for minimum statutory rights (like demand for minimum wages) is met with severe reprisal.
- There is a tendency to circumvent and evade statutory

responsibility in the matter of enforcement of industrial/mining safety.

- There is utter lack of surveillance and vigilance on the part of both the management of the enterprise and the State.
- The preventable crisis is not prevented but is allowed to reach enormous proportions.
- The tragedies are not reported to the statutory authority under the Workmen's Compensation Act, Factories Act and Mines Act.
- Instead, there is a determined and deliberate attempt to exonerate oneself, to disown moral and even statutory responsibility.
- Advancements in science and technology have not been backed by a humane and sensitive understanding of the factors which cause accidents and handling of affairs of human beings qua human beings, far less citizens and workers and even less by a desire to recognize the dignity, beauty and worth of their lives.

VII

Why is this so? Political scientists describe society as an integral unity but in reality it is not so. Consisting of numerous layers and sub layers within layers it is known for its heterogeneity—too many nationalities, castes and classes, too many tribes, too many sects, too many languages and dialects, too many faiths and beliefs. All living beings on this planet are born differently, grow differently, live and think differently. They have different traits and characteristics, some of which are partly genetic and some partly acquired. These differences tend to accentuate themselves in a highly stratified society where societal and individual relationships are often governed by artificial barriers.

The role of the state as an agent of the society lies in harmonizing differences (since differences in a democracy cannot be wiped out) and creating a multicoloured garden of beauty and radiance where thousand flowers with diverse hues could gently flutter in the breeze sending their fragrance to all sections of humanity regardless of differences.

The State has to do a lot more than harmonizing differences. It has to ensure basic minimum needs (education, primary health care, immunization of pregnant mothers and children, nutrition, environmental sanitation and hygiene) of those who have been deprived of the same. It has to protect the weak and defenceless against the tyranny and oppression of the strong. It has to open up opportunities for employment, income, decent livelihood and a minimum standard of living for those who have been deprived of the same. It has to restore the balance or equilibrium in a situation of uneven progress, unethical and immoral acquisition of material prosperity and affluence by a few at the cost of many, unmerited enjoyment of the fruits of progress by a microscopic minority at the cost of enjoyment of basic minimum needs by an overwhelming majority.

At the early stages of industrialization elsewhere and at the early stages of experimentation with mixed economy and democratic socialism in India State intervention did create conditions for development through development of both physical and social infrastructure. Through the first and in particular through investment in irrigation, power, transport and communication, cost of inputs used by industry could be brought down and demand for goods could be increased. Through the second, workers could be educated and trained in skills, which would enhance the productive capacity of human capital.

On the basis of the strength of this experiment we could assume that the State is capable of playing a harmonizing, protective and anti-exploitative role. Our assumption gets reinforced and buttressed, in the Indian context, by the provisions of Indian Constitution (in particular those in Chapter III and IV), by the fact that we have a free press, an impartial judiciary many of whose interventions have come like breaths of fresh air, an open Parliament and a number of Constitutional statutory and administrative bodies like

- the National Human Rights Commission
- the National Commission for Women
- the National Commission for SC and ST

- the National Commission for Minorities
- the National Backward Classes Commission
- Two National Commissions on Labour, which have since completed their mandate in 1969 and 2002 respectively.
- National Commission on physically, orthopaedically and visually handicapped
- National Commission on Farmers
- National Commission on Rural Labour (1987-1991)
- National Commission on Safai Karmacharis (Sweepers)
- National Commission on micro-enterprises in the unorganized sector.

In actuality, however, this may not be so. The executive organ of the state—the elected government in power may be plagued by serious limitations (manpower, quality of human resource, procedural wrangles, financial resources) in creating conditions for economic democracy where the poor, the deprived and the disadvantaged would not only breathe freely but would actually lead a life of dignity, equality, decency and freedom. The State may suffer from a class bias that may prevent it from effectively playing its desired role. The State may have a corporate interest of its own. Willy nilly it may sometimes be prompted to act in a manner which may promote and sub serve vested interests (Sam Benegal's film 'Manthan' on Cooperative movement vis-à-vis vested interests). Acting in such manner may not help in improving economic conditions of average women and men on the street.

VIII

Art. 12 of Indian Constitution has defined 'State' in a manner which makes it co-terminus with government at the Central, Provincial and even local level. To quote: 'The State includes the Government and the Parliament of India and the Government and Legislatures of each of the States and all local and other authorities within the territory of India or under the control of Government of India'.

It is not a question of what the State cannot do or should

not do. It is a question of doing even a small fraction of what it can do or should do with dedication, devotion and determination.

We have a good number of examples, which bear ample testimony to the grit, courage and determination with which government has attended to some of its avowed tasks. Take for example Article 23 of the Constitution, which provides for prohibition of traffic in human beings and forced labour. There are two major international instruments on the subject namely ILO Convention No. 29 (1930) on forced labour and ILO Convention No.105 (1957) on abolition of forced labour. There were other international instruments such as UN Declaration of Human Rights (10.12.48) and UN Supplementary Convention on the Abolition of Slavery (1956), which dealt with the subject of slavery and debt bondage. India had ratified the ILO Convention on forced labour No. 29 (1930) in 1954 (it ratified the other ILO Convention on abolition of forced labour No. 105 (1957) only in 1999) but had not taken any concrete steps to give effect to the Provisions of the Convention which once ratified become legally binding. It is only on 25.10.1975 that Government promulgated the Bonded Labour System (Abolition) Ordinance which was later converted to a law namely Bonded Labour System (Abolition) Act, 1976 passed by both Houses of Parliament on 9th February 1976. 'Bonded Labour System stands abolished and shall be declared illegal wherever it exists', thus read the old 20 Point Economic Programme announced to the Nation on 1st July 1975 by the then Prime Minister—Smt. Indira Gandhi. A centrally sponsored scheme on rehabilitation of freed bonded labourers was introduced in May 1978. The subject was once again included in the New 20 Point Economic Programme on 14.1.82. The State Governments/UT proceeded with a lot of gusto/tempo for about 10 years (1975-85) before the fervour died out. As of now there is practically no fresh initiative for identification, release and rehabilitation of bonded labourers.

Take another example namely Art. 24 of the Constitution of India which provides for prohibition of employment of children in any factory or mine or in any other hazardous employment. As many as 20 ILO Conventions on the subject have been adopted by the International Labour Conference culminating with Convention No. 182 on elimination of the worst forms of child labour adopted on 19th June 1999 by the ILC. India has ratified 6 of these Conventions. It has also ratified Convention on the Rights of Children (CRC) adopted by the General Assembly of UN on 20th November 1989. Government of India have formulated and adopted 2 National Policies on Children and Child Labour in 1974 and 1987 respectively. The old law, 'Employment of Children Act, 1938' has been repealed and replaced by a new law, 'Child Labour (Prohibition and Regulation) Act, 1986. A national programme on rehabilitation of Children through special schools (NCLP) has been launched since 1988 and as of now over 100 such projects have been made operational. (This is likely to go up to 250 by the end of the Tenth Plan). A parallel programme captioned "Education for all Children" is also operational for about 5 years. India was also the first signatory to the International Programme on elimination of Child Labour (IPEC) in May 1992 and over 150 projects under auspices of IPEC have been implemented. Despite all these initiatives—national and international, India continues as home to the single largest number of working children in the whole world. Millions of petals of childhood wither away in wilderness before blossoming to the flowers of youth and manhood.

Similar bold and imaginative initiatives have been taken by the national government to protect and safeguard interests of migrant labour. Freedom of movement in any part of the territory of India is a fundamental right guaranteed by Article 19 of the Constitution. Migration being movement of human beings for better employment, better wages and better standard of living there is nothing wrong or objectionable in migration per se. It becomes objectionable only when it leads to exploitation culminating in human misery and suffering. Recognising the dangers inherent in both domestic as well as overseas migration, Government of India enacted Interstate Migrant Workmen (Regulation of Employment and Conditions of Service) Act, 1979 and Emigration Act, 1983. These laws are on the statute book for 26 and 22 years respectively. Elaborate administrative and enforcement machinery is in place to protect and safeguard the interests of migrant labour. All these notwithstanding nearly 30 million workers are constantly on the move from one part of the territory of India to another and are victims of cheating, manipulation and exploitation of innumerable intermediaries who are blind to their suffering. Same is the story about exploitation of emigrant workers though the number involved is comparatively small and intensity of exploitation comparatively less than their domestic counterparts.

IX

Bonded labour, migrant labour and child labour belong to the category of distress labour and they deserve special treatment in terms of prohibition of employment (bonded labour and child labour) and amelioration (migrant labour) of their misery and suffering. Labour occurs in the concurrent list of distribution of powers and both Central and State Governments have been empowered to enact laws for labour in their respective domains. This is how over 250 legislations have been enacted in a variety of areas and themes which can be divided broadly under the following categories:

- Employment Relations related.
- Wages related.
- Conditions of employment and service in factories, plantations and mines related.
- Social Security related.
- Specific category of employment related (Merchant Shipping Act, Motor Transport Workers Act, Shops and Commercial Estts. Act) Beedi and Cigar Workers Act, Sales Promotion Employees Act).

There is a basic rationale and philosophy inherent in these legislations regardless of the category to which they belong. The ramifications of this rationale must be clearly understood and internalized. The ramifications are:

- Consistent with the physical growth, health and biological energy of a person there must be a minimum age of entry to the world of work. Such an age should not in any case be below 14 and above 18.

- The hours of work should be limited to 8 hrs a day and 48 hrs a week. Such hours cannot be stretched indefinitely. The principles of weekly off (payment of wages for full 7 days for 6 days of work), spread over (minimum period of rest between the minimum and maximum working hours) and OT must be respected.
- Wages/remuneration has to be fair and need based. All aspects of wage namely periodicity, quantum, adequacy, equity and security deserve careful consideration.
- Welfare at the work place cannot be viewed as a substitute for denial of dignity, decency and freedom.
- Measures for occupational health demand thorough screening of the status of health of every worker at periodic intervals and adopting both preventive and corrective measures against occupational diseases.
- Accidents are both man made and machine made. Considering the ignorance, illiteracy and backwardness of workers drawn from a traditional background a process for injecting thorough critical awareness of causes of accidents and measures for their prevention will have to be launched.
- Industrial safety is to be viewed not as mere routine compliance with statutory regulations but as an instrument for recognizing the dignity and worth of lives of workers as human beings.
- Social protection (including social security) is necessary and desirable for all categories of workers—serving and retired, young and old, able and disabled who look up to the State for provision of this barest minimum which is otherwise guaranteed by the Constitution as their legitimate claim.
- Rationalisation, retrenchment and displacement of workers means a colossal waste of human resources. The principles of industrial engineering should be so applied as to have the right man for the right job through a rational and scientific job study, job description, job classification and job analysis and to

preclude the possibility of initial over staffing and later rationalization.

- One rationale about gender dimension may be illustrated. This dimension lies in non-discrimination or equality of opportunities in matters of employment/ equality of treatment. In essence it implies that gender differences basic to women and men should not lead to discriminatory treatment at the work place. This philosophy gave birth to two ILO Conventions namely Convention No. 100 and Convention No. 111. The first implies that for work of equal value women and men should be paid the same remuneration while the second implies non-discrimination on grounds of class, colour, creed, gender, faith/belief, political ideology, social origin and national extraction. India has ratified both the Conventions and 'Equal Remuneration Act' was enacted in 1976 in pursuance of the ratification of C.No. 100 in 1958 but discriminatory treatment at the work place related to caste, class, gender, religion and political ideology persists. Added to this is the increasing incidence of sexual harassment of women at the work place and its serious repercussions on the dignity and decency with which women deserve to be treated. This perverse practice goes on unabated despite the judgment of the apex Court in Visakha *vs.* State of Rajasthan and others.

X

Why are there aberrations in practice despite laudable intentions behind enactment of a law in general and law relevant to labour in particular. Every labour law like any other law is a framework, an enabling mechanism and it evolves in response to the specific needs of a particular time, to strengthen the foundations of a planned economic growth and ensure a fair deal to the working class. Being products of a particular time they get considerably influenced by the social milieu, political ethos and economic policy obtaining at that point of time. Besides, in the process of consultation with the concerned interests (and in case of labour laws such consultation is tripartite) the draft framework of the law itself undergoes so much of change that the original objectives get blurred beyond recognition. In the process of reconciling many irreconcilable interests the original draft loses its basic identity.

Against this background it is futile to expect that any law far less labour can be foolproof. It is futile to expect that it can be a panacea against all our ailments—social, economic and political.

Law enforcement has broadly two parameters. One is through inspection of establishments and the other is through the system of judicial redress. Both have severe limitations. This is because the area of law enforcement is large and scattered and the enforcement machinery is small and its mobility is severely restricted. The system of seeking judicial redress is cumbersome, expensive and time consuming. The trend of Public Interest Litigation (PIL) and the system of appointment of socio-legal investigating Commissioners by the Supreme Court is no doubt laudable; it has aroused a lot of hope and assurance for the common man and numerous grass root level agencies fighting for them but it is also beset with severe limitations. This is because the courts are saddled with too many routine original jurisdiction cases. Even if they succeed in disposing off some public interest litigation cases in less time and cost, giving thereby some semblance of relief to the aggrieved, the relief itself becomes elusive as the judgment of a Court in a PIL case has necessarily got to be implemented by the very same enforcement agency whose indifference and callousness prompted the aggrieved to seek judicial redress. It is futile to expect that there will be a radical change overnight in the attitude and approach of the enforcement machinery.

This by itself does not belittle or minimize the directions of the apex Court in vital issues affecting the dignity, decency, equality and freedom of labour. In interpreting law it has sought to fill in a number of gaps, remove a lot of doubts, disputes and ambiguities and provide a balanced construction which will be beneficial to all sections of the society namely the producer, the consumer, the provider of services and the voiceless and marginalized who are at the bottom layer of the society battling for generations against disaffection, discrimination, dehumanization and denial. This can be illustrated with reference to a number of case laws.

1. When a sub-contractor supplies raw materials to a worker and takes recourse to rejection of finished products on the ground that they did not conform to laid down specifications and the question arose whether there is employer employee relationship between the two, the apex Court decided in the affirmative citing element of supervision as the ground.
2. No industry has a right to exist unless it is able to pay its workmen at least a bare minimum wage. Employment of labour on Starvation Wages cannot be encouraged or favoured in a modern democratic welfare state.

   [Crown Aluminium Works *vs.* Their Workmen 1958-1 LLJ1 (SC)].
3. A worker's wage is no longer a contract between an employer and employee. It has the force of collective bargaining under the law. Each category of the wage structure has to be tested at the anvil of social justice, which is the live fibre of our society today. Keeping in view the socio-economic aspect of the wage structure we are of the view that it is necessary to add the following additional components as a guide for fixing the minimum wage in the industry. (v) Children's education, medical requirement, minimum recreation including festivals/ceremonies and provision for old age, marriage etc. should further constitute 25 PC of the total minimum wage.

   [Workmen Reptakos Brett and LTD *v* Management 1992 1 LLJ 340]
4. No one shall be forced to provide labour or service against his will even though it be under a contract of service.... We arc, therefore, of the view that where a person provides labour or service to another for a remuneration which is less than the minimum wage, the labour or service provided by him clearly falls within the scope and ambit of the words 'forced labour' under Art. 23. [People's Union for Democratic Rights

and others *v* Union of India and others AIR 1982 SC 1473]

5. When interpreting the provisions of the Constitution conferring fundamental rights, the attempt of the Court should be to expand the reach and ambit of the fundamental rights rather than to attenuate their meaning and content.
   [Maneka Gandhi *v* Union of India, AIR 1978, SC 597]
6. Right to life guaranteed under Art. 21 is not confined merely to physical existence or to the use of any faculty or limb through which life is enjoyed or the soul communicates with outside world but it also includes within its scope and ambit the right to live with basic human dignity and the State cannot deprive any one of this precious and invaluable right because no procedure by which such deprivation may be effected can ever be regarded as reasonable, fair and just.
   [Francis Coralie Mullin *v* the Administrator, UT of Delhi AIR 1981 SC 746]
7. Ordinary course of human affairs would show, indeed judicial notice can be taken of it, that there would be no occasion for a labourer to be placed in a situation where he is required to supply forced labour for no wage or for nominal wage, unless he has received some advance or other economic consideration from the employer and under the pretext of not having returned such advance or other economic consideration, he is required to render service to the employer or is deprived of his freedom of employment or of the right to move freely wherever he wants. [Bandhua Mukti Morcha *v* Union of India and others AIR 1984 SC 802]
8. Where judicial redress is sought of a legal injury or legal wrong suffered by a person or a class of persons who by reason of poverty, disability or socially or economically disadvantaged position are unable to approach the Court and the Court is moved for this purpose by a member of the public by addressing a letter drawing the attention of the Court to such legal

injury or legal wrong, Court would cast aside all technical rules of procedure and entertain the letter as a writ petition on the judicial side and take action on it.

[Judges Appointment and Transfer case, AIR 1982, SC 149]

Human freedom, dignity and decency of labour is sacrosanct but cannot and should not be allowed to degenerate into a licence. As and when, therefore, supplies and services essential to the life of the individual and community are disrupted or public order is jeopardized by unilateral and irresponsible acts of individuals or groups of individuals the courts cannot sit idle as a mute spectator and must intervene to countermand such irresponsible acts. This is what the High Court of Kerala did by declaring all *bandhs* (cessation of economic activities) as illegal and unconstitutional. [Bharat Kumar, K. Palichan and another *v* State of Kerala and another AIR 1997 (Kerala) 291]. The apex court on appeal confirmed the judgement of the High Court on 12th November 1997 [Communist Party of India (Marxist) *vs.* Bharat Kumar and others 1998 SCC 201].

There have also been occasions when the judgments of the Court have created a stir on a similar issue though in a slightly different context. The apex Court while disposing off an appeal (Civil Appeal No. 5556 of 2003 arising out of SLP No. 12224 of 2003 with writ petition nos. 298, 308 and 330 of 2003 arising out of SLP No. 12577 and 13102 of 2003) under Art. 32 of the Constitution filed by the State of Tamilnadu against the order of Madras High Court made the following pertinent observations:

- Government employees have no fundamental, statutory or equitable moral right to go on strike as such strikes affect the society as a whole.
- There is no moral justification in pressurizing the state through recourse to strike to redress grievances.

Under Art. 141 of the Constitution the law declared by the apex court shall be binding on all courts within the territory of India. It is not my intention, therefore, to express any view on a judgment pronounced by the apex court which has become the law of the land but as a student of political science for over 40 years and as an avid observer of the social scene which gets affected by such directions I think it may be useful to lay down a few broad principles on which further dialogue and debate can take place:

1. Art. 19 gives to every citizen the right to form association, which includes the right to freedom of expression. The right to association logically implies the right to resent, resist and protest against a decision of the State, which is unreasonable, unjust and unfair.
2. Those who sell their labour power are often confronted with the unequal might, unresponsiveness and intransigence of the buyer of that power. Do they have any alternative but to withdraw their labour collectively when their reasonable pleas go unheard and grievances go unredressed?
3. Taking away the right to strike from the government employees and industrial employees would tantamount to taking away the civil and democratic rights.
4. Right to go on strike may not, however, be absolute in the same sense as right to freedom of expression is not absolute. It should be subject to certain reasonable restrictions. The nature and character of such restrictions may be determined through constructive social dialogue.
5. Institutional mechanisms should be in place for ventilation and redressal of genuine grievances of all workers (including government employees).

In the ultimate analysis the relationship between state, market and labour will have to rest on a set of basic principles. The basic principles are:

- Every worker is first a human being and secondarily a worker.
- Like any other ordinary human being, every worker has his hopes and aspirations, strength and weaknesses; there need to be viewed with empathy and sensitivity.
- Human life has a sacrosanctity, which deserves to be

protected. Whether it is employment relations, freedom of association and collective bargaining, occupational health and safety, social security they must be woven around the sacrosanctity of human life.

- Nothing needs to be done which will cause the slightest injury to the life and limb of a worker as a human being nor will hurt him mentally and emotionally.

Despite an excellent track record in terms of a consistently high rate of GDP growth since 24th July 1991 (when the New Economic Policy was adopted and the economy was opened up in a bid to integrate it with the global economy) and initiation of a series of path breaking exercises (like the right to information, employment guarantee scheme etc.) to bring about a balance between growth and equity there are doubts as to whether the above principles have been respected in letter and spirit. Such doubts are genuine; they emanate from the class structure of the society overlapping with divides of caste and religion. They also emanate from the fact that there are compulsions of electoral politics, which influence the nature of the State as much as the dictates of caste and class. They emanate from the fact that the State has represented the social and economic interests of the dominant classes who constitute the ruling elite. The vested interests of these classes or the elite have perpetuated a cynical politics of soft options as a result of which the State has shied away from hard decisions. It simultaneously craves for political legitimation from the poor, deprived, disadvantaged and under privileged. This in turn breeds a competitive politics of populism under which one political party vies with another in wooing the voters by sops around election time. The relationship between State, Political Parties and the propertied class is a symbiotic one characterised by a lot of nepotism (distribution of spoils), bribery and corruption. The net result of all this is:

- Trials and tribulations in eking out a decent livelihood are far too many;
- Growing unemployment with dwindling job opportunities;
- Rising prices of essentials of life in relation to income;
- Declining per capita food availability contributory to

under nutrition;

- Proper nutrition beyond the reach of most families;
- Scarce housing in cities with disproportionately high rent;
- Rising incidence of pollution of air and water; no environmental sanitation;
- Minimal public health care is becoming a dream;
- Lives of SC, ST, and linguistic, cultural and religious minorities exposed to additional stress and strain, risks and hazards.
- Rising invasion of privacy of lives of all households by multiple agencies.

Placed as we are in such a mess we need to have neither an idealistic nor a fatalistic but only a pragmatic view of the State. There are multiple weaknesses and infirmities but there are also potential strengths to be harnessed. We need, in particular, to draw up a checklist of items as to what the State should do and what it should not. The list could be long but to mention only a few.

- Excessive State intervention is as bad as State indifference and inaction.
- State must take cognizance of all instances of forced/ bonded labour, child labour in exploitative situations, discrimination on the basis of caste, class, gender, religion, sexual harassment at the work place, atrocities on SC, ST, minorities and women either suo moto or on the basis of intelligence reports or on the basis of newspaper reports and must intervene instantaneously.
- There are areas, which must remain as exclusive domain of the State (education, primary health care, potable water, nutrition, immunization, sanitation, etc.).
- Basic needs of workers (a roof above the head at a reasonable price, access to potable water and sanitation, access to education and primary health care of children, immunization of pregnant mothers and children etc.) must receive undiluted priority attention of the State.
- The State must institutionalize a social safety net to deal with the speedy and full rehabilitation of

rationalized, retrenched and displaced workers (since NRF instituted in 91-92 has since been wound up). Such rehabilitation should be both physical and psychological.

- The State must institutionalize joint study teams comprising of representatives of originating and destination States to deal with the problems of 30 million workers who are constantly on the move and to provide special protection to them. A similar protection to overseas emigrants and to promote their welfare through a welfare fund will have to be thought of. The coverage of students (potential workers) in skill training programmes available through polytechnics, *i.e.* NVTI, RVTIs etc. is less than IPC. This needs to be substantially stepped up by augmenting financial allocations to the skill-training programme. A programme for review and replacement of all obsolescent skills (which are no longer market relevant) should also simultaneously be launched. Markets like government are human institutions. Trading in the market can never be free or fair. Markets tend to underproduce information; they also manipulate access to information. They may even create misinformation in pursuit of profit. The competition is also inadequate. There will always be monopolies or oligopolies. It is futile, therefore, to think of perfect and efficient solutions to the mind-boggling problems of 400 million of workers in India through the market. The market will be least bothered in taking decisions actuated by consideration of distributive justice. It may not also produce and supply goods (public goods) and services, which are considered desirable for all sections of the society. Market solutions may lead to under investment in some sectors or under provision for R & D and innovation in other sectors. Market failures, therefore, will be as disturbing as the failures on the part of the State.

The State and the market should not, therefore, be perceived as opposed to each other or as alternatives to each other vis-à-vis genuine interests of workers. Both *laissez faire* and central planning have their frailties and shortcomings and they need self-correcting mechanisms. Proper functioning of a market needs the support and at times, the guidance of other institutions, especially that of the State. Conversely, the State cannot do without the market. Whether it is the tyranny of inspector *raj* or excesses of *babu raj* (clerkdom) or plunders of kickback *raj* neither the State nor the market is foolproof and both need checks and balances to remain on the right track and to achieve the desired objective of holistic/human development.

2

THE LABOUR MOVEMENT AND THE STATE: A GLOBAL PERSPECTIVE

*A. Venkateswarlu**

I. Introduction

"The history of all hitherto existing society is the history of class struggles" as per the authors of *Communist Manifesto*. The reason for the struggle in any social formation is the contradiction between the classes; one class the labouring class that generates surplus product or surplus value and the other, the non-labouring class that appropriates the surplus. There could not have been any problem between generation and appropriation of surplus product or surplus value, if man were not capable of producing in one working day more means of subsistence, which would signify in the strictest sense, more agricultural products than every labourer needed for his own reproduction; if the daily expenditure of his entire labour sufficed merely to reproduce the means of subsistence indispensable for his own individual requirements. Further, while concurring with Physiocrats, Marx (1971b, p. 786) says:

> "An agricultural labour productivity exceeding the individual requirements of the labourer is the basis of all societies, which disengages a constantly increasing

* I am very grateful to my teacher Prof. G.K. Chadha, who has encouraged me. I am also thankful to Prof. S. Mahendra Dev, Director, CESS, Hyderabad and Prof. S. Galab for their help at various stages.

> portion of society from the production of basic foodstuffs and transforms them into 'free heads' ... making them available for exploitation in other spheres."

That is, the labourers, required for engaging in non-agricultural capitalist production, were to be released by the rural and agricultural economy. Keeping European history in view, this amounts to say that the economic structure of capitalist society has grown out of the economic structures of feudal society (Marx, 1971b, p. 668). The immediate producer, the labourer, could only dispose of his own person after he had ceased to be attached to the soil and ceased to be slave, serf, or bondsman of another, *i.e.*, only after the labourer would be expropriated from his means of production and from the guarantees of existence afforded by the feudal arrangements. But, this history of expropriation has been written in the annals of mankind, in blood and fire, as per Marx (1971a, p. 669).

Though, the capitalist is assumed to be progressive, compared to the feudal lord, the capitalist system placed the labourer at the mercy of capitalist who had to provide employment to the labourer. The labourers were subjected to exploitation by the capitalist, as there was great exodus of labourers from the rural areas (from British experience); that led to over supply of labourers.

Therefore, competition among labourers (proletarians), these workers were in constant competition among themselves as were the members of the bourgeoisie among themselves. The power-loom weaver was in competition with the handloom weaver, the unemployed or ill-paid handloom weaver with him who had work or was better paid, each trying to supplant the other. This competition among the workers themselves was the sharpest weapon against the proletariat in the hands of the bourgeoisie. If the workers would get united in the form of associations, they would be able to counter the bourgeoisie by demand for the rise in wages and for the betterment of working conditions. Hence, the effort of workers to nullify the competition among themselves by their associations generated hatred among the bourgeoisie against the association of workers. Further, *the bourgeoisie could take the help of the state* which could operate on their behalf by applying force against the workers (Engels, 1845, Chapter 4). Engels, in the case of Britain's experience, tells us how in the name of 'free choice', the proletariat was exploited.

> "The proletarian is helpless; left to himself, he cannot live a single day. The bourgeoisie has gained a monopoly of all means of existence in the broadest sense of the word. What the proletarian needs, he can obtain only from this bourgeoisie, which is protected in its monopoly by the power of the state. The proletarian is, therefore, in law and in fact, the slave of the bourgeoisie, which can decree his life or death. It offers him the means of living, but only for an "equivalent", for his work. It even lets him have the appearance of acting from a free choice, of making a contract with free, unconstrained consent, as a responsible agent who has attained his majority."

The proletarians had no other choice to accept the condition of the bourgeoisie, if they would not like to starve or freeze to death. The bourgeoisie would be protected in its monopoly by the power of state, if the proletariat united under their associations. That is why, Engels (1845) says:

> "If all the proletarians announced their determination to starve rather than work for the bourgeoisie, the latter would have to surrender its monopoly. But this is not the case… is instead, a rather impossible case... so that the bourgeoisie still thrives. To this competition of the workers among themselves there is one limit; no worker will work for less than he needs to subsist. If he must starve he will prefer to starve in idleness than in toil."

On realizing the importance of forming into association, the proletariat were ready to form associations; but the bourgeoisie through state power could resist in England till 1824, as the freedom of association was not granted to the British working class, due to *the intervention of the state in favour of bourgeoisie.* It is in this connection, Adam Smith noted the imbalance in the rights of workers in regard to owners (or "masters") in *The Wealth of Nations* (in Chapter 8).

Smith says:

> "We rarely hear, it has been said, of the combinations of masters, though frequently of those of workmen. But whoever imagines, upon this account, that masters rarely combine, is as ignorant of the world as of the subject. Masters are always and everywhere in a sort of tacit, but constant and uniform combination, not to raise the wages of labour above their actual rate... *[When workers combine,] masters... never cease to call aloud for the assistance of the civil magistrate, and the rigorous execution of those laws which have been enacted with so much severity against the combinations of servants, labourers, and journeymen.*"

Further, the classical political economy emphasised the positive role of the state in the economy in the interest of the capital accumulation and considered state to be an impartial arbitrator between the proletariat and the bourgeoisie to correct the limitations of the private sector. But, Marx, in his *Critique Political Economy,* stressed that the state as 'the concentrated and organised force of society' becomes *the dispenser of brutal force* for creating conditions for capitalist development in the early stages where *force was an economic agent* itself. Once the capitalist mode of production established itself on a general mode of production, the brutal force of state would become necessary only exceptionally (Chattopadhyay, 1985). It is clear that for a long time the state acted as an obstruction for the formation of association of workers among themselves though secret organisations of workers were there. Thus, to understand the process of labour movement and the state's response is important.

II. Objective

The main objective of the study is to explore the genesis and development of the labour movement. However, the specific objectives are:

(i) to explore the pre-conditions for the labour movement and state's response in England, which was *the workshop of the world;*

(ii) to analyse the labour movement and state's role at global level; and

(iii) to examine in brief the relevance of the thesis of 'end of labour' and 'end of labour movement'.

III. The Necessity of the Labour Movement and State's Response in England Till Mid-1840s

The history of the proletariat in England began with the second half of the 18th century. By 1843, the England was the classic land of industrial revolution, where the proletariat could be studied in all its relations and from all sides, as per Engels (1845). In this section, we take up the effects of the Labour Statutes, the conditions of the working class in the early phase of industrial revolution, and then the concomitant necessity of labour movement.

1. Labour Statutes in England against Labour from Mid-14th to Mid-19th Century

Shortening of working day and rise in the minimum wages are the two important aspects to improve labourers economic conditions, apart from improvement in the other living conditions and work environment. The state began to act in this direction only from the middle of 19th century, and prior to that it was acting against these aspects.

But the most important aspect of Labour Statutes in England in the beginning was: *(i)* to lengthen the working day, and *(ii)* to make the labourers work compulsorily. As per Marx (1971a), the establishment of a normal working-day was the result of centuries of struggle between capitalist and labourer. The history of this struggle showed two opposed tendencies, if we compare the English factory legislation of 19th century with the English labour Statutes from the 14th century to well into the middle of the 18th century. Whilst the modern Factory Acts compulsorily shortened the working day, the earlier statutes tried to lengthen it by compulsion.

(i) The background of the Statute of Labourers of 1349

First, the demise of feudalism which was being replaced by capitalism; *second,* the Black Plague, sometimes called the Black Death or the Bubonic Plague of 1348-1349, caused massive carnage, killing almost a third of England's population. The poor died at a much higher rate than others which caused a severe shortage of labor. These forces were breaking down the feudal system and created economic dislocation as more people left the feudal manors and roamed the land looking for better work and begging. There was no guarantee of labor for the lord anymore, and some of the liberated serfs were roaming the country as vagrants, migratory workers. The effect of the Black Plague was to immediately create a scarcity of workers and an upward push on wages administering a shock "unparalleled in severity" to the feudal system.The already ailing feudal system would never recover (Quingley, on net).

(ii) Lengthening of the Working Day

The lengthening work day or compulsory work for labourers was the intention of the first Statute of labourers, which was enacted in 1349, in England. The 1349 Statute contained four methods to regulate the workers: *compulsory work; reduced compensation and control of wages; imprisonment as penalty for quitting work before the term ended; and stiff enforcement through a special justice system created to hear disputes over the statute.* The statute began with a method to eliminate able-bodied beggars, provide much-needed laborers, and roll back wages to those prevailing in 1346; coercion to work and to accept prior wages. It mandated that every able-bodied man or woman under 60 was required to work. That meant anyone not already working could be made to work involuntarily for whoever wanted their work (Quingley, *on net*).

(iii) Fixing Lower Wage Rate

The 1350 Statute of Laborers supplemented and reinforced certain points of the 1349 statute, which had been left vague. The act abandoned the prior concept of generally trying to roll back wages three years (1346) and instead legislatively fixed the maximum amount that could be paid to workers (Marx, 1971a).

The spirit of the Statute of Labourers of 1349 and of its offshoots came out clearly in the fact, that *indeed a maximum of wages was dictated by the State, but on no account a minimum.* It was forbidden, under pain of imprisonment, to pay higher wages than those fixed by the statute, but the taking of higher wages was more severely punished than giving them: ten days' imprisonment was decreed for him that would pay the higher wages, but twenty-one days for him that received them. A statute of 1360 increased the penalties and authorised the masters to extort labour at the legal rate of wages by corporal punishment (Marx, 1971a).

For more than 400 years laws had been made for the maximum, beyond which wages absolutely must not rise, Whitbread in 1796 proposed a legal minimum wage for agricultural labourers. Pitt opposed this, though confessed that the "condition of the poor was cruel". Finally, in 1813, the laws for the regulation of wages were repealed.

(iv) Continuation of the Labour Statutes

The Labour Statutes, also called Poor Laws, were intended to make the vagabonds and paupers work forcefully. The fathers of the present working-class were chastised for their enforced transformation into vagabonds and paupers. Legislation treated them as "voluntary" criminals, and assumed that it depended on their own good will to go on working under the old conditions that no longer existed. In England this legislation began under Henry VII and took different turns under Henry VIII, Edward VI, Elizabeth and others. Only the poor those who could not work used to be given Licence of beggar. As per the Law of 1530 under Henry VIII, the beggars old and unable to work had to receive a beggar's licence. On the other hand, whipping and imprisonment for sturdy vagabonds They were to be tied to the cart-tail and whipped until the blood streams from their bodies, then to swear an oath to go back to their birthplace or to where they had lived the last three years and to put themselves to labour. In the Law of 1572, under Elizabeth, the unlicensed beggars above 14 years of age were to be severely flogged and branded on the left ear unless some one would take them into service for two years; in case of a repetition of the offence, if they were over 18, they were to be executed, unless some one would take them into service for two years; but for the third offence they were to be executed without mercy as felons.

Every Labour Statute that was hitherto enacted in England was useful for the capitalists to exploit the workers by lengthening the working day and paying less wages to the workers. If they had to demand either individually or in some associational form, the workers were subjected to punishment and penalties under those Statutes. As per Quingley, the laws considerably enhanced the authority of employers. *The laws broadened the employers' legal options when dealing with their servants and further shifted the balance of power against the workers.*

2. *The Condition of the Working Class in England*

The proletariat created by the breaking up of the band of feudal retainers and by the forcible expropriation of the people from the soil, this "free" proletariat, could not possibly be absorbed by the nascent manufactures as fast as it was thrown upon the world. They were turned *en masse* into beggars, robbers, vagabonds, partly from inclination, in most cases from stress of circumstances. (Marx, 1971a).

The factory system of production was started with the invention of the steam-engine and the use of machinery for working cotton. These inventions gave rise to an industrial revolution, a revolution that altered the whole civil society. Depending on Engels (1845), the conditions of the working class is described, as prevailed in England by the early 1840s.

The working conditions were so bad that when society placed hundreds of proletarians in such a position that they would inevitably meet a too early and an unnatural death, one which was quite as much a death by violence as that by the sword or bullet. *Had the production of textiles and other manufactured goods been for the domestic market, the conditions would have not been so worse.* But, the conquest of foreign markets constantly and rapidly increased the demand for manufactured goods.

The involuntary and mechanical toil was the source of demoralisation, due to destroyal of the body and soul, among the workers. The long hours of work amounted to 14-17 hours a day. In many families the wife, like the husband, had to work away from home, and the consequence was the total neglect of the children, who were subjected to accidents or even killed by falling, drowning, or burning, as in the great cities and towns of England. The unmarried female workers started working from their 9th year. Men were displaced by women and girls in spinning and weaving, because flexible and slender fingers were required there. Thus, due to crowding out of adult males in mills, female workforce dominated in the mills to the extent of one-half to three-fourths. As a result, the family life was disturbed, and accidents to child labourers increased.

The problems faced by the workers were: Long standing hours brought bone problems in spinal column and legs. Several health disorders used to arise due to restless work and lack of breath of fresh air. Stunted growth and premature oldage became common. Injuries and fatal accidents used to occur often. The woman specific problems for young beginners were the undergrowth of female parts, and pregnant women had to work till delivery.

The dwellers in cities were more exposed to acute, and especially to inflammatory affections than rural populations. The working-people's quarters of all great towns and cities, had the bad state of the dwellings in the matters of ventilation, drainage, and cleanliness—in single ill-built, ill-kept streets of smaller places. All these conditions used to engender fever, typhus.

As the workers in the factory system became worse slaves than the Negroes in America or the serf in the feudal society. *The free working-man had no guarantee whatsoever, because he had a place in society only when the bourgeoisie could make use of him; in all other cases he was ignored, treated as non-existent.*

In addition to the exploitation in the wage market, the worker also was subjected to exploitation under the arrangements of the truck system and the cottage system. In *truck system* the manufacturer used to supply the provisions to the operatives against wage mostly at higher rates and though the system was made illegal by the Truck Act 1831, it was continued in disguise. In *cottage system,* the manufacturer used to build dwellings to rent them to the operatives at higher rates.

The bourgeoisie and the State did not do much for the education and improvement of the working-class. The day schools were rare. The evening schools, supposed to be attended by children who were employed during the day, were almost abandoned or attended without benefit. Thus, lacking cultural advancement, the workers used to involve in the drunkenness and sexual irregularities to forget the toil and forgive the bourgeoisie.

3. *The Necessity of Labour Movement*

Despite falling real wages, the wages were not allowed to be risen due to legal control on wages in the manufacturing and mining also, which were important for the capitalist development. By the Statute of Elizabeth, the justices of the peace were empowered to fix certain wages and to modify them according to the time of the year and the price of commodities. James-I extended these regulations of labour also to weavers, spinners, and all possible categories of workers. As per the Labour Statutes (the Poor Laws) forming associations was illegal. George-II extended the laws against coalition of labourers to manufactures. In the cities, all combinations, contracts and oaths by which masons and carpenters reciprocally bound themselves, were declared null and void.

Thus, unions were illegal for many years (till 1824). *There were severe penalties for attempting to organise unions, up to and including execution, as the state was in favour of the bourgeoisie.* But, the workers were compelled to strive to escape from this brutalising condition, to secure for themselves a better, more human position; and this they could not do without attacking the interest of the bourgeoisie, which consisted in exploiting them. So the unions were formed to fight against the unilateral wage cuts and to get improvements in the working conditions, by shortening working day.

(i) Luddite Movement

The revolt of the workers began soon after the first

industrial development, and passed through several phases. The earliest, crudest, and least fruitful form of this rebellion was that of crime. Later, as a class, they first manifested opposition to the bourgeoisie when they resisted the introduction of machinery at the very beginning of the industrial period, to get relief from the labour displacement. The first inventors, Arkwright and others, were persecuted in this way and their machines destroyed. Later, there took place a number of revolts against machinery, in which the occurrences were almost precisely the same as those of the printers' disturbances in Bohemia in 1844; factories were demolished and machinery destroyed. This form of opposition is called as Luddite Movement. Marx (1971a, p.404) pointed out that this movement gave the anti-jacobian governments a pretext for the most reactionary and forcible measures and *it took both time and experience before the work people learnt to distinguish between machinery and its employment by capital and to direct their attacks, not against the material instruments of production, but against the mode in which they used.*

(ii) Repeal of anti-Trade Union Laws

Thus, *coalition of the labourers was treated as a heinous crime from the 14th century to 1824, the year of the repeal of the laws against Trades' Unions.* The barbarous laws against Trades' Unions fell in 1824 before the threatening bearing of the proletariat. *This law repealed all laws by which coalitions between working-men for labour purposes had hitherto been forbidden. The working-men obtained a right previously restricted to the aristocracy and bourgeoisie, the right of free association.* Secret coalitions had previously existed, but could never achieve great results.

(iii) The Spread of Trade Unions

When the working-men received in 1824 the right of free association, these combinations were very soon spread over all England and attained great power. In all branches of industry Trades Unions were formed with the outspoken intention of protecting the single working-man against the tyranny and neglect of the bourgeoisie. Thus, they tried to settle with the capitalists a scale of wages to be universally adhered to.

They aimed further to keep up the demand for labour by limiting the number of apprentices, and so to keep wages high; to counteract, as far as possible, the indirect wages reductions which the manufacturers brought about by means of new tools and machinery; and finally, to assist unemployed working-men financially. To attain these ends, a President and Secretary were engaged at a salary and a committee collected the weekly contributions and watched over their expenditure for the purposes of the association. When it proved possible and advantageous, the various trades of single districts united in a federation and held delegate conventions at set times. *The attempts were made several times (in 1830 for the first time) to form one universal trades association for the whole United Kingdom, with a separate organisation for each trade.*

The strike was used as a weapon. The strikes were necessitated to oppose every reduction in wages. Especially in the case of partial strikes the manufacturer could readily secure recruits from the black sheep or knobsticks (strike breaking workers), and rendered fruitless the efforts of the united workers. Knobsticks were opposed in all possible ways: threatened, insulted, beaten, or otherwise maltreated. But, the law-abiding bourgeoisie had the power in its own hands, so that the force of the Union was broken almost every time by the first unlawful act, the first judicial procedure against its members. The history of these Unions was a long series of defeats of the working-men, interrupted by a few isolated victories.

The major success of the formation of the unions was that they could destroy the competition of the workers among themselves, so that the competition could not be exploited by the bourgeoisie. This was possible the moment the workers resolved to be bought and sold no longer. The Unions contributed greatly to nourish the bitter hatred of the workers against the property-holding class.

4. *Chartism—Its Charter of Demands*

Since the working-men did not respect the law of the bourgeoisie, they wanted to put a proletarian law in the place of the legal fabric of the bourgeoisie. This proposed law was the People's Charter. Chartism was the compact form of their opposition to the bourgeoisie. In Chartism it was the whole working-class which arose against the bourgeoisie, and attacked, first of all, the political power, the legislative rampart with which the bourgeoisie had surrounded itself. The Chartist movement not only fought for political power, particularly for democratic governance (as per 1st petition of People's Charter, 1838), but also struggled for the better working conditions of the labourers (as per 2nd petition of the Charter, 1842). In 1838 a committee of the General Working-men's Association of London, with William Lovett at its head, drew up the People's Charter (1st Charter), whose six points were as follows (Engels, 1845):

1. Universal suffrage for every man who is of age, sane and unconvicted of crime;
2. Annual Parliaments;
3. Payment of members of Parliament, to enable poor men to stand for election;
4. Voting by ballot to prevent bribery and intimidation by the bourgeoisie;
5. Equal electoral districts to secure equal representation; and
6. Abolition of the even now merely nominal property qualification of £300 in land for candidates in order to make every voter eligible.

It also intended to submit its 3rd petition to parliament in 1848, by mass march. But this was disturbed and suppressed by the ruling class. Later, it began to decline. It lacked consistent proletarian leadership. But it had a tremendous influence on the international working class movement. It is easy to understand its importance, as by the early 1880s, the five of six demands of Charter of 1838 were fulfilled (the left out being annual parliaments).

5. *Enactment of Labor Laws in Favour of Workers*

The apprentices, the young children rented by the manufacturers before the factory system and new machinery came, were lodged, fed, and clothed in common, and were completely the slaves of their masters, by whom they were treated with the utmost recklessness and barbarity. As early as 1796, the public objection to this horrible system found opposition from the people; and in 1802 Parliament passed the Apprentices' Act of 1802, by which the most crying evils were removed. Gradually the increasing competition of free workpeople crowded out the whole apprentice system; factories were built in cities, machinery was constructed on a larger scale, and work-rooms were made more airy and wholesome; gradually, too, more work was found for adults and young persons.

The Factory Laws started emerging in England depending on the agitations and struggles of the working class. Thus came *the Factory Acts of 1819, 1825, and 1831, of which the first two were never enforced, and the last only here and there. This law of 1831 provided that in cotton mills no one under twenty-one should be employed between 7.30 p.m at night and 5.30 a.m in the morning; and that in all factories young persons under eighteen should work no longer than twelve hours daily, and nine hours on Saturday. But since operatives could not testify against their masters without being discharged, this law helped matters very little.* Later, restricting children's working hours to 6½ hours and compulsory school attendance for children were proposed by 1845, as per Engels (1845).

IV. Labour Movement: Global Level

In the most common acceptance of the term, the labour movement refers to the trade union movement, as per Gallin (2005). It also comprises the political parties created by workers to defend their interests, such as socialist or social-democratic or labour parties. This is also inspired and organised by ideologies, like Marxism, syndicalism and Christian social doctrines. It is influenced by the values of human dignity, equality, justice and solidarity and of freedom from oppression and exploitation. The labour movement also has been differentiated from the earlier liberation movements from its nature of international character.

Following Gallin (2005), the history of the international labour movement is divided into four phases: *(i)* from its origins to World War-I; *(ii)* the inter-war years (1914-1945); *(iii)* the period from the end of World War-II to the collapse of socialism in Eastern Europe and USSR (1945-1991); and *(iv)* the present period of globalisation (1991 onwards).

1. International Labour Movement: Origins to World War-I

In the preceding section, it has been elaborated how the necessity of labour movement arose in England, *the workshop of the world*. The labour movement first developed in England and then expanded into other West European countries and the USA. The Labour movement being discussed in this subsection is mostly related to the movement aiming at capturing state power.

In this first period, the foundations of the movement were laid. It relates to formation of Communist League leading to emergence of the *Communist Manifesto*, and the effects of the First International, the Paris Commune (1871), the Movement of 1886 in Chicago, the Second International. This phase of the movement comes to an abrupt end on August 1, 1914. During this period, the state played its role in favour of the ruling classes, and against the working class.

(i) Communist League and Communist Manifesto

While the Chartist movement was going on in the England; the Communist League, the first international communist organisation of the proletariat was founded by Marx and Engels and it existed from 1847 to 1852. The League, which was secret at that time, commissioned Marx and Engels to draw up for publication a detailed theoretical and practical programme of the Communist Party. They first published the Communist Manifesto, in February 1848. It brought out the prominence of class struggle through the materialist conception of history, whereby ultimately the workers had to emancipate themselves by their own action, as no one was going to do it for them. The Manifesto declared that the first step in the revolution of the working class was to raise the proletariat to the position of ruling class, to win the battle of democracy. Further, the proletarian movement was the self-conscious, independent movement of the immense majority, in the interests of the immense majority. It conveyed the message that the proletarians had nothing to lose except their chains, by the communist revolution, whereby they had a world to win. It ended with the message of solidarity "Working Men of All Countries, Unite".

The message of the Manifesto influenced the working classes of England, Germany, France, Switzerland, Poland and other West European countries and the USA. They waged struggles against the bourgeoisie.

(ii) The First International (1864-1876)

The First International (International Working Men's Association) came into being in 1864 in London, when the working class of Europe had gathered sufficient strength to fight the bourgeoisie after some lull. Its aim was to weld together into one huge army the whole militant working class of Europe and America. Marx prepared the Inaugural Address and Rules for this Association. The First International was open to local and national workers' societies, known as sections and included all possible forms of workers organisations, viz., political parties and propaganda groups, unions, cooperatives and mutual aid societies (Gallin, 2005). The first congress of the International, the first International Labour Congress ever held, met in Geneva in September, 1866. By 1868, the International grew rapidly, as unions developed in many countries.

The workers of the USA also participated in organised labour movement, and it was to their credit that first they recognized the criterion of limiting working day to 8-hour working day. Marx (1971a) noted that the National Labour Union (the General Congress of Labour) in the USA, at Baltimore, on August 16, 1866, declared:

> "The first and great necessity of the present, to free the labour of this country from capitalistic slavery, is the passing of a law by which eight hours shall be the normal working-day in all States of the American Union. We are resolved to put forth all our strength until this glorious result is attained."

At the Geneva Congress of the First International, in September, 1866, it resolved that the limitation of the working-day was a preliminary condition without which all further attempts at improvement and emancipation must prove abortive and the Congress proposed eight hours as the legal limit of the working-day.

The achievements of the First International were all the more remarkable. It gave the first practical expression to labor internationalism and established the first regular contacts between labor organisations of different countries, which survived its demise and became the basis of its successor organisations. The First International ceased to exist as an international organisation in 1872, when its headquarters were removed from London to New York, although it was not officially disbanded. The conflict between Marxists and anarchists led to several splits and eventually contributed to the demise of the International in 1876. Marx became the political leader of the International, but was challenged by the anarchists, because of differences in dealing with the *state power* (Gallin, 2005):

> "Whereas Marxists held that the labor movement had to conquer the State through political action, the anarchists believed that any State could only be authoritarian by nature and therefore had to be destroyed and replaced by federated system of community-based bodies. The syndicalist variant of this school of thought held that trade unions could simply replace the State: since their members were running production and services anyway, political superstructures were redundant and parasitical."

(iii) Paris Commune (1871) – The Impact of the First International

The Paris Commune, the *first proletarian government,* came into existence on March 18, 1871, when the Paris workers overthrew the French government, despite Marx's warning of autumn of 1870 not to take arms. However, Marx greeted this proletarian revolution with the greatest enthusiasm. The new government—composed of radical democrats, socialists and anarchists of various tendencies—proclaimed a democratic republic and introduced some progressive social legislation such as establishment of *a minimum wage, the prohibition of night work in bakeries, reform of public education, etc*. The Commune governed in Paris for eleven weeks. In May, troops under the command of the conservative national government occupied Paris in a week of bloody street fighting. As per

Lenin (1974, p. 27), about 30,000 Parisians were shot down by the bestial soldiery, and about 45,000 were arrested, many of whom were afterwards executed, while thousands were transported or exiled; and thus Paris lost about 100,000 of its best people. In connection with the collapse, Marx and Engels noted "the working class cannot simply lay hold of the ready-made state machinery and wield it for its own purposes." Later, the required state machinery took the form of the proletariat dictatorship. As per Marx, the Commune had demonstrated the ability of workers to exercise power democratically and to reorganise society and the State, and was thus the prototype of the coming socialist revolutions. *The decline of the International was attributed to the repression of the Paris Commune,* which was directly or indirectly the contribution of the French members the International.

(iv) The 1886 American Workers Strike for 8-Hour Working Day

It is historically important that it was the American working class, that had first resolved on August 16, 1866, for 8-Hour working day, under the leadership of the National Labour Union (NLU), which wanted the workers to fight against the capitalist slavery, through independent political action. This attracted the attention of Marx. Thus, in September 1866, the Congress of the First International, at Geneva, on the proposition of the London General Council, resolved:

> "the limitation of the working day is the preliminary condition without which all further attempts at improvements and emancipation must prove abortive ... the Congress proposes eight hours as the legal limit of the working day", (Marx, 1971a, p. 285).
>
> "As this limitation represents the general demand of the workers of the North American United States, the Congress transforms this demand into the general platform of the workers of the whole world", (Trachtenberg).

Later, despite the demise of the International, the American workers were strong on this demand. The Federation of Organised Trades and Labour Unions of the US and Canada, formed in 1881, (later known as the *American Federation of Labour*), at its 4th convention on October 7, 1884 resolved that eight hour day should constitute legal day's labour from May First 1886, and recommended all their organisations to conform to that resolution. This Federation sought collaboration and solidarity of another labour organisation, the Knights of Labour, and made preparations for the strike.

The workers of the Federation and workers of the Knights of Labour, despite the sabotage of the latter's leadership, participated in the strike on May First 1886, for the implementation of the eight-hour day (Trachtenberg). Totally 500,000 workers participated in the strike. The strike was most aggressive in Chicago. At a workers meeting of striking workers on May 3, firing was made killing 6 workers and wounding many. On May 4, at Haymarket Square, the workers gathered in a protest meeting; but bomb was thrown by the police on the mob, which turned into bloody place. Thus, as a mark of commemoration, every year May First has been celebrated as Labour Day since 1890. In this connection, Engels wrote letter on June 3, 1886 to Kelly Wischnewetzky assessing the movement:

> "Our and your bourgeois thought that America stood above class antagonisms and struggles. That delusion has now broken down, the last Bourgeois Paradise on the earth is fast changing into a Purgatorio ... and now they (the proletariat of America) appear all of a sudden in such organised masses as to strike terror into the whole capitalist class." (*Biography of Engels*, Moscow, p. 405)

Engels anticipated a working-class movement on a national scale, a year early despite the opposite opinion in the USA:

> "In February 1885, American public opinion was almost unanimous on this one point; that there was no working class, in the European sense of the word, in America; that consequently no class struggle between workmen and capitalists, such as tore European society to pieces, was possible in the American Republic; and that,

therefore, Socialism was a thing of foreign importation which could never take root on American soil." (Engels, 1845, Preface to American edition, January 26, 1887).

(v) The Second (Socialist) International and World War-I

Several attempts were made to revive an international labor organisation in the 1880s. In this period, socialist mass parties arose in Central and Western Europe, with close links to the trade union movement, much stronger and more representative. Strong anarcho-syndicalist unions also emerged in Southern Europe. The founding of the Second (or Labor) International in Paris in July 1889 (the centennial year of the French Revolution) reflected these developments (Gallin, 2005). Like the First International it was based essentially on the European labour movement, but very much larger than its predecessor. The Second International was essentially a loose federation of parties and trade unions.

One of the most significant decisions of the Paris congress was to declare the First of May as an international day of struggle for the eight-hour day. When May Day 1890 came around, it turned out to be a more forceful and impressive demonstration than its organisers had dared to hope, and the Labor International was revealed, to its enemies and to its followers, as a new political and social reality. The congress of the International in August 1891, noted that the May Day demonstrations had given a tremendous impulse to the labor movement worldwide. May Day became the official day of struggle, of remembrance and of celebration of the international labor movement, which it has remained to this day. *After 1900, the Second International evolved into an organisation of socialist parties.*

At Basle, on November 24-25, 1912, at its congress it adopted a manifesto on war, known as the Basle Manifesto. It warned the peoples against the imminent danger of an imperialist world war and called on the workers of all countries to wage a determined struggle for peace. In case of war, the manifesto recommended socialists to take advantage of the economic and political crisis brought about by the war for carrying out a socialist revolution, thereby initiating a civil war within each country as it would be easy to win the battle when the ruling class and its military was involved in the world war. But, when the world war actually broke out on August 1, 1914 the opportunist leaders of the Second International, including Karl Kautsky, supported their imperialist governments in "defence of fatherland"; and only the Russian, Serbian and Hungarian parties remained true to the principle of the International. Thus, as per Lenin, the international was dead after the outbreak of the World War-I.

(vi) International Federations

International Federation of Trade Unions (IFTU) was formed with workers union non-members in the Second International. The first attempts to establish an international organisation of the trade union federation movement was established in 1901, when the first conference of secretaries of national trade union federations was held at Copenhagen, on the occasion of the Scandinavian Labour Congress. Seven countries were represented, namely: Belgium, Denmark, Germany, England, Finland, Norway and Sweden. By 1903, there were fourteen national trade union federations affiliated to it in 1903. In 1908 the trade union federations of Finland and Croatia were admitted; and in 1909 Bosnia, Rumania and the United States of America became affiliated. In the year 1911 the Bulgarian trade unions were expelled until such time as the rival trade union federations of that country had amalgamated. The Transvaal joined the Federation in 1913. At the outbreak of the World War no less than 20 national trade union federations were organised within the International Federation of Trade Unions. The war stopped the development of the international organisation (Gallin, 2005).

International Trade Secretariats (ITS) were organised for workers solidarity. Twenty eight ITS had been formed by 1911, with a total membership of 6.3 million. The International Transport Workers' Federation (ITF) was founded in 1896 as the International Federation of Ship, Dock and River Workers, adopting its current name in 1898 when it expanded to include transport workers in non-maritime industries. After the First World War started, the Federation virtually ceased to exist in 1915 (Gallin, 2005).

2. The Labour Movement in the Inter-War Period (2nd Period)

In the second phase, the period from the Russian Revolution to the outbreak of the Second World War was dominated by the bitter and increasingly irreconcilable split between the social-democratic and the Communist movements. *In this period, the success of socialist revolution in the USSR encouraged the state to play a somewhat favourable role for the working class, to pacify the revolutionary spirit of the working classes, by supporting the unionisation and collective bargaining. Whereas the capitalist class was on the defensive.*

As the World War-I was going on; in 1917, revolution broke out in Russia: in April, the Tsar was overthrown and replaced by a center-left Constituent Assembly; that government was overthrown in November and replaced by a coalition government of revolutionary socialists, where the radical wing of Russian Social-Democracy, the Bolsheviks, were the dominant political force. Thus, the Union of Soviet Socialist Republics came into existence. In June 1918, *a decree was issued nationalizing the land and the main industries.*

The Third International (The Communist International) was formed in March 1919, in Moscow, under the Bolsheviks. The conference was held to from the new International instead of reconstituting the Second International. Thus, the new International was less representative. The conference, however, adopted a manifesto calling on workers to rise and to establish Soviet republics on the Russian model, called for an uncompromising struggle against all other socialist parties and movements that were not prepared to accept their leadership, adopted provisional statutes and elected a provisional executive committee. In June 1921, immediately after the third congress of the Communist International, an international congress of trade unionists in Moscow established a new trade union International: the Red International of Labor Unions (RILU), a coalition of communist and syndicalist unions, with a close connection to the Communist International.

After the end of the War, the IFTU conference was held at Berne on February 5-9, 1919. The conference focused on achievement of peace and of unity in the labour movement.

Their attitude towards the capitalist system was expressed in terms of open hostility; and their final aim was defined as the abolition of the capitalist system of production. Reforms did not mean a surrender of trade union aims but a preparatory step to their accomplishment. ITF was re-established in 1919, with an Amsterdam office, under the secretaryship of Edo Fimmen, joint secretary of the International Federation of Trade Unions. By 1939, the imminent outbreak of war caused the International Transport Workers' Federation to move to England, initially to a temporary war-time home in Bedford and later to London. Further, International Federation of Christian Trade Unions (IFCTU) was formed in 1920. These unions were made up of Catholic workers mainly from the European countries. Most of those unions were supported politically by Catholic Parties (Gallin, 2003).

International Labour Organaisation (ILO) was formed in 1919, as the Allied Powers met a long-standing demand of the social-democratic labor movement, as a part of the Versailles Peace Treaty. In the context of the time when it was established, *it was meant to be a reformist alternative to the revolutionary threat from Russia*. The ILO, a tri-partite institution with representation from government, employers and workers (in general but not always represented by unions), survived the Second World War and is now part of the United Nations system.

By the time of the emergence of the Second World War in 1939 and after, fascism had wiped out the labour movement in most of Europe: first in Italy and Portugal, then in Germany and Austria, then in Spain, as the German armies occupied nearly all of the continent, everywhere except in Britain and a few remaining neutral or unoccupied countries. The Jewish Labour Bund was destroyed together with the population that supported it.

In this phase, the Bolshevik revolution made two impacts on the labor movement. On the one hand, it greatly strengthened the working class movement, with improved collective bargaining in the developed countries as well as the colonies of West Europe. Further the state began to assume the role of the welfare state, because higher degree of exploitation and repression and suppression might make the working class attracted towards communism. At the same time, Bolshevism caused a deep rift in the socialist movement. Most socialist parties and unions rejected the Bolshevik system of a political dictatorship supported by terror and stressed that political democracy was an inseparable part of socialism.

3. *Labour Movement in the Post Second World War Period (3rd Period)*

This period starts with the end of the Second World War and ends with the collapse of Soviet socialism in 1991. The period, *1945-1980,* may be treated as the early period, which was favourable to the working classes all over the world. But, the latter period, *1980-1991,* may be treated as reactionary phase. During this latter period, the IMF-World Bank forced the Structural Adjustment Programme (SAP) upon almost all the Third World Countries, which was intended to withdraw the state from economic affairs, paving the way for liberalisation, privatisation and globalisation (LPG).

(i) The Early Period in Third Phase (1945-1980)

As the USSR worked with the anti-Fascist capitalist countries including the USA, during the Second World War, this wartime alliance was also reflected in the trade union movement. A united trade union organisation, World Federation of Trade Unions (WFTU), was formed in Paris, in December 1945; as the western social democratic unions cooperated with the unions of the USSR. Thus, the IFTU had to be dissolved. The International Transport Workers' Federation (ITF) continued to flourish since the end of the Second World War from its base in London and engaged in world-wide campaigns on a range of issues. *In fact, the state became more favourable to the working classes in the post-Second World War phase. Keynesian revolution, which emerged as aconomitant of the Great Deppression of late 1920s, highlighted the role of public sector, by favouring the state's interference in economic affairs. Thus, the state acted in favour of collective bargaining and unionisation.*

After the Marshall Plan was declared for the recovery of war-shattered Europe, the communist labour unions opposed this Plan, whereas it was welcomed by the social democratic unions. There were splits in the labour movement in France, Germany and Italy. Among the American unions, American Federation of Labour (AFL) left the WFTU, but Congress of the Industrial Organisations (CIO) remained with WFTU. ITS also, disagreeing with the communist unions, broke of relations with the WFTU. All the non-communist labour unions, which left the WFTU, formed in 1949 a separate federation called International Confederation of Free Trade Unions (ICFTU). Thereafter, the WFTU continued as the Soviet controlled federation, with the Soviet bloc unions and a few communist-led unions of Europe, of Asia and Latin America. International Federation of Christian Trade Unions (IFCTU), which was formed in 1920, reorganised on its own in 1945. It expanded outside Europe, with affiliations in Canada, in the former French colonies in Africa where the French Christian unions had established branches, in Latin America and in Asia. It decided to broaden its membership to include unions based on other religious affiliations (like the Buddhists of South Vietnam) and, in 1968, changed its name to World Confederation of Labor (WCL). At the same time, it developed an anti-capitalist program, incorporating elements of liberation theology, and seeking to position itself somewhere to the left of the ICFTU (Gallin, 2005).

The Communist labour movement emerged very strongly at first, as a dominant force in France and Italy, but also strong elsewhere in Europe, building on its prestige in the resistance movement (which it had joined only after 1941, when Nazi Germany attacked the USSR) and by the prestige of the USSR as the principal land-based power in Europe that had defeated Nazi Germany. The social-democratic labour movement emerged from the war superficially victorious, actually greatly weakened by its losses, and far more dependent on the State than it had been before the war (Gallin, 2003).

(a) Cold War Conditions: A Compromise between the Capital and Labour

In the post Second World War period, most of the Third world countries, which were either colonies or semi-colonies, became independent. In 1949, China liberated itself and emerged as the communist China. At this point, the Cold War became the new global political reality. Each of the two superpowers were deploying tremendous financial and political resources to control the labour movement in support of their bloc. The labour movement became polarized. In fact, along with *the Cold War* conditions, adoption of Keynesian *economic policies* and application of *Fordist mass production* system contributed for the strengthening the labour movement. But by the end of this early Phase, the conditions for weakening the labour movement (through *Toyatist flexible production system*) also appeared.

In post Second World War, Keynesian revolution got upper hand, as it stressed state interference in Demand management. The Development Economics joined hands with Keynesianism. During the period of dominance of Keynesian economics, the developed capitalist countries supported state-intervention for industrialization (through planning process) and also involved in solving the food problem of the developing countries through the export of food grains for some time and later by the export of green revolution. It seems, all this was done as a strategic compulsion, due to cold war conditions, for the fear that the developing countries might fall into the orbit of socialist bloc, if the people would get revolutionised by communist ideology.

There was a *compromise* between the capital and labour, because of constant threat to the world capitalism that working class might take the path of Russia or China. Due to Keynesian influence, *the role of state* increased in the economic affairs turning it into a *welfare state*. In most of the developing countries public sector assumed importance in production of capital goods and provision of public utilities and services. In Western Europe, the state appeased the working class by providing social security and free provision of the health and education.

(b) Change in Production Conditions: Strengthening to Weakening of Labour Movement

By the end of this early phase of the Third period (1945-1980), there were changes in the production system of industrial organisation from Fordism to flexible production system. Ford's production system was an outcome of the application of scientific management of Taylorism, which depended on the minute level division of labour. This brought into existence, the *worker* of the assembly lines, the 'mass worker'. *Already organised by their employers, they were easily mobilized on behalf of their own interests.* In every developed country, labor unions emerged as the best-organised and often the most powerful political force. Their preferences were reflected not only in labor laws, but also in public policy generally. *They were the architects and chief supporters of the postwar Keynesian welfare state, with its goals of full employment, social security, and income parity. Indeed, some refer to the welfare state as the Fordist state.* During the development of the working class, it discovered the secret of the production of relative surplus value and learned to exploit this knowledge in its struggle for a fairer share of the product of the national economies of the industrialised world. This in part explains *the powerful workerist movements of the 1940s-1980s.* Due to increase in the deskilling of labour, the unskilled assembly workers eventually reaped substantial gains from increased industrial productivity. In the English-speaking world, unions enforced artificial scarcity to win supra-competitive wages for their members—sometimes on their own, sometimes in cooperation with other unions, and sometimes in collusion with specific firms (Thompson).

But as per Gramsci, this phase of industrial organisation would yield to a new phase leading to displacement of the labour:

"Taylor is in fact expressing with brutal cynicism the purpose of American society—developing in the worker to the highest degree automatic and mechanical attitudes, breaking up the old psycho-physical nexus of qualified professional work, which demands a certain active participation of intelligence, fantasy and initiative on the part of the worker, and reducing productive operations exclusively to the mechanical, physical aspect. But these things, in reality, are not original or novel: they represent simply the most recent phase of a long process which began with industrialism itself. This phase is more intense than preceding phases, and manifests itself in more brutal forms, but it is a phase which will itself be superseded by the creation of a psycho-physical nexus of a new type, both different from its predecessors and undoubtedly superior. A forced selection will ineluctably take place; a part of the old working class will be pitilessly eliminated from the world of labour, and perhaps from the world tout court". (*Prison Note Books,* on internet)

This new phase was introduced through Toyatism, *the flexible production system (FPS),* which dramatically reduced the demand for unskilled labor. Flexible production required numerate and literate workers, capable of a high degree of self-direction. As a consequence, the number of unskilled industrial workers in the developed world has been falling for nearly thirty years. Decreased numbers have been reflected in political decline, as unskilled labor lost its leading role in the union movement and union influence in general has waned, and also in falling relative or, in some cases, real wages. Increasingly, workers are forced to choose between full employment (the US choice) and job security (Western Europe's).

Like Fordism, *this second transformation* extends well beyond process engineering. It is transforming not only how we make things, but also how we live and what we consume. It reflects the declining importance of both scale and scope and is driven by reductions in communications, logistics, and information processing costs—reductions stimulated if not caused by the introduction of computers and by our increasing ability to use them. Thus, new system of production is in a position to cut the costs, mainly labour costs, while increasing the profits of the capitalist class.

(ii) The Latter Period in Third Phase (1980-1991)

By early 1980s the Western Europe and the US were affected by stagflation. In Poland and East European countries the internal contradictions were being blown up. In the former countries, there had been severe recession during 1980 and 1981 and further projections showed slower rates of growth for these countries. But, slower rates of growth were insufficient to sustain: *(i)* high standard of living of their people and *(ii)* social security system there. In the US also, there was decline in the productivity and decline in the competitiveness, fuelled by cold war and the cult of deterrence (Dubey, 1992). Thus, the stage had come for Structural Adjustment Programme (SAP) in their own economies of the developed countries. But instead of this, the developed countries imposed the structural adjustment on the developing countries, as they were suffering from the debt crisis, through the Bretton Woods Institutions (BWI), viz. World Bank and IMF. Reagan and Thatcher under the influence of the Supply side economics (under the SAP) repressed the internal lablour movement, while encouraging the collapse of socialism in the East European countries and the USSR by 1991.

The phase of international economy (up to late 1980s) gave scope for the unity of imperialist powers of the capitalist world, as against the socialist bloc countries, with a threat of communist alternative. This collusion of imperialist capitalist powers was called *'Ultra-imperialism' by* Kautsky, at the beginning of this century. Lenin opposed the thesis of Kautsky (Patnaik, 1995). But it became a reality soon after the World War-II, though Lenin's thesis of imperialism held correct till that time. Somewhat less aggressive and hesitating collusion of imperialist powers has been further strengthened by the downfall of socialist bloc countries, with continuing ultra-imperialism under the uni-polar world.

The collapse of socialism was an outcome of discontentment among the working classes of the East European countries and the USSR, after the experience of the *Solidarity movement* in Poland. At the same time, the other European social-democratic unions had stopped asserting their political and ideological identity. The collapse of socialism, during 1989-91, threw the labour movement into an unprepared crisis: ideologically, politically, organisationally. The labour movement could not offer political alternative.

By the time of collapse of socialism in the Eastern Europe and the USSR, came globalisation on the agenda of liberalization. The advanced capitalist countries imposed globalisation on the developing countries, when they approached BWI for loans and help. While giving loans, Bretton Woods Institutions attached conditionalities to liberalise imports of the developing countries and devalue their currencies to facilitate the entry of the MNCs or foreign companies into their territories to capture their markets and exploit their natural resources. This is in the name of competition (Dasgupta, 1997). Involvement in international trade is prescribed as panacea for all the problems of the developing countries.

After the end of Cold War, the capitalist classes of the developed capitalist countries are free from the fear of communism; and the feeling of 'End of History' has been prevailing. For them, the capitalism had triumphed on all fronts and for the capitalists the compromise with labour (of the cold war) was no longer necessary. Now the capitalist forces could pursue their narrow economic and political interests with fewer inhibitions. The historical and economic preconditions for such a compromise are no longer there, and the most important product of this compromise, *the welfare state*, is under increasing pressure (Wahl, 2004).

The general question of the World Order is put to the working class in very urgent and pressing terms. They are facing an onslaught on their movement, world wide, of a kind that they have not experienced since the 1930s. They are facing this onslaught at every level: in the industrial democracies, social welfare and social protection are being dismantled, democratic rights and union rights are being eroded; the rest of the world is caught in a poverty trap, often maintained by repression, from which there seems no escape. This obviously calls for a global political response (Gallin, 2003a).

4. *The Labour Movement in the Globalisation Period (4th Period)*

This phase starts from 1991 onwards. After the collapse of East European and Soviet socialism; the liberalisation, privatisation and globalisation (LPG) policies have been adopted in the advanced as well as the developing countries, in the name of TINA (there is no alternative). As a part of liberalisation package, the state withdrawal from economic affairs led to undermining the state's support to the working classes, through minimum wage laws and other labour protective laws. As a result, the conditions for constraining labour movement that germinated by the end of the third phase have developed to the higher level in this fourth phase.

In this phase, the following changes have taken place to weaken labour movement in the formal as well as the informal sectors of the developing economies.

(i) Flexible Production System

Added to the changes in the socio-political dimensions, another dimension is the changes in the production system, as already explained in subsection-4.3. Toyatist production system has been developed out of Fordist method. Toyatism is seen in different forms: Lean Production, Just in Time (JIT), Macdonaldisation, Total Quality Management (TQM). All these are part of Flexible Productions Systems (FPS). In workplaces worldwide lean production is being introduced, where a managerial control system pioneered by Japaneese automobile companies. This management has abandoned Taylorism and substituted more humane and worker-centred factories and offices (Yates, 2001). Capital is continuously in search of either reducing work by replacing humans with machines and/or intensifying the process further through management methods of reengineering and restructuring (Varman and Chakrabarthi, 2003).

In the name of empowerment of labour, quality circles, *kaizens*, team work, multi-skilling etc., the lean production leads to actual disempowerment of the workers, as per Chandra (2004):

> "Lean production is mean production. What it implies is that the enterprise would retain a few highly skilled workers in its core competency areas as its regular highly paid employees and employ casual and contract labour, part-time workers and mostly source out the jobs to informal sectors across the globe that is coterminus with bad jobs with low wages, long working hours, inhuman working conditions, total insecurity of employment and income. The so-called decentralisaton of production amounts to this shift from organised sector to the informal sector.... The labour market characteristics of the informal sector mainly derive from the fact that the workers of this sector remain unorganised. To the extent labour is getting

> disorganised in the organised sector as reflected in the decline of the trade union membership, there is at least the attrition of the bargaining power of the workers in this sector as well."

As per Reddy (2005), flexibilisation has become the thrust of organisation of production and labour markets. Flexibility of work takes many forms. The numerical flexibility leads to the adjustment of the number of workers suited to employer's needs. Externalisation can put part of the work for subcontracting. Internal flexibility adjusts working hours. Functional flexibility involves in modifying workers' jobs. Wage flexibility may also be there. To this list, spatial or geographical flexibility may be added, which means that geographically concentrated and socially homogeneous industrial working class of semi-skilled factory labourers are being increasingly replaced by socially diverse and geographically dispersed labour forces. Due to adoption of flexibilisation, during last two decades, through de-industrialisation and industrial reorganisation, there has been dismantling of many of the forces and institutions of traditional (blue-collar and unionized) working class forms of power.

(ii) Rising Share of Service Sector Employment

As per Antunes (2001), in the world of labour today there is a reduction of manual proletariat, steady factory workers, typical of the Taylorist and Fordist period. The shrinking of this proletariat has happened all over the world, though obviously there are differences due to the particularities of each country, of its insertion in the international labour division, though there was tendency of rising labour in absolute terms in the 1960s, 70s and 80s.

Further, the share of employment in productive sectors, in the total non-agricultural workforce, has been going down. As per Braverman (1994), in the USA, the share of employment of manufacturing, mining and construction sectors together in total non-agricultural workers formed nearly 50.0 percent during 1820-1920; but, by 1970, this share came down to 33.0 percent. This happened so because of the displacement of the workers in the productivity rising sectors (while employment rising in quite less proportion) to be absorbed in the non-productive sectors, such as, the banking, the insurance, the investment, the brokerage, the real estate industries; the accounting and control industries including those operated by the government in the form of regulatory or tax agencies; the relief industries, such as those which deal with unemployment compensation or welfare.

In the developed countries, in the globalization era, by mid-1990s, the share of employment in services sector formed about 60.0 percent of the total employment; which is an indication that those developed economies are getting increasingly geared to catering to the fancies of the affluent, instead of providing food, clothes, shelter etc., to the millions of the hungry, naked and roofless populations of the world (Roy, 1995). In the USA, at present the service sector is occupying nearly 80.0 percent of the total employment. Yates (2001) says that these are mostly skilled workers like the new crafts workers are business managers, consultants, and marketing and financial experts as well as scientific and technical researchers and computer specialists. The new skilled workforce must be treated with respect by the employer and made a full participant in the running of the enterprise. Modern management now focuses on the team nature of production, and workers, often called "associates," are no longer treated as hands to be manipulated but as members of the corporate team. Indeed, employers now routinely concern themselves with the development of the whole person and urge workers to think of the company as a place where their social life and their work life merge into a creative whole. Stock options and profit sharing further merge the interests of associates and firm. These workers may not have any interest in labour movement, because of the so-called *Hawthorne effect*.

(iii) Rising Precurious Employment

Antunes (2001) notes that parallel to the reduction of stable jobs, there has been a boom of jobs for part time men and women and for temporary jobs. This is a strong manifestation of this new segment that composes the working class today, an expression of this new proletariat. As per Gapasin and Yates (2005), besides damaging workers directly, the class war waged by employers has also radically restructured employment. Worldwide, there are many hundred million persons who are either openly unemployed or engaged in extremely marginal informal employment. This group includes millions of displaced peasants living in the sprawling urban slums surrounding the great cities of the global South. Among the rest of the working class, various kinds of contingent employment have spread rapidly—homeworkers, temporary workers, contracted workers, self-employed (and self-exploited) workers. Full-time, year-round employment is much less common, even in the rich nations, than it was in the generation following the Second World War. What is more, workers once secure in their employment must now face the likelihood of being uprooted and forced to move both within and among countries to find work, making the working class of every nation more ethnically and racially diverse. And everywhere, work stress and work danger are on the rise. *Needless to say, all of these changes create difficulties for workers trying to organise themselves into unions and political organisations.*

(iv) Feminisation of Labour

There is an increase of feminine work in the labour world, not only in industry, but also and essentially in the services sector. Working class has always been as much feminine as masculine. Only that now the proportion has altered considerably. In England, for example, working women have outstripped working men. In several European countries, about 40.0 to 50.0 percent or more of the whole labour is feminine. Even the more are the part time jobs spreading; the more the feminine labour penetrates this universe, as per Antunes (2001). Ghosh (2003) notes the fact that in South East Asian and East Asian countries, in export processing zones and export-oriented manufacturing, the share of female employment exceeds 70.0 percent. The reasons for this feminisation of work are: (a) women have lower reservation wage, (b) women accept to work longer hours, (c) they agree to work in unpleasant, unhealthy and hazardous factory conditions, (d) they can be easily hired and fired, (e) they do not claim permanent contracts, and (f) most importantly they do not have unions for collective bargaining.

(v) Exclusion of the Young from Employment

There is a terrible exclusion of the young and of the "old" in the sense given by the destructive capital. The young are those who graduate from high schools and colleges and still do not have a space in the labour market. Young Europeans, young Americans and also young Brazilians see that there is no guarantee of room for them in the labour market. In Europe, the only thing they can be sure of is unemployment. This is also a characteristic of our labour market. And workers of 40 or more are now considered old by the capital. Once they lose their jobs, they do not return to the labour market (Antunes, 2001).

(vi) Lack of Solidarity among the Working Classes

As Reddy (2003) notes, the globalisation has created serious hurdles for cross-border solidarity especially between the workers of the less-developed countries and those of the developed countries. Tensions are created between the unions in developed countries and those in less-developed countries that the cheap labour-based exports from the latter would lead to loss of jobs in the developed countries. The multinational corporations attribute the high unemployment rates in the developed countries to the poor workers of the Third World (as they work for lower wages), as part of the design to divide the labour movement. Also, the MNCs appeal to the workers in the developed countries to cut down their wages, or keep wages flat, under the threat that the work would be outsourced to the workers of the less-developed countries. This also causes bone of contention for the unions in the developed countries.

V. Is there 'End of Labour' and Non-Necessity of Labour Movement?

As there is a void kept by the labour movement in opposing the global capitalist class in a befitting manner, the independent movements are developing, called *the social movements,* single issue movements and protest movements against globalising capitalism dominated by transnational corporations. They are capable of forming powerful coalitions: the World Social Forum is one of their platforms. Some originate in authoritarian traditions; most are anti-authoritarian as well as anti-capitalist.

The vast majority of the world working class today is not organised. Now about 90.0 percent of the world's workers are not organised. This is so because partly the working class has changed, and partly over a large part of the world trade unionism is repressed. One of the major changes in the world working class is the growing informalization of work and the growth of the informal economy, which is outside of the scope of traditional union organizing. Organizing in the informal economy again requires political skills and the creation of alliances, in this instance principally with women's organisations. Such political skills, much less a political vision, are not currently much in evidence (Gallin, 2003a).

Organising women workers is also important, by taking into account the specific needs of women such as equality of opportunity and treatment (Reddy, 2003). Further, the working class is as feminine as it is masculine, and socialism will not be built only by the masculine part of the class. The class trade unions will not be those of men-only. Today it is predominant in many areas, in diverse sectors, and especially in the sector of part time jobs, which has been spreading all over the world in these last years. Precisely because capital has realised that women do polyvalent activities, at home and in their jobs out of home, it has exploited this polyvalence intensely. Capital has become aware of the polyvalence in it. It has already been exploiting feminine work in the domestic chores, in the sphere of reproduction, and now this exploitation is amplified to embrace also the factory and services space (Antunes, 2001).

Chandra (2004) rightly raises about the role of working class in regard to the maintenance of ecological and environmental balance. Such issues will be useful in allying with other social movements, such as social justice unionism, social unionism, transformative unionism, class struggle unionism and social movement unionism (Hassan, 2000).

Hassan says:

> "The labour left not only need to advance a programme of labour solidarity, but it also needs to promote intermovement of solidarity and that the sharing of experiences in the different sectors and trades, in order to deatomise the experience of workers. Learning about and from other social movements can have a direct impact on the strategies and tactics that unfold within organised labour. In this sense, the term social movement unionism has a particular ring. This has been historically demonstrated and is true today."

In many countries the relationship between the trade union movement and its historical allies, the social-democratic and labor parties, has become difficult. Yet, the trade union movement needs a political dimension, because *all trade union activity is political by nature*. In the present situation, restoring the political dimension to the trade union movement cannot mean re-establishing allegiances and much less dependencies with respect to existing political parties, nor taking control of a political party. But the politics of the trade union movement have to be reinvented, taking as a point of departure the interests of its members at the point of production (Gallin, 2005). Further, the working class has the urgent political tasks: *stopping privatisation and deregulation, repealing anti-union legislation imposed on us by disgraceful governments and maintained by other disgraceful governments. One such piece of legislation is the virtual outlawing of solidarity strikes, particularly international solidarity strikes, in most industrialised countries. In a globalised economy, that is precisely the right to strike we most need, and that we must take back* (Gallin, 2004).

David Bacon—who reviewed Kim Moody's book, *Workers in a Lean World*—highlights Moody's stress on the political aspect as the dominant factor for the trade union movement or the labour movement but not economic aspect alone, so as to mount a militant opposition to defeat neo-liberalism. For this, a radicalized labour movement is required. As per Yates (2001) the new labor movement should embrace a struggle for at least the following:

> "(1) Employment as a right; (2) meaningful work with maximum integration in every job, of our uniquely human capability to conceptualize and carry out work tasks, and a sharing of society's more onerous tasks; (3) a good deal of consumption fully socialized, including education at all levels, health care, care for the aged, child care, transportation, and recreation; (4) maximum democratic control of production, whether by workers or communities or both; (5) hours of work as low as possible; (6) work as nondestructive of nature as possible; (7) no discrimination of any kind; and (8) equality (not just some sham equality of opportunity) seen as a good in itself."

Recently there are some positive symptoms of improvement for the Unity of labour movement at the global level, as the 'New Voices' leadership of the Amercan Federation of Labour-Congress of Industrial Organisations (AFL-CIO), since 1995, has been showing change in its policies from those of the past, and now it is openly critical of free trade and imperial intervention in other parts of the world (Reddy, 2003).

"End of Labour" has been a thesis presently echoed in the capitalist circles, as the humans are being replaced by the machines; and in fact, this is also in line with the theses of "end of ideology' and "end of history." There is a view that as the worker friendly environment, with less hazardous work, is provided by the recent technologies, there is no necessity of labor movement and so the labour unions are anachronisms (Yates, 2001). Whatever the level of technology, the human agency is required in the process of production of goods and services, because *living labour has to coordinate and cooperate with dead labour always* (Antunes, 2000). It is a fact that though there is no 'end of work', there is informalisation of work (Varman and Chakrabarti, 2003). Thus, the necessity to organise all informal sector working class as for the part-time workers, contractual workers, temporary workers and casual labourers. Not only in the sense of proletariat, but all the salaried workers are to be taken into this fold (Antunes, 2001).

VI. Conclusion

As seen from the exploitative characteristics of the capitalism, which resulted in *the self-estrangement and the estrangement of the thing* for the working people (Marx, 1977), there was a historical necessity for the genesis and development of labour movement, in the sense of not losing anything but chains. By the middle of 19th century, when the industrial revolution was on the full speed, the roots of labour movement formed in the West Europe, particularly in England. The capability of working class to fight against the ruling class, when this class was same as the exploiting class (bourgeoisie), was proven unequivocally from the Paris Commune of 1871 first, and later by the capturing of state power in Russia. Till the Second world war, and till the imperialist capitalist countries colluded into ultra-imperialism, the working class movement was not satisfied with the economic agenda alone and there was political agenda to capture state power. After Russia's victory in defeating fascist Hitler and the formation of communist China, the ruling classes, who were separate from the exploiting classes but serving their interests, began to compromise with the working classes, by adopting Keynesian state-interventionist policies with pro-labour bias; for the fear that working classes might take over power. Thus, the bargaining power of the labour was improved. The ruling classes all the world over adopted the welfare state, with relative autonomy to state. This also made the working classes to pacify themselves, confining to the economic benefits in the advanced countries particularly, and they kept aside the political agenda of capturing state power.

Till late 1970s, the Fordist production system of assembly line developed labour movement, because the unity developed among deskilled multitudes of workers on the shopfloor or within the factory premises. As gradual adoption of flexible production system (Toyatist methods), accompanied by scientific and technological progress, has been picking up; the engaged labour in the heavy industries is being reduced by the capitalist classes in the developed countries and in the developed sectors of the developing countries. In fact, Taylorist-Fordist-Toyatist combination of production and management methods caused reduction in regular employment and increased casual, part-time, contractual and temporary employment. Further, subcontracting and outsourcing work on-shore and off-shore are being increasingly practiced by the multinational corporations. This practice along with the informalisation of work has created insecurity among the working classes of the world, thereby undermining the labour moment. Exactly at this time, globalization united the capitalist classes of the world, and began to threaten the working classes keeping them in precarious employment conditions, as there is no fear of the working class taking the communist path, due to collapse of socialism in the East Europe and the USSR.

Now the working classes are realizing the importance of achieving unity among themselves allover the world, by organising all sections of the informal sector workers including women workers, by joining hands with all social movements including those in favour of environment and peace and against wars. The agenda no more confines to economic benefits alone. The political agenda of capturing state power is gaining strength. Thus, there is no *end of labour,* and no end of labour movement.

References

Antunes, Ricardo (2000), "The Tansformation in the Working Class", *Marxism Alive,* October.

_______ (2001), "The New Proletarians of the World at the Turn of the Century", *Marxism Alive,* June.

Braverman, Harry (1994), "The making of the U.S. Working Class", *Monthly Review,* Vol. 46, No. 6, November.

Chandra, Navin (2004), "Collective Bargaining in the Era of Lean Production", The *Indian Journal of Labour Economics,* Vol. 47, No. 4, October-December.

Chattopadhyay, Paresh (1985): "On the Problematic of the State as Capitalist and its Significance for the Third World: An Essay in the Critique of Political Economy", in Ashok Mitra (ed.), *The Truth Unites,* Subarna Rekha, Calcutta.

Dasgupta, Biplab (1997) "SAP: Issues and Conditionalities–A Global Review", *Economic and Political Weekly,* May 17-24.

Dubey, Muchkund (1992): "Political Economy of the Uruguay Round of Trade Negotiations", *Mainstream,* May 30, June 6 and 13.

Engels, Fredrick (1845/1887), *The Condition of the Working Class in England,* Marx and Engels Archives on internet.

Gallin, Dan (2003a), "The International Labour Movement: History and Ideologies", Center Praxis Conference: *The Anti-Totalitarian Left: Between Past and Future,* Moscow, June 21-22, available GLI website.

_____ (2003b), "Strategies for the Labour Movement", Conference on *Globalisation 2003,* LO Skolen, Helsingør, August 20-22, available GLI website.

_____ (2004), "Contemporary Issues in the International Trade Union Movement", T&GWU Seminar: *Globalisation, Development and International Trade Union Movement,* Eastbourne, April 16-23, available GLI website.

_____ (2005), "The Labor Movement", A shorter version of this paper will be published by Harvard University in 2005 as part of a textbook on social movements (working title: *Claiming Global Power: Transnational Civil Society and Global Governance),* available GLI website.

Gapasin, Fernando E. and Michael D. Yates (2005), "Labor Movements: Is There Hope?", *Monthly Review,* Vol. 57, No. 2, June.

Ghosh, Jayati (2003), "Changes in the World of Work", *The Indian Journal of Labour Economics,* Vol. 46, No. 4, October–December.

Hassan, Khalil (2000), "The Future of the Labour Left", *Monthly Review,* Vol. 52, No. 3, July/August.

Lenin, V.I (1974), *On the Paris Commune,* 1974, Progress Publishers, Moscow.

Marx, Karl (1971a), *Capital, Vol. I,* Progress Publishers, Moscow.

_______ (1971b), *Capital, Vol. III,* Progress Publishers, Moscow.

_______ (1977), *Economic and Philosophic Manuscripts of 1844,* Progress Publishers, Moscow.

Patnaik, Prabhat (1995), "Nation-State in the Era of Globalisation", *Economic and Political Weekly,* August 19.

Pruijit, Hans (2002), "Repainting, Modifying, Smashing Taylorism", *Journal of Organisational Change Management,* Vol. 13, No. 5, November 14.

Reddy, D. Narasimha (2003), "Changing World Economic Order and World of Workers: New Trends in Organising Labour", *The Indian Journal of Labour Economics,* Vol. 46, No. 2, April-June.

_______ (2005), "Challenges of Decent Work in the Globalising World", *The Indian Journal of Labour Economics,* Vol. 48, No. 1, January-March.

Roy, Ajit (1995): "Civil Society and Nation State in the Context of Globalisation", *Economic and Political Weekly,* August 5-12.

Thompson, Fred (n.d), *Fordism, Post-Fordism and the Flexible System of Production,* Public Management and Policy Centre, Atkinson Graduate School of Management, Williamette University, Salem, Oregon, 97301, USA; (available on net).

Trachtenberg, Alexander (1932), *The History of May Day,* International Pamphlets, 1932 (marxists.org)

Varman, Rahul and Manali Chakrabarti (2003), "Workers Struggles in Times of Globalisation: A Critique of Trade Unions in Historical Perspective", The *Indian Journal of Labour Economics,* Vol. 46, No. 4, October-December.

Wahl, Asbjorn (2004), "European Labour: The Ideological Legacy of the Socialist Pact", Monthly *Review,* Vol. 55, No. 8, January.

Young, Robert M. (1974), "Braverman's *Labour and Monopoly Capital*", *Radical Science Jouranl,* No.4, pp.81-93.

Yates, Michael (1999), "Braverman and the Class Struggle", *Monthly Review,* Vol. 50, No. 8, January.

_______ (2001), "The 'New' Economy and the Labour Movement", Monthly *Review,* Vol. 52, No. 11, April.

3

STATE INTERVENTION AND LABOUR MARKET IN INDIA: ISSUES AND OPTIONS

Dipa Mukherjee & Rajarshi Majumder

I. Introduction

Interaction between State and Labour came into being as work became organised and some sort of regimentation of workforce started. Historically, laws and acts concerning labour originated to ensure regular and disciplined workforce to the modern sectors of production—mines, plantations and factories. This was done to ensure that wavering commitment of workers migrating from the traditional agricultural sector to these sectors does not create recurring shortages of labour and irregular production. As surplus rural workers came to perceive that the wages offered by these modern sectors were substantially higher than they were earning at home, transition of labourers became more permanent and regular. With abundant labour supply, the balance of power shifted towards the employers who now began to exploit the workers—by paying little, employing children and women who were paid even less, paying no attention to working or living conditions, operating 18 hour shifts, and offering no provision for leave of absence. This has been the experience worldwide—from the first industrial revolution in Britain to the newly industrialising economies of Asia and Africa. As a result, while the initial laws were pro-employer, laws in the later periods were pro-employee, enacted to prevent inhuman exploitation of the workers and offer them a dignified living. However, while the objectives of State intervention into matters related to Labour are justified and commendable, the effect of these interventions has not always been commensurate to their aims. In this paper we attempt to look at State policies towards Labour in India and the major impact of such policies on the labour market and the economy.

II. Labour Policies in India—An Overview

There have been two basic tenets of labour policies in India related to the fields of (a) Employment security, and, (b) Minimum wages and other benefits. These laws have also moved through the same phases as discussed earlier.

1. Employment Security

The first piece of labour legislation, *The Workmen's Breach of Contract Act, 1859* was enacted to make any breach of contract by workers punishable by law as a crime. Though it was repealed in 1926 allowing trade unions to function, employment regulations till 1947 (e.g. *Trade Disputes Act, 1929; Rule 81-A of the Defence of India Rules, 1942*) aimed to secure uninterrupted production, not employment security. In addition, predominance of foreign owned enterprises meant that Indian workers were struggling against the colonial masters.

After independence, labour laws were enacted to eradicate labour exploitation and to shift the balance of power from the employers to the workers. The other objective was to enhance the welfare of the workers in general so that they can live with dignity. This was expected to spread prosperity to a larger mass of people in the long run. Employment security was provided through regulations and State interventions, and market forces were substituted by forcing employers to ensure certain minimum standards. In cases of the contractual conditions being lower than the legal minima, the legal conditions would supersede the contractual agreements. The plethora of labour related laws in Independent India started with the *Industrial Disputes Act, 1947* that succeeded the *Industrial Employment (Standing Orders) Act, 1946*. This Act puts in black and white the rights and obligations of employees and employers related to almost every aspect of organised employment. The earlier law provided for settlement of disputes regarding termination, through compulsory adjudication by appropriate authority in absence of mutually satisfying agreement between employer and employee. There were no restrictions on retrenchment until 1976 if an employer followed reverse chronological order, gave a month's notice or pay in lieu of notice, paid half a month's average pay for every year of continuous service or any part in excess of six months and informed the government. For retrenchment following closure, the requirement of sixty days' notice was introduced in 1972 but retrenchment remained the sole prerogative of the employer till 1976. Amendments to the Industrial Disputes Act in 1976 and 1982 placed severe restrictions on employers and required three months' notice and prior permission from 'appropriate government' for retrenchment or closure in industrial establishments employing 100 or more workers. While these provisions were disputed in court, in 1984 these were reintroduced through an Amendment to the Constitution. Certification of service rules under the Industrial Employment (Standing Orders) Act, 1946 has been another source of employment security. Along with these, *The Shops and Establishments Act, 1953* attempts to provide statutory obligation and rights to employees and employers in shops and establishments.

2. *Wages and Benefits*

State intervention in determining wages has also been quite substantial in India, and quite pervasive in the organised sector. The basic framework was set out in *The Report of the Committee on Fair Wages, 1948* following which the government designed fairly elaborate methods of intervention. For the organised sector, Tripartite Wage Boards were established to guarantee a decent minimum wage to the workers. For Central Public Sector Undertakings (CPSUs), there are periodic wage settlements by the Department of Public Enterprises and the state-level PSUs follows the Central PSUs. Rules related to indexation compensate workers for rising cost of living through Dearness Allowances. In addition, *Payment of Bonus Act, 1965* provides statutory bonus. Workers and employees have automatic annual increments to basic wages and in some establishments receive welfare benefits and other allowances. The government has also attempted to limit wage inequality through the *Indian Companies Act, 1956*. The main instrument for ensuring minimum wages in the unorganised sector is the *Minimum Wages Act, 1948*, under which minimum wages for an eight-hour work-day has been fixed for certain types of jobs where the market conditions expose the workers to exploitation.

To these were added *The Factories Act, 1948* ensuring adequate safety measures, health and welfare of the factory workers; *The Employees State Insurance Act, 1948* providing health cover, medical care and cash benefits for sickness, etc.; *The Employees Provident Funds and Misc. Provisions Act, 1952* making provisions for old age security or death benefits; *The Maternity Benefit Act, 1961* providing relief to women workers; *The Contract Labour (Regulation & Abolition) Act, 1970* stipulating 9 hours work for them between 6 A.M. and 7 P.M. only; *The Payment of Gratuity Act, 1972; The Equal Remuneration Act, 1976* ensuring equal remuneration to men and women workers for similar work; *The Inter-state Migrant Workmen (Regulation of Employment and Conditions of Service) Act, 1979*. Taken together, these legislations ensure a dignified work environment, a certain minimum remuneration, and aims to prevent discrimination and exploitation in the labour market.

Thus there have been a plethora of laws and acts in the post-independent India, mainly directed to protect the workers from the vagaries of employers. We have to look at what has been the practice under this maze of State interventions in the labour market.

III. Implementation of Labour Policies—The Practice

While the labour laws have been commendable in their declared intentions to protect fundamental rights of workers, they are hardly implemented in any meaningful way for most workers in the country. Moreover, as the Second Labour Commission points out:

"... our labour laws have not flowed from any vision

of a harmonious and just social order that takes into account the needs of an efficient and non-exploitative society, or a vision of the rights, duties and responsibilities of the different social partners to themselves, to each other, and to the totality of the community." (Report of Second National Commission for Labour, Chapter 1, page 12.)

They have been imposed from above and it has been presumed that it is solely the State's responsibility to protect the workers' interests. Consequently, development of labour market in India has been stifled and various institutions needed to ensure welfare of the workers have not come up. These laws are also alleged to be directed towards a meagre proportion of the working class in India—those in the organised sector. It is true that the laws were aimed mainly at the 'industrial' sector, but there were sufficient reasons for doing so in the early days of our planning. It had been assumed that a Lewis type economic transition will take place in India. If a large part of the workers were ultimately to be engaged in the modern sector, it was natural to ensure that a model working conditions and regulations were in place for this sector. However, such massive transformation did not take place and in 1999-2000, only 7 per cent of the workers were in the organised sector, and 2 per cent in the organised industries (Table 1). Assuming that all the laws for the organised sector are fully implemented (which they are not) the coverage of most of the pro-labour legislations are therefore very restricted.

Table 1

Employment (in millions) in the Organised and Unorganised Sector

	Total Employment		*Industrial Employment*		*Growth Rate of Total Emploment*		*Growth Rate of Industrial Employment*	
	Organi-nised	*Unorga-nised*	*Organi-nised*	*Unorga-nised*	*Organi-nised*	*Unorga-nised*	*Organi-nised*	*Unorga-nised*
1983-84	24.03 (7.9)	278.93 (92.1)	6.96 (2.3)	27.24 (8.9)				

1987-88	25.71	293.88	7.15	30.05	1.75	1.34	0.68	2.58
	(8.0)	(92.0)	(2.2)	(9.4)				
1993-94	27.41	349.64	7.12	36.55	1.10	3.16	-0.07	3.61
	(7.3)	(92.7)	(1.9)	(9.7)				
1999-00	27.95	369.01	7.78	41.49	0.33	0.92	1.54	2.25
	(7.0)	(93.0)	(1.9)	(10.4)				

Note: Figures in parenthesis are percentages to total workers. Growth Rates are over previous time point.

Source: Monthly Abstract of Statistics, Govt. of India, CSO (Various Years).

The only recourse that the 'left-out' mass of workers in the unorganised sectors have is the *Minimum Wages Act, 1948*. But the practice in this regard too is poor. Minimum wage rates are revised very infrequently, in absence of indexation their real values erode in the intermediate years, and in some cases the revised rates are lower in real terms than the pre-revision rates. Significantly, in most cases, such statutory minimum wages have not been sufficient to enable a regular worker to remain above the official poverty line. Even then, enforcement has been poor and actual wages have mostly lagged behind statutory minimum wages. Only exception has been the agricultural sector where market wages have been higher than minimum wages and their long run growth have been quite substantial and uniform across the states. Since no perceptible difference in enforcement mechanism exists in this sector this can be attributed to substantial increase in agricultural productivity, and the organisation of agricultural workers (ILO-ARTEP, 1993).

The only area where labour laws—both regarding job security and adequate income have been implemented with some fervour in India has been that of organised industries and the public sector. Wages here have been 'fixed' to ensure certain living standards, revisions to wages have been fairly regular, full indexation have been used in the intermediate periods, annual increments have been systematic, and bonus and other welfare payments have been consistent. It is however peculiar, that the recommendations of Central Pay Commissions, specifically appointed to fix salaries of central government employees, usually serve as reference points for the Wage Boards and the DPE, and then for state PSUs and private enterprises as well. Therefore, it is virtually impossible to consider factors like productivity growth, skill formation, profitability, etc. while revising wages. Money wage growth is thus ensured over time. As a result, per employee emoluments in the industrial sector has increased consistently both in monetary and real terms (Table 2). The rate of wage increase has been faster in the public industries compared to the private industries, and even greater in public services and administration.

Table 2

Growth of Wages in the Registered Factories

	Average Annual Growth Rate over the Previous Period (%)		
Year	*Money Wages*	*Prices*	*Real Wages*
1970-1975	13.81	9.23	4.58
1975-1980	12.78	6.14	6.64
1980-1985	17.96	14.50	3.46
1985-1990	15.35	9.53	5.82
1990-1995	17.10	4.87	12.23
1995-2000	11.66	15.52	-3.86

Source: Annual Survey of Industries, CSO, Govt. of India (Various Years).

The prevalent labour policies have thus created and perpetuated *Dualism* in the Indian labour market. On one hand a small group of workers are immunised from retrenchment, obtain decent wages and other benefits, enjoy automatic annual increments and indexation, and for whom pay-revisions are regular and has no link with productivity. On the other hand, we have a large mass of workers who do not have any job security, whose wages have lagged behind statutory minimum wages and are not adequate to keep them above poverty line. These later group also do not enjoy any additional benefit in most cases, indexation of their wages are absent, revisions of the legislations for them are irregular and infrequent. While the former group enjoy both employment security and income security, lack of job security for the latter group prevent them from organising themselves and demand even decent income security. This inequality has initiated and propagated certain scheme of reactions in the economy to which we turn in the subsequent section.

Table 6
Work Participation, Employment and Unemployment Trends in India

	Usual Employment Rates							Usual Unemployment Rates						
	Number of persons employed/unemployed per 1000 workforce													
	Rural			Urban			Total	Rural			Urban			Total
	M	F	T	M	F	T		M	F	T	M	F	T	
1983	97.9	98.6	98.1	94.1	93.2	93.9	97.3	2.1	1.4	1.9	5.9	6.9	6.1	2.7
1987	98.2	97.6	98.0	94.8	93.8	94.6	97.2	1.8	2.4	2.0	5.2	6.2	5.4	2.8
1993	98.6	99.4	98.9	95.9	93.9	95.6	98.1	1.4	0.6	1.1	4.1	6.1	4.4	1.9
1999	98.3	99.0	98.6	95.6	94.6	95.2	97.8	1.7	1.0	1.5	4.5	5.7	4.7	2.3

	Current Daily Employment Rates							Current Daily Unemployment Rates						
	Number of persons employed/unemployed per 1000 workforce													
	Rural			Urban			Total	Rural			Urban			Total
	M	F	T	M	F	T		M	F	T	M	F	T	
1983	92.5	90.8	92.0	90.8	89.8	90.6	91.7	7.5	9.0	7.9	9.2	10.5	9.4	8.3
1987	95.4	93.2	94.8	91.2	88.0	90.6	93.8	4.6	6.7	5.2	8.8	12.0	9.4	6.2
1993	96.8	96.6	96.9	93.2	89.4	92.4	95.7	3.2	3.4	3.1	6.8	10.6	7.6	4.3
1999	92.8	92.7	93.0	92.8	90.2	92.2	92.8	7.2	7.0	7.1	7.3	9.4	7.7	7.3

Source: Author's Calculations based on NSSO (1983, 1990, 1992, 1994, 2001).

IV. Dualistic Labour Market—Impact on the Economy

There have been certain unwarranted outcomes of the labour policies practiced in India. These impacts have been different across different segments of the economy.

1. Public Sector

The labour policies related to job security and income enhancement are more rigorously followed in the public sector—both industrial and services. The State, in its bid to behave like a model employer, have always looked at the external economies of sustaining a well paid industrial and administrative workforce, and not at the costs and external diseconomies.

Table 3

Growth of Employment in the Public Sector

Year	*Employment (in millions)*		*Average Annual Growth Rate (%) over previous period*	
	Total	*Manufacturing*	*Total*	*Manufacturing*
1980-81	15.48	1.50		
1990-91	18.77	1.87	2.13	2.47
1999-00	19.31	1.53	0.31	-1.85

Source: Monthly Abstract of Statistics, Govt. of India, CSO (Various Years).

Since government jobs are best paid (ratio of public sector wage to private sector wage has varied between 1.25 to 1.75 over the 1970-2000 period, increasing consistently) and there are practically no efforts to even measure productivity, supply of labour to this sector has been infinite, and efficiency low. This has resulted in accumulation of surplus labour in the PSUs and the government services without proportional rise in output and income (estimated to be about 16 per cent of total workforce in 2001). Since these workers also enjoy substantial wage-increases periodically irrespective of profitability of the enterprises, the financial burden on the State in terms of wage payments and other benefits multiplied manifold over the years till they became unsustainable. Units became sick and fiscal prudence asked for closure of units and rationalisation of workforce. This has resulted in slackening growth of employment even in the Public sector in recent times (Table 3). On the other hand such a huge fiscal burden prevented the State to take up programmes which could have generated employment in the unorganised, especially the rural sector. A major cause of declining rural employment in the nineties has been attributed to declining public expenditure in the rural areas and dwindling infrastructure (Mukherjee, 2003).

2. *Organised Private Sector*

The labour policies have been applicable to the organised private sector as well, especially for the factories. However, as rational employers, they have faced the laws as restrictions imposed on their decision making process and have attempted to maximise their returns nevertheless. Firstly, rules regarding closure of enterprises entail substantial compensation for retrenchment. Secondly, temporary or casual labour is used cautiously as after a specified time of employment they would be deemed to be permanent and entitled to higher benefits. Thirdly, wage legislations have raised the cost of hiring workers—both current wages and present value of future benefits that are to be offered to the workers in cash and kind. Such wage legislations are also practically exogenous in nature—pay revisions for government employees take place at regular intervals; this leads to wage revisions in PSUs; there is a demand for wage revision in private sector as well and real wages are revised upwards. Thus the employers face a peculiar dilemma—once they hire someone they cannot fire her; the costs of retaining is substantial and ever increasing, having no link with productivity and profitability; the cost of retrenchment (if permitted) is exorbitantly high. All these push cost of labour far above the prevalent wage level and makes labour relatively dearer compared to capital, or at least the relative price of labour compared to capital goes on increasing.

Table 4
Terms of Trade between Capital and Labour and Capital-Labour Ratio in Registered Factories

Year	*Terms of Trade*		*Capital-Labour Ratio*	
	Level	*Index*	*Level*	*Index*
1980-81	0.90	100	0.37	100
1985-86	1.34	148	0.63	170
1990-91	1.04	116	0.81	219
1995-96	1.30	145	1.19	320
2000-01	1.37	152	1.44	387

Note: Terms of Trade between Capital and Labour is calculated as the ratio between Emolument per Worker and Interest per unit of Outstanding Loan; Capital-Labour Ratio is measured as Fixed Capital per Employee in Rs. Lakh in constant 1980-81 prices.

Source: Annual Survey of Industries, CSO, Govt. of India (Various Years).

Table 5
Movements of Factor Returns in Registered Factories (Base 1980-81 = 100)

Year	*GVA per Employee*	*Employment per Employee*	*Profit per unit Invested Capital*	*Interest per unit Outstanding Loan*
1980-81	100	100	100	100
1985-86	169	155	103	104
1990-91	218	174	126	150
1995-96	323	222	194	153
2000-01	373	261	135	172

Source: Annual Survey of Industries, CSO, Govt. of India (Various Years).

This has surely happened in India where, in the registered factories, labour cost (measured by per employee emoluments and benefits) relative to capital cost (measured by interest payment per unit of borrowed capital) has been increasing throughout (Table 4). Such rise has also been faster than the rise in profitability (measured by profit per unit of invested capital) (Table 5). That productivity (measured by Gross Value

Added per employee) has increased faster than emoluments is of little consolation as this has followed substitution of labour by capital by employers in response to exogenous changes in wages to enhance labour productivity. This is corroborated from Table 4 where we find that capital-labour ratio has almost quadrupled during 1980-2000. Such steps however adversely affect the prospects of employment increase in the medium to long run. In the initial years any rise in costs due to rise in wages (and other factors too) were tacitly passed on to the consumers. In a closed economy framework this suited the employers, the employees and the State. But in the new global economy framework, such mechanisms are suicidal. Domestic enterprises have to compete with MNCs both for international and domestic markets and so price and cost competitiveness is of utmost importance to employers. This has prompted them to search for escape routes, especially since mid 1980s when the *Industrial Disputes Act* with new restrictions was put into place and soft liberalisation took away the protective shield from domestic industry. One of them, the substitution of labour by capital, has already been mentioned. Other avenues taken up by innovative entrepreneurs include entering into 'contracts for services' with individuals, middlemen and agencies for labour supply; engaging workers for specific time-determined piece-meal contracts; inducing workers to form cooperatives and submit bills for work done instead of drawing wages; classifying workers as apprentices or trainees and specifying that employment is not offered; changing record of names several times a year; hiring casual workers; designating workers as consultants who submit periodical bills; etc. Another method taken up by employers has been to set up number of independent small units instead of one large unit. Though this method prevents realization of economies of scale, the resultant losses are outweighed by the combined advantages of labour flexibility and the saving on labour costs.

3. *Unorganised Sector*

The fallout of the slackening employment growth in the public sector and the private organised sector is a tremendous growth of employment in the unorganised sector in India, growth rates in the latter being almost three times that of the former during the 1987-93 and 1993-99 periods (Table 1). As a result, while its share in total employment had been above 90 per cent even in 1983-84, it has been increasing throughout the last two decades, except a marginal fall during 1983-87. For the industrial sector, the share has been increasing since 1983-84 itself. This is quite natural as the employers seeking escape from the laws pertaining to the organised sector are increasingly resorting to ancillarisation and sub-contracting. In addition, workers not finding entry into the organised sector are resorting to self-employment and setting up small units as means of livelihood. While a part of the unorganised sector are growing in tandem with the organised sector through the linkages of sub-contracting and supplying of semi-finished inputs, a major part of them are distress units. It is observed that at least for the unorganised manufacturing sector (UMS) such a dual force is clearly operative with the comparatively larger units (the DMEs) growing along with the factories in the urban areas and along with agricultural development in the rural areas.[1] On the other hand, the smaller units (OAMES and NDMEs) are growing in spaces of relative economic hardship (slackening growth of factories and agricultural sector, high poverty, low per capita income, etc.). However, as the DMEs are lesser in number and worker base (in 2000, DMEs constitute only 4 per cent of the units and 17 per cent of the workers in UMS), and their characteristics are more like the organised sector, it would be justified to infer that much of the 37 million workers in UMS are in distress and have taken up the profession to fend away complete unemployment. It is also to be noted that a major part of these workers are unpaid household workers (in 2000, more than 75 per cent of workers in UMS were household labour) and the share of part time workers in this sector have increased from 10 per cent in 1989-90 to over 18 per cent in 1999-2000. For the hired workers, the story has not been very different. Emoluments per hired worker in the UMS in real terms (1989-90 prices) have increased from Rs. 3029 in 1989-90 to Rs. 4193 in 1999-2000, averaging a growth of around 3.6 per cent p.a. Compared to about 7.3 per cent p.a. rise in per employee emoluments in the factory sector over the same period, it is quite clear that the workers in the unorganised sector are getting a raw deal. On one hand, they are practically not covered by any job-security legislation. On the other, the only legislation that they can resort to, that of income security, is not effective.

V. Effect on Employment – A Comprehensive View

It is thus evident that stringent labour laws have provided strong incentives to present and prospective employers, especially those in the organised sector, to minimise hiring of regular workers. The public sector has already passed the threshold limit of its carrying capacity as far as providing jobs is concerned and is desperately trying to shed flab through various early separation schemes. This has had serious impact on employment growth in the economy and also on the nature and quality of jobs that are available.

1. *An Analytical Model*

Analytically, the dual labour market policies are expected to trigger off the following mechanism in the labour market.[2] As evident, there are two segments of the labour market – the Organised sector where workers are protected (both in terms of secure jobs and adequate income), and the Unorganised sector where there are practically no coverage.

Figure 1

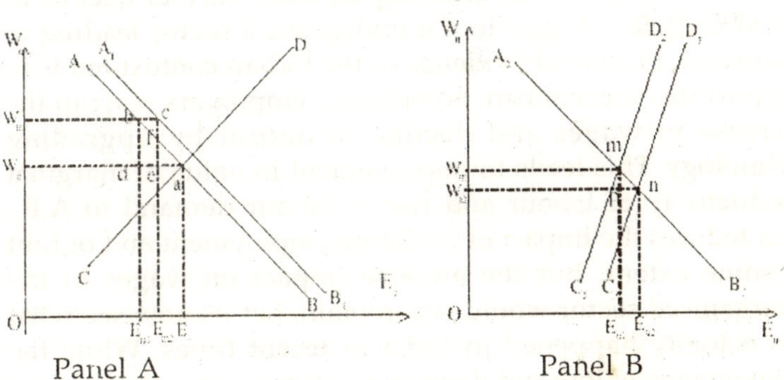

Panel A Panel B

Let the two markets be represented in Panel A and Panel B respectively of Figure 1. AB and CD are the labour demand and labour supply curves in the organised sector. Market clearing wage rate is W_o and employment is OE_o. However, due to various legislations and pro-worker policies, the effective minimum wage rate is W_{m1}. It is quite natural that in a labour surplus developing economy W_m has to be substantially higher than W_o. The gap W_oW_{m1} is the premium enjoyed by workers in the organised sector. Facing this wage rate, employers employ only OE_{m1} amount of labour. There is thus loss of employment of the magnitude E_oE_{m1}, which we may call notional displaced workers due to labour legislations. Output also reduces by E_oabE_{m1} amount. If we consider the unorganised sector as the balancing sector where all those seeking but not finding jobs in the organised sector are absorbed, then the labour supply curve would be almost vertical, as depicted by C_2D_2 in Panel B. In absence of any protection, wage rate in this sector is determined by market forces. Expectedly, this wage W_{u1} would be lower than W_o. After implementation of legislations in the organised sector, the notionally displaced workers enter the unorganised labour market, expanding labour supply to C_3D_3. As a result, employment in the unorganised sector increases from OE_{u1} to OE_{u2} but wages decrease to W_{u2}. Thus employment increases by $E_{u1}E_{u2}$ and output increases by $E_{u1}mnE_{u2}$. The incremental employment and output are however lower than the loss in employment and output in the organised sector as $E_oE_{m1} > E_{u1}E_{u2}$, and $W_m > W_o > W_{u1} > W_{u2}$. The result is therefore a net loss in employment and output, and a further decline in the already low wages in the unorganised sector leading to inequality. Empirical evidence in the Indian context tends to support this mechanism. Sometimes, employers react to the increase in wages and decline in output by upgrading technology. This leads to improvement in value of marginal productivity of labour and rise in labour demand to A_1B_1. This reduces the impact of declining employment and output to some extent, but the adverse impact on wages in the unorganised sector would still remain. Let us now see what has actually happened in India in recent times. While the phenomenon of low and depressing wages in the unorganised sector has already been mentioned, let us examine the effect on employment scenario.

2. Employment Growth

The absolute level of employment growth has decelerated in recent times, especially in the post-1990 period. Both Usual and Current status employment rates have decreased during 1993-99 leading to a rise in open unemployment rates (Table 6). The only exception to this broad trend is the urban female group, where the employment rates have increased in the post-reform period. However, this is not a sign of enthusiasm as it is observed to be caused by a decline in usual employment and a more than proportional decline in size of workforce. It is generally accepted that when work is not available even after a long wait, a substantial proportion of females withdraw themselves from the labour force rather than report as unemployed. The post reform increase in current employment rate for urban female is due to an increase in workforce along with a more than proportional increase in employment. The virtue of this phenomenon too has been questioned on grounds of increased availability and employment of females in irregular and low paid jobs especially in the service sector.

Such deteriorating employment scenario is the main outcome of the sluggishness of employers to take in more labour. This phenomenon of *jobless growth* will be more evident if we look at the elasticity of employment with respect to output in the economy (Table 7). In all the major sectors of the economy this elasticity has consistently declined, with negative elasticity experienced in the Mining and Electricity-Gas-Water Supply sectors during 1993-99 period. If we consider the 2001-02 thin sample survey of NSSO, then the elasticities are negative in the Primary and Tertiary sectors during 1999-2001 period. Though too much should not be read from thin samples, yet the unsatisfactory performance of the services sector, hailed as the engine of employment creation in the new era, invites serious concern and asks for deeper exploration. At the sub-national level, such decline in elasticity levels are evident in all the major states except Delhi, Gujarat, Kerala, Madhya Pradesh, and Punjab.

Table 7

Elasticity of Employment with respect to Output Growth by Sectors

Sector	*1983-87*	*1987-93*	*1993-99*
Agriculture	0.20	0.34	0.14
Mining & Quarrying	1.17	0.43	-0.44
Manufacturing	0.31	0.30	0.16
Elec, Gas & Water	0.60	0.31	-0.10
Construction	-0.61	2.39	0.96
Services	0.87	0.39	0.23
Total	0.35	0.33	0.18

Source: Same as Table 6, and Estimates of State Domestic Product, Govt. of India, CSO.

3. *Quality of Work*

The impact has not been restricted to loss of jobs only. Even the jobs that have escaped the axe have become less regular and less secure. There is a marked trend towards casualisation of the workforce both at the usual principal and the usual principal and subsidiary status (Table 8). Proportion of casual workers among all workers have increased in all segments during 1979-99 period except for urban females in 1993-99. That this may have been caused by withdrawal of females from the workforce has already been indicated.

Table 8

Distribution of Usually Employed by Category of Employment

		Usual Principal Status Per 1000 Workers			*Usual Principal & Subsidiary Status Per 1000 Workers*		
Sector	*Year*	*Self Employed*	*Regular Employee*	*Casual Employee*	*Self Employed*	*Regular Employee*	*Casual Employee*
Rural	1978-1979	622	108	270	628	106	266
Male	1983-1984	595	106	299	605	103	292
	1987-1988	575	104	321	586	100	314
	1993-1994	569	85	346	579	83	338
	1999-2000	544	90	366	550	88	362

Rural	1978-1979	563	37	400	621	28	351
Female	1983-1984	541	37	422	619	28	353
	1987-1988	549	49	402	608	37	355
	1993-1994	513	34	453	585	28	387
	1999-2000	500	39	461	573	31	396
Urban	1978-1979	399	472	189	404	464	132
Male	1983-1984	402	445	153	409	437	154
	1987-1988	410	444	146	417	437	146
	1993-1994	411	427	162	417	421	162
	1999-2000	412	419	169	415	417	168
Urban	1978-1979	422	308	270	495	249	256
Female	1983-1984	373	318	309	458	258	284
	1987-1988	393	342	265	471	275	254
	1993-1994	364	355	281	454	286	258
	1999-2000	384	385	231	453	333	214

Source: NSSO (2001).

Apart from casualisation of usual workers, lack of regular employment (Underemployment or Semi-open unemployment —SOU) itself has to be highlighted.[3] The difference between Current Daily Status Unemployment and Usual Status Unemployment would give us a measure of underemployment or SOU—people who are usually employed but not currently employed. It is observed that the nineties have witnessed rising magnitude of SOU after a consistent decline of it in the earlier decade (Table 9). SOU is more severe for the female workers, the proportion being almost 4-5 times of the corresponding male figures in both rural and urban areas.

Thus, in the face of stringent labour laws, wage-gap between the organised and unorganised sector has been increasing, while the share of organised sector itself is decreasing. In addition, both open unemployment and underemployment are increasing, widening further the gap between the small mass of protected labour and the remaining millions of vulnerable workers and job-seekers. Decreasing elasticities of employment also paint a pessimistic picture of the labour market in the medium run. How to face this situation is studied in the next section.

VI. Issues and Options

The objectives of State intervention in labour market have not been fulfilled in India. It has often been argued that such interventions have achieved *'employment at the cost of employability'*. Legislations based on job type and working conditions criteria have institutionalised, propagated, consolidated and perpetuated dualism in the labour market. The assumption that slowly more and more workers will enter the formal sector where the model legislations are operative has not come true. On the contrary, employment have increased in the form of *informal* jobs where employers are not encumbered by rules related to security of jobs and minimum wages and therefore can exploit the workers. The very intention of providing protection to the working class has created a small enclave of 'protected' labourers leaving out the teeming millions to fend for themselves in the *market*. This has gone against our proclaimed principle of social equity leading to persistence poverty and economic inequality. To meaningfully provide solutions to this peculiar paradox, we must summarise the issues and options before us carefully.

Table 9
Underemployment Trends in India

	Number of persons per 1000 workforce						
	Rural			*Urban*			*Total*
	M	*F*	*T*	*M*	*F*	*T*	
1983	11.6	41.2	22.6	7.2	27.8	11.5	20.4
1987	8.7	44.1	21.6	6.8	32.6	12.3	19.6
1993	6.4	31.5	15.4	4.6	22.4	8.3	13.6
1999	9.8	31.6	17.3	5.2	19.0	7.9	15.0

Source: Same as Table 6.

It is argued that in light of our experience and in the context of globalisation, labour market reforms are necessary for stimulating long-term growth of output and employment in the Indian economy. The attack has mainly been focused against the regulations restricting retrenchment and closure i.e. those that impede employment flexibility. While it is true that restrictions to flexibility have prevented unemployment during downturns, it has also dampened employers' incentive to expand employment during upswings. These regulations have obstructed expansion of flourishing sectors, prevented restructuring of dying sectors, and hence constrained growth in both output and employment. Also, high actual labour costs act as a restraint to foreign investment and confines it to capital-intensive sectors. In the face of growing external competition, the clamour for restructuring has gained momentum. It is argued that if introduced, the right to hire and fire will enable employers to compete with MNCs enjoying flexible conditions and help them to actually prosper, lifting employment figures upwards.

However, this proposition cannot be welcomed without blinking. Employment flexibility can be introduced only when appropriate labour market institutions are in place. Hiring and firing itself leads to substantial social and personal loss unless retrenched workers are able to find suitable jobs. This requires upgradation of their employability quotient through training and rehabilitation programmes. This calls for sufficient labour market information available to the workers, training centres imparting useful and *in-demand* skills, and providing means of sustenance in the intermediate period between jobs. In absence of such provisions, taking away job security from the workers will only create a sense of despair and despondency among them. Our experience with labour redundancy in the public sector and National Renewal Fund (NRF) seems to corroborate this thinking. Only the Voluntary Retirement Scheme (VRS) programme under the NRF has made any progress while those related to counselling, retraining and redeployment hardly has advanced anywhere. Most of the workers who have taken VR have deposited their capital in Post Offices and Banks and are living on interest income. Though some workers, mostly from managerial cadre, have gone into the private sector, very few workers have taken up new assignments. Even if they were to enter the job market, they would most probably have gone into the unorganised sector, worsening the conditions of those already employed therein. One way out of this mess can be linking of retrenchment and closure permissions with the 'Area Regeneration Programmes'. Entrepreneurs desirous of winding up an unit would be permitted only if the capital released is used for setting up of unit(s) of similar employment potential in the same area—albeit of a *sunrise* sector. This will enable employers to restructure without job loss. Workers would have to be paid Allowances in the intermediate period and retrained to be employable in the new venture. A major part of this cost would have to be borne by the State no doubt. Another way to prevent labour being relatively dearer would be to link wages with productivity and severe the link between pay rise in government administrative sector and those in production sectors.

One may argue that what happens to this protected minuscule part of our workforce is of little importance. That however is not the situation. Giving carte blanche to formal employers to retrench and close down will have its impact on the unorganised sector too. Once job security in the organised sector is withdrawn, vulnerability of workers in that sector would increase. They would no longer be able to organise themselves and collectively bargain for preservation of their income security. Once that happens, demonstration effect will create immense pressure on unorganised workers and make their task of being organised and press for better working conditions more difficult.

In this light the recommendations put forward by the Second Labour Commission has to be evaluated. It seems that the commission has proposed a relaxation of retrenchment and closure restrictions along with linking of wages with productivity for the organised sector. On the other hand, a host of social security and minimum wage policies have been proposed for the unorganised sector. While the intentions of the commission are commendable, there are certain issues that need to be sorted out. It is not the fact that there have been no income security or pro-worker legislation covering the unorganised sector. The problem is that the sheer size of the sector has made implementation a monumental task. A major part of the sector is hidden through unpaid and unaccounted household labour and being unorganised they lack political clout to form pressure groups for execution of relevant laws. Even with all the good intentions such an umbrella protection will need huge fiscal commitment from the State, which is hard to materialise under present economic dispensation. Therefore, passing laws to protect unorganised workers will hardly work and only the easier recommendations like relaxation of rules for the organised sector will get implemented in the immediate run. This will be much like putting the cart before the horse and will create further distortions in the labour market. While balancing the two segments and breaking the dualistic character is important, one should be careful to avoid deteriorating conditions in both the sectors in the name of uniformity.

Under such situation one may consider few other options as well. While in principle flexibility in the labour market is welcome, they should be implemented in a careful and phased manner. Apart from linking closure with regeneration as already mentioned, one may also look at possibilities of allowing employers to transfer workers between units and departments, even across regional and national boundaries. This will make the employers responsible for skill upgradation of the workers and allow them to pursue flexible specialisation too.[4] Such restricted flexibility in the short run will have to be followed by adequate institution building in the medium run. However, such institutions are to be built up not through State legislations solely. A major reason of the present disorder is that the present legislations have been imposed from above and not followed through labour organisations and labour struggles. So, the policies and legislations should emerge from consultations among, discussions with, and active participation of the workers themselves. The relatively better position of agricultural workers, especially in West Bengal and Kerala, bear testimony to the necessity of organising the unorganised workers before passing laws for them. Efforts made in this direction by VV Giri National Labour Institute in Madhya Pradesh, Rajasthan, Tamil Nadu, and Uttar Pradesh have also borne fruits (NLI, 2000). Institutions that require State sponsorship and guidance are those that would impart retraining and assistance in job search. The institutions conceived under the NRF are Employee Resource Centres, Employee Assistance Centres, and Area Regeneration Councils. These should not be restricted to retrenched workers only, but should be extended to all workers presently positioned or intending to join unorganised sector. Also, the programmes must be directed more towards self-employment rather than wage employment. Additional support to these workers in form of smooth and cheap credit, scientific and technical consultancy, incentive to form cooperatives, preference in purchase of materials would also go a long way in improving the conditions of unorganised workers. Ideal situation would see an integrated network of institutions, managed jointly by the government, trade unions and employers' organizations functioning in a mutually interactive and supportive manner. In addition, it must be noted that investment, employment creation and growth are significantly affected by infrastructural availability, credit flow, and human resource embedded in the workers, along with labour costs. Improving the endowment of those other factors would also help in creating a more job-friendly environment. The State should understand that reforming labour legislations in a piecemeal manner would only deteriorate the already vulnerable position of workers countrywide.

Notes

1. This has been explored extensively by Mukherjee (2004).
2. This has been adopted from Brown et al (1982).
3. The concept was first discussed loosely by Joan Robinson (1960), and then by Gautam Mathur (1999). Pioneering work in these two issues was by Mathur (1999) who concentrated at the national level. Mukherjee (2003) has explored these issues in detail.
4. Such delinking of job permanency from income security has also been advocated by ILO-ARTEP (1993).

References

Brown, C. C. Gilroy, and A. Kohen (1982), "The Effect of the Minimum Wage on Employment and Unemployment", *The Journal of Economic Literature*, June.

GOI (2001), Report of Second National Commission for Labour, (downloaded from website http://labour.nic.in/lcomm2/nlc_report.html)

ILO-ARTEP (1993), "India: Employment, Poverty and Economic Policies", New Delhi.

Mathur, Ashok (1999), "Economic Reforms, Employment and 'Non-Employment': Theory, Evidence and Policy", Keynote paper for Technical Session VI of 82nd Annual Conference of the Indian Economic Association, December, 1999.

Mathur, Gautam (1999), "The Analysis of Responsibility of Poverty", in B. Satyanarayan and Ch. Raghuram (eds.) *Essays in Political Economy: Selected Papers of Prof. Gautam Mathur*, Concept Publishing Company, New Delhi.

Mukherjee, Dipa (2003), "The Changing World of Work and No-Work", *Indian Journal of Labour Economics*, Vol. 46, No. 4, 2003.

_________ (2004), "Informal Manufacturing Sector in India: Pre- and Post-Reform Growth Dynamics", *Indian Journal of Labour Economics*, Vol. 47, No. 2, 2004.

NLI (2000), "Report on Organising the Rural Labour", VV Giri National Labour Institute, mimeo.

NSSO (1983), "Report on 3rd Quinquennal Survey on Employment and Unemployment, NSS 38th Round, Report No. 341 and 341/1 to 341/17", Government of India, New Delhi.

_____ (1990), "Report on 4th Quinquennal Survey on Employment and Unemployment, NSS 43rd Round", *Sarvekhsana*, Special Issue, September, Government of India, New Delhi.

_____ (1992), "Report on 4th Quinquennial Survey on Employment and Unemployment, NSS 43rd Round", *Sarvekhsana*, Special Issue, January, Government of India, New Delhi.

_____ (1994), "Report on 5th Quinquennial Survey on Employment and Unemployment, NSS 50th Round, Report No. 409, Government of India, New Delhi.

_____ (2001), "Report on 6th Quinquennial Survey on Employment and Unemployment, NSS 55th Round, Report No. 455, 458/1, and 458/2, Government of India, New Delhi.

Robinson, Joan (1960), *Exercises in Economic Analysis*, Macmillan, London.

4

STATE, MARKET AND LABOUR: AN INDIAN EXPERIENCE

K. Alamar & N. Murali

Labour reforms, an offshoot of the liberalisation policy, are currently attracting a good deal of attention and debate. It is argued that reforms in the labour market facilitate the speeding up of structural adjustment programme. The assumption is that there are rigidities and distortions in the labour market, which create obstacles to structural adjustment in general and industrial restructuring in particular. Hence one of the important objectives of economic reform policies pursued by India during the last one and a half decades is to ensure labour competitiveness for industrial growth.

The neo-liberal economists are of the opinion that permanency of employment acts as a major drag on the profitability of the organised sector. So the labour market flexibility is crucial for increasing private investment, improved productivity and overall growth, which in turn will improve external competitiveness that is essential in a globalised environment. They further argue that because of the rigid labour laws there is a dualism in the labour market in India, which is a source of conflict between organised worker and unorganised worker. Organised workers who have strong trade union ignore the problems of workers in the informal sector. Protection given to organised workers allows or even militates against the improvement of conditions of unorganised workers.

Labour Flexibility: A Solution for Overall Growth?

The protagonists of labour market reforms put forth that any restrictions on the employer's right to dismiss the workers at will and stipulate some degree of permanencies of employment act as a barrier against the growth of their concerns and further act as a block to compete with other firms which have flexible labour relations. Much security is bad for growth—that people with greater security of employment and income put less effort into their work and so is less productive. In other words, greater security reduces output and growth. But in reality, the empirical evidence is mixed. High levels of security, for instance, in some public sector enterprises may make adjustments and innovation difficult, and so adversely affect economic performance. But country such as Sweden, which may have maintained high level of employment security, or countries such as Netherlands, which have ensured high levels of income security, have also performed well in terms of output and employment (Datt, 2003). A shift towards more contract-based system of labour relations, with no assumption of permanency of employment is required to ensure economic progress. But insecurity makes the employee morale low and productivity will get affected. The advantages provided by the flexible labour market may be short-lived and illusory if the productivity of the labour stagnates. Labour standards by creating a productive on versatile workforce may provide wider option for adjustment. Free and creative labour is the prime source of economic and social progress. The great English economist William Petty believed that "labour is the Father and active principle of wealth, as Lands are the Mother". Unlike the western countries where thanks to comprehensive social security network, the workers made redundant know that they will not starve. There is no such guarantee in India. Given the low wage levels, provident fund balances do not offer sufficient cushion. Contract system does not work in a society like ours where the welfare support is missing.

Protection of Organised Labour – At the Cost of Unorganised Labour

The supporters of labour reforms put forth that the organised workforce takes away a large chunk of benefits accrued from growth at the expense of unorganised workforce. Hence privileges extended to organised sector workers can be withdrawn since they are anyway so much better off than most other workers in the economy. This kind of ideologies are propagated to attack on organised workers to reduce their bargaining power which ultimately end in even more exploitation of unorganised workers. In such context greater flexibility of labour markets might simply mean the perpetuation of low wage and more exploitation by the employer. The ultimate goal of any democracy should be the removal of exploitation in any form.

Okun's Law – Not Operational in a Liberalised Labour Reform Scenario

Okun's law states that a rise in GDP of an economy is accompanied by a fall in unemployment rate. But it is possible there could very well be contradiction between jobs and growth in the present global scenario, where cost cutting and competitiveness hold the key to success. The private sector is bound to concentrate on enhancing profits and exports, facing competition and not exactly on creating employment opportunities. Competition among the different firms forces them to introduce labour saving devices to cheapen their products. Those firms, which are unable to replace labour by mechanisation, are squeezed out of the race. The automation process, which increases the production on the one side and replaces labour on the other goes against the Okun's law.

One of the most crucial problems facing the Indian economy has been the acute problem of unemployment. The employment of elasticity of 1980s and early 1990s of 0.52 went down to 0.16 in the late 1990s. The available data from different rounds of quinqunnial survey shows that there has been a remarkable fall in annual growth rate of total employment in the economy from 2.04 percent during 1993-94 to 0.98

percent during 1999-2000. India experienced higher growth rate of GDP in the 1990's as compared to 1980's. But this growth has been a service sector driven growth, which has made a negligible impact on employment. Such a growth of GDP unaccompanied by a fall in unemployment rate which is incompatible with the Okun's law of growth and expand the entitlement of people to various social and economic opportunities. The Planning Commission Task Force also arrived at the same conclusion—the employment-elasticity of the output has declined which indicates that there had been a fall in economy's labour intensity in the post–reform period.

Pigouvian Wage Cut and Full Employment Relation—Not hold good

Pigou stated that a reduction in wage rate is the key to bring out more investment and full employment in the economy. The argument was that the general reduction in wages will result in general reduction in commodity prices and it will increase the consumption. Similarly lower wage will result in higher investment. This relationship may be found to be true for a particular industry where cut in money wages will increase the investment and employment by reducing cost of production. If the same policy is adopted for the economy as a whole it will result in reduction of investment and employment. In producers' drive for profit, they seek not only to expand production but also to check the growth of wages and salaries and this tends to be circumscribed paid-up demand and consequently limit the marketing of the commodities. It has been found that the wage cut may result in more unequal distribution of income as it may be shifted from the poor who have higher marginal propensity to consume to the producers who have lower marginal propensity to consume. It is therefore clear that wage cuts, by redistributing the income in favour of the rich causes decline in income, output, investment and employment. The expansion of market tends to lag behind the expansion of production, which outturns sales. The discrepancy between supply and demand is deepened by the anarchy of market economy. No country can sustain growing unemployment rates in the long run because diminishing demand at some point limits the economic growth. Cut in wage rate will also result in unrest and would bring a decline in the overall growth rate of the economy. Keynes admitted that crises and unemployment were not accidental and that the market mechanism behind the haphazard self-regulation of the economy could rid capitalism of crises and unemployment.

Kuznet's Version of Shift in Labour Force—Not occurring

Kuznet's version of economic development relates to a shift in the labour force from agriculture to non-agriculture, in particular to manufacturing. A.G.B. Fisher in this connection writes that "........ in every progressive economy there has been a shift in employment... from the essential primary activities to secondary activities of all kinds and to a still greater extent to tertiary production." Five-year plans in India have aimed at rapid structural changes in GDP and workforce. However one of the paradoxes of the Indian economy is that the decline in the share of agricultural workers has been slower as compared to the decline in the share of GDP. The agricultural sector has been more labour intensive, as compared to the manufacturing sector. But the elasticity of employment with respect to output in agriculture has declined over time. The employment elasticity of the manufacturing sector showed a gradual deceleration from 1.14 during 1973-78 to 0.33 during 1988-94. It shows that even if we have high growth rate of GDP in manufacturing sector it may not lead to greater absorption of labour.

Commodification of Labour

Labour reforms lead to lay-off, retrenchment and closure of industries which force the workers to sell themselves in a piecemeal manner like any other commodity and consequently expose them to all vicissitudes of competition and fluctuations of the market. Labour force in India exhibits unmistakable signs of deprivation consequent to labour reforms. The bottom of the economic pyramid is being crowded with more and more people getting precipitated downwards, increasing the ranks of unorganised and informal sector workers. Despite wrestling huge concession from successive pliable governments and acquitting the role of permanent advisors the private sector has nothing much to show as far as offering employment to the people of the country. Exploitation thus continues unabated with increasing value being added due to the toil of the industrial workforce for which they get lesser and lesser wages. A comparison of the compound annual rates of growth over1990-98 reveals that while employment has grown at a sticky 2.46 percent the net value added per worker has increased by a much more healthy 5.6 percent. This indicates that with increased mechanisation, newer technologies and more workloads workers are adding much more value as time passes. Thus we see that in the organised sector in general, employment opportunities are declining, workload is increasing and wages are declining. The workers in the organised sector have largely been coerced to opt for early retirement and the compensation paid to the workers has been poor. A sizeable section of the retired workers have specific commitments in the areas of non-productive expenditure that they had to meet out of meager funds that they receive after retirement. The residual has been inadequate for starting a self-employment. The current funeral rites of progressive labour legislation will only spell a more open and vicious attack on the working people, already suffering from declining living standards.

Attack on Right to Work—A Design to Enslave Labour

The recent Supreme Court verdict on Government employees strike has dealt a severe blow to organised labour movement in India. It is true that strikes cause inconveniences to the public and also damage the smooth functioning of administration. But employers are unreasonable at times and are also intransigent and insensitive to fair demands of employees that there can arise horrendous situations in which the employees have no effective mechanism for redressal of their grievances and are left with no option but to resort to strike. Curbing workers right to strike to realise just demands is unjustifiable. Strikes empower the disempowered to fight injustice in oppressive cases when no constructive option is left. It is a weapon against subjugation and exploitation. Hence any attack on labour organisation and the right to association and collective bargaining goes against ILO conventions 87 and 98, which specifically relate to the rights of those employed in public services. In the absence of such a right it leads to enslaving of labour. Labour flexibility will give employers unbridled rights of exploitation and trespassing the legitimate rights of workers. There is a need to bring about a balance between the interest of labour and employer so as to promote growth.

Government and Labour Rights

Article 41 of the Directive Principles states that "The State shall, within the limits of its economic capacity and development, make effective provision for securing the right to work, to education and to public assistance in cases of unemployment, old age, sickness and disablement, and in other cases of undeserved want. Similarly, there is attention to the conditions of work and the level of wages in Articles 42 and 43, which state that "The State shall make provision for just and humane conditions of work and for maternity relief.... The State shall endeavour to secure, by suitable legislation or economic organization or in any other way, to all workers, agricultural, industrial or otherwise, work at a living wage, conditions of work ensuring a decent standard of life and full enjoyment of leisure and social and cultural opportunities and, in particular, the State shall endeavour to promote cottage industries on an individual or co-operative basis in rural areas. Despite these declarations, in fact the State in India has not been particularly successful in promoting the right to work, even in terms of the promises of the Constitution. Low levels of productive employment generation in the aggregate, the persistence of poverty and low educational levels probably are the most significant failures of the Indian development strategy this far. And the problem as far as employment goes has probably intensified rather than ameliorated in the recent past. The reality regarding employment prospects for most people in our country is alarming.

The government should address the livelihood concerns of the workers and think of them while taking major policy decisions. The government should give primacy to the removal of the unemployment and 'right to work' to be recognised as a basic human right and a new model of GDP growth and employment be developed to provide, firstly 'work for all' and then 'decent work for all'. In the present globalised scenario, training and retraining needs are continuous since the sector composition will constantly undergo changes under new innovative technologies. It should also chalk out a completely new approach to blend growth and employment generation. As per the Census of 2001, the number of workers in India is as large as 402.05 million. Of these 235.1 million or 58.4 per cent are employed in agriculture as cultivators and agricultural labourers. By giving appropriate policy this sector can still be a gold mine for generating faster employment by changing the sectoral composition of agriculture in favour of labour intensive high value areas like horticulture, floriculture, agro-forestry, minor irrigation, water shed, etc. (Planning Commission, 2002). The National Rural Employment Guarantee Act, which has been recently legislated by the Parliament of India, is a major move in the right direction. It can provide much-needed employment for the rural poor and can become the basis for the necessary regeneration of the rural economy, without which sustainable aggregate growth is not possible. (Ghosh, 2005). Small and medium scale enterprises contribute nearly 80 per cent of manufacturing employment and its employment elasticity is relatively 3.8 times more than the organised sector. Thus, to achieve more favourable effect on employment what is needed is a shift in the percentage of composition of manufacturing in favour of small and medium enterprises. Transport and construction are equally equipped for higher growth and employment intensiveness. Unlike China the economic changes have not created large job opportunity in the manufacturing sector in India; factory sector workers as a proportion of total workers was only 2 per cent in India in 2001. The IT sector needs to build strong linkages with primary and secondary sectors of the economy for it to create a serious impact on the problem of unemployment in the country.

Otherwise, it will remain an island of high wages creating very little benefits to the rest of the economy and even increasing the existing inequalities in the country. Banning strikes would neither be feasible nor wise in a democracy. Even today workers strike work but it is not their first, most pleasant option. The impasse created by the Supreme Court verdict on the right to strike be cleared by bringing before the parliament an appropriate legislation guaranteeing all sections of workers their democratic right to strike. There should be freedom of association, freedom from discriminations, freedom from forced labour and freedom from child labour. The government should introduce a comprehensive social security schemes for all, including workers in unorganised sectors.

On the workers' part, the workforce should strike a balance between realising demands and maintaining productivity. They need to demonstrate degree of flexibility in redesigning workloads and welcome the assessment and accountability as they have strong implications for productivity and competition in a globalised scenario. The remuneration paid to the workers should be based on the quantity and quality of an individual's work. The pay scale is also determined mainly by his performance on the job, his technical level and his actual contribution. Good performance of a labour makes a great contribution to society. To ensure good performance, it is imperative to institute a system for the evaluation of work. The evaluations must be strict, comprehensive and regular. Promotions in jobs will be based on the result of these evaluations. This will act as a moral encouragement to the workers. On the other hand, if a person has no achievement to his credit after several years of effort, he should be asked to switch over to some other occupation. The point of all this is to encourage people to make progress. But the government must ensure a minimum security and dignity to all positions including the lowest within the occupational system.

References

Abalkin, L. (1983), *Political Economy,* Progress Publishers, Moscow, p.148

Dutt, Ruddar (2003), *Economic Reforms, Labour and Employment,* Deep and Deep Publications, New Delhi, p. 185.

ILO Global Employment Trends, 2004 cited by Alok Mukherjee "Global Unemployment on the rise" *The Hindu,* 20 June 2004, p. 10.

Ghosh, Jayati (2005), "The Right to Work and Recent Legislation in India", *The Indian Journal of Labour Economics,* Conference Issue, Vol. 48, No. 4, October-December, p. 699.

Mahendra Dev, S. (1997), "Growth, Employment, Poverty and Human Development: An evaluation of changes in India since Independence with emphasis on rural areas" *Review of Development and Change* II/2, July-Dec., p. 250.

Pandit, B.L. (2004), "Jobless Growth?", *Economic Times,* July-11, p. 6.

Pigou, A.C. (1943), "The Classical Stationary State, *Economic Journal* L111, Dec. p. 343.

Planning Commission, 'Report of Special Group on Targeting Ten Million Employment Opportunities per Year', Government of India, 2002, p. 2.

Khasnabis, Ratan and Sudipti Banerjee (1996), " Political Economy of Voluntary Retirement: Study of Rationalised Workers in Durgapur" *Economic and Political Weekly,* Dec 28, p. L-71.

Ghosal, Ratan Kumar (2004), "GDP Growth and Feel Good Factor" *Economic and Political Weekly,* Vol XXXIX, No 20, May 15-21, p. 6.

Werner, Sengenberger (1991), The Role of Labour Market Regulation in Industrial Restructuring in Guy standing and Victor Tokman (eds) *Towards Social Adjustment: Labour Market Issue in Structural Adjustment,* ILO, Geneva.

Varma, Subodh (2002), "Labour: Who's Who and Why?" *The Indian Economy 2001-2002—An Alternative Survey,* Rajasakthi Book House, Hyderabad, p. 78.

Petty, William (1667), *A Treatise of Taxes and Contribution,* London, Printed for Nath, Brooke, at the Angel, p. 47.

5

WAGE POLICY FOR PUBLIC SECTOR EMPLOYEES IN INDIA

S.V. Hariharan

I. Introduction

The administrative machinery of the government is operated by the employees of the Government Departments and they are the back bone of the government system. The salaries paid to the government employees are periodically increased and revised based on the cost of living index. Indeed, the government employees are the most privileged group enjoying first the timely compensation for the decline in real income caused by the inflation.

However the rise income through the rise in dearness allowances and pay revision compensates the rise in prices caused by inflation is an important aspect needs to be examined. Of late, there is a common opinion among the public that the government employees are unduely paid and frequent hikes in their salaries are paid by the government. Further, whether the real income of the public sector employees increases over the time is another important hypothesis to be tested. An analysis of these aspects will help to understand the actual situation of the government employees and to answer the question whether they are overpaid.

II. Main Objectives

1. To study the growth of the total emoluments paid to

the government employee in current and constant prices.

2. To examine whether the increase is in average wage is in proportion to the increase in cost of living index.
3. To study the association between increase in the average wage and consumer price index.
4. To study the growth in real wage.
5. To examine the growth of total emoluments to the public sector employees as a proportion of GDP, Government Revenue and Tax Revenue.

III. Methodology

(i) Data Requirements

The data on total emoluments paid per year, percapita emoluments, the number of public sector employees, population, consumer price index, GDP, total government revenue and total tax revenue have been used for the analysis. The total emoluments paid to the public sector employees is taken as the wage bill and the percapita emoluments per annum is taken as proxy for the average wage

(ii) Period of Study

Thirty years period from 1971-72 to 2000-01 has been taken for this analysis. This period is divided in to three sub periods, each consisting of 10 years. The choice of this period is mainly due to the availability of data.

(iii) Sources of Data

The required data have been taken mainly from Economic Survey and Statistical Outline of India.

(iv) Analysis of Data

The annual average increase in size of the public sector employees, the increase in total emoluments paid to them, increase in the annual average emoluments have been estimated through the Simple Linear Trend Models and their compound growth rates are estimated through the Semi-log Linear Regression Models. The trend and growth rates of total emoluments and average emoluments are estimated for the data on current prices and also for the data expressed in 2000-01 prices. The data expressed in constant prices will measure the growth in real wages.

The association between money wage and consumer price index is studied through the Simple Linear Regression Models where consumers price index is taken as the independent variable and the percapita emoluments as the dependent variable. The regression coefficient in this case will measure the increase in money wage when the consumer price index goes up by one point.

The elasticity of money wage with respect to consumer price index number is estimated through the Double Log Linear Regression Models. The regression coefficient of this model measures the increase in percapita emoluments in percentage terms when consumer price index increases by one per cent. The parameters of the regression models are estimated through the Principle of Least Squares Method and the estimated parameters are tested for their significance using 't' test. The compound growth rates are estimated through the regression coefficient of the Semi-log Linear Regression Models. The results of the regression analysis have been given in Tables 2, 3 and 4.

The growth of total emoluments as a proportion of GDP is studied by converting the total emoluments as a percentage to the GDP. The share of the total emoluments in total government revenue and in total tax revenue have also been worked out to know the proportion of government revenue and tax revenue spent on the public sector employees.

IV. Analysis of the Results

1. Growth in the Employment of Public Sector

In 1971-72, there were 7.01 lakhs of public sector employees and the strength increased to 18.39 lakhs in 1980-81. However, the growth was slowed down in the next decade, and the strength was 22.19 lakhs in 1990-91. In the decade 1991-92 to 2000-01, the strength of the public sector employees started declining and came down to 17.40 lakhs.

The trend models reveal that the strength of the public sector employees increased, on an average, by 1,12,900 persons per year during the decade 1970-72 to 1980-81. The average increase in the next decade was 30,700 persons only. However, during 1991-92 to 2000-01, the strength of the public sector employees was reducing by 46,100 persons per year.

The Semi-log Linear Regression Models indicate that the compound growth rate of the public sector employees was 10.75 per cent during 1971-72 to 1980-81, and it came down to 1.51 per cent in the next decade. The compound growth rate became negative (-2.27 per cent) in 1991-92 to 2000-01.

2. *Total Emoluments to the Public Sector Employees in Current Prices*

The total emolument expressed in current prices was Rs. 415 crores in 1971-72 and it increased to Rs. 2619 crores in 1980-81. In the next decade, it reached Rs. 10912 crores and during 1991-92 to 2000-01, it reached Rs. 38223 crores from Rs. 12311 crores.

Measured through the regression coefficient of the trend models, the total emoluments of the public sector employees increased by Rs. 238.36 crores during 1971-72 to 1980-81, by Rs. 852.41 crores during 1981-82 to 1990-91 and by Rs. 2607.54 crores during 1991-92 to 2000-01.

The compound growth rate of the total emoluments was 21.89 per cent in the first period, and 14.68 per cent in the second period. It declined further to 12.63 per cent during the last period. Thus, even though the total emoluments show tremendous increase in absolute terms, the growth rate is reduced in the second and third periods.

3. *Total Emoluments to the Public Sector Employees in Constant Prices*

To analyse the growth of total emoluments is constant prices, the data on the total emoluments in current prices are deflated to 2000-01 prices using consumer price index numbers. The deflated data reveal that the total emoluments was Rs.4734 crores in 1971-72 and it increased to Rs. 14303 crores in 1980-81. It was growing further and touched Rs.

25126 crores in 1990-91 and then to Rs. 31705 crores in 2000-01.

The trend models fitted to the total emoluments in 2000-01 prices point out that the average increase in total emoluments per year increased marginally from one decade to another decade. The increase in the first decade was Rs 1116.46 crores and it was Rs. 1119.75 crores in the second decade. It was Rs. 1123.30 crores in the last decade Hence, the total emoluments to the public sector employees expressed in 2000-01 prices was increasing approximately by Rs. 1100 crores every year during the period under investigation.

The compound growth rate was 13.42 per cent in the first period, and it was 5.65 per cent in the second period. The compound growth rate came down further to 3.76 per cent in the last decade.

4. Per capita Emoluments in Current Prices

The percapita emoluments expressed in current prices grew from Rs. 5920 in 1971-72 to Rs. 219672 in 2000-01. During the first period it increased by 2.40 times, in the second period by 3.04 times and in the third period by 3.75 times.

The results of the trend models suggest that percapita emoluments in current prices grew by Rs. 960/- per year during 1971-72 to 1980-81, by Rs. 3585/- per year during 1981-82 to 1990-91 and by Rs 15797/- per year during 1991-92 to 2000-01. Hence, the percapita emoluments increased by the highest amount during 1991-92 to 2000-01.

The compound growth rate of percapita emoluments was 11.40 per cent in the first period and it was 12.97 per cent in the second period. However, in the third period, the percapita emoluments increased at the compound growth rate of 15.03 per cent.

Hence, the money wage has recorded the highest growth both in terms of absolute value and compound growth rate during 1991-92 to 2000-01. It means that the money wage to the public sector employees increased by the highest amount during 1991-92 to 2000-01.

5. *Per capita Emoluments in 2000-01 Prices*

The percapita emoluments expressed in terms of 2000-01 prices was Rs. 67525 in 1971-72. It recorded a declining trend till 1974-75 and then started increasing. It increased to Rs, 77764 in 1980-81 and to Rs. 114251 in 1990-91. Finally it touched Rs. 219672 in 2000-01. In the first period, percapita emoluments grew by 1.15 times, in the second period by 1.44 times and in the third period by 1.84 times. Thus, the increase in percapita emoluments in real terms is the highest during the decade 1991-92 to 2000-01.

Measured through the trend models, the average annual increase in percapita emoluments was Rs. 2302/- in the first period, Rs. 3909/- in the second period and Rs. 9066/- in the third period. Thus the percapita emoluments in real terms have grown by the highest amount only during the third period.

The compound growth rate of percapita emoluments in 2000-01 prices is also the highest (6.08 per cent) during 1991-92 to 2000-01. In the first period, it was 3.56 per cent and in the second period, it was 4.23 per cent. Hence, the real percapita emoluments has been growing since 1971-72 and the growth is the highest during 1991-92 to 2000-01.

6. *Association between Percapita Emoluments and Consumer Price Index*

To analyse how percapita emoluments increase whenever there is an increase in consumer price index, Simple Linear Regression Model is fitted by taking the consumer price index number as the independent variable and the percapita emoluments as the dependent variable.

The regression coefficient estimated for the first period suggests that percapita emoluments increased by Rs. 40.91 when consumer price index number increased by one point. The increase in the second period was Rs. 67.25 and for the third period, it was Rs. 121.99 for the increase in consumer price index by one point.

The regression coefficients are significant at one per cent level and the value of adjusted R^2 exceeds 0.78. Hence, consumer price index number alone is capable of explaining around 80 per cent of variations in percapita emoluments.

7. *The Elasticity of Percapita Emoluments with respect to Consumer Price Index Number*

The results of the Double Log Linear Regression Models reveal that the percapita emoluments increased by 1.25 per cent when consumer price index number increased by one per cent during 1971-72 to 1980-81. In the second period, the percapita emoluments increased by 1.5 per cent and in the third period, it increased by 1.68 per cent. Therefore, the percapita emoluments recorded the highest elasticity only during 1991-92 to 2000-01. This means that the proportion of increase in percapita emoluments is greater than the proportion of increase in consumer price index in all the three periods and in the third period; the proportion of increase in percapita emoluments is the highest.

8. *Emoluments to the Public Sector Employees as a Portion of GNP*

The total emoluments paid to the public sector employees as a percentage to GNP are given in the last column of Table 1.

The value of total emoluments as a percentage to GNP varies from a minimum of 0.93 per cent to a maximum of 2.32 per cent. It was minimum in 1971-72 and touched the highest value in 1988-89. Since then it is fluctuating within a marginal range and touched 2.02 per cent in 2000-01.

The public sector employees formed 0.27 per cent of the population in 1980-81. The percentage was reduced to 0.26 in 1990-91 and then to 0.17 in 2000-01.

The total emoluments paid to the public sector employees formed 10.66 per cent of total government revenue in 1980-81. It was 9.87 per cent in 1990-91 and 9.72 per cent in 2000-01. The total emoluments measured as a percentage to the total tax revenue works out to 13.20 per cent in 1980-81, 12.44 per cent in 1990-91 and 12.48 per cent in 2000-01. Thus approximately one eighth of the tax revenue and one-tenth of the government revenue are spent on public sector employees.

V. Conclusions

The total emoluments paid to the public sector employees even though recorded a remarkable growth in current prices, it maintains its share around 2 per cent to the GNP. Further as a proportion to the total government revenue and total tax revenue, it has not showed much variation and indeed, the proportion is declining marginally. The percapita emoluments measured in constant prices is growing and it has recorded the highest growth rate during 1991-92 to 2000-01. Hence, the government may maintain this stage, if increase is not desirable. However, the increase in percapita emoluments needs to be linked with productivity. The wage policy of the government should see that the benefit of increased real wage should be provided not only to the employees of public and organized sectors, but also to the workers of unorganized sectors. Further, a strict control over inflation will check the rise in prices, and in turn the rise in consumer price index and there by reduce the commitment of the government to spend more to pay the dearness allowances to the public sector employees. This will also help to check the redistribution of income caused by the disproportionate increase in income between the different sections of the people and especially check the redistribution of income from the salaried group to the business community.

Table 1

Emoluments to the Public Sector Employees

Year	*Total Employees (in lakhs)*	*Total Emoluments (Rs. in crores) Current Prices*	*Percapita Emoluments (in Rs.) Current Prices*	*Total Employees (Rs. in crores) 2000-01 Prices*	*Percapita Emoluments (in Rs.) 2000-01 Prices*	*Tot. Eml as % to GNP*
1971-72	7.01	415	5920	4734	67525	0.95
1972-73	9.32	541	5804	5724	61405	1.10
1973-74	13.44	749	5573	6561	48819	1.24
1974-75	14.32	1000	7402	6909	51137	1.41
1975-76	15.04	1352	8083	9282	55491	1.79
1976-77	15.75	1408	8940	10244	65045	1.74
1977-78	16.39	1646	10048	11126	67917	1.78
1978-79	17.03	1908	11210	12624	74169	1.91

1979-80	17.75	2213	12468	13462	75847	2.03
1980-81	18.39	2619	14219	14303	77764	2.01
1981-82	19.39	3133	16158	15213	78461	2.06
1982-83	20.34	3649	18029	16443	81242	2.16
1983-84	20.72	4485	21549	17956	86275	2.27
1984-85	21.07	5126	24328	19289	91544	2.31
1985-86	21.54	5576	25887	19696	91440	2.25
1986-87	22.11	6371	26820	20701	87145	2.30
1987-88	22.14	7193	32537	21403	96815	2.30
1988-89	22.09	8683	39415	23681	107504	2.32
1989-90	22.36	9742	43665	24953	111844	2.25
1990-91	22.19	10912	49179	25126	113251	2.17
1991-92	21.79	12311	58508	24987	118751	2.13
1992-93	21.52	13983	64983	25842	120095	2.11
1993-94	20.70	14913	72043	25676	124036	1.89
1994-95	20.62	17015	82517	26573	128896	1.84
1995-96	20.52	21931	106876	31147	151789	2.07
1996-97	20.08	22219	110662	28844	143657	1.81
1997-98	19.50	25385	129582	30834	157396	1.84
1998-99	19.00	26254	136179	28619	148448	1.65
1999-00	18.06	30402	168339	31705	175554	1.74
2000-01	17.40	38223	219672	38223	219672	2.02

Source: For columns 2,3 and 4: Economic Survey, 2003-04, p. S51.
For columns 5, 6 and 7: Computed from the data given in columns 2, 3 and 4.

Table 2. Results of the Trend Models

S.N.	*Variable*	*Period*	*a*	*b*	SE_b	*Adjusted* R^2
1.	Employment (in lakhs)	I	8.23	1.13*	0.16	0.848
		II	19.70	0.31*	0.04	0.842
		III	22.45	-0.46*	0.04	0.948
2.	Total Emoluments in current prices (Rs in Crores)	I	74.13	238.36*	10.33	0.983
		II	1798.73	852.41*	48.60	0.971
		III	7922.13	2607.54*	230.21	0.934
3.	Total Emoluments in 2000-01 prices (Rs in Crores)	I	3356.40	1116.46*	43.70	0.986
		II	14287.50	1119.75*	51.18	0.982
		III	23067.30	1123.30*	242.51	0.694
4.	Percapita Emolument in current prices (in Rs)	I	3865.40	960.60*	79.42	0.842
		II	10039.00	3865.40*	286.70	0.945
		III	26948.50	15997.80*	1752.34	0.901

5.	Percapita Emoluments in 2000-01 prices (in Rs)	I	51848.90	2302.36**	867.93	0.401
		II	73052.50	3909.01*	459.07	0.888
		III	98965.10	9066.25*	1652.88	0.764

* Significant at one per cent level ** Significant at five per cent level

Table 3. Results of the Semi-log Linear Regression Models

S.N.	Variable	Period	a	b	SE_b	Adjusted R^2	CGR
1.	Employment (in lakhs)	I	2.041	0.096*	0.210	0.698	10.75
		II	2.980	0.015*	0.020	0.801	1.51
		III	3.109	0.023*	0.002	0.937	-2.27
2.	Total Emoluments in current prices (Rs in Crores)	I	5.997	0.198*	0.014	0.957	21.89
		II	7.950	0.137*	0.003	0.994	14.68
		III	9.296	0.119*	0.006	0.977	12.63
3.	Total Emoluments in 2000-01 prices (Rs in Crores)	I	8.402	0.126*	0.080	0.969	13.42
		II	9.611	0.055*	0.003	0.975	5.65
		III	10.073	0.037*	0.008	0.720	3.76
4.	Percapita Emolument in current prices (in Rs)	I	8.460	0.108*	0.008	0.955	11.40
		II	9.569	0.122*	0.005	0.984	12.97
		III	10.799	0.140*	0.007	0.978	15.03
5.	Percapita Emolument in 2000-01 prices (in Rs)	I	10.869	0.035**	0.014	0.354	3.56
		II	11.223	0.041*	0.004	0.907	4.23
		III	11.572	0.059*	0.009	0.855	6.08

* Significant at one per cent level ** Significant at five per cent level

Table 4. Associated between per capita Emoluments and Consumer Price Index: Results of Linear and Double Log-linear Models

S.N.	Period	Model	a	b	SE_b	Adjusted R^2
1.	I	Simple Linear	-3313.56	40.91*	7.03	0.785
2.	II	Simple Linear	-15334.60	67.25 *	3.06	0.982
3.	III	Simple Linear	-83522.30	121.99*	8.52	0.888
4.	I	Double Log	1.977	1.245*	0.230	0.759
5.	II	Double Log	0.515	1.500*	0.500	0.990
6.	III	Double Log	-0.778	1.676*	0.129	0.949

*Significant at one per cent level

Note: 1. I Period: 1971-72 to 1980-81 2.CGR: Compound Growth Rate
II Period: 1981-82 to 1990-91
III Period 1991-92 to 2000-01

6

ARE RETRENCHMENT LAWS INEFFICIENT?*

Errol D' Souza

It is argued that anti-retrenchment laws end up hurting the workers they were designed to protect because firms decrease their demand for labour in anticipation of surplus labour during downturns. If free contracting between workers and firms is allowed we show in an efficiency wage set up that both firms and workers can behave opportunistically requiring third-party enforcement of employment protection legislation.

I. Introduction

The issue of flexibility in the labour market has attracted a lot of attention in policy debates in India. The lack of flexibility in the labour market is often cited as the reason for poor performance of the labour market in terms of employment generation and productivity growth. A popular view is that increased integration of the economy and technological change require structural change in the organization of production in firms and the lack of flexibility in the labour market does not permit accommodation of this change. It is often pointed out that many labour market institutions such as wage settlements that are binding on whole sectors and dismissal regulations are relevant to only a small part of the workforce in what is called the formal sector, which is not expanding

* Reprinted with permission from *Indian Journal of Labour Economics*, Vol. 48, No. 4, 205, pp. 939-944.

at a sufficiently rapid pace. This has led to recommendations that these institutions be altered in order that the allocative function of the labour market be improved.

The important piece of legislation that has attracted all the attention is the Industrial Disputes Act (IDA) of 1947, which applies to establishments employing fifty or more workers in the organized sector. The IDA was amended under pressure from the trade unions in 1976 and 1982. The 1976 amendment of the IDA requires that if a firm employs 300 or more workers, then the workers cannot be laid off or retrenched without the permission of the government. The 1982 amendment of the IDA made this provision of government permission applicable to all firms employing 100 or more workers. This provision is known as Chapter V-B of the IDA, which stipulated prior permission from government for layoff, retrenchment or closure. There is an exception for retrenchment resulting from power shortages or natural disaster but the penalty for retrenchment or closure without permission includes a fine and a prison sentence for the employer. Chapter V-A requires an establishment employing 50 or more workers to provide workers with 30 days notice and 15 days pay for every year of continuous work by the worker in case the firm retrenches workers for valid reasons. Circumvention of these laws by firms has taken many forms—managements using lockouts as a means towards closure, subcontracting to pressurize workers to leave of accept voluntary retirement schemes, and transferring ownership, as it is not incumbent on new owners to retain employees.

Basu (2002) has argued that legislation against retrenchment or dismissal of labour as in the IDA of 1947 can backfire because of failure to distinguish between what is good ex ante and what is good ex post. A law that makes retrenchment difficult is of course good for workers who are already employed. However, firms will be more wary of employing workers making labour a less valuable input and decreasing the demand for labour. As a result wages will fall and workers who benefit from more secure jobs lose out by having lower wages. Thus workers may be worse off as a result of legislation meant to make them better off. A formal statement of this argument is in Basu, Fields and Debgupta (2001). Basu recommends on this basis that contracts between firms and employees should not be exogenously fixed by law (such as the restrictions on firing) but that there should be free contract between workers and firms which depending on preferences (including risk aversion) would see some contracts with low wages and long tenure for employees and some contracts with high wages and firing rights with employers. This argument that free contract leads to efficiency is an outcome of the traditional, perfectly competitive story in which workers and firms implicitly bargain for the efficient level of employment security. This as we argue below is a very unsatisfactory way of carrying out the analysis because in a competitive model when wages adjust the unemployment rate remains unchanged or zero.

A satisfactory model for the analysis of employment protection must be able to demonstrate not only that wages are endogenous but also that equilibrium unemployment is possible because labour markets like credit markets do not clear. Such an explanation is provided by efficiency wage models. In one variant of these models workers are paid in excess of their marginal contribution and reservation wages in order to reduce shirking and increase labour productivity at the risk of involuntary unemployment (Shapiro and Stiglitz, 1984). In another version, which is the deferred payment incentive version, the wage is initially less than the worker's marginal product and then increases as tenure in employment increases in order to induce effort over time. In both variants the threat of termination and loss of the efficiency wage deter employee shirking. However efficiency wage models also do not consider the possibility that when efficiency wage exceed worker's marginal contribution, firms have an incentive to terminate workers before the wages are paid. The response to this moral hazard as we argue is to introduce employment protection. Hence, labour protection laws may be necessary to deter employer opportunism. We first present the argument advanced by Basu (2002) in the next section and then employ a version of an efficiency wage model that considers the incentives of firms to terminate workers to illuminate the requirements for retrenchment laws.

II. The Basu Approach

The Basu approach compares two alternative legal regimes—one in which employers are free to retrench workers at will (the free retrenchment or F regime) and another in which no retrenchment is allowed (the no retrenchment or N regime). In the simple version of the model there are n identical firms, each with a production function given by

$$q = \phi f(L) \tag{1}$$

where q is output, L the labour employed by the firm, and f is a stochastic shock independent across firms and across time that takes the values of 1 and 0 with probability p and (1–p) respectively. Each period a randomly selected pn firms have $f = 1$ and $(1-p)n$ firms have $f = 0$. We can think of $f = 1$ as a good production year for the firm and $f = 0$ as a bad year. In a good year a firm maximizes profits given by $f(L) - wL$ and demands labour according to the condition $f'(L) = w$. The demand for labour is then given by

$$L = f'^{-1}(w) \tag{2}$$

In a bad year with $\phi = 0$ the firm will not demand any labour. The labour in the F regime is then given by

$$L^F = \Sigma f'^{-1}(w) == npf'-1(w) \tag{3}$$

If the production function is quadratic, *i.e.*

$f(L)=(A/B)L-L^2/2B$ *with* $A,B>0$ (and $L < A$ *then* $w=f'(L)=(A/B)-(L/B)$ *and* $f'^{-1}(w)=L=A—Bw$. Hence,

$$L^F == np\,[A-Bw] \tag{4}$$

In the no-retrenchment N-regime a risk neutral firm that does not know the value of f in advance will maximize expected profits $pf(L) - wL$ and demand labour according to the condition $pf'(L) == w$ or,

$$L = f'^{-1}\left(\frac{w}{p}\right)$$

As the firm ex ante identical the aggregate demand for labour is given by

$$L^N = nf'^{-1}\left(\frac{w}{p}\right) \tag{5}$$

For the case of the quadratic production function,

$$L^N = n\left[A - B\frac{w}{p}\right] \tag{6}$$

The two labour demand curves L^F (equation 4) and L^N (equation 6) are graphed in Figure I. The supply curve of labour as drawn in Figure I is the standard upward sloping supply function $S = S(w)$, where, $S'(w) > 0$. Now, if the initial regime is one where retrenchment is freely allowed, then, equilibrium in the labour market is at point E^F. Suppose now that a new law is legislated that does not allow firms to retrench labour, then, the equilibrium shifts to E^N. Clearly both wages and employment decline and workers are adversely affected by this legislation that was

intended to benefit them. Intervention meant to protect workers ends up hurting them. Basu argues on the basis of this that by severely limiting the scope of voluntary contracting between workers and employers India's labour laws have harmed workers and could have contributed to industrial strife.

III. Efficiency Wage Model

In an efficiency wage set up the problem of employment protection is best addressed in a simple two- period framework. At time t_0 the firm and the worker agree to a contract to be executed in period t_1. The contract states that the firm will play the worker ($w > 0$) if the worker expends effort ($e>0$) but the worker will be terminated from service without compensation ($w=0$) if the worker is caught shirking ($e=0$). The worker's disutility of effort is e. the effort provided by the worker is not easily observable by the employer or verifiable by a third party such as a court. The output generated due to the effort expended by the worker, however, is observable and verifiable.

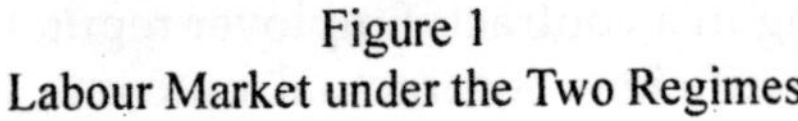
Figure 1
Labour Market under the Two Regimes

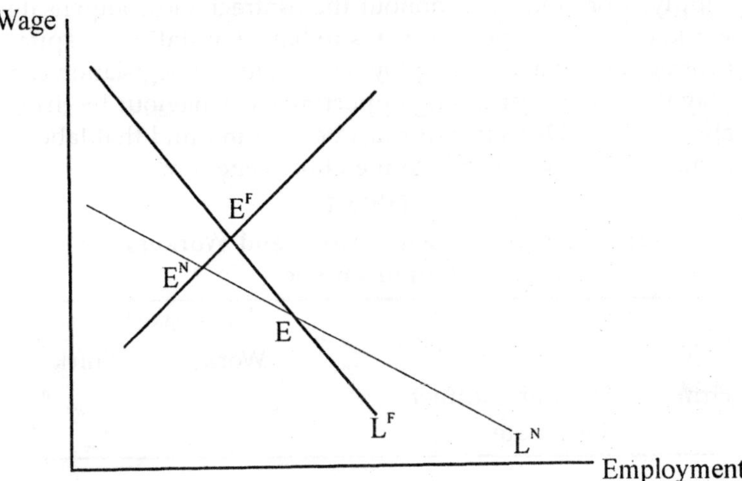

At time t_1 the worker has the options of either working or shirking. If effort is expended the firm's gross benefit is y and if the worker shirks then expected output is *py* where (1-*p*) is the probability of detecting a shirking worker. The firm also has two options before it[2] -to fulfill the contract or to behave opportunistically and terminate the worker. If the firm is opportunistic and the contract is terminated by it then it captures the full rents generated from the employee's efforts. If the firm honors the contract it pays the worker for effort or fires a shirking worker detected with probability (1-*p*). Hence, the worker can be dismissed for two reasons- employer opportunism and verifiable shirking. The expected payoffs of the firm are in the lower left- hand corner of each cell in Table 1 and that of the worker in the upper right hand corner of each cell.

Table 1 depicts the opportunism faced by both firms and workers. The worker has an incentive to shirk if the wage is too low and monitoring is imperfect and the firm has an incentive to exploit the worker. When both firm and worker anticipate the other will behave opportunistically the worker will shirk and the firm will fire the worker and neither benefits from engaging in a contract. Employer reputation effects may result in the efficient contractual outcome where workers supply effort and firms honour the contract and compensate workers. But to expect all firms to have reputational capital is unwarranted and so employment protection legislation can play the role of restraining opportunistic behaviour by firms and workers. Of course, it must be kept in mind that labour protection laws can reduce the effectiveness of

Table 1

Efficiency Wages when firms and Workers are Opportunistic

		Worker			
		Work		Shirk	
Firm	Honour contract	y-w	w-e	p(y-w)	pw
	Terminate	y	-e	py	0

efficiency wages and reduce worker productivity if it is a blunt instrument. An employment protection legislation whilst alleviating the worker's fear that he may be opportunistically terminated must at the same time allow the firm to terminate the worker if he is caught shirking. If there is third-party verifiable evidence of shirking then legislation should be such as to induce the expectation in the worker that termination of his services will occur.

There of course is the second variant of efficiency wages where workers are given deferred payments in order to elicit a performance bond in the form of effort over time (Lazear, 1981). Here even if the worker is fired with verifiable evidence he loses compensation due to him in terminate services before the full term is served. To safeguard against this type of opportunism contractual safeguards in the form of a penalty on the firm in case of premature firing is called for. This function is typically performed by severance packages which specify a fraction of the worker's contractually established wage benefits to be paid to the worker if the firm chooses to respect to quality warranties are used to signal quality attributes. Similarly in labour markets when firms and workers may behave opportunistically with when firms and workers may behave opportunistically third- party enforcement of employment protection legislation is called for. This legislation should not be written in stone but accommodate firing in case shirking by workers is established and severance payments in case firms wish to terminate workers regardless of shirking.

IV. Conclusion

Employment protection involves a whole range of measures apart from severance payment. These are designed so as to limit the employer's ability to dismiss workers without delay or cost. The idea is to protect both workers and employers from opportunistic behaviour- tying their hands so as to make both better off by deterring them from short-termism. Some forms of employment protection need not entail immediate financial gains to either party. Administrative procedures such as writing to an employee concerned giving reasons for dismissal, specifying lengths of time that the employer has to wait for a response, and notices of termination where may be issued but not become effective, etc., are employment protection measures that do not entail a direct transfer from the employer to the worker. These are often wise to include in employment protection legislation (as in the case of Chapter V-A) so as to delay dismissals and induce employers to negotiate over termination and not behave opportunistically.

One could argue that this increases job tenures and gives power to established workers with adverse effects on job creation. However, given opportunism, the only way that workers and firms will invest in a job is if there are speed breakers to opportunism. The unintended consequence that this may reduce turnover is an outcome that is an indirect cost of the gains to protection. Employment protection is usually thought of as creating redistribution towards labour, especially established workers, and is held responsible for creating rent seeking and efficiency losses. However, such policies also create immense insurance benefits by deterring opportunism. The challenge is to ensure that the efficiency losses are contained whilst the insurance gains are furthered. Employment protection should not be so rigid that it prevents change and preserves the status quo. It should not be so blunt that it is unable to distinguish between termination for shirking and opportunistic termination. Serious employment protection is counter productive when it is protectionist to vested interests and does not promote economic progress. Data-Chaudhuri (2001) appropriately quotes Justice Mehta, a former Chief Justice of a High Court, when he states that the view taken by many judgments "that to favour labour is the only goal of the stature (the IDA) is counter productive in as much as it ultimately harms the cause of labour itself."

Job security regulations are often seen as a source of rigidity and resulting in rents for organized labour. However, these regulations often emerged as a response to the threat of unemployment and income insecurity and are more a social insurance than rent seeking. Moreover, markets if left to themselves will not be able to device contracts that provide an efficient level of employment security. In a temporal world if workers tradeoff working with shirking, employers can similarly tradeoff honoring a contract with termination of employees. Opportunistic behaviour is often difficult to observe or to verify. In product markets opportunism can be nipped through signals such as the offer of warranties. In labour markets both firms and workers are susceptible to opportunism and verifying breach of contract is difficult. A meaningful way to get workers to invest in a job and employers to honour contracts is to legislate employment protection. The difficult task, of course, in reality is to ensure that employment protection does not become protectionist and enemy of economic progress. It is premature to conclude that anti-retrenchment laws are inefficient and end up hurting workers.

Notes

1. Of course, the labour supply curve can be to the right of point E in which case legislation that does not permit retrenchment raises wages and employment, benefiting workers. The effect of the anti-retrenchment law is thus theoretically ambiguous but that is not important to our critique expounded below.

2. For simplicity assume that at time the worker's effort decision is made simultaneously with the decision of the firm as to whether to honour the contract.

References

Basu, K. (2002), "Ideology, Economics and Labour Market Policy", in Mohon, Rakesh (ed.), *Facets of the Indian Economy—The NCAER Golden Jubilee Lectures,* Oxford University Press, New Delhi, pp. 248-264.

Fields, G.S. and Debgupta, S. (2001), "Retrenchment, Labor Laws and Government Policy: An Analysis with Special Reference to India", Paper written for the world Bank, *Shrinking Smartly Research,* Washington D.C.

Data-Chaudhuri, M. (2001), "Labour Markets as Social Institutions, in India", in Satu, Kahkonen and Lanyi, Anthony (eds.) *Institutions, Incentives and Economic Reforms in India,* Sage Publications, New Delhi, pp. 449-468.

Lazear, E. (1981), "Agency, Earnings Profiles, Productivity, and Hours Restrictions", *American Economic Review,* Vol. 71, September, pp. 606-620.

Shapiro, C. and Stiglitz, J.E. (1984), "Equilibrium Unemployment as a Worker Discipline Device", *American Economic Review,* Vol. 74, No. 3, pp. 433-444.

7

GROWTH OF LABOUR PRODUCTIVITY, WAGE SHARE AND TOTAL FACTOR PRODUCTIVITY IN ORGANISED MANUFACTURING DURING 1981-99: THE EXPERIENCE OF WEST BENGAL

Maniklal Adhikary & Ritwik Mazumder

I. Introduction and Objectives

The Indian economy is passing through a distinct phase of transition where a combination of market forces and partial government intervention are ruling most sectors—manufacturing industries being a typical example. Current experiences show that the greater the importance of the market in this blend in a sector or industry, higher is the echelon of discontent amongst Leftist political forces—their main apprehension being the adverse impact of market forces on employment. Succumbing to international pressure (mostly from international financial/lending institutions) India was compelled to implement an economic reforms programme following an acute balance of payments crisis in July 1991. Initially, the reforms programme comprised of macroeconomic stabilisation measures along with some key structural modifications. The objective was to give an impetus to output growth in order to break the shackles of poor industrial and macro-economic performance of the mid and late 1980's. On the one hand, the regime of regulation and control did not grant the public sector the autonomy necessary for commercial viability. On the other hand, protective trade policy did not compel both public and private sector enterprises to improve efficiency and product quality.

While the 1980's saw rather partial deregulation and liberalisation of a few aspects of the pre-existing control regime, the reforms of the 1990's, by contrast (in the areas of industry, banking, and trade among others), were much more extensive. Perhaps the most radical change in the policy resolution of 1991 was the withdrawal of government intervention from market oriented business activities. Successive governments have tried to implement this policy by disinvestment of PSUs, of course not without stiff resistance from leftist forces. The relaxation of government control gained momentum since 1997-98.

The key element of Economic Reforms—New Industrial Policy of 1991-92, witnessed some fundamental changes—abolition of industrial licensing, relaxing rigidities due to MRTP and FERA, reducing list of industries to be reserved for the public sector, automatic approvals of foreign technology agreements and 51 percent foreign equity, among others. For the first time, 100 percent FDI was invited in power production and in basic infrastructure (e.g., highway development)—another drastic policy change. The opening up of the domestic market to foreign producers had the potential of enhancing productivity and efficiency of Indian industries as it put in some coercive pressure by creating, rather suddenly, a harshly competitive environment for domestic players. It may however be argued that output growth in manufacturing (not necessarily indigenous) would accelerate following a boost in demand owing to the opening up of the domestic economy that would provide variety to domestic buyers.

For over more than a decade now, domestic manufacturers are exposed to global competition and the industries in West Bengal, a state that has seen almost three decades of leftist political rule, are by no means outside its purview. Incidentally, the topic of industrial performance and productivity in West Bengal during post-1977 years is debatable. Popular journalistic writings would suggest that the Left Front regime in West Bengal is characterised by industrial stagnation and inefficiency of contemptible degree. Firm resistance to liberalisation has been primarily responsible for poor investment climate, poor work-culture, especially in State owned production units, and hostile worker-employer relations originating from destructive rather than constructive leftist trade unionism have created a vicious circle. Policies like disinvestment of PSUs and inviting FDI inflows to core sectors as infrastructure are presently debated by the state leadership. The apprehensions often projected through public discussions and debates are—rise in unemployment in the organised sector (mainly manufacturing), closure and extinction of both small and medium scale indigenous units (due to incompetence at the international level) and the like. Clearly, resistance to reforms has neither improved the investment climate nor helped the cause of FDI inflows to the state.

In the backdrop of these events the present study covering the period 1981-1999, has been undertaken with two major objectives in mind. On the one hand an attempt is made to enquire whether such firm resistance to market oriented reforms in West Bengal is based on sound economic logic. On the other hand, the study aims to delineate the performance and growth of productivities of labour and capital in the manufacturing sector in the state across different phases of liberalisation during 1981-1999. It further examines whether the increased competitiveness following market oriented reforms have succeeded to raise factor productivity growth (partial and total) and efficiency of the manufacturing sector in the state.

In view of these objectives, this paper examines the performances of 16 selected industry groups (see Appendix 1) aggregated at the 2-digit level of ASI (NIC-1970) classification in the state over the said period on the basis of industry level ASI data. For this purpose we begin by studying growth patterns of performance indicators as outputs and inputs, capital intensity, partial and total factor productivities along with their decompositions across different phases of liberalisation during 1981-82 to 1999-00 for each of these 16 industry groups. The sub-periods 1981-82 to 1985-86 (Regime-1) and 1986-87 to 1990-91 (Regime-2) are considered as two phases of weak liberalisation and respectively (Dutt, 1993). We take the sub-periods 1991-92 to 1995-96 and 1996-97 to 1999-00 (Regime-3 and Regime-4), as two phases of strong liberalisation. Like most Indian researchers in this field, 'value added' is taken as a suiTable substitute for 'output'. Labour has been measured by the number of production workers as reported by ASI and not by labour time. Labour and fixed capital are the only inputs considered. The growth of total factor productivity (TFPG) is computed by both Tornqvist and Solow Divisia index of growth accounting using time series data on value added, labour and capital stock. Growth of labour productivity is decomposed into contribution of capital intensity and TFPG for each industry group across all regimes. Regime wise, pooled estimates of a trans-log production function are utilised to find the rate of technical progress and its bias with respect to the two inputs. Further, cross-sectional technical efficiency levels of each industry group at the macro-economic level of production are computed by estimating a deterministic frontier production function (Corrected Ordinary Least Squares or COLS). For this purpose the entire manufacturing sector is considered where a cross-section comprises of the 16 major industry groups. In the absence of information on output prices we left out three industry groups viz., repairing works, water, gas and steam producing industries.

The aim is to elicit the impact of economic reforms on factor productivity growth and performance of major industry groups in West Bengal. The major limitation of the study crops up from the degree of heterogeneity that results from aggregation of various industries and industry groups implicit at the 2-digit level (NIC–1970) of industrial classification. However a credible study of the manufacturing sector at the state level, which requires further disaggregation, is beyond the reach of the present exercise.

There have been a number of studies on spatial and inter-temporal variations in manufacturing sector performance and productivity in India. An overview of a few leading works in this area can build up an approach to this paper. Ahluwalia (1985) estimated Solow and Translog indices of TFPG at different levels of industrial disaggregation for the period 1959-

60 to 1980-81 with two sub-periods 1959-65 and 1966-80. She made four alternative estimates of TFPG for the entire manufacturing sector and for use-based and input-based classification of industries. Her study reveals declining TFPG during the first and second sub-periods, interpreted as decline in productivity performance. Her observations support the view that industrial performance did not appear to have deteriorated after 1965 though there was some decline in efficiency of factor use. Goldar and Seth (1989) studied trends in industrial output in 12 major States for the period 1960-61 to 1985-86. The purpose of their study was to investigate the causes of industrial deceleration since mid-sixties. Their work reveals that all 12 states experienced a deceleration in the rate of industrial growth after mid-sixties and most states experienced a recovery after mid-seventies. They concluded that in general those states which gained more from public sector investment during 1950-60 experienced greater deceleration in the rate of industrial growth after mid-seventies. Pradhan and Barik (1998) observed trends in TFPG over a longer period ranging from 1963-64 to 1992-93 in selected polluting industries. Their study reveals a positive trend of TFPG with a marked deceleration in the 1980s. An important finding of their exercise was that TFPG in Indian manufacturing followed a fluctuating path. Based on ASI data for the period 1974-75 to 1988-89, Coondoo, Neogi and Ghosh (1993) observed that capital intensity has been rising at a pace faster than that of labour productivity in Indian manufacturing industries. According to this study the rise in labour productivity was the result of rising capital intensity and not due to pure productivity increase. Neogi and Ghosh (1994) have found that technical efficiency in Indian manufacturing has been declining over time till the late 1980s. Further Neogi and Ghosh (1998) studied the impact of liberalisation on the performance of selected industries on the basis of firm level data over the period 1989 to 1994. They concluded that productivity growth and efficiency levels did not improve in these industries to the expectation level during this post-liberalisation period. Very similar are the conclusions drawn in more recent studies conducted by Adhikary and Mazumder (2004 and 2005) They show that efficiency levels in the entire

manufacturing sector in West Bengal did not rise during post reform years vis-à-vis pre-reform years. They found declining TFP at the state level during pre-reform years in West Bengal but rising TFP during post reform years. None of these studies however focus specifically on issues related to industrial workers, labour productivity, labour efficiency and wage share.

In the light of these studies the present exercise should ideally have been carried out at the 2-digit level (NIC 1970) of industrial classification for all other major industrialised states in India to compare the performance and productivity standards across states. Evidently, the study cannot assist us in bringing out the relative performance of the manufacturing sector in West Bengal vis-à-vis other industrially growing states but it can assist in identifying the better performing and more productive industry groups as well as those, which use resources more efficiently than others. There is of course an opportunity to compare the results of our study with those obtained in similar other studies conducted. Throughout the text the terms 'output' and 'value added' are used alternately since value added is taken as a suiTable proxy for output.

The paper is presented in the following sections. Methodological issues of the study including model specifications and data sources, described in section 2. Section 3 deals with empirical results and Section 4 presents a brief summary and conclusions.

II. Methodological Issues

2.1 Growth Rates

In order to see the trends in the growth of the variables of interest for different regimes we use Poirier's (1974) spline function approach. Assuming a linear time trend, the postulated model is

$$\begin{aligned}
&\text{Regime1:} && \ln Y_t = \alpha_1 + \beta_1 t + u_t && \text{for } t \le 1985 \\
&\text{Regime2:} && \ln Y_t = \alpha_2 + \beta_2 t + u_t && \text{for } 1985 < t \le 1990 \qquad (2.1) \\
&\text{Regime3:} && \ln Y_t = \alpha_3 + \beta_3 t + u_t && \text{for } 1990 < t \le 1995 \\
&\text{Regime4:} && \ln Y_t = \alpha_4 + \beta_4 t + u_t && \text{for } 1995 < t \le 1999
\end{aligned}$$

We now define the following variables:

$$w_{1t} = t, \forall t = 1,2,......,19\,; \qquad w_{2t} = \begin{cases} 0 & \text{if } t \le 1985 \\ t-1985 & 1985 < t \end{cases}$$

$$w_{3t} = \begin{cases} 0 & \text{if } t \le 1991 \\ t-1991 & 1991 < t \end{cases} \text{ and } w_{4t} = \begin{cases} 0 & \text{if } t \le 1995 \\ t-1995 & 1995 < t \end{cases} \qquad (2.1a)$$

and reparameterise the function as

$$\ln Y_t = \alpha_1 + \delta_1 w_{1t} + \delta_2 w_{2t} + \delta_3 w_{3t} + \delta_4 w_{4t} + u_t \qquad (2.2)$$

The expression $[\exp(\beta_i)-1]*100$ will yield the percentage growth rate for the *i*-th regime (i = 1,..,4), where $\beta_1 = \delta_1$, $\beta_2 = \delta_1 + \delta_2$, $\beta_3 = \delta_1 + \delta_2 + \delta_3$ *and* $\beta_4 = \delta_1 + \delta_2 + \delta_3 + \delta_4$ Equation (2.2) was employed to compute the growth rates of desired variables for each industry group across regimes. The variables, which capture the growth rates in the four different regimes, are w_{1t}, w_{2t}, w_{3t} *and* w_{4t} respectively. The growth rate for the entire period 1981-82 to 1999-00 is computed by estimating the equation

$$\ln Y_t = \alpha + \beta t + u_t \qquad (2.3)$$

The variables we shall consider are listed as under.

Y: Gross value added; K: Gross fixed capital stock; L: Labour as measured by no. of production workers; Y/L: Average product of labour; Y/K: Average product of capital; CAPIN or K/L: Capital intensity i.e., Gross fixed capital stock per worker ; W/Y: Wage share in value added; TFPG-1: Tornqvist index of Total factor productivity growth ; TFPG-2: Tornqvist index of Total factor productivity growth when factor shares are replaced by output elasticities with respect to inputs; TFPG-3: Solow–divisia index of total factor productivity growth; CLOG: Contribution of labour to output growth; CKOG. Contribution of capital to output growth

2.2 *Factor Productivity Growth and Technical Efficiency*

Growth of factor productivity has been conventionally recognised as the principal determinant of economic growth. Considering the supply side, growth of output in an economy or an industry or a firm is determined by the rate of expansion of its productive resources and by improvements in their efficiency; i.e. by TFPG. Nishimizu and Page (1982), introduced change in technical efficiency as a source of productivity growth. Output growth under this specification is determined by the rate of expansion of productive resources, rate of technical progress and change in technical efficiency. However for the present study we ignore the technical efficiency term and interpret TFPG as the combined effect of autonomous disembodied type of technical progress along with efficiency of factor use. In order to compute the growth of total factor productivity, we use Tornqvist Index of TFPG. Tornqvist index is an important variant of the divisia index used by Solow. Under the specification of a translog production function under constant returns to scale, Diewart (1976) proved that the Tornqvist index is the exact measure of technical change. Thus, if we have a transcendental logarithmic production function as

$$\ln Y_t = \alpha_0 + \alpha_t t + \beta_{tt} t^2 + \sum_{i=1}^{k} \alpha_i \ln X_i + \frac{1}{2}\sum_i \sum_j \beta_{ij} \ln X_i \ln X_j + \sum_{i=1}^{k} \beta_{it} t \ln X_i + u_t \quad (2.4)$$

then Tornqvist approximation of the divisia index, as introduced by Jorgensen and Grilliches (1967), is expressed as

$$\overline{DI}_t = \ln\left(\frac{Y_t}{Y_{t-1}}\right) - \sum_{i=1}^{k} \overline{Sh}_i \ln\left(\frac{X_{i,t}}{X_{i,t-1}}\right) \quad (2.5)$$

where $\overline{Sh_i} = \frac{1}{2}\left[Sh_{i,t} + Sh_{i,t-1}\right]$, sh_i being the share of the i-th input in value added. The average rate of technical change, $\overline{DI}_t$, is also called translog index of technical change or TFPG. The expression in (2.5) implicitly assumes that share of each input in value added is equal to the corresponding elasticity of value added with respect to inputs. In other words, it is assumed that first order conditions of profit maximisation are satisfied so that factor prices are paid according to their marginal products. This in effect implies the presence of constant returns to scale. Computation of TFPG time series (TFPG-1) is initially done using the expression in (2.5). However doing away with the assumption of constant returns to scale (CRS) and replacing the factor shares sh_i's by the partial elasticities of output with respect to inputs [by estimating the regime–wise output elasticities (η_i) with respect to inputs], we get another TFPG time series (TFPG-2)—a minor modification of the Tornqvist divisia index in (2.5). Further, the contribution of factors and TFPG to output growth is computed. In contrast to the studies cited, the factor contribution to output growth is computed as the partial elasticity of a factor times its growth rate. The sum of output elasticity (partial) weighted input growth is deducted from growth of value added to compute the Solow residual measure of TFPG (TFPG-3).

The translog measure of TFPG is not significantly different from the Solow residual measure under two conditions. First, the elasticity of substitution is not significantly different from 1. Second, variation in the growth rates of inputs over time is not significant (see, Ahluwalia 1991). Admittedly, the trans-log approach does not distinguish between total factor productivity growth and the rate of technical progress. Higher the rate of technical progress, higher will be the growth of output relative to inputs. Under the specification of production function as in (2.4), the expression for the rate of technical progress (or TFPG) is

$$\frac{\partial \ln Y}{\partial t} = \alpha_t + \beta_{tt} t + \sum_i \beta_{it} \ln X_i \qquad (2.6)$$

where α_t is the rate of autonomous growth of total factor productivity, β_{it} is the bias in the growth of total factor productivity and β_{tt} is the rate of change in growth of total factor productivity. $\beta_{it} = 0$, implies technical progress is Hicks neutral and $\beta_{it} > 0$, implies technical progress is non-neutral in the Hicksian sense and is biased with respect to the *i*th input. From (2.4), output elasticity with respect to i-th input is

$$\eta_i = \frac{\partial \ln Y_t}{\partial \ln X_i} = \alpha_i + \sum_j \beta_{ij} \ln X_j + \beta_{it} t \qquad (2.7)$$

(2.7)

Also from (2.7), $\frac{\partial \eta_i}{\partial t} = \beta_{it}$, i.e., technical progress may raise or lower the value of output elasticity with respect to i-th endogenous input depending on the sign of β_{it}. Under the strong assumptions that competitive equilibrium prevails and factor prices are paid according to their marginal products, we have $\eta_i = sh_i$, i.e., output elasticity is same as factor share. If β_{it} is statistically significant in the estimation of the parameters of the trans-log production function, we can proceed to compute a time series of the amount of input bias in technical progress from the expression

$$BIAS_t(X) = \frac{1}{sh_i}\beta_{it} + RTP \qquad (2.8)$$

Our estimations will be done on the basis of one output i.e., value added and two inputs—labour and fixed capital. Following Hulten and Schwab (1984) and Mullen and Williams (1994) we decompose growth of labour productivity into contribution of capital intensity and Solow divisia measure of TFPG by assuming a Cobb-Douglas production function.

$$\frac{d \ln (Y/L)}{dt} = \frac{d\, A(t)}{dt} + \alpha \frac{d \ln (K/L)}{dt} \qquad (2.9)$$

Here α is the output elasticity with respect to capital. In the absence of CRS growth of labour productivity can only be decomposed into the sum of TFPG and output elasticity weighted sum of the logarithm of inputs. The advantage of (2.9) is that it exposes the part of labour productivity growth due to capital intensity growth and reveals the portion unexplained by input growth (TFPG).

A deterministic production frontier at the state level (comprising of 16 industry groups) is estimated using the corrected ordinary least squares method (COLS) after Winsten (1957). For this purpose a Cobb–Douglas production function in its log-linear form is estimated separately for each regime by applying OLS to pooled observations. COLS intercept is estimated consistently by $\hat{\alpha}_0^* = \hat{\alpha}_0 + \max\{\hat{u}_i\}$ where $\hat{u}_i$'s are the OLS residuals and $\hat{\alpha}_0$'s are the OLS intercepts. OLS residuals are corrected in the opposite direction so that $-\hat{u}_i^* = \hat{u}_i - \max_i\{\hat{u}_i\}$. COLS residuals $\hat{u}_i^*$ are non-negative with at least one being zero and can be used to get consistent estimates of the technical efficiency of each industry group by $TE_i = \exp\{-\hat{u}_i^*\}$. Since only the OLS intercept is corrected, COLS has a restrictive property in the sense that the structure of the best practice technology is same as that of the central tendency technology (Kumbhakar and Lovell, 2000).

Following the common practice in most empirical studies on Indian industries, data source for the study is the Annual Survey of Industries: *Summary Results for Factory Sector* (various issues). The data relates to aggregate industry level at the 2-digit level of NIC 1970 classification. Admittedly, at the 2-digit level of classification, the level of aggregation is quite high which makes the data set heterogeneous. We converted all nominal values to real values using suitable deflators—wholesale price index numbers from RBI Report on Currency and Finance (various issues). We deflated the gross value added of each two-digit industry group by the wholesale price index of output of the respective industry. The price indices of machinery and equipments were used to deflate nominal value of fixed capital as provided by ASI. Since credible information about daily or hourly labour-time is unavailable, we measure labour by number of workers directly engaged in production.

The study uses estimates of gross fixed capital stock. Gross fixed capital stock at constant prices was computed by the *perpetual inventory accumulation* method (Goldsmith, 1951). Gross fixed capital stock at replacement cost for the benchmark year (1980-81), was approximated using the rule of thumb after Roychaudhury (1977), "...doubling the value of fixed capital stock at book value at current prices for the benchmark year..." to arrive at estimates of the replacement cost figures of machinery and equipments.

III. Results and Discussion[1]

The computed values of TFPG-1 for each of the 16 industry groups across 4 regimes are presented in Table 1.

Table 1. Regime Wise Average Annual Growth Rate of Total Factor Productivity (TFPG-1)

Industry Group code	*Regime 1 (1981-85)*	*Regime 2 (1986-90)*	*Regime 3 (1991-95)*	*Regime 4 (1996-99)*
20-21	16.7	4.1	3.7	-8.3
22	-5.1	4.1	7.2	-11.3
23	0.1	4.2	-1.6	8.1
24	-1.5	-4.7	-22.1	13.6
25	-5.5	-5.0	-5.3	-3.2
26	-3.5	-13.3	2.7	-8.2
27	-8.8	7.8	9.6	29.8
28	-9.8	4.6	-2.3	3.6
29	0.7	-0.9	18.9	23.5
30	10.0	49.2	0.3	-4.7
31	3.4	8.9	2.8	7.0
32	-22.2	-50.3	-17.3	23.9
33	-7.3	3.8	-1.5	-8.4
35-36	-6.0	0.2	3.0	-3.3
37	-3.4	8.6	-6.4	3.9
40	-10.4	-2.5	5.4	51.1
State average	-3.3	1.2	-0.2	7.3

If TFPG is taken as a performance indicator, basic chemical industries (31) have performed consistently well. In contrast to our findings here, Neogi et al (1998) observed declining TFPG (-7.32%) for the chemical industries at the all India level on the basis of firm level data over the period 1989-94.

Strong liberalisation apparently has had a deteriorating impact on certain industry groups. Food processing industries, beverages tobacco and related products, plastic, rubber and petroleum are examples. With occasional periods of declining TFPG textiles, finished wood and leather industries are other good performers. The poorest performers are jute and basic metal and alloy industries where TFPG is found almost always declining. Paper, printing and publishing as well as transport equipments have experienced fluctuating TFPG. However there are certain industry groups that have recovered during the second phase of strong liberalisation. Synthetic fibre, non-metallic mineral products and power show sharp recovery during second phase of strong liberalisation. Manufacturing of machinery and equipments have suffered a set back during post 1996. As many as 11 industry groups registered falling TFP in Regime 1. The figure became 6, 7 and 7 in subsequent years. Average TFPG is highest during the 2nd phase of strong liberalisation. In spite of the industrial slowdown of the mid and late 1990s, rising TFP at the state level is undoubtedly satisfying to liberalisation protagonists. The performance of the power sector in West Bengal is remarkable in this respect. Alternative estimates of TFPG using output elasticities with respect to inputs give very similar results.

Table 2. Regime Wise Average Annual Growth Rate of Total Factor Productivity (TFPG-2)

Industry Group code	*Regime 1 (1981-85)*	*Regime 2 (1986-90)*	*Regime 3 (1991-95)*	*Regime 4 (1996-99)*
20-21	12.4	1.3	2.1	-1.2
22	-3.1	2.5	5.2	-9.5
23	0.1	2.4	-2.1	8.1
24	-5.9	-5.2	-29.9	11.5
25	-6.5	-5.1	-6.5	-3.9

26	-4.6	-19.2	2.1	-8.9
27	-9.9	6.2	8.6	23.1
28	-9.9	4.0	-2.3	2.4
29	0.6	-1.0	16.5	21.6
30	7.0	38.9	0.2	-2.6
31	3.0	7.9	2.8	6.0
32	-20.3	-46.1	-6.5	30.0
33	-5.6	4.7	-0.9	-6.6
35-36	-2.3	1.0	3.6	0.1
37	-2.1	9.9	-2.7	5.0
40	-5.6	-1.0	7.0	59.0
State average	-3.3	0.1	-0.2	8.4

Solow residual estimates of TFPG, i.e., TFPG-3, growth rate of value added and contributions of labour and capital to growth rate of value added are presented in Table-3. No clear pattern is observed in growth rates of value added. Interestingly the more capital intensive sectors have suffered setbacks during the second phase of strong liberalisation. This may be indicative of the macroeconomic slow down of the late 1990s where basic and heavy industries suffered the most. Broadly the growth pattern of value added indicates that the more labour intensive sectors have picked up while the more capital intensive sectors have suffered in the era of economic reforms and macroeconomic slowdown. An interesting observation is that, the more labour intensive industry groups show higher contribution of capital to output growth during post 1991 years with the exception of food processing industries. Regarding contribution of TFPG, the manufacturing sector in West Bengal has had a mixed experience. It is generally observed that labour intensive sectors in the state have picked up while the more capital intensive sectors have suffered amidst global competition and macroeconomic slow down of late 1990s.

Table 3. Contribution to Output Growth and Solow Residual (Percentage Averaged over years)

Industry Group code	*Variables*	*Regime 1 (1981-85)*	*Regime 2 (1986-90)*	*Regime 3 (1991-95)*	*Regime 4 (1996-99)*
	Y growth	21.5	13.3	2.2	23.0
20-21	CTFP	15.9	1.8	-4.0	1.4
	CLOG	-0.8	-0.8	-0.4	27.1
	CKOG	6.3	12.3	6.6	-5.5
	Y growth	0.2	-8.0	27.6	34.2
22	CTFP	-6.5	-5.5	-10.7	-39.0
	CLOG	-1.8	-1.1	9.5	35.1
	CKOG	8.6	-1.4	28.8	38.1
	Y growth	-1.0	0.0	-1.0	14.3
23	CTFP	-1.1	3.2	-1.7	4.0
	CLOG	-3.6	-5.4	-1.3	2.8
	CKOG	3.7	2.2	2.0	7.6
	Y growth	6.6	11.5	-21.3	44.5
24	CTFP	-6.3	-8.1	-29.4	-4.7
	CLOG	0.9	1.4	-3.9	9.1
	CKOG	12.0	18.2	12.0	40.2
	Y growth	-5.6	-2.4	3.4	-3.5
25	CTFP	-6.1	-4.9	-5.8	-3.3
	CLOG	-1.9	-0.9	7.4	-4.6
	CKOG	2.3	3.4	1.9	4.5
	Y growth	-1.2	3.4	26.1	-0.4
26	CTFP	-10.0	-10.3	7.1	-10.2
	CLOG	0.6	-1.2	7.0	-1.5
	CKOG	8.3	14.9	12.0	11.3
	Y growth	-5.5	19.7	12.4	37.5
27	CTFP	-9.1	4.1	8.9	29.3
	CLOG	-1.1	1.2	-1.9	0.3
	CKOG	4.7	14.3	5.4	7.9
	Y growth	-8.2	7.5	6.6	13.5
28	CTFP	-12.7	3.2	-2.8	5.9
	CLOG	-2.9	-1.2	2.2	2.8
	CKOG	7.4	5.5	7.2	4.8

29	Y growth	2.5	3.6	27.1	40.5
	CTFP	-0.1	-1.7	18.4	-4.6
	CLOG	-1.5	1.9	-0.8	4.7
	CKOG	4.1	3.3	9.5	40.3
30	Y growth	14.2	66.1	6.6	-0.7
	CTFP	5.3	47.7	-0.2	-7.8
	CLOG	-2.2	2.3	0.4	-0.6
	CKOG	11.0	16.0	6.4	7.8
31	Y growth	5.4	10.9	9.3	10.7
	CTFP	2.9	8.6	-2.1	6.6
	CLOG	-0.8	-0.3	-0.5	-0.5
	CKOG	3.3	2.6	11.8	4.6
32	Y growth	-18.1	-46.0	3.4	29.7
	CTFP	-24.2	-51.0	-5.2	15.6
	CLOG	-1.9	-0.5	0.8	-2.1
	CKOG	8.1	5.5	7.7	16.2
33	Y growth	5.1	1.3	9.8*	-3.6
	CTFP	-9.5	1.1	-1.6	-6.7
	CLOG	1.8	-3.3	-0.2	2.6
	CKOG	12.8	3.5	11.6	0.4
35-36	Y growth	0.0	7.3	9.7	0.5
	CTFP	-6.6	-0.8	2.6	-4.6
	CLOG	-1.1	-0.2	-0.6	-1.1
	CKOG	7.7	8.3	7.6	6.3
37	Y growth	-1.3	9.5	-0.1	6.2
	CTFP	-4.0	7.1	-8.6	3.9
	CLOG	-3.2	-1.6	3.6	-0.3
	CKOG	5.9	4.0	4.9	2.5
40	Y growth	2.0	4.3	14.8	60.7
	CTFP	-11.2	-2.8	3.6	54.1
	CLOG	2.3	-1.0	0.9	-0.1
	CKOG	10.9	8.1	10.4	6.7

Only six industry groups have registered lower average CLOG during post 1991 years. Leaving out wood products, the rest of these six industry groups are more capital intensive. The more capital intensive sectors show lower average contribution of labour to value added growth during period of strong liberalisation. CKOG is found to be lower on an average for most of the more capital intensive industry groups during post 1991 years. However the more labour intensive industry groups experienced higher contribution of capital to output growth in the post reform era. If TFFG is taken as a rough indicator of efficiency promotion then West Bengal has had a mixed experience in the industrial sector. Declining TFPG during post reform years is observed in as many as 9 industry groups. Though it is difficult to pinpoint the exact cause of deceleration in TFP for such heterogeneous groups, we can assume with due reservations that the industries which registered positive TFPG during pre-1991 years but experienced falling TFP during post 1991 years are the ones hurt due to strong liberalisation. By this definition, food products, rubber, plastic and petroleum products and transport equipment industries are the ones hurt due to the strong liberalisation of 1991.

Performance wise, the power sector has surpassed all other industry groups in terms of growth rate of value added and TFPG. Falling CLOG is observed in this industry group on account of the long term strategy of the government to down size staff strength of the State Electricity Board in both production and distribution. Remarkably, CKOG is lower during the second phase of strong liberalisation so that value added growth is due to pure TFPG. Recent efforts of the state government to revitalize the power sector by promoting automation, computerization etc, apart from raising efficiency standards in production and distribution seems to have worked. Introducing rational pricing of power together with its gradual implementation also might have contributed positively.

Average annual growth rates of capital stock, labour force and share of wages in value added are presented in Table 4. An important observation is that with occasional fluctuations the capital stock is seen to grow positively. But declining labour force is seen in all industry groups during pre-1991 years and liberalisation cannot be blamed. In many cases there has been a turn around in growth of labour force after the onset of reforms. That is after exhibiting a falling trend during pre-liberalisation years labour force is seen rising during post 1991 period in as many as 11 industry groups. The point is that, strong liberalisation can in no way be held responsible for declining work force in registered manufacturing in West Bengal. This is just because declining work force is more common during pre-liberalisation years. Having said that, the second phase of strong liberalisation has not entirely been employment friendly. Eight industry groups show falling labour force during 1996-99 following a positive phase of growth during 1991-95. However post 1991 observations are too few, and based on that, it would be unwise to draw any conclusion regarding the impact of reforms on employment in organised manufacturing in the state.

Importance of labour as a factor of production can be somewhat captured from the share of total wages (to workers) in value added. As the figures in Table-4 show, falling wage share is common across the manufacturing sector in West Bengal both during pre-1991 and post-1991 years. Amongst the more labour intensive industry groups food processing seems to be relying the least on labour. Steadily growing capital stock and declining labour force is suggestive of this. During regime-4 falling wage share is witnessed in as many as 9 industry groups. But this falling wage share is not the consequence of strong liberalisation as wage share is seen falling even during regimes 1 and 2. Declining employment and wage share is perhaps the end result of the policy of manufacturers (government included) to shed off excess staff in production, maintenance and managerial cum supervisory posts. This actually is a direct consequence of automation. Note that the larger problem is that of falling employment and wage shares, observed even during 1981-90, and strong liberalisation can hardly be held responsible for the falling trend in these variables in the registered manufacturing units of West Bengal. Reforms might have aggravated this pre-existing trend although the contrary is observed in a few industries. Ironically, prolonged Leftist rule along with active and rigid trade union practices have failed to protect workers' interests.

Table 4. Regime Wise Average Annual Growth Rates of Labour, Ccapital and Wage Share in Percentage

Industry Group code	*Variables*	*Regime 1 (1981-85)*	*Regime 2 (1986-90)*	*Regime 3 (1991-95)*	*Regime 4 (1996-99)*
	K	9.6	14.6	8.6	5.1
20-21	L	-2.8	-1.9	-1.3	42.9
	W/Y	-9.1	-0.8	3.7	-6.3
	K	10.7	-0.9	13.1	14.8
22	L	-6.3	-4.4	36.6	60.0
	W/Y	20.2	3.9	1.3	5.5
	K	13.1	5.0	5.3	6.8
23	L	-5.2	-6.9	-2.1	-0.7
	W/Y	1.1	-0.6	7.8	-46.5
	K	13.3	23.2	8.5	41.4
24	L	1.9	4.8	-15.1	32.6
	W/Y	0.7	-2.4	9.0	2.5
	K	14.9	12.9	5.2	10.8
25	L	-1.2	-1.0	8.6	-8.9
	W/Y	4.4	-4.2	3.2	-11.6
	K	0.2	27.0	17.5	12.9
26	L	-2.4	-4.9	12.6	-15.3
	W/Y	97.4	-4.0	34.2	-17.7
	K	8.1	14.7	14.0	6.3
27	L	-2.7	2.0	-1.8	10.7
	W/Y	7.3	-12.4	45.7	60.6
	K	8.3	7.4	11.4	10.9
28	L	-6.9	-2.9	6.2	-8.7
	W/Y	-0.9	-3.1	5.1	-10.2
	K	5.6	8.1	12.0	7.1
29	L	-4.0	-3.2	-2.1	18.8
	W/Y	-2.9	75.2	6.0	-27.4
	K	9.2	17.8	6.8	7.7
30	L	-7.0	8.7	2.9	-7.6
	W/Y	6.1	72.7	-2.8	-2.6
	K	3.8	3.5	8.0	4.7
31	L	-3.1	-2.5	-1.2	1.5
	W/Y	-3.5	-7.1	3.3	3.3

	K	10.4	8.9	15.2	18.0
32	L	-4.2	-1.6	2.9	-11.4
	W/Y	2.3	-0.5	-8.0	10.8
	K	20.4	5.9	19.1	2.5
33	L	2.5	-2.7	-0.8	1.3
	W/Y	4.5	25.2	-4.8	36.4
	K	10.0	9.8	9.5	6.0
35-36	L	-4.7	-0.8	-2.3	-15.3
	W/Y	6.4	-5.7	-8.4	2.1
	K	10.4	5.4	4.8	8.0
37	L	-7.4	-2.6	7.0	-6.9
	W/Y	2.3	-7.5	11.1	-2.8
	K	16.1	10.5	11.2	7.3
40	L	7.6	-3.4	3.5	-2.4
	W/Y	-1.0	-13.6	12.1	-44.2

Table 5. Average Annual Growth Rates of Capital Labour Ratio

Industry Group Code	*Regime 1 (1981-85)*	*Regime 2 (1986-90)*	*Regime 3 (1991-95)*	*Regime 4 (1996-00)*
20-21	12.4	16.5	9.8	-37.8
22	17.0	3.5	-23.4	-45.2
23	18.3	11.9	7.4	7.5
24	11.4	18.4	23.7	8.8
25	16.1	14.0	-3.4	19.7
26	2.6	31.8	4.9	28.2
27	10.8	12.7	15.8	-4.4
28	15.2	10.3	5.2	19.7
29	9.6	11.3	14.2	-11.7
30	16.2	9.1	3.9	15.3
31	6.9	6.0	9.2	3.2
32	14.6	10.5	12.3	29.4
33	17.9	8.6	19.9	1.2
35-36	14.7	10.6	11.8	21.3
37	17.8	8.0	-2.1	14.9
40	8.5	13.9	7.7	9.8

Growth rates of capital labour ratio i.e., *CAPIN* are presented in Table 5. *CAPIN* has been rising in most industries. Moreover none of the high capital intensive industries exhibit falling capital labour ratio. But in 14 out of 16 industry groups post 1991 growth rates of capital labour ratio are lower than in previous years. Strong liberalisaton did not raise the pace of capital stock growth relative to labour force growth. If capital intensity growth is taken as a first hand indicator of automation then strong liberalisation did not raise the pace of automation in the manufacturing sector. In the absence of detailed information of firm level experiences, this is difficult to explain.

Table 6
Average Annual Growth Rates of Average Product of Capital

Industry Group	*Regime 1 (1981-85)*	*Regime 2 (1986-90)*	*Regime 3 (1991-95)*	*Regime 4 (1996-00)*
20-21	11.8	-1.3	-6.3	17.9
22	-10.5	-7.1	14.4	19.4
23	-14.1	-5.0	-6.2	7.5
24	-6.8	-11.7	-29.9	3.1
25	-20.5	-15.3	-1.8	-14.3
26	-1.4	-23.6	8.5	-13.3
27	-13.6	5.0	-1.6	31.2
28	-16.5	0.1	-4.8	2.6
29	-3.1	-4.6	15.1	33.3
30	4.9	48.3	-0.2	-8.4
31	1.6	7.4	1.2	6.0
32	-28.5	-54.9	-11.8	11.7
33	-15.2	-4.6	-9.3	-6.1
35-36	-10.0	-2.5	0.2	-5.4
37	-11.7	4.1	-4.9	-1.8
40	-14.1	-6.2	3.7	53.4

Table 7. Sources of Labour Productivity Growth (average Growth rates in percentage)

Industry Group code	*Variables*	*Regime 1 (1981-85)*	*Regime 2 (1986-90)*	*Regime 3 (1991-95)*	*Regime 4 (1996-99)*
	Y/L GROWTH	24.3	15.2	3.5	-19.9
20-21	Contribution of K/L	8.4	13.4	7.5	-21.4
	TFPG	15.9	1.8	-4.0	1.4
	Y/L GROWTH	6.5	-3.6	-9.0	-25.8
22	Contribution of K/L	13.1	1.9	1.7	13.2
	TFPG	-6.5	-5.5	-10.7	-39.0
	Y/L GROWTH	4.2	6.9	1.1	15.0
23	Contribution of K/L	5.3	3.7	2.8	11.1
	TFPG	-1.1	3.2	-1.7	4.0
	Y/L GROWTH	4.6	6.7	-6.2	11.9
24	Contribution of K/L	11.0	14.8	23.2	16.6
	TFPG	-6.3	-8.1	-29.4	-4.7
	Y/L GROWTH	-4.4	-1.4	-5.2	5.4
25	Contribution of K/L	1.7	3.6	0.6	8.7
	TFPG	-6.1	-4.9	-5.8	-3.3
	Y/L GROWTH	1.2	8.3	13.4	14.9
26	Contribution of K/L	11.3	18.6	6.3	25.0
	TFPG	-10.0	-10.3	7.1	-10.2
	Y/L GROWTH	-2.7	17.6	14.2	26.8
27	Contribution of K/L	6.3	13.5	5.2	-2.4
	TFPG	-9.1	4.1	8.9	29.3
	Y/L GROWTH	-1.3	10.4	0.4	22.3
28	Contribution of K/L	11.4	7.2	3.1	16.4
	TFPG	-12.7	3.2	-2.8	5.9
	Y/L GROWTH	6.5	6.8	29.2	21.6
29	Contribution of K/L	6.6	8.5	10.8	26.2
	TFPG	-0.1	-1.7	18.4	-4.6
	Y/L GROWTH	21.1	57.3	3.7	6.9
30	Contribution of K/L	15.8	9.7	3.9	14.7
	TFPG	5.3	47.7	-0.2	-7.8
	Y/L GROWTH	8.5	13.4	10.5	9.2
31	Contribution of K/L	5.6	4.7	12.6	2.6
	TFPG	2.9	8.6	-2.1	6.6

	Y/L GROWTH	-13.9	-44.3	0.4	41.1
32	Contribution of K/L	10.4	6.7	5.6	25.5
	TFPG	-24.2	-51.0	-5.2	15.6
	Y/L GROWTH	2.7	4.0	10.6	-5.0
33	Contribution of K/L	12.1	2.9	12.1	1.7
	TFPG	-9.5	1.1	-1.6	-6.7
	Y/L GROWTH	4.7	8.1	12.0	15.8
35-36	Contribution of K/L	11.3	8.9	9.4	20.5
	TFPG	-6.6	-0.8	2.6	-4.6
	Y/L GROWTH	6.1	12.1	-7.1	13.1
37	Contribution of K/L	10.0	5.0	1.5	9.2
	TFPG	-4.0	7.1	-8.6	3.9
	Y/L GROWTH	-5.6	7.7	11.4	63.2
40	Contribution of K/L	5.6	10.5	7.8	9.1
	TFPG	-11.2	-2.8	3.6	54.1

Refer to Table 6. During pre-reform years average product of capital is found declining on most occasions on account of lower output growth relative to capital stock growth. Falling output capital ratio is synonymous with rising capital output ratio. Note that 13 industry groups exhibit falling average product of capital in regime-1. This figure was just 6 in regime-4. Ahluwalia (1985) *op cit* took rising capital output ratio as an indicator of declining efficiency of factor use. Interpreted in that way our results indicate that strong liberalisation has raised efficiency of factor use since most industry groups (10 to be exact) registered rising capital productivity during 1996-99. Growth of labour productivity and its decomposition is presented in Table 7.

In as many as 11 industry groups growth rates of labour productivity is higher during post liberalisation years. Almost all high capital intensive groups show rising labour productivity with the exception of basic metal and alloys. Low capital intensive industry groups as food processing and beverages, tobacco and related products mostly show falling labour productivity. In as many as 11 industry groups contribution of capital intensity to growth of labour productivity is higher during post 1991 years. Our general observation is that reforms have raised the contribution of capital intensity to labour productivity growth. For the wood products industries negative contribution of capital intensity is associated with rising labour productivity during regime-4 implying that output growth is purely due to in high growth of TFP.

Table 8. Average TE across Regimes in Percentage

Industry Group	*Regime 1 (1981-85)*	*Regime 2 (1986-90)*	*Regime 3 (1991-95)*	*Regime 4 (1996-00)*
20-21	34.5	35.4	27.2	14.1
22	57.5	77.3	34.0	28.6
23	26.4	24.5	18.1	28.8
24	68.8	60.2	43.8	50.9
25	33.4	30.0	20.0	24.7
26	64.6	52.7	46.5	37.8
27	27.9	29.5	14.3	13.8
28	41.4	40.1	29.3	33.4
29	58.0	41.0	41.0	76.6
30	83.0	80.9	96.6	91.9
31	53.6	73.1	85.5	64.7
32	46.4	37.4	34.4	31.0
33	44.8	26.6	33.9	29.3
35-36	83.9	85.7	72.2	76.5
37	62.0	60.4	35.7	36.1
40	49.2	54.2	53.8	84.1
State Average	52.2	50.5	45.0	42.9

Regime wise average technical efficiency (TE) figures (using COLS) for each industry group are presented in Table 8. Average TE during post 1991 years are clearly lower for 12 industry groups compared to the same during pre 1991 years. Efficiency standards of both high and low capital-intensive industries have fallen in the era of strong liberalisation. Growing capital stock and capital intensity may have contributed positively to labour productivity in many occasions but that did not enhance the efficiency of factor use during post 1991 years. Hence, technical efficiency levels did not rise as per expectation in major industry groups of

West Bengal during the period of strong liberalisation. Remarkable improvement in TE is observed in case of leather, rubber, plastic, petroleum and coal products, chemicals and power industries during post reform era. Throughout all regimes rubber, plastic, petroleum and coal products industries are found to be technically most efficient. Not only do most industry groups show poor TE levels, but also most of them are too inefficient compared to a selective few and inter-industry variations in efficiency are substantial. 12 out of the 16 industry groups show lower average TE levels during post reform years and it would not be inappropriate to infer that the first and second waves of globalization have been disappointing from the view point of efficiency promotion for the manufacturing sector in West Bengal. Neogi (1998) *et al* arrived at similar conclusions for selected Indian industries. Finally efficiency of factor use and TFPG are not related. High TFPG may or may not be associated with high technical efficiency. Average TFPG at the state level is higher during post liberalisation years although average TE at the state level is seen falling across regimes.

Table 9

Regression Estimates of Rate of Technical Progress and its Bias for the Entire Manufacturing Sector in West Bengal (computed values of t-statistic are presented in parenthesis)

Regimes	*Coefficient*⁺ *of*						
	Time	*Time*	*time* × *lnK*	*time* × *lnL*	R^2	*F*	*D.W. Statistic*
Regime 1 1981- 85	-0.029 (-0.835)	-0.013 (-0.483)	0.006 (0.200)	0.0015 (0.033)	0.90	82.1	1.98
Regime 2 1986-90	-0.665 (-1.669)	0.026 (0.809)	0.023 (0.607)	0.024 (0.455)	0.88	49.5	2.07
Regime 3 1991-95	-0.413 (-1.436)	0.004 (0.159)	0.017 (0.629)	0.019 (0.517)	0.91	31.2	1.97
Regime 4 1996-99	0.002 (0.986)	-0.136 (-0.234)	0.106 (0.575)	-0.074 (-0.290)	0.86	27.0	1.74

** Significant at 1% level.

* Significant at 5% level.

Estimates of those coefficients of the time variant trans-log production function (using value added, labour and capital), which are necessary for estimating the rate of technical progress and its bias in technical progress are presented in Table 9. The coefficients of the aggregative (state level) production function were directly estimated from pooled observations separately for each regime, a cross-section consisting of sixteen industry groups. The coefficient of time gives the rate of autonomous technical progress and that of time squared gives the rate of change of technical progress. The coefficient of time multiplied by logarithm of labour measures the bias in technical progress with respect to labour. Similarly, coefficient of time multiplied by logarithm of capital measures the bias in technical progress with respect to capital. As seen in Table 9, all the coefficients relevant for estimating bias in technical progress are statistically insignificant across all regimes. Only during regime 4 there is a hint of a bias in technical progress in favour of labour but as the estimates are statistically insignificant we simply consider technical progress to be neutral.

IV. Summary and Conclusions

This paper studies the performance of 16 major industry groups in West Bengal (see Appendix 1) aggregated at the 2-digit level (NIC-1970) of classification for the period 1981-99 on the basis of industry level (2-digit) ASI data. Growth patterns of performance indicators as value added and inputs, capital intensity, partial and total factor productivities are seen along with their decompositions across different phases of liberalisation during 1981-82 to 1999-00 for each of these 16 industry groups. The periods 1981-82 to 1985-86 (Regime-1) and 1986-87 to 1990-91 (Regime-2) are considered as two phases of weak liberalisation and respectively. The periods 1991-92 to 1995-96 and 1996-97 to 1999-00 (Regime-3 and Regime-4), are taken as two phases of strong liberalisation.

'Value added' is taken as a suitable substitute for 'output'. Labour and fixed capital are the only inputs considered. The growth of total factor productivity (TFPG) is computed by both Tornqvist and Solow Divisia index of growth accounting. Growth of labour productivity is decomposed into contribution of capital intensity and TFPG for each industry group across all regimes. Regime wise, pooled estimates of a trans-log production function are used to find the rate of technical progress and its bias with respect to inputs.

Finally, cross-sectional technical efficiency levels of each industry group at the macro-economic level of production are computed by estimating a deterministic frontier production function (Corrected Ordinary Least Squares or COLS). The entire manufacturing sector is considered for this purpose where a cross-section comprises of the 16 major industry groups.

Broadly, the growth pattern of value added indicates that the more labour intensive sectors have picked up while the relatively more capital-intensive sectors have suffered in the era of economic reforms and macroeconomic slowdown. The more labour intensive industry groups experienced higher contribution of capital to output growth in the post reform era. If TFPG is taken as an indicator of efficiency then West Bengal has had a mixed experience in the industrial sector. Declining TFPG during post reform years is observed in as many as 9 industry groups. Apparently, food products, rubber, plastic and petroleum products and transport equipment industries are the ones hurt due to the strong liberalisation of 1991. Performance wise, the power sector has outclassed all other industry groups in terms of growth rate of value added and TFPG.

Declining employment in the manufacturing sector in West Bengal is clearly seen during pre-reform years. It could be the outcome of long-term strategy of employers to shed of excess staff strength. The post- reforms labour growth figures are marginally higher for most industries. Thus strong liberalisation cannot be held responsible for falling employment in the organized manufacturing sector in West Bengal. Probably, trade union pressures along with delay in labour reforms are responsible for the check in the rate of decline of employment during the post-1991 period. Apparently they have failed to resist automation and worker displacement during the study-period as observed from the steep capital intensity growth figures. Labour market reforms have the potential of reviving the industries along with generating employment, as it offers greater freedom to employers. Skepticism in this regard is entirely justified as because initially labour market reforms may adversely affect employment. In spite of several initiatives, West Bengal was not been able to attract much FDI in manufacturing (except in petro-chemical industries) till late 1990s. Only few large-scale units (capable of promoting bulk employment) have been established during post-reforms possibly due to the grim investment climate in the state. As such the falling tendency in employment could not be resisted. Capital intensity shows tremendous growth in all periods but has declined during post-reforms on account of marginal rise in employment growth. On the whole, reforms have raised the contribution of capital intensity to labour productivity growth.

It must be mentioned here that it is beyond the scope of the state government to decelerate the pace of automation. Nevertheless, it can combat the falling tendency of employment by raising the pace of industrialisation in the state, as there is still a lot of scope for expansion of manufacturing sector's share in state GDP as the state is far from being industrially saturated. Greater private investment (both foreign and domestic entrepreneurs) in expansion of basic infrastructure is another alternative to re-employ the displaced workers. A financial safety net for displaced workers, no matter how impermanent, is yet another option but hardly a pragmatic one from the view-point of the existing conditions of the state exchequer. It is here that the Centre can come to the rescue. In our opinion, a comprehensive national policy (at least for organised manufacturing) in this direction could well provide a humane touch to the greater issue of worker displacement due to automation (among many others), which in turn is a direct consequence of unrestrained entrepreneurial freedom.

Wage share (in value added) is on the decline for all industries indicating a drop in relative importance of workers in the production process. Reforms cannot be blamed since the rate of decline is higher during pre-1991. Evidently trade union practices have failed to protect and promote workers' welfare since our findings illustrate that rising labour productivity is accompanied by falling employment and wage share.

Seemingly, reforms have not been conducive to efficiency of factor use. Technical efficiency is found declining across regimes on many occasions. For most industry groups technical efficiency is lower on an average during post 1991 years. Firm level evidence may explain this better. Inter industry variations in efficiency are substantial. Technical progress is found to be Hicks neutral.

Summing up, economic reforms have had a depressing effect on the relatively more capital-intensive industry groups in West Bengal. Performance of relatively more labour-intensive industry groups have improved in terms of value added, partial and total factor productivity growth during post 1991 era. Considering all evidences, economic reforms cannot be held responsible for falling employment and wage share in the state manufacturing. However strong liberalisation may have been detrimental to efficiency of factor use.

References

Adhikary, M.L., and R. Mazumder (2004), "Manufacturing Sector Productivity In India Across Phases of Liberalisation During 1981-97: A Study of Selected States", *Arthaniti,* Vol 3, Nos. (1-2), pp. 49-65.

Adhikary, M.L., and R. Mazumder (2005), "Economic Reforms and Manufacturing Sector Productivity in West Bengal: An Industry Level Study", *Indian Journal of Regional Science,* Vol. XXXVII, No. 1, pp. 82-91.

Ahluwalia, I.J. (1985), *Industrial Growth in India: Stagnation since Mid-Sixties,* Oxford University Press, New Delhi.

Ahluwalia, I.J. (1991), *Productivity Growth in Indian Manufacturing,* Oxford University Press, New Delhi.

Coondoo, D., C. Neogi and B. Ghosh (1993), "Technology Intensive Industrialisation in LDCs: Experience of Indian Industries", *Economic and Political Weekly,* 28, M43-M52.

Diewert, W.E., (1976), "Exact and Superlative Index Numbers", *Journal of Econometrics,* pp. 115–45.

Dutt, R. (1993), "New Economic Policy and its Impact on Industrial Relations and Employment in India", *Indian Journal of Labour Economics,* vol. 36, No. 1, Jan.–Mar., pp. 66-76.

Ghosh, B. and C. Neogi (1993), "Productivity Efficiency and New Technology: The Case of Indian Manufacturing Industries", *The Developing Economies,* Vol. 31, (3), Sept., pp. 308-28.

Goldar, B. and V. Seth (1989), "Spatial Variations in the Rate of Industrial Growth in India", *Economic and Political Weekly,* June 3, pp. 1237-1240.

Goldsmith, R.W. (1951), "A Perpetual Inventory of National Wealth", *Studies on Income and Wealth*, NBER, vol. 14, pp. 169-72.

Gorman, W.M. (1970), *Notes on Divisia Indices*, (Unpublished) University of North Carolina, Chapel Hill, North Carolina.

Hillinger C. (1970), "Comment on Invariance Axiom and Economic Indexes", *Econometrica*, 38, pp. 773-74.

Hulten, C.R. (1973), "Divisia Index Numbers", *Econometrica*, Vol. 41, No. 3, pp. 213–36.

Hulten, C.R. and R.M. Schwab (1984), "Regional Productivity Growth In US Manufacturing: 1951-78", *The American Economic Review*, Vol.74, No. 1, pp. 153-62.

Jorgenson, D.W. and Z. Griliches (1967), "The Explanation of Productivity Change", *Review of Economic Studies*, 34, pp. 349-82.

Kumbhakar, S.C. and C.A.K. Lovell (2000), *Stochastic Frontier Analysis*, Cambridge University Press, New York.

Mullan, J.K. and M. Williams (1994), "Convergence, Scale and the Relative Productivity Performance of Canadian-US Manufacturing Industries", *Applied Economics*, Vol. 26, pp. 739-50.

Neogi, C. and B. Ghosh (1994), "Intertemporal Efficiency Variations in Indian Manufacturing Industries", *Journal of Productivity Analysis*, October 5.

Neogi, C. and B. Ghosh, (1998), "Impact of Liberalisation on Performance of Indian Industries: A Firm Level Study", *Economic and Political Weekly*, February 28, pp. M16-M24.

Nishimizu, M. and J.M. Page (1982), "Total Factor Productivity Growth, Technological Progress And Technical Efficiency Change: Dimensions of Productivity Change in Yugoslavia, 1965-78", *The Economic Journal*, vol. 92, pp. 921-36.

Poirier, J.D. (1974), *The Econometrics of Structural Change*, North-Holland, Amsterdam, Chapter 2.

Pradhan, G. and K. Barik, (1998), "Fluctuating Total Factor Productivity in India: Evidence from Selected Polluting Industries", *Economic and Political Weekly*, February 28, pp. M25-M30.

R.B.I. *Report on Currency and Finance*, Govt. of India (various issues).

Roychaudhury, U.D. (1977), "Industrial Breakdown of Capital Stock in India", *The Journal of Income and Wealth*, vol. 2, April, pp. 504-35.

Winsten, C.B. (1957), "Discussion on Mr. Farrell's Paper", *Journal of the Royal Statistical Society*, Series A, General, 120, Part 3, 282-84.

Appendix 1
National Industrial Classification-1970

NIC Code	*Description of Industry Group*
20-21	Manufacture of food products
22	Manufacture of beverages, tobacco and related products
23	Manufacture of cotton textiles
24	Manufacture of wool, silk and man made fibre textiles
25	Manufacture of jute and other vegeTable fibre textiles
26	Manufacture of textile products (including wearing apparel)
27	Manufacture of wood and wood products; furniture and fixtures
28	Manufacture of paper and paper products; printing and publishing
29	Manufacture of leather and leather products, fur and leather substitutes
30	Manufacture of rubber, plastic petroleum and coal products
31	Manufacture of basic chemical and chemical products
32	Manufacture of non-metallic mineral products
33	Basic metal and alloy industries
35-36	Manufacture of machinery and equipment—electrical and non-electrical
37	Manufacture of transport equipment and parts
40	Electricity–generation, transmission and distribution

[1] Two digit Industry codes are presented in Appendix 1.

8

IRRESPONSIBLE STATE, PREDATORY CAPITAL AND VULNERABLE LABOUR: EVIDENCES FROM INDIA

G.B. Nath

I. Introduction

After India enter in to a globalised world economic order the status of labour has under gone radical change. State was playing crucial role in shaping the labour market institution from the beginning of the capitalist economy. But as capitalism enter into the phase of globalization the character of the state has under gone radical change. Correspondingly the capital labour relationship has also changed. In the wake of WB, IMF, WTO dictated globalization and liberalization drive enormous changes are taking place in Indian economy. Basically this is a out word oriented, market driven, export led growth strategy. This strategy has not taken human development as an integral part of the development policy; on the contrary it has forced the state to retreat from its historical role. As a result of which this development strategy has reduced the social and human development expenses and eroded the food security by reducing subsidies and increasing administrative prices. Flexibilisation of the labour market has worsened the situation. Employment of atypical, nonstandard, part-time, home working and casual has increased. State has become a soft state towards implementing the social security measures enshrined in the Indian constitution. Capitalism has retreated from the welfare capitalism to predatory capitalism and correspondingly state has changed from a welfare state to an irresponsible, oppressive, and police state. This is sometimes described as 'hollowing out of the state', 'de-centred state', 'retreat of state' 'spanning out of the state' etc.

The objective of this paper is three fold: (1) to highlight on the changing nature of state corresponding to the changes in capitalism as an economic system; (2) to understand the relation between state and labour in India in a globalize scenario and (3) the consequences of the globalization on the working class due to the on going changes. In the sections that follow I explore in: (1) the political economy of capitalism and globalization; (2) the relationship between globalization, state and labour; (3) the consequences of globalization on the labour market in India; (4) the resistance movement against globalization.

II. The Political Economy of Capitalism and Globalisation

Capitalism as an economic system is constantly changing and adapting to new system. Hence capitalism, which started in Europe in 15th and 16th century, is not the same as it is today. As a system, capitalism is capable of creating destroying and recreating it-self because whenever there are symptoms of malfunctioning within the system some of the well-known defender of capitalism have staunchly advocated reform of the system. Capitalism has survived despite two World Wars, Great Depression of 1930s', emergence of Soviet Union and later on its demise in 1989, Oil crisis, War in gulf countries, and serious recessions in 1967,69,74,81, and so on. The solution sought for such a recession ridden economy was to apply Keynes prescription of massive state intervention along with lowering of Central Banks' lending rates and budget deficits. The classical idea of non-interference of state in the economic activities or complete *laissez–faire* of Smithian type was abandoned and in its place State intervention was sought.

As Karl Marx has said, capitalism is always global in nature. What today we call globalization is nothing but international expansion of capitalistic relation of production along with capitalist ethics, morals and values. In essence it refers to widening and deepening of the international flow of trade, capital, technology and information within a single integrated global market. Stiglitz (2002) defines globalization as 'Fundamentally, it is the closer integration of the countries and peoples of the world which has been brought about by the enormous reduction of costs of transportation and communication and the breaking down of artificial barriers to the flows of goods, services, capital, knowledge, and (to a lesser extent) people across borders'.

Another feature of globalization is the internationalization of production, characterized by the growth of huge global multinational corporations (MNCs) and transnational banks. After the collapse of the soviet system now we are in a unipolar world and which is under the hegemony of the US imperialism. In a sense there is Americanization of the world economy. Thus in 1998 out of the top 500 firms 244 alone belong to U.S.A. where as only 46 belong to Japan and 173 to European countries, (Petras and Veltmeyer 2001). These MNCs with direct help from their government, World Bank, IMF and WTO serve to accelerate the capital export in order to establish productions units all over the world.

In a globalised economic scenario capital is in search of cheap labour and raw material. This has given rise to new international division of labour. Hence MNCs increasingly relocating their industries of a part of their operation into areas of abundance of cheap labour and cheap raw materials. The recent revolution in IT and communication system has speed up this processes. All this have given rise to a new global production system where MNCs shifting their work from South Korea, Taiwan, Hog Kong, Singapore to Malaysia, Philippines, Vietnam, China, India etc. Therefore the MNCs are clamoring for a world without borders for free flow of goods, services and capital between various countries.

Globalization has also lead to the emergence of internationalization of finance capital. The 20th century marks the turning point from the old capitalism to the new form of domination of capital in general to the domination of finance capital. For Lenin this is the stage of imperialism the highest stage of capitalism. However Patnaik (2002) has differentiated the Lenin's concept of finance capital from globalization of capital as finance' in three counts: (i) Lenin's finance capital represents banking and industrial capital, while contemporary finance capital is an autonomous entity with little interest in production as such and concerned primarily with quick speculative gains though rapid global movements. (ii) Lenin's finance capital is nation based while inter imperialist rivalries are far more muted in contemporary finance capital. What we have observe today is a unprecedented degree of internationalization of finance capital. In this era of globalization investment is taking place in speculation with a aim of making immediate financial gain. International banking institutions are helping the speculators in their game plan. Thus the dominance of the flow of speculative capital-flows not backed by any flow of goods and services and not used for productive purposes is one of the defining characteristics of globalization. The international financial network is like a chain of gambling casinos where trillions of dollars changed hands. Even powerful nations states have become helpless spectators to this global gambling played by the major international banks and financial manipulators. There is no international mechanism to regulate the financial flows across the national borders. The currency speculators, the share brokers, international bond holders the real estate manipulators and other financial swindlers have the power to lead even a mighty nation state to the verge of ruin and bankruptcy.

III. Pre-Economic Reform Policy Regime, State and Labour

Soon after the transfer of power at political level in 1947, in order to decolonize the Indian economy there was consensus to assign greater role to the state. Besides, on 26th January 1950 the Indian constitution was adopted and in its directive principles of state policy it was stated that the state shall strive to promote the welfare of the people by securing and protecting as effectively as it may a social order in which justice, social, economic and political would be ensured. Going a step further the Indian National Congress (the then ruling party of India) in its Avadi session in 1954 accepted a resolution that objective of national policy would be the building of a socialist pattern of society. Hence all these ideas have reflected in the Industrial policy resolution of 1948 and 1956. in the 1948 industrial policy resolution certain strategic and defence industries like atomic energy, railway, defence goods industries were kept exclusively for the state. New undertakings in basic and key industries like coal, iron and steel, aircraft, ship building. Telecommunication were henceforth be undertaken by the state. However there was no watertight classification and the division between public and private sector was made flexible. The public sector was kept at the commanding height of the economy. Hence what the private sector was unable or unwilling to undertake and what was unprofitable for private enterprise to undertake, especially in lumpy industries state started taking responsibilities. With an attempt to build a solid public sector state resorted to nationalization of major sectors like banking, insurance, coal, copper, air transport etc. The Imperial bank was nationalized in 1955. 14 major commercial banks were nationalized in 1969, life insurance was nationalized in 1972, coal fields were nationalized in 1973.

Capitalism had made an alliance with feudalism during British rule and there was prevalent of feudal land relation. State wanted to relies the productive forces arrested under colonial influence stagnating agriculture. In response to this various land reform majors, which included the abolition of intermediary right in land, security of tenures, fixation of ceiling on land and their distribution were initiated. In order to convert the weather bound traditional agriculture state take of various measure to step up agriculture production and productivity. These include investment in irrigation, pesticide, HYV seeds, fertilizers etc. Peasants were brought to the orbit of market and subsistence farming gave way to commercial farming. Credit is a critical input in agriculture and in order to provide institution credits at a cheaper rate to the peasantry, banks were nationalized, interest rates were cut down and peasants were provided with credit with a priority basis.

The organized labour in India, though there number is only within 10 percent have achieved a lot of social security measures through their protracted struggle. They are Minimum Wage Act, 1948, Equal Remuneration Act, 1970, Child Labour Provision and Regulation Act, 1986, Industrial

Dispute Act, 1947, Employees provident Fund Act, 1952, Employees State Insurance Act, 1948, Trade Union Act 1926, Environment Protection Act, 1986, a few to mention. These statutes regulations terms of employment, conditions of employment social security and status of working class have gone in long way in maintaining employer employee relation in India. These measures have been in conformity with the constitutional provision and statures and the state has ensured their enforceability by establishing various institution. Hence the role of the state has become a referee between the employees and employer. Without such a positive state intervention the working class would not have been enjoyed the benefits given to them by statutes and regulations. Hence the state was a 'welfare state' in the sense that it is the duty of the state to intervene in the economy in favor of the poor.

However it is important to note that the growth of public sector or nationalization of the key sector of the economy was not to established socialism or communism therefore the private sector was not afraid in the growth of public sector. It was in no way a thereat to there interest. Rather it was complementary to private sector (Martinussen, 2002; Myrdal, 1968). Even the Indian monopoly capitalist like Tata and Birla had brought out a plan of economic development for India (1944) known as the Bombay Plan (1944) otherwise call Tata Birla Plan. This plan also advocated for greater role to state for infrastructural development. Absolutely there was no socialistic objective in the state intervention rather what the state was building was state capitalism. In the scheme of state capitalism there were rooms for close collaboration between Indian monopoly capital and British finance capital; it is also important to note that the post colonial state in its first industrial policy resolution of 1948 assured all foreign capital that not only would their interest be safeguarded, they would also be free to expand. Thus the Nehruvian model of planning and development was not only in the interest of the Indian monopolist capitalist and landlords but also at the same time in the interest of the foreign finance capital.

IV. Post Reform Policy Regime and Retreat of the State

In its attempt to built state capitalism the industrial sector in India, during the first fifteen years of planning registered a fairly rapid growth. But there after there was industrial deceleration (Rangarajan 1982, Desai 1981) and the deceleration is more in case of capital goods and basic industries sector. Ramana (1984) Shetty (1987) describe the decline in the growth rate of industrial sector as the structural retrogression in Indian economy while Chandra (1982) characterized it as stagnation. The slowing down of industrial growth accompanied by progresssive deceleration in the elasticity of employment in industrial sector. The explanation for deceleration of industrial growth and consequent reduction in the labour absorption capacity in Indian manufacturing sector includes a strong preference for maximum use of capital in place of labour as a result of excessive protective legislation and trade union activities (Visalia and Minhas 1991; Ahluwalia, 1991). Employer considered the indeed neo-classical economist envisaged flexible labour market as an instrument of efficiency and growth.

The euphoria of massive state intervention did not last long. Even the efficiency the public sector was questioned. It was alleged that the PSU's are inefficient; there is poor utilization of capacity, over capitalization, political and bureaucratic interference lake of autonomy etc. It was even alleged that the public enterprises are being use for private purpose (Choudhury, 1994) all these allegation provide a legitimacy for liberalization and privatization of PSU's in India. Again there was over all micro imbalances in the economy, particularly unmanageable balance of payment difficulties accompanied by deficit financing. It was in this context that the then ruling party in India approached the IMF for a loan. The loan was granted with the conditionality that India would initiate Structural Adjustment Programme. In order to fulfill the conditionality the roll assign to PSUs in 1948 and 1956 policy was withdrawn, the area reserved for public sector was thereafter open for private sector, the process of denationalization stated by privatizing the public sector undertaking. The license permit Raj was brought to an end and MRTP Act restriction was removed. State was exposed to openness in areas of trade, finance, fiscal policy etc. Automatic approvals were given for direct foreign investment up to 51% in a wide range of industry. Liberalization in trade policy was encouraged. Quantitative restrictions on all imports were withdrawn. The slogan of "export promotion and import substitution" was substituted for "export or perish".

In the post reform period the WTO, WB led growth strateg forced the Indian state to retreat from the agrarian restructuring initiated earlier. Even the policy of land reforms was abandoned on the plea that it is conflict with the 'laissez faire' market driven principles of the new economic policy. On the contrary the state resorted to reduction of subsidies on agricultural inputs, deregulating the grain market, liberalization of policies regarding International trade in agricultural commodities, scaling down of government procurement operations, reduction of role of Food Corporation of India (FCI) dismantling the public Distribution System (PDS), modifying tenancy laws etc. These policy changes pursued under the dictates of the Britton wood institutions have exposed the true character of the state. It is now argued that these measures would improve the terms of trade infavour of agriculture, Indian farmers would reap the benefits, the rigors of inflation can be softened and the income and employment opportunity can be widened etc.

V. Impact of State Retreat on the Working Class in India

Work Flexibilisation

Since 1990's World bank and its protagonists arguing that widespread government interference in the labour market and work place in the form of minimum wage legislation, social security measures and trade union rights have distorted the working of the labour market, leads to higher labour cost, lower accumulation, inhabit technological advancement, misallocate scarce resources and make the industry uncompetitive. This has, as a consequence adversely affected productivity, growth and efficiency in the economy. Hence it has been argued to dismantle the protective labour legislation and the legal sanction to hire and fire workers, fix their wages and work allocation should be with the management. This is what is called labour market flexibility or work flexibilisation is associated with wage and employment flexibility. Of course this is beneficial to the capitalist to accelerate the capital accumulation by cutting wage cost and becoming competitive in the world scale.

However, work flexibilisation has resulted in introduction of exit policy, Closure of industries, retrenchment, lay off, cut in the social security measures, withdrawal of trade union rights etc Bhattacharya (1994) investigates labour market flexibility vis-à-vis employee leasing in the post liberalization era on the basis of a survey of 200 employees and 50 trade unionist drawn from 10 industrial units located in and around Calcutta. The result of this study shows that to withstand price competition. Indian industries now required to workout possible avenues of cost minimization. Institutionalized approach to contact labour system i.e. employees leasing can enable Indian industries to save non wage labour cost, burden in addition wage cost for idle hours can also be saved substantially when employees are hired from leasing companies. It is apparent from the survey that employees reject concept of institutionalizing employees leasing due to the fear of losing job security and free time and leisure period in the work place. Trade unionists are in general averse to the proposition of institutionalizing employee leasing in Indian organization for it would take India back to the era of pre-historic days as workers would enjoy no better status than slaves. (Bhattacharyya, 1994)

In recent years Fordist method of mass production has given way to flexible specialization. This has given rise to non-standardized product, multipurpose machines, multitasking and multi-skilling of work force etc. Based on the experience of advance countries attempts have been made to introduce flexible specialization in India restricting device. However, experience from the developing countries show that flexible specialization, encourages segmentation of workforce between 'core' and 'periphery'. A low road strategy will create demand for unskilled and casual labour and they would prone to exploitation and a high road strategy will require skilled and semiskilled labour those who are better paid and protected. This has been highlighted by Knorringa (1996) for Agra's foot ware industry and garment making and clothing companies. Thus work flexiblisation has led to work informalisation, which the following sections deal with.

Work Informalisation

Less developed countries are characterized by labour market dualism where there is a co-existence of modern sector with traditional sector. Labour market dualism variously described as 'organized' and 'unorganized' sector, 'Formal and 'Informal' sector 'Rural' and 'Urban' sector ' Primary' and 'Secondary' sector etc. In recent years partly due to protective labour legislation (Visaria and Minhas, 1991) and partly due to structural retrogression in Indian economy (Shetty, 1987) there has been progressive deceleration in the elasticity for employment in the industrial sector. There is also deceleration in the elasticity of employment in the agricultural sector. In view of the low labour absorption in organized industrial sector and traditional agricultural sector it is now the non-farm non-manufacturing sector, which considered as a major absorber of labour force. Informal sector act as a 'sponge', which absorbs the abandoned workers for whom there is no place in the formal sector.

In a labour abundant country like India the liberalization and globalization policy of the state has encouraged more in formalization of work in the economy. Employment in formal sector on a permanent basis is no doubt, providing regularity, stability, security and social dignity. But employers are resorting to cost reduction in order to be competitive, ignoring the labour legislation and they are replacing the permanent employees with casual, contract worker, hired from the labour suppliers or contractors on lease basis. The textile mill closures in Ahmedabad cost over one lakh of jobs and resulted in the ir formalization of vast majority of sacked workers due to the liberalization policy in 1985 by the Government of India. the exploitation and exclusion of this sacked workers in the informal sector tells volume about the changing world of work in the globalised scenario (Breman 2002; Unni, 2002) has shown from a survey of informal activities in Ahmedabad city that a large proportion of regular employees are infact informally employ without enjoying the benefits due the formal workers. G Vijay (2003) has also observed that in Kothur industrial town, Andhra Pradesh various formal industrial units has informalised the labour market the restructuring process has affected the quality of employment wage, social security and emoluments etc. Khasnabis and Banerjee's (1996) study on the rationalized workers in Durgapur industrial area of the West Bengal; Chowdhury's (1996) study on the Ahmedabad Textile mill workers, Nath's (2001) study on the voluntarily retired steel workers in Rourkela Steel Plant, Orissa, show how the restructuring of the Indian economy has pushed the secure workers to the sea of economy as own account worker, petty producers, small capitalist producers, steel vender, floating or footloose labour. World Development Report (1995) has glorified this type of downward mobility of labour from formal to informal sector, from security of employment to insecurity, from permanent to temporary or part time job as 'independent producers' or 'self employed' persons. Following World Bank there is a sea change in the political thinking level to withdraw the social protection given to the formal sector worker even if their number is within 10% of the working class in India. Thus the policy changes in the economy were threatened majority of worker, mostly women who are most vulnerable social class.

Gender Based Segregation

Gender based discrimination in the work place is natural phenomena in the capitalist society. In the post globalised scenario women workers are pushed in to more vulnerability. For the policy changes displace women from their traditional job without creating any new opportunities and this may be treated as the continuation of female marginalization. After the policy of globalization various countries have pursued flexibility in their labour process, organizational structure and as a requirement of this has casualised the permanent workforce, subcontracted the product, relocated the industries to low wage cost areas. Hence the work has been pushed out of the factory into the sweatshops and homes. Food processing, textile, garment, catering, lace making, bidi and cigar rolling, packaging industry where the skill required is relatively low they employ considerable number of temporary, part-time home based peace rate female worker. Shah and Gandhi's (1998) study shows that the plastic processing industry which employ a substantial number of women worker are molding their temporary workers, both men and women to do each other's task which could allow them to take care of absenteeism without adding new employment and optimally use machines even during lunch hours. Thus along with flexibilisation of the work force there is attempt at multi-skill task. They have observed that workers are getting less than minimum wage in tiny small medium and large-scale plastic processing industries. Even more than 50% of women workers don't get any paid holidays. Often workers are left out of the minimum wage and other social security measures accruing to the permanent work by dubbing them as 'trainees', 'learners', 'contact labour', 'casual labour' etc. Vanamala's (2001) study on an engineering unit shows women workers were paid less than minimum wage in the name of 'trainees' even though they are put 8 to 16 hours of works. Industrialization process in Valsad region located in south Gujrat after liberalization has led to casualisation and feminization of the local work force. Employers were increasingly employing contract labour enlisted by officially approved contractors (Streekeru 2001).

The success story of Indian software professionals in western countries is tremendous. Nayyar (2003) opines that 'globalization has made them as mobile as capital, indeed we can think of them as globalised people who are employable almost everywhere in the world. The world is their oyster'. However this may be true for a few software professionals those who are getting high salary and social status. But large numbers of them are regarded as 'computer coolies'. Similarly of late large no of call centers are opening in India employing bright young software professionals considered as 'cyber coolies'. Umadevi (2002) has recounted the experience of Indian women on the HIB or H4 visa, which highlights the deepening contraction between the economy restructuring and emancipatory potential it offers women in the labour market. The long and irregular office hours of software professionals coupled with frequent travel forced their wives to adjustment in their career aspiration. Globalization and exodus from India of a large number of professionals has exposed a large number of women to strain in their conjugal relationship and the strain is more in the wives than their husband. (Umadevi 2002)

Trade, Technology and Labour Redundancy

Trade policy reform in India, which initiated during 1980s and deepened in the 1990s rapidly dismantled the Quantitative restriction on imports and exports, substantially reduced tax on them and resorted to adjust the exchange rate. Briefly speaking there has been shift from import substation to export promotion growth strategy. The inward looking protective trade and technology policy has given rise to an outward looking liberalized trade and technology policy. However this has raised the import intensity of country exports destroyed the market for the indigenous capital goods sector and import of technology from abroad has driven the country from self-sufficient import substation to assembly led industrialization. As a result there may be take of technology and skill accumulation in the economy affecting long-term growth and employment generation.

It is believed that MNCs would transfer the technology and upgrade the skill of Indian workers. But the MNCs want to exploit the low labour cost situation and other fiscal incentives and normative environmental laws. Hence they were emphasizing the introduction of microcomputers, robots, computer numerical machines, automation etc. these are adversely affect on the overall demand for labour. Hence there is 'downsizing, redundancy, early separation, lay off, retrenchment' etc.

De-unionization of the Working Class

In recent years through various formal and informal way workers are prevented from forming any trade union and when formed are prevented from functioning efficiently. The employers are using numerous devices like closure, lockouts, sub–contracting, and transfer of ownership etc. to intimidate workers. Both in magnitude and intensity the lockout were severe than the strikes. Illegal retrenchments of workers, VRS, transfer of ownership etc. are liberally utilized as employee's offensive on labour. In the globalization process the position of capital has strengthened where as position of labour has weakened. (Nayyar 2003) Today trade unions are the passive specters in the changing economic scenario. After globalization workers are on defensive and employees are on the offensive. Sometimes managements has gone to the extend of liquidating trade union leaders or threatening the workers and leaders of dire consequences if they would not fall in line with the prerogatives of management. Murder of Sanker Guha Niyogi and the consequent set back to the Chattisgarh Mukti Morcha struggle in Bhilai-Rajnandagaon-Raipur industrial belt of Madhya Pradesh is a case point (*EPW* Editorial, 1992; PUDR Report, 1991). Similarly the direct, brutal and necked attack by the Haryana police on the striking workers of Honda Motorcycles and Scooters India (HMSI) on 25th July, 2005 has shown the strain labour-management relation in the MNCs. The Workers Solidity Report (2005) says, "Honda management's intention to thwart the process of union formation is the crux of the event that have unfolded over the last two months. The suspension, dismissal, false cases, attacks on union leaders, and use police violence, all show to what depth managements, multinationals of otherwise, can stoop to break unions and undermine working class solidarities. In this, managements are completely assisted by the police, by different office of the administration, and local political leaders. This powerful nexus of state and capital has over the last decade tried its utmost to undermine workers interest to invite investment from companies—foreign and national". P. Sainath (2005) has reported that Gurgaon was about police and administration increasingly actively acting as enforcement agents of big corporations. It has been happening for some years in Kasipur and other parts of Orissa. There police and local officials have functioned almost as a private army of mining companies. Opposition leaders, even elected representatives, have been attacked when reaching there to inquire in to violence. (Sainath 2005) Khare (2005) has commented on the Gurgaon brutality that the new economy has produced new politics where State has shown its sensitivity to defend the entrepreneur and industrialist but it has shown its insensitivity towards the working class.

Agricultural Reforms, State and the Peasantry

Liberalization policies regarding international trade in agricultural commodities have adversely affected the poor peasants and agricultural labours by raising the domestic price of agricultural products. The new policy has removed the restriction on the import of food grains and other agricultural products as part of the WTO agreement. This has displaced the peasantry from their traditional occupation, income and livelihood. Fiscal compression in the economy, in India, has been achieved in part, through cutback in agricultural infrastructure like power, irrigation, fertilizer etc. the institutional credit to rural sector has been reduced following the recommendation of the Narasimham Committee report and this has now raised cost of credit to agriculture. Similarly in order cut back fiscal deficit, Government has resorted to reducing the subsidies on fertilizer, power, water etc. This has result in loss of income and fall of production. Capital intensive agriculture imposed by the MNCs with lure of profit has created heavy debts for purchase of costly inputs. The seed policy, which encourages privatization of the seed sector, has led to change in the cropping patterns. Which is not suitable for the vast mass of marginalized peasantry. The WB/WTO induced trade liberalization policy has led to the distress sale of their farm produce by the small and marginal peasants in all most all states. This has worsened the income distribution pattern of the peasants affecting their standard of living adversely. In certain cases the peasants have resorted to suicide as in Andra Pradesh, Karnatak and Panjab (Deshpandhe, 2002).

Globalisation and Erosion of State Power

Historically state has taken the responsibilities in providing the socio economic space for labour by curtailing the unrestricted freedom of capital, but now State is retreating from its historical role. On the contrary state has given complete freedom to capital. One can argue that State has surrender to the international finance capital. It is now they who dictate term on what should be our fiscal policy, monetary policy, budgetary policy etc. State has become a 'soft state' towards implementing the social security measures enshrined in the constitution. Stiglitz (2001) has remarked that "unfortunately we have no world government...instead we have a system that might be called global governance without global government, one in which a few institution-the world a Bank, the IMF, the WTO—and a few players—the finance, commerce, and trade minister closely linked to certain financial and commercial interest—dominate the scene but in which many of those effected by their decision are left all most voice less". Patnaik (2002) has shown on the emergence of a super state when he says— "finance capital transcending its national origins, significant segments develop a loyalty to the world imperialist super state in addition to, and perhaps even overriding, what they feel towards there own nation state". Of course Chandhoke (2003) has argued that the state has not disappeared. It has been pluralized and now shares power with sub-national government, proliferating forms of network and partnership organizations, a variety of quasi-public and private organizations, NGOs and international agencies and other forms of supranational governance (Chandhoke, 2003).

VI. Growing Resistance against Globalisation and the Response of the State

The hollowing of the State giving rise to the market forces in its place by the imperialist globalization lobby headed by global super states has adversely effected various section of the working class. Hence there is growing outrage against the imperialists' globalization world over (Narasimha Reddy, 2002). The resistance movement has got regional dimension too. But weather the protest movement are local, national, or global does not matter, since they have been directed against the globalization policy of the IMF, WB, WTO, World Economic Forum and the G8. Unprecedented and militant demonstrations were organized in the meetings of G8, world Economic Forum, WTO ministerial meeting etc. in Seattle, Washington, Melbourne, Prague, Geneva, Genoa, Brussels against the dominance of the global capital. Most interestingly these protests were organized not through the conventional trade union framework or traditional political outfits. On the other hand the participants are drawn from all walks of life, those who are disillusioned and discontented against globalization policy like civil liberty groups, democratic mined individuals, intellectuals, public sector employees, environmentalists, independent trade union, workers in unorganized sectors etc.

In this global resistance movement India is not far behind. Each day from each corner of the country, protest movements against the predatory capitalist system, thrust upon the working class by the ruling class on behalf of the WB, IMF, and WTO, is going on. We can mention the all India strike on December 11, 1998, paralyzing the Indian economy. There have been repeated strikes of bands and insurance industry against privatization. The electricity workers in UP, Maharashtra and in several other states have demonstrated against the plan of state electricity boards to privatize them. There was also historic strike for two months by the BALCO employees against the privatization and sale of BALCO to Sterelite. In December 3rd 2001 mine workers went on three days successful strike against proposed amendment to the nationalization of the coalmines act. There was general strike and Bharat Band call on 21st May 2003 by the trade unions run by the left parties in India against the threat posed by the state to the public sector in India. These few evidences show that new form of resistance movement were taking place as a discontentment against the exploitation of the working class with the active participation of the state. They are demanding the states be more responsive towards the vulnerable section of the society. They are demanding that the state should serve the interest of the working class instead of global capital of multinational corporations.

Despite worldwide resistance, as we have seen above, there is little tangible achievement of these resistance movements. This is due to the fact that some of the movements are scattered, fragmented and unorganized. Of course World Social Fourm (WSF) sphere hading and co-coordinating the scattered movements with the slogan that' another world is possible 'However WSF in its conference organized in Bombay in 2004 has faced certain resistance from the radical groups in India called Mumbai Resistance or MR 2004. The allegation of MR 2004 is that the protagonists of Globalisation have initiated the WSF process with a view to taming the anti-globalization wave. This type of controversy is natural since certain groups are fighting to give globalization a human face. Hence they want the modus operandi of WB, IMF, WTO, should be changed. Stiglitz (2002) has not favored the abandon globalization rather he calls for reform in the governance of the international institutions like World Bank, IMF and WTO assigning greater role to the Third World countries. But certain resistance movements are totally against globalization and they want to smash the international institution, which are adding and abetting and facilitating the globalization process. For the protagonists of the globalization there is no alternative (TINA) but for the working class there are many alternatives (MITA) to globalization.

The responses of the state towards this resistance movement are lukewarm. Sometime as it is above State take the sides of Capital leaving little for labour consequently, almost all the resistance movements have to face state terror.

VII. Conclusion

Historically State was playing most crucial role shaping the labour market institutions for the beginning of the capitalist economy. But as capitalism enters to the phase of globalization the nature of state has undergone a radical change and corresponding the state-capital labour relationship has also undergone enormous change. Taking evidence from India we have seen that the post colonial state its pre–reform period, in India was an interventionist developmental, and welfare oriented one. The vulnerable section particularly the working class was expecting all possible help from the state. But in the post reform period the state opted for globalization and liberalization of the economy. Stabilization and Structural Adjustment policies were adopted. Basically this is a outward oriented, market driven, export led growth strategy instead of taking human development it has taken material development as a integral part of development policy. This policy has put tremendous impact on the world of work and workers world. It has introduce the flexible labour market policy in India which has raised the issue of loss of direct control of jobs, changes of job content and responsibility, job redundancy and redeployment. It has also imformalised and segregated the labour market. Hence employment of atypical, non-standard, part time, home working and casual type has increased.

After globalization of economy there has been a considerable erosion of state power. State has withdrawn from many areas where it was active and responsible. In the name of structural adjustment the most vulnerable section, particularly working class was left to the anarchy of the market. Thus state in its active support strengthened capital and weakened labour.

The working class in India as else where have responded with bitter battle against the wage cut, speed up, retrenchment, scrapping of wages, welfare measures, landlessness, homelessness and withdrawal of other traditional rights etc. They have cut across caste, gender, party line spontaneously. United due to the objective situation created by the globalized world. The neoliberal slogan is, there is no alternative to globalization. But the working class slogan is that there are many alternatives to WB, IMF, WTO led globalization.

References

Ahluwalia, I.J. (1991), *Productivity and Growth in Indian Manufacturing*, Oxford University Press, Delhi.

Bhattacharyya, D.K. (1994), "Employee Leasing and Labour Market Fexibility—An Empirical Study of its Problems and Prospects in Selected Manufacturing Units", *IJIL*, Vol. 37, No. 4, Oct.-Dec., pp. 551-57.

Breman, Jan (2002), "An informalisation Labour System End of labour Market Dualism", *Economic & Political Weekly* (EPW), Vol. 36, No. 52, pp. 4804-21.

Chandhoke, Neera (2003) "Governance and the Pluralisation of the State-Implications for Democratic Citizenship", *EPW*, Vol. 38, No. 28, July 12-18.

Chandra, N.K. (1982), "Long Term Stagnation in the Indian Economy 1900-75", *Economic and Political Weekly*, Annual Number.

Chaudhuri, Sudip (1994), "Public Enterprise and Private Purpose", *EPW*, Vol. 29, No. 22, May 28.

Choudhury, S.R. (1996), "Industrial Restructuring, Union and The State: Textile Mill Workers in Ahmedabad", *EPW*, Vol. 31, No. 8, Feb 24, pp. L7-13.

Deshpande, R.S. (2002),"Suicide by Farmers in Karnataka: Agrarian distress and possible Alleviatory Steps", *EPW*, Vol. 37, No. 26, June 29.

EPW (1992), "Bhilai Workers: Mounting Repression", Editorial, No. 27, July 4.

Khasnabis, Ratan and Sudipti Banerjee (1996), "Political Economy of Voluntary Retirement: Study of Rationalised Workers in Durgapur, *EPW*, No. 52, Review of Labour, Dec. 28, pp. l-64-72.

Knorringa, Petter (1996), "Operationalisation of Flexible Specialization: Agra's Footwear Industry", *EPW*, No. 52, December 28.

Khare, Harish (2005), "A Metaphor for the New Insensitivity", *The Hindu*, dated 27th July.

Martinussen, J.D. (2001), *Policies, Institutions, and Industrial Development Coping With Liberalisation and International Competition in India*, Sage Publication.

Myrdal, Gunnar (1968), *Asian Drama*, Vol. 11, Allen Lane, The Penguin Press, G. Britain.

Narasimha Reddy, D. (2002), "Globalisation, its Discontents and the Power of the People's Resistance" in Krishna Row, Y.V. and Narasimha Reddy, D. (eds) *Corporate Globalization and People Resistance*, NRR Research Centre, Hyderabad.

Nath, G.B. (2001), *Impact of Voluntary Retirement Sceme on the Labour Market in India—A Micro Study on RSP*, A Report submitted to the UGC, New Delhi.

Nayyar, Deepak (2003), "Work, Livelihoods And Rights", *IJLE*, Vol. 36, No.1, pp. 3-13.

Patnaik, Prabhat (2002), "Globalisation and Emerging Global Politics", in Krishna Rao, Y.V. and Narasimha Reddy, D. (eds), *Corporate Globalisation and People's Resistance*, NRR Research Center, Hyderbad.

Petras, James and Henry Veltmeyer (2001), *Globalisation Unmasked*, Madhyam Books, New Delhi.

Ramana, R. (1984), 'Performance of Capital Goods Sectors in India 1955-76; A Theoretical Study', *EPW*, Annual Number.

Rangarajan, C. (1992), Industrial Growth; Another Look, *EPW*, Annual Number.

Sainth, P. (2005), 'Malls of the Few, Chawls of the Many', *The Hindu*, 28, July.

Shah, N. Gandhi, (1978), "Structural Retrogression in Indian Economy since the Mid-Seventies", *EPW* Special Number 1978.

Stiglitz, J.E (2002), *Globalisation and its Discontents*, Allen Lane, London.

Streefkerk, Hein, (2001) "Thirty Years of Industrial Labour in South Gujarat: Trends and Significance", *EPW*, Vol. 36, No. 26, pp. 2398-11.

Uma Devi, S. (2002), "Globalisation, Information Technology and Asian Indian Women's Workforce Participation", *IJLE*, Vol. 42, No.4, Oct-Dec.

Unni, Jeemol (2001), "Gender and Informalisation in Labour Market in South Asia", *EPW*, Vol. 36, June, pp. 2360-78.

Visaria, Praveen, and Minhas, B.S. (1991), "Evolving an Employment Policy for the 1990s: What Do the Data Tell Us", *EPW*, No. 15, April 13.

Worker's Solidarity (2005), "Police Attack on Honda Workers", *Workers Solidarity*, New Delhi.

9

NEO-LIBERAL LABOUR MARKET REFORMS AND WORK STOPPAGES: COMPARISONS OF INDIA, INDONESIA, UNITED STATES AND AUSTRALIA*

L.J. Perry

Introduction

There is a voluminous literature on the economic and social impact of neo-liberal economic policy reforms.[1] Many writers are convinced neo-liberal economic policies are responsible for many of the world's enduring woes. Others argue the same policies are a source of economic salvation. Most writers see pluses and minuses, and depending upon the weights attached to the pluses and minuses, come down for or against or undecided. Surprisingly little attention has been given to the impact of different neo-liberal reforms on the pattern of work stoppages in different economies. To be sure, individual country studies have been made in which the issue of labour market reform has been broached. However, there has not been much attention paid to making international comparisons, and when international comparisons are made, there has been a tendency to focus on the experience of developed economies.

* This paper originally appeared in *The South Asian Journal of Management*, Vol. 13, No. 3, September 2006. My thanks go to the editors for kindly permitting the paper to be reproduced in this volume.

This paper seeks to compare the experience of four countries quite prominent, in one way or another, around the rim of the Indian Ocean: India, Indonesia, the United States and Australia. India and Indonesia are the two most heavily populated countries along the rim. Australia is lightly populated, but it is the wealthiest on a per capita basis and also has the second largest economy[2] that is geographically located along the rim. The United States is, of course, not geographically located on the Indian Ocean rim, but it is the largest and most influential economy in the world and also one of the most important trading partners to all of the countries in the region.

The four countries provide an interesting mix of diverse features. India and Indonesia are both relatively underdeveloped, heavily populated and have at various times been troubled by sluggish economic growth. On the other hand, the United States and Australia are both relatively well-developed with low population densities (particularly Australia) and both have also been troubled at times by sluggish economic growth. All countries currently enjoy harmonious political and economic relations with one another, and all have been affected, in one way or another, by the emergence of neo-liberal thinking providing an intellectual framework for managing the economy. It is of interest to compare the experience of these rather diverse countries to identify notable differences and similarities in their experiences of labour market reform and changing patterns of work stoppages.

To address the issue of the relation between work stoppages and neo-liberal labour market reforms, we proceed as follows. The next section of this paper reviews the notion of neo-liberalism. This is followed by a comparative analysis of the pattern of work stoppages, with some attention given to measurement differences and definitional changes. Stoppages can be looked at in terms of their frequency, worker involvement and duration—all of which affect the aggregate number of work days lost due to stoppages. The penultimate section reviews the links between neo-liberal labour market reforms and work stoppages, as well as the influence of other factors, such as labour market conditions, inflation and trade union density, on dispute rates. Some concluding thoughts are offered in the final section.

Neo-Liberal Labour Market Reforms

What is meant by neo-liberal reform?

Neo-liberal reform involves a movement towards markets, deregulation and private enterprise. The 'liberalism' in neo-liberalism refers to the notion of *laissez-faire* which is usually identified with the writings of Adam Smith in *The Wealth of Nations,* where the 'unfettered' actions of individuals, limited only by minimal rules of exchange, automatically promote a maximal level of social well-being. As individuals buy and sell goods in order to promote their own wellbeing they unintentionally promote the wellbeing of others. Smith, like later 'liberals', was deeply sceptical of government direction and actions claimed to be made in the public good.

> 'Every individual necessarily labours to render the annual revenue of the society as great as he can. He generally indeed neither intends to promote the public interest, nor knows how much he is promoting it. He intends only his own gain, and he is in this, as in many other cases, led by an invisible hand to promote an end which was no part of his intention. By pursuing his own interest he frequently promotes that of the society more effectually than when he really intends to promote it. I have never known much good done by those who affected to trade for the public good.' (*The Wealth of Nations,* 1776, Vol. 1, p. 456).

The 'neo' in neo-liberalism refers to the 'new' or contemporary use to which Adam Smith's perspective on markets and individual actions has been put. The contemporary liberal favours limited regulation of local and international trade, limited involvement of government in business activity, limited labour market regulation and limited interference in the market place choices that individuals make. Globalisation has come to be associated with neo-liberalism. Globalisation, which is simply the contemporary word for increased international commerce, is seen by writers of a neo-liberal bent, to be an effective vehicle for promoting specialisation in trade and thus greater output and higher living standards.

Neo-liberalism, globalisation and associated market liberalising approaches to economic management have risen in importance during recent decades. Key international bodies like the World Bank and the International Monetary Fund have promoted neo-liberal strategies to address the various problems that nations have faced—especially those that are experiencing financial crises. India and Indonesia have, for example, acted on IMF and World Bank advice in recent years.

So far as labour markets are concerned, neo-liberalism has been associated with policies favouring: *(a)* reduced government regulation of labour markets, *(b)* greater employer choice in hiring and firing workers, usually referred to somewhat euphemistically as labour market 'flexibility' and *(c)* reduced legislative and/or administrative support for unions in the workplace.

In this paper we will seek to identify changes in labour market policies and see if these have been associated with apparent changes in the pattern of industrial disputes. But first let us take an overview of the broad historical differences in stoppages for our four economies, as well as review some important differences in collecting and compiling practices.

Measuring Work Stoppages

For the four countries in this study, there are some notable—and at times disturbing—differences in the methods that different countries have used in collecting and compiling statistics on work stoppages.

First, the minimum criteria for inclusion in the collection for Australia and India are quite similar. For India, only those stoppages involving 10 or more workers are included; for Australia only stoppages involving 10 or more working days lost are included. It is unclear what the minimum criterion is for Indonesia. In 1982 the USA radically changed its minimum criteria for tallying stoppages. The collecting procedure changed from counting all stoppages involving *6 workers or more* to counting all stoppages involving *1000 workers or more* and lasting at least one full shift. This effectively meant that the USA ceased counting small-scale stoppages and, instead, counted only large-scale stoppages. Up until the introduction of the new minimum criteria, large-scale stoppages account for around 70 per cent of all working days lost due to stoppages. The reason given for the change was 'due to financial stringencies'.[3] Thus, after many decades of collecting data on both small- and large-scale stoppages, the world's most powerful and wealthiest nation found its financial resources insufficient to report fully and accurately on this central and fundamental labour market measure.

Second, India alone among the four countries collects and publishes separate data on: *(i)* lockouts and *(ii)* strikes. All of the other countries lump strikes and lockouts together and refer to them collectively as industrial disputes or work stoppages. These different collections of strikes versus lockouts may be of interest when comparing the effect of neo-liberal labour market changes on lockouts versus strikes.

Thirdly, Australia, unlike the other countries, includes in its tally political strikes. For Australia, these stoppages have been, at times, quite sizable. However, over the entire period under review (1960-2004), they have averaged out at around 14 per cent of all days lost due to work stoppages.

Finally, it can be noted that these data are unlikely to be fault-free. First, as noted above, there has been a radical definitional change in the USA data, so that after 1981 it counts only large-scale stoppages. Of all those countries actively recording data on labour stoppages, the USA is the only country in the world to purposefully exclude small-scale stoppages from its tally. Second, according to Datt (2003), there appears to be some inconsistency in Indian national government figures and certain state government collections. Third, Indonesian national data collections are at times substantially different from the International Labour Organization's tally. Part of this difference may be attributable to the Indonesian data being expressed in terms of *hours* not worked due to stoppages versus *days* not worked (Perry, 2005a). The Indonesian data used in this paper are from the national collection after 1980 (with some minor adjustments[4]) and ILO data prior to this date. Lastly, it is worth pointing out that at least two studies (Kelly and Nicholson, 1980 and Kopi, 1981), though rather dated now and Europe-focussed, found evidence of under-enumeration of small-scale work stoppages. It would be surprising if this problem has not affected the stoppage tallies for at least some of the countries discussed in this paper. Nevertheless, it is unlikely that this under-enumeration affects the accuracy of the trend displayed in the data or, for that matter, the broad accuracy of the number of days lost due to stoppages (Turner, 1969).

To provide a framework for reviewing and analysing work stoppages, this paper will focus on four dimensions of work stoppages. These are: *(a)* time lost due to work stoppages, *(b)* the frequency of work stoppages, *(c)* average involvement in stoppages and *(d)* the average duration of stoppages. Below we comment further on these measures.

(a) Time Lost due to Work Stoppages

This is the number of working days lost per annum per thousand labour force members. This is the broadest measure of work stoppages. Moreover, it is the least likely to be affected by problems such as under-enumeration and minimum selection criteria changes (Turner, 1969). To give a quick overview of relative dimensions of time lost, the average values for our four countries for the period 1960-2004 are reported below:

- United States 232 (estimate)
- Australia 209 (adjusted)
- India 77
- Indonesia 7

The estimate for the USA is based on the combination of actual time lost for large-scale stoppages plus actual small-scale stoppages for 1960-81 with estimated small-scale stoppages from 1982-2004. The estimates draw from econometric estimates in Perry and Wilson (2004). The Australian data are adjusted to exclude political strikes, as such stoppages are excluded from the tally for the other countries. If USA large-scale strikes alone were calculated, time lost would have been 154. If Australian stoppages included political strikes, time lost would have been 240.

The above figures give an instructive overview of stoppage rates in the four countries. The USA and Australia have, on average, had similar rates of time lost, and their experience shows them to be substantially more strike prone than India and Indonesia. India appears to be middle ranking among the four countries. However it is important to keep in mind that the measure of time lost being employed here is workdays lost per thousand *labour force members*. If an alternative denominator, such as the number of employees had been used for all countries, India's measure of time lost would increase more than tenfold. This is because formal sector employment in general and formal sector employee numbers in particular have represented a relatively small proportion—around 7 per cent—of the total labour force for India. Unions and work stoppages are largely confined to the formal sector in India. Thus the denominator (labour force members) tends to mask the fact that for India's relatively small formal sector, its disputation rate is amongst the highest in the world.

It is notable that time lost in Indonesia has been, on average, substantially lower than that for the other countries. Indonesia's experience of relatively low rates of time lost due to work stoppages is, incidentally, quite similar to that of most other East and South-East Asian economies on average.

Figures 1 to 4 chart time lost due to stoppages for our four economies. Focussing on the total stoppages for each of the economies, a visual inspection of the figures indicates that there has been a fair degree of similarity in the pattern of time lost due to stoppages in India, the USA and Australia.[5] The same does not apply for Indonesia. Table 1 reports the correlation coefficients between the four countries for the period 1960 and 2004. Some variations are allowed for with respect to Indian stoppages (strikes plus lockouts versus strikes alone) and USA large-scale stoppages versus total estimated stoppages. All in all, there are positive associations between all of the countries experiences of stoppages, except for Indonesia. For India, for example, there is quite a strong positive correlation between Indian strikes and Australian stoppages (the vast bulk of Australian stoppages have been strikes), a weaker but positive association between Indian stoppages and USA stoppages, but a negative association between Indian and Indonesian stoppages. We will return to these broad similarities and differences later on in this paper.

Time lost due to stoppages can be decomposed (or divided) into three dimensions. These three dimensions are: *(i)* the *frequency* or number of work stoppages, *(ii)* the number of workers *involved* in work stoppages, and *(iii)* the average *duration* or length of stoppages.[6] An independent increase (or decrease) in any of these dimensions will cause time lost to correspondingly rise (or fall). By decomposing time lost due to work stoppages into these three dimensions for each of the countries under review, we can get a fuller appreciation of underlying differences and similarities in the 'shape' of work stoppages for the countries under consideration. These three measures are now discussed below under subheadings (b) to (c).

(b) Frequency of Work Stoppages

This is the number of work stoppages per annum per (say) million labour force members. This measure does not reflect either the average number of workers involved in stoppages or the average duration of stoppages. It is thus a much narrower measure of stoppages than time lost (discussed under subheading (a) above). Nevertheless, it does represent an important partial measure of stoppages. To give a quick overview of relative dimensions of the frequency of work stoppages, the average values for our four countries for the period 1960-2004 are reported below in descending order:

- Australia 234
- United States 30 (estimate)
- India 6.8
- Indonesia 1.2

It is notable that Australia has a much higher frequency of work stoppages than is the case for the other countries. This, indeed, has been a feature of the Australian labour relations scene; that is, a relatively large number of brief strikes, very often designed to register a protest over some issue or other, but typically lasting just a couple of days. The USA data are based on an estimate of smaller scale stoppages. Essentially the missing figures for the total number of stoppages are calculated by grossing up the figures for large scale stoppages. The grossing-up factor is the ratio of number of all (large-scale plus small-scale) stoppages to large-scale stoppages for the period when these data overlapped (1960-81). Given that the there was quite a reasonable degree of stability in this ratio and given also the overall similarity in the pattern over time of the two series (the frequency of all stoppages and the frequency of large-scale only stoppages), it is suggested that the estimate given above is not unreasonable. It is certainly more instructive than simply using the current flawed large-scale only data that is available officially. Note that India's frequency of disputes is much lower than Australia's, even allowing for the use of the labour force denominator. Note also that the average frequency of Indonesian disputes is well below that of the other countries.

(c) Involvement in Stoppages

This is the average number of workers involved in a typical stoppage. This (like frequency) is a much narrower measure of stoppages than time lost, as it does not take into account the duration of stoppages or the frequency. To give a quick overview of the relative dimensions of involvement in work stoppages, the average values for our four countries for the period 1960-2004 are reported below in descending order:

- India 903
- United States 555 (estimate)
- Australia 521
- Indonesia 350

There has not been the same degree of international variability in the average level of involvement in stoppages as there has in the various other measures of work stoppages. India ranks highest, followed by the USA and Australia, which are much the same, followed lastly by Indonesia, which has the lowest level of involvement.

(d) Duration of Stoppages

This is the average number of days an average worker is involved in a stoppage. Again this is a much narrower measure of stoppages than time lost, as it does not take into account the number of stoppages or the average number of workers involved. To give a quick overview of relative dimensions of the duration of work stoppages, the average values for our four countries for the period 1960-2004 are reported below in descending order:

- United States 20 (estimate)
- India 18
- Australia 2
- Indonesia 1.4

The USA estimate is based on the average duration of large-scale disputes. This is because for the chosen overlap period (1960-81), the average durations of small-scale and large-scale stoppages are almost identical. Note the marked difference between India and the USA versus Australia and Indonesia. The latter two countries have generally short stoppages of a day or two on average, the former experience disputes that generally last a month (recall there are typically 5 working days in a week and about 22 working days in a month). These are quite marked and notable differences.

Labour Market Reform, Strikes and Lockouts

Drawing in the main from the existing literature, this section discusses the background role and impact of neo-liberal economic policies over the last four decades or so in each of the four economies. We commence with India.

India

Major neo-liberal reforms were put into place in India in 1991, though a number of lesser reforms were introduced during the late 1980s during Rajiv Gandhi's administration of 1984-89. Zagha (1999, p.171) refers to these earlier attempt at reform as 'partial liberalisation'. Regardless of how we might choose to label them, the 'partial liberalisation' of the later 1980s did not avert a currency crisis during 1991 (Bhagwati, 1993; Bhattacherjee, 2002). At that stage India had essentially run out of sufficient foreign exchange to pay for its imports. The Narasimha Rao government, with Manmohan Singh as Finance Minister, introduced, over time, a package of general market-oriented reforms, including a substantial depreciation of the local currency. Labour market reforms were much more difficult to legislate. As a result, many neo-liberal labour reforms have been introduced via judicial rulings, government administrative rulings and by state governments. (Kuruvilla *et al*, 2002; Beasley and Burgess, 2002; Sanyal and Menon, 2004; Sharma, 2004) In addition of course, reforms elsewhere in the economy had ramifications for labour markets.

In its review of the Indian economy in 1997, *The Economist* magazine, a notable defender of, and advocate for, neo-liberal reforms made the following observations:

> '[Government rules and regulations] ... go to great lengths to protect existing jobs. For instance, permission to sack workers in firms employing more than 100 people must be obtained direct from state government. Only very rarely is such permission granted. [..] Firms with more than 25 workers have to inform official labour exchanges of any vacancies, and fill them from that source. This gives armies of civil servants a vested interest in the system, and offers valuable opportunities for graft. The government also regulates ("certifies") job specifications: firms of a certain size—all firms in some states—must notify the authorities of changes to job content or employee status. Some states forbid any such changes unless every worker consents to them.'

In fact labour markets appear to have been amongst the slowest of markets to reform. *The Economist* (1997, p. 19) noted that: '... except for the indirect effect of increased competition, the reforms of 1991-93 left the labour market untouched'. In a more recent comparative review of the Indian economy and Chinese economy, *The Economist* (2005, p. 14) came to much the same conclusion about the extent of direct labour market reform:

> 'Firing workers remain hard in India, which deters firms from hiring them in the first place. This has a big impact on productivity. Many firms feel unable to reap economies of scale, because once they employ more than 100 people they become subject to restrictive labour laws.'

In spite of the absence of major labour-market legislative changes, the changes introduced in the early 1990s were nevertheless quite profound. (Zagha, 1999; Sodhi and Plowman, 2001; Vankata Ratnam, 2001; Bhattacherjee, 2002; Krueger and Chinoy, 2002; Tendulkar, 2003; Sharma, 2004; Desai, 2005). Two questions arise. The first is: have these changes been associated with major changes in work stoppages? The second is: how might we measure such an effect? To answer the first question, we must initially address the second question.

To get an overview of the possible impact of neo-liberal reforms in 1991 in India on work stoppages, we will compare India's reform period, 1991 to 2004 with its equivalent pre-reform period, 1978 to 1991. (See Datt, 2003a for a similar methodology, though for a briefer timeframe.)

Let us initially consider the broadest measure of work stoppages—time lost in Table 2. Compared to the pre-reform period, the reform period has witnessed, on average, a relative decline in total stoppages. On the surface, then, neo-liberal reforms, such as they have been, have been associated with declining stoppages. But other macroeconomic changes may also explain some of the decline in time lost. First, inflation has been lower, on average, during the reform period than before. Less inflation tends to be associated with a reduced need for militancy to maintain the purchasing power of wages. Second, the unemployment rate has been higher, on average, during the reform period. A high underlying unemployment rate is more likely to act as a dampener on militancy than is a low unemployment rate. Nevertheless, the *change* in the unemployment rate has, on average, been one of decline during the reform period, as indicated in Table 2. Third, union density (the percentage of formal sector employees who are members of unions[7]) has, on average, declined. Again, this tends to be associated with a declining capacity to strike; though it may be the case that neo-liberal reforms have themselves been partly responsible for declining trade union density, in which case some of the decline in stoppages attributed to falling trade union density is in fact ultimately attributable to neo-liberal reform rather than to a presumed autonomous decline in density. Finally, real GDP growth has been greater during the reform period than during the pre-reform period. The effect of this on strikes is unclear. Strikes may be moderated by a greater economic capacity to reward labour more generously. On the other hand, strong growth, coupled with declining unemployment, may embolden labour to agitate for a bigger slice of the cake[8].

It is notable that the decline in time lost due to strikes is much more pronounced than the decline in lockouts. Neo-liberal reforms tend to directly favour capital over labour (Datt 2003a, 2003b), and the fact that strikes have declined much more sharply than lockouts, may suggest that the bargaining position of capital has been strengthened by neo-liberal reforms. Figure 5 charts the ratio of time lost due to lockouts to time lost due to strikes. While it is true that the ratio has increased quite markedly in recent years, it should also be noted that relative increase in lockouts commenced well before the introduction of neo-liberal reforms. Sen Gupta and Sett (2000) argued that lockouts have risen in importance in India because of the application of rigid labour market regulations. Lockouts are a legal way of reducing short-term employment levels, when it is legally near impossible to retrench employees (Mathur, 1991). Lockouts also keep downward pressure on wage costs, especially when product demand is low. In some ways, then, lockouts may be a consequence of the failure of neo-liberal labour market reforms to materialise, as much as being a consequence of neo-liberal reforms in general. In other words, if labour employment and retrenchment rules were more flexible in the first place, employers would not need to resort to lockouts as a means of reducing labour costs.

Let us next turn to the three dimensions of work stoppages: frequency, involvement and duration of stoppages.

Table 2 indicates that, as with time lost, the average frequency of stoppages—but particularly the frequency of strikes—has declined markedly during the reform period. In fact the proportional change in time lost and frequency are almost identical. The average duration of disputes—but again particularly strikes—has declined during the reform period, as indicated in Table 2.

Involvement in strikes and lockouts, on the other hand, has risen sharply. Most of the rise in involvement has occurred over the last few years. The extent of the rise in involvement in strikes and, to a lesser extent, lockouts is quite spectacular, and quite unprecedented. During 2004, the average number of workers involved in strikes reached more than 7000 workers. The average involvement in strikes up until 1999 was 700—which is around one tenth of the value of the 2004 figure. Note that, in spite of the rise in numbers involved in an average dispute, the overall amount of time lost due to work stoppages has still declined. This is because the decline in the frequency of and duration of stoppages has more than offset the increase in involvement.

All in all, the decline in time lost due to work stoppages in general and the decline in strikes in particular are what we might expect from the introduction of neo-liberal reforms. However, we can also note that other factors such as lower inflation, higher unemployment rates and lower union density (independent of density declines produced by neo-liberal reforms themselves) may also have acted to bring down the amount of time lost due to work stoppages in India.

Indonesia

Major neo-liberal economic reforms, of one ilk or another, have often accompanied major political and economic crises in Indonesia. For the period under review, the first major changes occurred during the mid-1960s. During this period, President Sukarno's policies, which were anti-Western, confrontational and an economic failure, were replaced by President Suharto's antithetical policies. When Suharto took over, he acted on the advice of Western-trained technocrats. He encouraged foreign investment, free enterprise (though often state and/or military owned) and was generally pro-business in his approach to economic development. While Suharto's authoritarian policies were more economically liberal than Sukarno's, they were not particularly liberal in the Smithian sense. Hadiz and Robison (2003) described Suharto's policies as a form of 'state capitalism'. Others have referred to Suharto's policies as a form of 'ersatz capitalism' (Yoshihara, 1988), meaning an inferior substitute for the real thing, a capitalism more than usually rife with nepotism, cronyism and corruption.

The second period, during which increased doses of neo-liberalism were administered, was during the 1980s '... following the dramatic collapse of oil prices in 1982 and 1986' (Hadiz and Robison 2005, p. 221). The most significant decline in real oil prices was in 1986. Real oil prices fell by around half (depending on the timeframe chosen). Oil was, at the time, Indonesia's principal source of export revenue. Hadiz and Robison point out that: 'Technocrats were able to push through a series of reforms in trade, banking, finance and to eliminate many monopolies as Indonesia's state revenues and foreign earnings came under threat' (p. 221).

The third wave of reforms occurred in the wake of the Asian financial crisis of 1997/98. On this occasion the IMF demanded '... more deregulation, dismantling the state owned sector, introducing institutional reforms in banking and public management and, significantly, diluting central state authority.' (Hadiz and Robison, p. 221)

The second and third wave of reforms did not, according to Hadiz and Robison (2005), result in any major movements towards the idealised neo-liberal paradigm embedded in the writings and arguments of its advocates. Instead, they contend, public monopoly power morphed into private monopoly power and old privileged business-government relations morphed into new relations, though still as questionable as before.

Table 3 indicates that during the first (1967-86) identified phase of the Suharto government, work stoppages—which were already low by international standards—were almost negligible during these years.

The Suharto government opposed having free trade unions. The national union, the SPSI, was under government control, being modelled on the type of quiescent unions established in Singapore and South Korea. Manning (1998, pp. 210-11) observes that:

> 'Promoting the interests of employers and workers depended on the government's willingness to allow SPSI to develop as an independent body, and resolve disputes of its members. As in South Korea under Park in the 1970s, neither of these conditions was fulfilled by the national trade union body. The SPSI emerged as a tool for government control of organised labour, rather than representing workers' interests in negotiations with employers.'[9]

During the second phase of neo-liberal reforms (1987-1997) there was an appreciable increase in time lost due to work stoppages (Table 3, Figure 2). The rise in stoppages, however, probably had little directly to do with neo-liberal reforms of either the first or the second phase identified above. Instead, the rise in industrial disputes during the second phase, but particularly during the early 1990s, have been linked to: *(i)* slow changing minimum and real wages, *(ii)* the failure of the SPSI to attend to the interest of workers (Agrawal, 1995; Manning, 1998; Rinakit, 1999)[10], *(iii)* a more informed, educated and motivated work force (Hadiz, 1997; Manning 1998; Robison and Hadiz, 2004), and *(iv)* the promise in the early 1990s of liberalising reforms (Hadiz, 1997; Manning, 1998).

The rise in disputes during the second phase of neo-liberal reforms does not appear to be linked to either inflation, which was steady, or the unemployment rate, which was edging upwards. Nevertheless, the 1990s, up until 1997, was a period of relatively strong economic growth. During the 1980s (1981-90) real per capita GDP growth averaged 4.5 per cent per annum; during the early 1990s (1991-96) it averaged 6.2 per cent per annum. In addition, growth of exports of goods and services during the early 1990s averaged 10.6 per cent per annum, compared to 1.4 per cent per annum during the 1980s. During this period the structure of Indonesia's exports changed from being principally oil exports to exports of manufactures. Industry sector growth during the early 1990s averaged 8.6 per cent per annum, compared to growth of 7.5 per cent during the 1980s. Thus, while the early 1990s presents a mixed macro-economic picture, there were some elements of an underlying expansionary environment which may have contributed, at least in part, to heightened expectations on the part of workers as to what the economy could and should pay them.

The year 1998, the worst year of the Asian Financial Crisis, has been isolated from the rest of the observations in Table 3. It was a period of collapsing output and a collapsing currency, both in terms of its domestic and international purchasing power.

The post-Suharto period (1999-2004) has been one of relatively low growth and declining work stoppages. The political freedoms won in the wake of the demise of the Suharto government and the frantic re-establishment of a free trade union movement (Rahayu and Sumarto, 2003; Mizuno, 2005[11]) has not been linked to a rise in work stoppages. In fact time lost due to stoppages declined. Why? With the benefit of hindsight, it is suggested that high unemployment, sluggish economic growth and a faltering recovery from the Asian financial crisis of (at its worst) 1998 and the global downturn of 2001-2002 help explain some the moderation in the time lost due to industrial disputes between 1997 and 2004.

All in all, the introduction of various forms of neo-liberal economic reform appears to have had little association with ups and downs of work stoppages statistics in Indonesia. One possible contributing factor to this negligible association may be that what we have chosen to label 'neo-liberal' reforms were, for Indonesia, at best a very pale imitation of the real thing. Likewise, the fluctuations in inflation appear not to be linked to time lost due to work stoppages. Indeed, inflation was relatively moderate, by Indonesian standards, during the mid-1990s at a time (around 1996) when work stoppages where at their highest for decades. Perhaps the underlying exuberance of the pre-crisis 1990s, the relatively strong real GDP growth, the sense that the Indonesian economy could perform as well as other successful neighbouring economies (Malaysia, Thailand, Singapore and China) all contributed to the heightened expectations of the times as well as the heightened level of industrial unrest during the 1990s.

United States

In many ways the USA is the home of neo-liberal economics. The capitalist system of private enterprise is embedded in the culture. Capitalism has some of its most effective advocates in the USA. Nevertheless, neo-liberalism was given a significant boost during the Reagan years (1981-1989).

Pivotal changes occurred in 1981with the Professional Air Traffic Controllers' Organization (PATCO) strike. The PATCO strike represented a major showdown between capital and labour in the US (Reagan, 1990; Johnson, 1991; Western, 1997). The outcome of the conflict was a major defeat for the striking unionists. The defeat of the unionists was symbolically important. It signalled to the wider labour market greater resistance to unionism in general, and a greater resistance to the relatively militant and strike-prone unionism that came to be associated with the late 1960s and 1970s.

The PATCO showdown in the USA and the defeat of the union acted as a fillip to neo-liberal and anti-union thinking in the USA and, arguably, elsewhere. And although the USA has never been anything but a bastion for capitalism, the outcome of the dispute managed to push the USA further towards, perhaps, a more strident form of neo-liberalism.

The changes wrought by the PATCO dispute were not legislative. Rather they were administrative. What this boils down to is that regulators have, since the Reagan Administration, taken a relatively hard line against union militancy (Western, 1997).

Given the importance of the PATCO dispute to USA labour Relations and neo-liberal government policies, we will compare briefly the time lost due to stoppages in large-scale stoppages, before and after the PATCO dispute. This is done in Table 4. There is a substantial drop in time lost due to stoppages during the Reagan years. However, inflation was relatively low and the unemployment rate a little higher on average during the Reagan years. Also, union density had been on the decline during and after the Reagan years, though the decline in union density itself may itself have been as much a response to the rise of neo-liberalism as it was an independent source of decline in stoppages. These factors, quite independent of the anti-union administrative arrangements introduced by Reagan, may have also acted to moderate time lost due to stoppages. On the other hand, the Ford/Carter years experienced a decline in stoppage rates relative to the Johnson/Nixon years, so it may be that that the Reagan years were, to some extent, merely the continuation of declining trend.

All in all, we cannot be entirely sure just how central the neo-liberal, anti-union policies of the Reagan Administration were to the decline in stoppages. Nevertheless it seems reasonable to suggest that the Reagan changes reinforced and, perhaps to some extent, pre-empted the fall in stoppages.

Australia

Neo-liberal reforms have been introduced gradually and progressively into Australia from around the mid-1970s. Most of the initial reforms were related to the operations of financial institutions. These sorts of reforms were then extended to foreign exchange markets, state-owned businesses (which were progressively privatised) and labour markets. The current government intends to extend neo-liberal labour market reforms during its present term in office. In December of 2005 the government enacted new detailed labour market regulation that will further entrench individual employer-employee, one-on-one wage bargaining, weaken union involvement in wage determinations and strengthen considerably the prerogative of management to hire and fire at will (Wooden, 2005).

Apart from the aforementioned newly-enacted changes of December 2005, perhaps the most noted labour marked reform involved the introduction of enterprise bargaining in the early 1990s and a movement away from a centralised and legalistic wage determining system. These neo-liberal changes involved both administrative changes and legislative changes, and were further developed in subsequent years. A recent study by Perera and Hodgkinson (2004) has argued that '... the move to enterprise bargaining has been the main determinant of strike volumes in the past decade ...' (p. 455). Using an error-correction model of work stoppages, they modelled enterprise bargaining for the period 1992 to 2003 via a legislative dummy variable and find that '... institutional factors now influence strike volumes, rather than economic conditions' (p. 439). Briggs (2004) has found an increase in the incidence of lockouts since the introduction of neo-liberal reforms, which represents, in a much diluted form, an outcome similar to that of India (Perry, 2006).

Table 5 compares the reform with the pre-reform period. Clearly there is a sizable decline in both time lost due to stoppages and the frequency of stoppages. Inflation and union density declines may explain much of the decline in stoppages, though again the decline in union density may be in part a response to neo-liberal reforms Inflation in particular has, for Australia since 1960, been positively correlated with time lost due to stoppages, though the up-kick in inflation (initiated by the introduction of a 10 per cent goods and services tax in 2000) has not been associated with a corresponding rise in stoppages (see Figure 4). This might be attributable to more severe restrictions placed on the rights of unions to strike since the introduction of enterprise bargaining in the early 1990s plus other subsequent limitations on the right to strike.

Some Concluding Thoughts

Clearly identifiable neo-liberal labour market reforms of one sort or another have been implemented in India, the USA and Australia. It is important to note though that reforms have been different in different countries. In the case of India, the reforms of 1991 had little if any direct impact on labour market legislation. Labour market reforms have occurred as an indirect result of reforms elsewhere in the economy as well as being a result of changes in state government regulations, judicial rulings and central government administrative initiatives. In the case of the United States, a country that has long espoused the benefits of a market-based economy, reforms—particularly during the Reagan years—were administrative rather than legislative with respect to labour market arrangements. In the case of Australia, reforms have been much more strongly driven by labour market legislative changes than has been the case for India or the United States.

The important point to note is not so much the exact shape of the neo-liberal reform in our selection of countries, but rather the *direction of change*. All countries have moved unmistakably in favour of neo-liberal policies, notwithstanding differences in timing and methodology. Just as unmistakably, there has been for India, the United States and Australia a marked declining trend in the pattern of time lost due to work stoppages during the various respective periods of neo-liberal reform. It is highly likely that a significant portion of the decline in work stoppages can be linked to various neo-liberal reforms, notwithstanding the fact that other factors, such as lower inflation and union density, have also contributed to the decline in stoppages.

The introduction of neo-liberal reforms has meant that management, labour and government are operating in a considerably different environment to the one, or ones, that prevailed earlier. Union militancy is considerably lower, the prerogative of management to determine wages and conditions has, by and large, been enhanced and government policymakers and business managers are less accountable to the demands of unions and unionists. The seemingly impersonal machinations of markets have increasingly become the arbiters of what, how and for whom to produce.

In the case of Indonesia, neo-liberal labour market and general reforms have been less clearly linked to declining rates of work stoppages. To be sure, the change in government in the mid-1960s saw a move, in a relative sense, towards neo-liberal policies, and an accompanying decline in stoppages. However, the decline in stoppages was more a result of government control of unions than it was a result of neo-liberal reforms.

The rising amount of time lost due to work stoppages in Indonesia during the 1990s up to the worst year (1998) of the Asian financial crisis has been linked to the relatively strong growth of Indonesia's manufacturing export sector, among other things. The moderation of time lost due to work stoppages during the post-Suharto years has been linked to Indonesia's relatively high unemployment rate and slow recovery from both the Asian financial crisis and the worldwide recession of the early 2000s. All in all, Indonesia's experience appears to be less linked to neo-liberal labour reform than has been the case for India, the United States and Australia.

The performance of all of our selection of countries over the next decade or so will provide valuable data for evaluating the effectiveness or otherwise of the various neo-liberal reforms they have thus far introduced.

FIGURES

Figure 1: India—Time Lost due to Work Stoppages

Days Lost per Thousand Labour Force Members

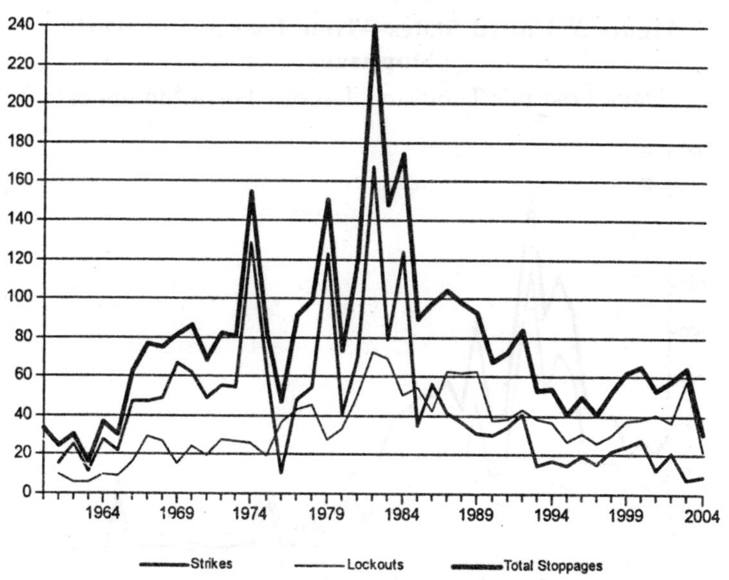

Figure 2: Indonesia—Time Lost due to Work Stoppages

Days Lost per Thousand Labour Force Members

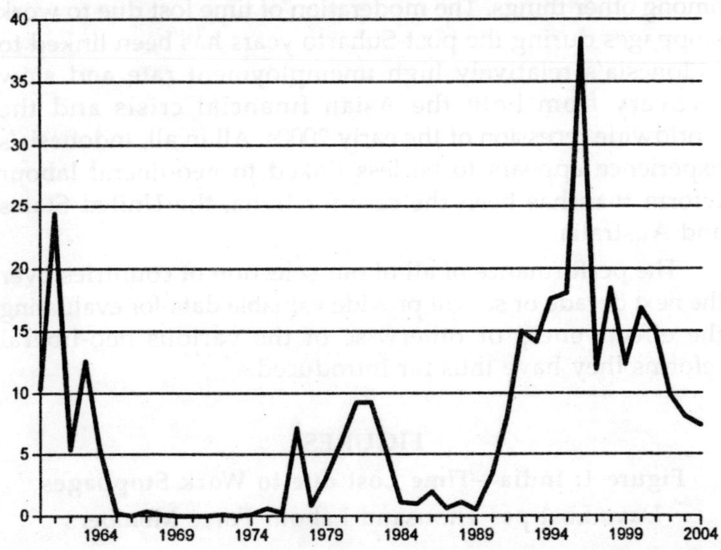

Figure 3: United States—Time Lost due to Work Stoppages

Days Lost per Thousand Labour Force Members

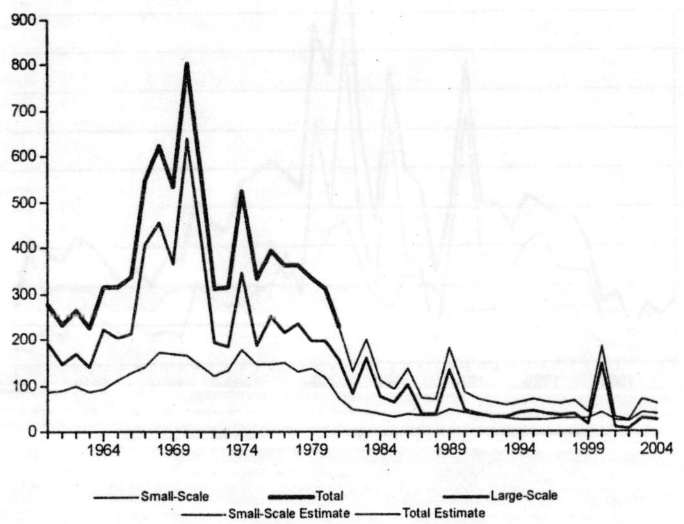

Figure 4: Australia—Time Lost due to Work Stoppages
Days Lost per Thousand Labour Force Members

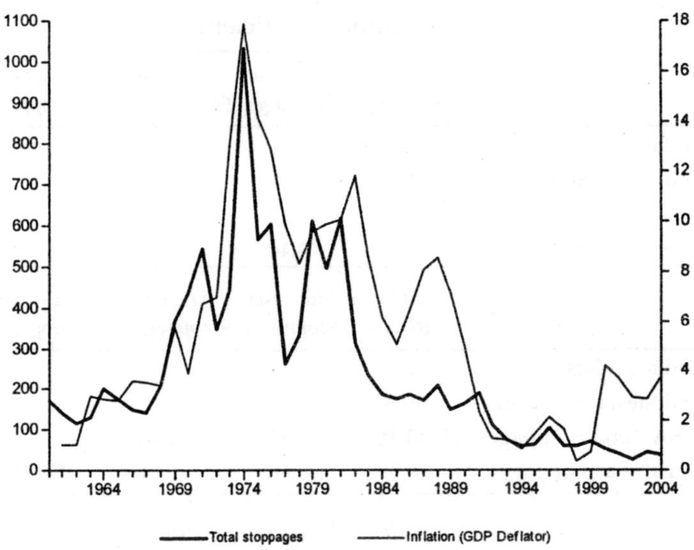

Figure 5: India—Ratio of Lockouts to Strikes
Time Lost

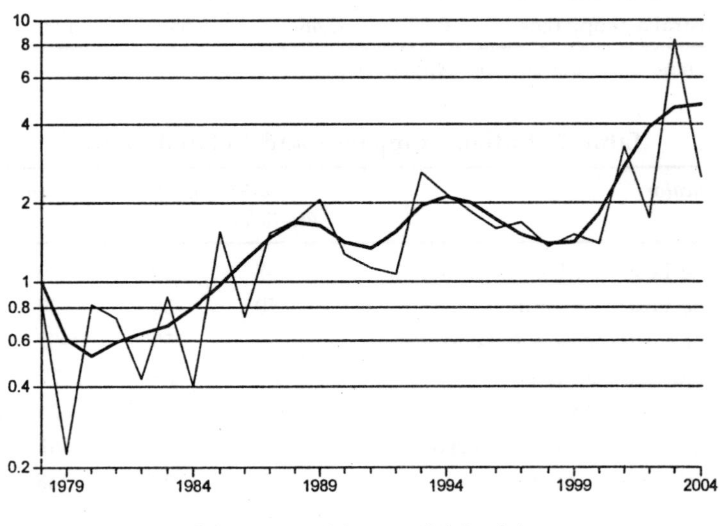

TABLES

Table 1: Time Lost Due to Work Stoppages Compared, 1960-2004

(Correlation Coefficients)

	India Stoppages	*Indonesia Stoppages*	*USA Total Stoppages (est.)*	*Australia Stoppages*
India Stoppages	1.00			
Indonesia Stoppages	-0.33	1.00		
USA Total Stoppages (est.)	0.09	-0.52	1.00	
Australia Stoppages	0.45	-0.46	0.61	1.00

	India Strikes	*Indonesia Stoppages*	*USA Total Stoppages (est.)*	*Australia Stoppages*
India Strikes	1.00			
Indonesia Stoppages	-0.37	1.00		
USA Total Stoppages (est.)	0.31	-0.52	1.00	
Australia Stoppages	0.59	-0.46	0.61	1.00

	India Strikes	*Indonesia Stoppages*	*USA Large Stoppages*	*Australia Stoppages*
India Strikes	1.00			
Indonesia Stoppages	-0.37	1.00		
USA Large Stoppages	0.30	-0.49	1.00	
Australia Stoppages	0.59	-0.46	0.55	1.00

Sources: See Data Sources Appendix.

Table 2: Indian Stoppages and Related Data

Indicator	*1988-91 Pre-Reform*	*1991-04 Reform*	*% Change*
Time Lost - Strikes	65	20	-70
Time Lost - Lockouts	50	36	-29
Time Lost - Strikes & Lockouts	116	55	-52
Frequency - Strikes	5.7	1.6	-72
Frequency - Lockouts	1.3	1.0	-24
Frequency - Strikes & Lockouts	7.0	2.6	-63
Involvement - Strikes	772	1918	148

Involvement - Lockouts	596	893	50
Involvement - Strikes & Lockouts	736	1466	99
Duration - Strikes	15	10	-33
Duration - Lockouts	69	52	-25
Duration - Strikes & Lockouts	24	21	-14
Inflation (GDP Deflator)	9.2	6.8	-26
Unemployment Rate (%)	7.5	9.2	24
Unemployment Rate Change	7.0	-1.0	-
Union Density (%) (a)	26.0	20.8	-20
GDP Growth (%)	4.7	5.9	24

Sources: See Data Sources Appendix. (a) 1982-91 compared to 1991-2000

Table 3: Indonesian Stoppages and Related Data

Indicator	*1967-86 Suharto I*	*1987-97 Suharto II*	*1998 Crisis*	*1999-04 Post-Suharto*
Time Lost - Strikes & Lockouts	2.3	11.6	18.4	11.5
Time Lost – Average Changes	0.1	0.9	6.5	-1.8
Frequency - Strikes & Lockouts	0.7	1.9	2.5	1.8
Involvement - Strikes & Lockouts	241	444	605	463
Duration - Strikes & Lockouts	1.1	1.3	1.2	1.4
Inflation (GDP Deflator)	29	10	75	9
Unemployment Rate (%)	2.0	3.6	5.3	7.9
GDP Growth (%)	7.1	7.4	-13.1	3.7

Sources: See Data Sources Appendix.

Table 4: United States Stoppages and Related Data

Indicator	*1966-73 (a) Johnson/ Nixon*	*1974-81 Ford/ Carter*	*1982-89 Reagan Reagan*	*1990-97 Bush/ Clinton*
Time Lost – Lage-Scale Stoppages	358	222	85	37
Frequency - Lage-Scale Stoppages	4.2	2.5	0.5	0.3
Involvement - Lage-Scale Stoppages	5199	4650	6683	7746
Inflation (GDP Deflator)	4.4	8.1	3.6	2.5
Unemployment Rate (%)	4.5	6.9	7.3	6.1
Union Density (%)	25	23	18	15
GDP Growth (%)	3.9	2.5	3.6	2.8

Sources: See Data Sources Appendix. (a) Presidential names are only approximate to various periods.

Table 5: Australian Stoppages and Related Data

Indicator	*1981-92 Pre-Reform*	*1993-04 Reform*
Time Lost - Strikes & Lockouts	179	56
Frequency - Strikes & Lockouts	191	67
Involvement - Strikes & Lockouts	571	550
Duration - Strikes & Lockouts	2.0	1.6
Inflation (GDP Deflator)	6.7	2.1
Unemployment Rate (%)	8.0	7.6
Union Density (%) (a)	44	28
GDP Growth (%)	2.8	3.8

Sources: See Data Sources Appendix.

Data Sources Appendix

General Sources

Asian Development Bank (2004), *Key Indicators 2004*, Asian Development Bank, Manilla.

Organization of Economic Cooperation and Development (OECD), *Economic Outlook*, various issues available through EconData Pty Ltd.

OECD, *Main Economic Indicators*, various issues available through EconData.

World Bank (2004), *World Bank World Tables*, Washington.

International Labour Office (ILO), *Yearbook of Labour Statistics*, Geneva, various issues plus ILO website: http://laborsta.ilo.org/.

International Labour Office (2003), *Statistics of Trade Union Membership*, Unpublished, ILO Statistics Bureau.

India

Datt (2003a)

Labour Bureau, Government of India, *Pocket Book of Labour Statistics Year 2003 & 2004*, GOI, Simla.

Labour Bureau, Government of India, *Labour Statistics*, GOI, Simla.

Indonesia

Departemen Tenaga Kerja Dan Transmigrasi Pemerintah Republik Indosesia (2005) Tabel 10.2, Kasus Pemogokan, Tenaga Kerja Yang, Terlibat Dan Jam Kerja Yang Hilang, 1980-2000. [The Department of Labour and Transmigration of the Indonesian Republic, (2005)

Table 10.2, The Case of Labour Strikes pertaining to Lost Working Hours, 1980-2000].

Depnakertrans, Ditjen PHI, (2005), Pemogokan, Tahun 2001-2003. [The Department of Labour and Transmigration: General Directorate of PHI, (2005) Strike Year 2001-2003].

USA

US Department of Labor, Bureau of Labor Statistics (BLS), *Monthly Labor Review*, various issues.

BLS, *Employment and Earnings*, various issues.

Hirsch (2003).

Statistical Abstract of the United States, U.S. Dept. of Commerce, Bureau of the Census, *Historical Statistics of the United States: Colonial Times to 1970*.

Australia

TRYM Model Database, various issues available through EconData Pty Ltd.

Australian Bureau of Statistics, AusStats Data, various.

References

Agrawal, N. (1995), 'Indonesia: Labor Market Policies and International Competitiveness', Policy Research Working Paper 1515, World Bank.

Bhagwati, J. (1993), *India in Transition: Freeing the Economy*, Oxford, Clarendon Press.

Bhattacherjee, D. (2002), 'Organised Labour and Economic Liberalisation in India:Past, Present and Future', in Jose, A.V. (Ed.), *Organised Labour in the Twenty First Century*, International Institute of Labour Studies, Geneva, pp. 307-345.

Bidwai, P. (1997), 'More than Murder', reproduced from *Mid-Day, Mumbai*, 27 January at http://www.proxsa.org/economy/labor/orglabr.html. Accessed 17.07.2005.

Beasley, T. and Burgess, R. (2002), 'Can Labor Market Regulation Hinder Economic Performance? Evidence form India', CERP Discussion Paper No. 3260.

Briggs, C. (2004), 'The Return of the Lockout in Australia: a Profile of Lockouts since the Decentralisation of Bargaining', *Australian Bulletin of Labour*, vol. 30, No. 2, June, pp. 101-112.

Datt, R. (2003a), *Lockouts in India*, New Delhi, Manohar.

Datt, R. (2003b), *Economic Reforms, Labour and Employment*, Delhi, Deep & Deep Publications.

Desai, M. (2005), 'Will India Ever Catch Up With China?', *South Asia: Journal of South Asian Studies*, n.s, vol. XXVIII, No. 2, pp. 321-336.

Ghosh, S. (2004), 'Dispute Incidence in Manufacturing and Co-movements in Economic Activity: Evidence from India', *Indian Economic Review*, Vol. XXXIX, No. 2. pp. 349-369.

Hadiz, V.R. (1997), *Workers and the State in New Order Indonesia*, Routledge, London.

Hadiz, V.R. (2001), 'New Organising Vehicles in Indonesia: Origins and Prospects' in Hutchison, J. and Brown, A. (eds.), *Organising Labour in Globalising Asia*, Routledge, London.

Hadiz, V. R. and Robinson, R. (2005), 'Neo-Liberal Reforms and Illiberal Consolidations: The Indonesian Paradox', *Journal of Development Studies*, Vol. 41, No. 2, pp. 220-241.

Hirsch, B. T. (2003), 'Union Membership and Coverage Database from the Current Population Survey: Note', *Industrial and Labour Relations Review*, Vol. 56, No. 2, January pp. 349-54

Hodgkinson, A. and Perera, N. (2004), 'Strike Activity Under Enterprise Bargaining: Economics or Politics', *Australian Journal of Labour Economics*, vol. 7, pp. 439-457.

Johnson, H. (1991), *Sleepwalking Through History: America in the Reagan Years*, Doubleday, NY.

Kammen, D. (1997), 'A Time to Strike: Industrial Strikes and Changing Class Relations in New Order Indonesia', Unpublished PhD thesis, Cornell University.

Krueger, A. O. and Chinoy, S. (2002), 'The Indian Economy in Global Context', in Krueger, A. O. (ed.), *Economic Policy Reforms and the Indian Economy*, University of Chicago Press, Chicago, pp. 9-46.

Kuruvilla, S., Das, S., Kwon, H. and Kwon, S. (2002), 'Trade Union Growth and Decline in Asia', *British Journal of Industrial Relations*, vol. 40, pp. 431-461.

Kelly, J. and C. Nicholson (1980), 'Strikes and Other Forms of Industrial Action', *Industrial Relations Journal*, Vol. 11, No. 5, pp. 20-31.

Korpi, W. (1981), 'Unofficial Strikes in Sweden', *British Journal of Industrial Relations*, Vol. 19, No. 1, pp. 66-86.

Manning, C. (1998), *Indonesian Labour in Transition: An East Asian Success Story?*, Cambridge University Press, Cambridge.

Manning, C. (1999), 'Labour Institutions: The Case of Indonesia' in Barlow, C. (ed.) *Institutions and Economic Change in Southeast Asia*, Edward Elgar, Cheltenham.

Mathur, A.N. (1991), *Industrial Restructuring and Union Power*, ILO-ARTEP New Delhi.

Mizuno, K. (2005), 'The Rise of the Labor Movement and the Evolution of the Indonesian System of Industrial Relations: A case Study', *The Developing Economics*, XLIII-1 March, pp. 190-211.

Perry, L. J. (2005), 'Industrial Disputes in Indonesia: A Reassessment', *Labour and Management in Development*, Vol. 6, No. 1, pp. 1-17.

http://labour-management.anu.edu.au/volumes/prt/volsix/6-2-perry.pdf

Perry, L.J. (2006), 'Lockouts and Strikes: Some Comments on the Experience of India and Australia', *Australian Bulletin of Labour*, Vol. 32, No. 1, pp. 74-102.

Perry, L. J. and Wilson, Patrick J. (2004), 'Trends in Work Stoppages: A Global Perspective', Working Paper No. 47, November, Policy Integration Department, Statistical Development and Analysis Unit, International Labour Office.

http://www.ilo.org/public/english/bureau/integration/departme/about/working.htm

Rahaya, S.K. and Sumarto, S. (2003), 'The Practice of Industrial Relations in Indonesia', SMERU Working Paper, The SMERU Research Institute, March 2003.

Reagan, R. (1990), *An American Life*, Simon & Schuster, NY.

Rinakit, S. (1999), 'Trade Unions and Labour Unrest,' in Baker, R. *et al.* (ed), *Indonesia: The Challenge of Change*, Institute of Southeast Asian Studies: Singapore.

Robison, R. and Hadiz, V.R. (2004), *Reorganising Power in Indonesia: The Politics of Oligarchy in an Age of Markets*, Routeledge Curzon, London.

Sen Gupta, A. . and Sett, P.K. (2000), 'Industrial Relations Law, Employment Security and Collective Bargaining in India: Myths, Realities and Hope', *Industrial Relations Journal*, Vol. 31, pp. 144-53.

Sanyal, P. and Menon, N. (2004), 'Labor Regulation and the Economics of Firm Geography: Evidence From India', Working Paper available from the SSRN Electronic Paper Collection.

Sharma, A.N. (2004), 'Globalisation, Labour Markets and Poverty: Towards an Agenda for Decent Work in India', paper prepared for the 1st Global Labour Forum held during the 5th Asian Regional Congress of the International Industrial Relations Association, June 23-26.

Smith, A. (1776), *An Enquiry into the Nature and Causes of the Wealth of Nations*, 2 Volumes, Liberty Classics, Reprint from Oxford University Press, 1976.

Sodhi, J. S. and Plowman, D. H. (2001), *Economic Change and Industrial Relations: India and Australia*, Scholastic Press Australia, Nedlands.

The Economist (1997), 'A Survey of India', 22 February.

The Economist (2005), 'The Tiger in Front', 5 March.

Tendulkar, S. D. (2003), 'Organised Labour Markets in India Pre and Post Reform', Conference on Anti Poverty and Social Policy in India, MacArthur Research Network on Inequality and Economic Performance, Neemrana Fort Palace, Alwar, Rajasthan, January 2-4.

Turner, H.A. (1969), *Is Britain Really Strike Prone? A Review of the Incidence, Character and Costs of Industrial Conflict*, Occasional Paper No 20, University of Cambridge, Department of Economics, Cambridge UP, Cambridge.

Venkata Ratnam, C.S. (2001), *Globalisation and Labour-Management Relations: Dynamics of Change*, Response Books, New Delhi.

Western, B. (1997), *Between Class and Market: Postwar Unionization in the Capitalist Democracies*, Princeton UP, Princeton.

Wooden, M. (2005) 'Australia's Industrial Relations Reform Agenda', 34th Conference of Economists Conference, University of Melbourne, 26-28 September.

http://www.melbourneinstitute.com/people/mwooden/ace05_%20ir_reform_agenda.pdf

World Bank (2004), *World Bank World Tables*, Washington.

World Bank (2005), *World Development Report 2005: A Better Investment Climate for Everyone*, Washington.

Yoshihara, K. (1988), *The Rise of Ersatz Capitalism in Southeast Asia*, Oxford University Press, Singapore.

Zagha, R. (1999), 'Labour and India's Economic Reforms' in Sachs, J. and Varshney, A. (eds), *India in the Era of Economic Reforms*, Oxford University Press, New Delhi.

Endnotes

1. See for example the entire February 2005 edition of *Journal of Development Studies*, Vol. 41, No. 2.
2. This is the case when Gross National Income is expressed in US dollar terms for the Year 2003. When expressed in purchasing power parity terms (PPP), Australia has the third largest economy after India and Indonesia for 2003. See World Bank World Tables.
3. See *Monthly Labor Review*, May 1982, p. 102 and June 1982, p. 111 (US Department of Labor, Bureau of Labor Statistics).
4. Official Indonesian data for the year 1988, during which the average duration of disputes was an aberrant 10 days, records

working hours lost as 607,265. Kammen (1997, p. 427), also reporting official government data from 'various media sources', records 60,726 working hours lost. Kammen's number implies an average duration of strikes of 1 day. This paper employs Kammen's number.

5. For worldwide comparisons see Perry and Wilson (2004).
6. Time lost due to stoppages is the product of the frequency, involvement and duration of stoppages. Thus: Time Lost ≡ Frequency × Involvement × Duration. Expressed differently: $WDL/LF \equiv NID/LF \times WI/NID \times WDL/WI$ where *WDL* refers to working days lost due to work stoppages, *LF* refers to the labour force, *NID* refers to the number of work stoppages and *WI* refers to the number of workers involved in work stoppages.
7. These data are not considered to be very reliable. See Venkata Ratnam (2001).
8. Ghosh (2004) found disputes in Indian manufacturing were pro-cyclical for the period 1964-1997.
9. See also Agrawal (1995), Manning (1999), Ranakit (1999) and Hadiz (1997, 2001).
10. This period saw the rise of unsanctioned unions and various non-government organizations championing workers rights. See Hadiz (1997).
11. Mizuno (2005, p. 190) notes that shortly after the resignation of President Soeharto in May 1998, greater freedom was granted to unions. With the coming to office of Habibie: 'Long-standing government intervention in the Indonesian labour movement was stifled with the ratification of the ILO Convention No. 87 on freedom of association and protection of the right to organise. This was done under Presidential Decree No. 83 in June 1998. This step helped increase the number of labour federations at a national level from 1 only under the Soeharto regime to 74 as of October 2003'. See Mizuno for further details.

10

RESTRUCTURING AND EMPLOYMENT ADJUSTMENT, JAPANESE EXPERIENCE: LESSONS FOR INDIA

Sib Ranjan Misra

In spite of Japan's profound success until 1994-95 as one of the most industrialized countries with least labour tensions and lowest unemployment rate, Japan witnessed some structural changes like demographic changes, institutional changes and social changes in recent years along with sluggishness in the economy since 1994. All these changes have exerted remarkable influence on the labour market, i.e., employment and methods of employment adjustment. Japan has been facing certain problems. One, the ageing society, fall in the birth rate and absolute decline in the younger population; two, the hollowing out of industries or 'de-industrialization' because of increasing transplantations of manufacturing operations abroad, may be, because of high cost structure and operational behaviour of market system in Japan. This relocation might outpace the creation of new jobs at home.

However, it should be mentioned that in spite of these, Japan's unemployment rate is much lower than unemployment rates in other countries.

Japanese wage levels are among the highest in the world. And finally, the amount of frictions and the low level of mandays lost due to strikes or lock-outs is the least. In 1994,

1,153 labour disputes were recorded in Japan, involving 4.5 lac employees. The number of days lost by these work stoppage amounted to 9.3 lac days which translates to 2.1 days per affected employee. In the USA, there were 4,800 disputes involving 1.7 million employees leading to 33 million working days lost. This translates to a much higher days, i.e., 19.4 days lost per affected employee.

Two observations are in order. One, a review of the relationship between the rate of growth in Gross Domestic Product (GDP) and the annual rate of increase of wages for all workers in Japan clearly reveals that the labour in Japan has been enjoying quite satisfactorily the benefits of economic growth in terms of high real wage rates. This is true even during the periods of recession when the real wage rates did not witness any decline whatsoever. There had been consistently higher increase in wages, in comparison to the average annual increase. An analysis of the data on increase in real wages during the period 1955-2000 of the top 1,000 companies listed in the Tokyo Stock Exchange will corroborate this. Second, by plotting the data on rates of growth of GDP and the rate of change in unemployment over the last four decades, it can be safely asserted even during recession, the unemployment rate used to remain stable. In effect, the returns to economic growth to the labour market which are reflected through an increase in wages and employment opportunities in Japan are remarkable. This helps maintain a sense of equity and social justice among the labour force participants.

10.1 Institutional Forces and Employment Adjustment Mechanisms in Japan

Unlike the practice of employment of labour pursued generally in different countries, the management and the employers in Japan used to lay emphasis more on employment security, rather than on job security. Once a person is employed in a company, he is required not to engage in a particular job. Once he is put on a payroll of a particular company, he may be required to work at different jobs or professions of the company. And so long as there is the guarantee or security of employment of a labour, enterprise unions respond flexibly to a variety of measures and policies adopted by the employers as and when required for employment adjustment. 'Employment security, and not job security of an employee in a particular company is a distinguishing feature of Japanese employment system (Rao, 1999).

For the excellent performance of Japan in maintaining a stable and low level of unemployment and at the same time, achieving employment adjustment without any frictions whatsoever, the following factors are generally considered responsible.

One, the unique or distinguishing characteristics of Japanese employment system, and two, also, in order to adjust, during the cyclical fluctuations, different methods employed by the employers.

Japan's favourable performance in employment market may be attributed to the distinguishing features of the market. They are, among others, life-time employment system, seniority-based wage system, enterprise unions, on-the-job training system, and severance payments.

10.1.1 Life-time Employment

The Japanese workers are under life-time commitment. It is only the tradition that dictates that a person once joins a company will continue to work. It is a custom or a practice, not enforced by any law or by contract. The system is a normative assumption mutually shared by management and workers rather than a set of objective rules and practices (Nakamura and Nitta, 1995). Employees neither quit nor refuse any job assignment; on the other hand, employers use not to fire or lay-off any employee of their company. The employees use to receive training and education within the company. They also receive experiences of various kinds of jobs through rotations and transfer in the course of which they obtain promotions. This system applies principally to employees of large enterprises, perhaps about 30 per cent of the regular full-time and mostly male workforce.

Large companies have become larger, because they have enjoyed monopolistic advantages in marketing and technology. Some of these advantages might have been accrued in the process as the result of growth, but for those companies, to become large, they must have possessed some advantages initially. They developed the advantages, because they employed people of better quality with more drive, better skills, and more professional knowledge. Life-time employment can be seen as a means of securing such people.

Japan was a latecomer on the scene of industrialization and grew much faster than western countries. Rapid industrialization meant a scarcity of skilled people. In order to meet their requirements, Japan's companies had to recruit people with good potential and training. If they lost such people after training, they would loose many things. They had to devise some measures to induce them to stay. As a guarantee of employment in the future, life-time employment scheme was such a measure (Dore, 1973).

The Japanese seem to have more obligations to the I E households, and to the ancestors and also to the society at large (Ranis, 1955). Business was not something that could be pursued single-mindedly, ignoring their obligations. Obligations to the IE, for example, made the employers considerate to the employees. Japanese put more emphasis on social needs, stable relationship and long-term interests (Abbeglen, 1958).

The psychological traits of the Japanese may have had something to do with the establishment of lifetime employment system. In fact, in Japan, there was practically no transition period from feudalism to capitalism. In Japan, although some traditions had to be modified to allow innovations, many retained, because the people just emerged out from the long-drawn feudal period, and were not completely ready for individualistic, predominantly pecuniary needs. Japanese capitalism had to start with a number of feudal values. Important among those are those derived from the low degree of horizontal mobility and the subsistence nature of the economy. There was a well-defined and stable social hierarchy and hence a great deal of co-operation in economic and social fields.

A system of long-time employment practices reduces employment fluctuations and provides stability for the economy as a whole. This practice is found to be highly effective with respect to job, in which teamwork is important and in relation to vocational abilities that require a build-up over time. For Japanese companies and the Japanese economy and society as a whole, it seems pertinent to focus on stabilizing employment, there by improving employees' morale and securing the flexibility needed for corporate growth. Hasty employment adjustment may sometime cause companies to loose credibility and make it more difficult to obtain required workers. The life-time employment ideal, in particular, works to eliminate employee resistance to technical changes and innovations. An employment system, based on the contract ideal, encourages employees to improve their specific skills or job qualifications. The life-time employment ideal, however, encourages employees to become familiar with the variety of skills they are likely to need during their lengthy employment with the firm. This is also made possible because the life-time employment system involves job rotations and job variety, making it more conducive to technological innovations.

The need for a sense of belonging—what the Japanese psychologists call AMAE—a sense of belonging, obligation, loyalty, integrity and consensus—fosters attitude of subordinate dependence and mutual dependence between the employers and the employees. The sense of loyalty is not typically from the subordinates to the superiors rather than a two-way reciprocal (Leibenstein, 1984).

In Japan, a generalist is valued more than a specialist. Hence, when an employee is trained in different sections of the company, he can very well understand the connections between different sections and he is more effective. Hence, the bidding away of a middle manager is not taking place in Japan. Employee's worth is company specific. Because of this system, employers have low transaction costs like advertising, and recruiting. Job turnover and the related costs are low. Japanese employees are identified with their employers.

On the other hand, the practice of long-term employment encourages investment in firm-specific human capital. With long-term commitment from workers, employers can safely invest in training their workers. Employees also do not quit after training. The system of deferred payments and steep wage-age profile help to enforce the practice.

Due to life-time employment, job rotation, commitment to the company and a steady movement in the same company hierarchy over time make the employees in Japan more motivated to work harder.

It, therefore, appears that the system provides reasonable benefits to both the employees and the employers

10.1.2. On-the-Job Training System

Wide and rapidly changing product lines require flexible production system, cycle-time reduction and generalist multi-skilled employees who could respond to changing needs. Japanese companies tend to proliferate products and features, serve all market segments, sell through multiple channels and emulate one another's approaches. The Japanese firms are reluctant to hire mid-career specialists; hence, they, on their own, had to design their programme for training their own employees.

In line with this spirit, there is a need for developing skills through training of the employees. In Japan, life-time employment is associated with human investment for this end in view. On-the job-training approach is an important method. The genesis of this approach was practically due to the existence of tight labour market along with the abundant supply of unskilled or semi-skilled labour during 1950s and 1960s. 'On-The-JobnTraining system' is considered more imperative for the blue-collar workers to acquire skills which is generally organized through job rotation among different production lines in the company.

10.1.3. Seniority-based Wage System—NENKO JORETSU

Long-term employment is linked to wages, which increase with seniority. Promotion and wage increase in Japan depend upon length of service an employee has put to a company, rather than upon merit. Under the scheme, the system is that the wages which were fixed at the time of recruitment would go on increasing automatically with an annual increment after the expiry of each year's services.

In the seniority wage system, the retirement benefits are sufficiently higher than proportional to the length of service. The earning prospects of an employee at retirement age depends upon their past work performance. The best workers may even be promoted to the position of management in the company or in one of its subsidiaries. The steep age-earning profile encourages for long job tenure by reducing the risk that workers will leave the company to work elsewhere. Moving to another company implies significant loss of income.

It appears that in Japan, a steep age-earning profile, promotion based on seniority and the lump sum payments at the time of retirement—all together act as the incentives for the employees to work hard and not to leave the existing firm.

10.1.4. Enterprise Unions—In-house Labour Unions

Enterprise unions are organized in Japan on the basis of individual enterprises or workplace rather than a trade or an industry. An enterprise union includes only employees of a single firm. All regular, non-managerial employees, including both blue-collar and white-collar employees may join. Line managers, supervisors and junior management personnel are also included. This has affected the style and attitude of unions in Japan by 'inhibiting militance, providing expertise and creating more contact and perhaps some egalitarianism between blue collar and white collar employees' (Gould, 1984). However, part-time and temporary employees are excluded. Membership is quasi-mandatory for regular employees in many enterprises, a situation which effectively locks out competing unions. Almost all large firms are unionized. But the organization rate is very low and falling in small and medium sized enterprises (SMEs). SMEs are defined as companies having less than 300 employees or which are capitalized at less than 100 million Yen. Since unions are company based, collective bargaining or consultation procedures usually take place at the level of the firm.

A major advantage of enterprise unions is that they are well-positioned to understand both the needs of the employees and also the financial position of the company when conducting collective bargaining. They are effective in promoting communication between labour and management.

Enterprise unions are organized to constitute industrial federations. They may be affiliated to the centralized national labour organization. Both the industrial federations and national organizations are entrusted with the responsibilities to deal with the issues, institutional and political, as and when required, which are difficult at the enterprise level to handle. Unions act as the mediating force between objective conditions like cost of living, profitability and wage outcomes.

Japanese enterprise unions play an active role in matters of direct concerns to workers such as wage fixation, employees benefits and working conditions. In addition, enterprise unions are said to have various advantages over trade unionism, which is typical in other countries. One advantage is that there is no jurisdictional dispute concerning union job. in enterprise unions. This permits flexibility in in-company training and job assignment and is conducive to greater labour productivity. Under enterprise unions, labour management relations have been quite co-operative.

Neither the union federations before 1987 nor the new RENGO since 1987 took part in collective bargaining with employers. It is the enterprise unions themselves that negotiate with the management of their firms in the annual Spring Offensive'. Rengo, however, serves as the voice for the unions in general and publicizes union's general demands concerning wages and other working conditions.

10.1.5. SHUNTO

In Japan, under the direction and co-ordination of national organizations and individual federations, each enterprise union negotiates with its management on wage levels and working conditions in each spring of the year. It refers to the unique institutionalized process in each spring. Spring is the appropriate time for wage bargaining, because April 1 is the beginning of the financial year in Japan. April is also the time when many companies recruit new workers, following the end of the school year in March and set up entry level wages and adjustment in the wage scales.

Representing the employers is the Japan's Federation of Employer's Association or NIKKEIREN. It counterbalances union's initial demand by publicizing the reasons for any wage restraint. By February of each year, individual enterprise unions put forward their own demand to their management, occasionally with some advice given at the industry or national level. The actual beginning also takes place at the enterprise level. Historically, settlements in few strategic industries like private railway workers, iron and steel industry workers, metal industry workers served as the pattern setters. The pattern of settlement reached in the private unionized sectors are closely followed by settlements in the public sectors. Small non-unionized firms also try to follow the same pattern with some variations because of the varying conditions in the small firms. Since the late-1980s, unions have included reduced working hours as part of their Shunto demands.

Annual wage revisions through collective bargaining repeat with ritual regularity since 1956. Wage functions depend upon independent variables like cost of living, labour market conditions, and firm's profitability, which largely explain how wages should change. In Shunto, the settlements of firms serve as unofficial guidelines for the rest of the economy. The system has provided the advantages of formally coordinated system, but it is more flexible. About 80 per cent of the organized workers participate in the Shunto. Government civil servants do not have the right to bargain over their pay.

10.1.6. Severance Payment—Taishoku kin

Almost every worker receives a severance payment. This amounts to two or three years of pay after retirement between the age of 55 and 60 years. Employees who leave jobs before the standard retirement age receive severance payment. This is more generous in the cases of discharges than that in the cases when the employees on their own take decision to leave, thereby discouraging indirectly employees from quitting. Corporate pension system is still not in practice in Japan.

10.1.7. Labour-Management Relations

The right to organize, to bargain collectively and to strike is provided by Japan's labour law for private sector employees.

Labour-management relations in Japan, however, are generally characterized by co-operation, and not confrontation. Since the first oil crisis, the number of labour disputes decreased steadily. Labour-management relations have been generally co-operative and harmonious.

This co-operative labour-management relations can be seen in a number of ways. Annual wage increases, for example, determined in an institutionalized bargaining process known as Spring Offensive with reasonable outcomes and without serious work stoppage. There is no denying the fact that, for example, the USA has a labour force nearly twice as large as that of Japan, but the number of workdays lost, for example, in the year 1989, was more than 77 times as large. Britain had a labour force that is slightly less than half that of Japan; but, its workdays lost in 1989 was nearly 19 times that of Japan.

As for reasons for low incidence of labour disputes in Japan, the conventional argument is that the rate of unionization among workers declined in the 1970s and 1980s, due to the decline of traditional industries which were highly unionized and the increased use of non-unionized temporary and part-time employees in the economy. But some economists attribute this harmonious kind of Japan's industrial relations to more fundamental reason which is that the company in Japan is a community with which all employees identify and in which they have important stakes in terms of profit sharing, bonuses, job security and participation in decision making (Abbeglen and Stalk, 1985, Dore, 1987, Ozako, 1991). Both Japanese management and unions operate within the same industrial culture 'Shimoda'. Workers are not treated as hired labour, bought and sold in the corporate labour market and the company is not the property of the stock-holders to be bought and sold as they wish. Thus the Japanese corporate model differs fundamentally from the western neo-classical model of the firm (Aoki, 1988).

Again, in Japan, the sense of corporate community on the part of the employees is strengthened by the fact that there are no marked differences between blue collar and white collar employees within a company both belong to the same enterprise union and income differences between top executives and the rank and file workers are relatively small. Employees are also trained by the company to acquire wide-ranging skills. This further blurs the distinctions between the blue collar and white-collar employees. All these contribute to what Koike calls the white-collarization of workers. Employee's sense of participation is also enhanced by such widespread practices as workers' participation in quality' control circles for product improvement, joint labour management consultation system concerning various aspects of work and complaint settlement system to adjudicate workers' grievances. In all these practices, the Japanese respect for consensus ensures that employees' views are taken into account seriously.

10.1.8. Decision Making

Japanese companies and other organizations in Japan generally try to seek a broad–based consensus in their decision-making. Two phases of the traditional decision-making process can be distinguished. The first one, sometime referred to as NEMAWASHI, is the informal pre-decision process of discussions and accommodation of views to prepare the ground for the formation of consensus. The second phase involves the formal drafting of a proposal for circulation among units of an organization for consultations, comments and approval. The procedure is referred to as the RINGI system, where RIN means submitting a proposal to one's superior for approval and GI means deliberations and decisions. In the procedure, a low-echelon management staff member first drafts a formal document 'RINGISO', outlining problems and his recommendations. The document is then reviewed and approved by the related units of the organization and finally evaluated and approved by the top-level management. After the approval, the document is returned to the original drafter for implementation. One implication of the system is that top executives lack the power to make quick 'top-down' decision. Even if the idea originally comes from a top executive, he would still entrust a lower staff member who would be involved in its implementation to draft the RINGI document. In this way the final decision would have the co-operation of more people after the proposal has gone through the due process.

As it appears, the system provides a mechanism for consultation with different departments, helps co-ordinate their activities and ensures the smooth implementation of the proposal. This consensus based decision making process reduces accountability and shields individuals from direct responsibility even if the proposal proves to be ill-advised and falls flat.

At the operational and shop floor level of an enterprise, decision making tends to be decentralized and organized on the basis of small groups. The famous Quality Control group is an example. True, this kind of decision making procedure is superior to the more centralized type, because it promotes sharing of technical knowledge among workers and cultivates a habit of thinking holistically on the part of the employees, thereby avoiding the demoralization and alienation of workers (Ozaki, 1991).

In view of the above mentioned features characterizing the Japanese employment market, practices and institutional forms, the unemployment rate used to remain stable for quite a long period.

Japan has become a major force in the world economy virtually in all fast growing high technology industries. Japan also has achieved this with relatively low level of unemployment and that too, with less frictions in the event of employment adjustment. This has made Japan a rare example of successful adjustment, in spite of the fact that the economy has to undergo quite often a very thorough structural adjustment process

10.2 Employment Adjustment Process in Japan—A Review

In Japan, labour and management used to give topmost priority to employment security of the employees. In the process of employment adjustment, this strategy is kept in mind. The following is the order according to which different steps are taken to conduct employment adjustment. Dismissal or retrenchment of an employee from a job is considered as the last resort.

Reduction of working hours is the first step.

Secondly, the company may adopt the step of personal transfer as the next.

To overcome redundant employees, the companies use to transfer an employee from one job to another within the same firm. Transfer of workplace is also common.

Thirdly, attrition and suspension of new hiring is the third step.

Fourthly, steps to reduce labour costs are taken by reducing over-time, bonus and sometime, wages.

Next comes temporary release of employees from work.

Sixthly, the company is to ask for voluntary retirement.

Seventhly, the company may ask for compulsory retirement.

And finally, the company may be required to dismiss and retrench employees.

10.2.1. Flexibility of Working Hours

Given the unwillingness of the firms to reduce regular full-time employee during economic down trend, firms have to take steps to absorb fluctuations in output by adjusting working hours per employee. The employees are, of course, kept on pay roll. Over-time will be reduced. And then scheduled working hours will be adjusted as and when necessary. It is true that the adjustment of working time in response to cyclical changes has made the variability of working hours relatively high in Japan which happens to be the highest in comparison to the variability in other countries like USA (standard deviation 1.4), Germany (standard deviation 1.6), and U.K. (standard deviation 1.7), in 1999. (EPA, White Paper, 1999). This, of course, stems from the fluctuations in over-time work.

Against this background, firms tend to hire part-time staff who tend to have fixed-terms contract. This provides firms with added flexibility in adjusting size of the work-force, thus enabling to maintain low labour costs. Firms need not have to pay benefits like pensions, health insurance and pay-roll taxes on employees.

10.2.2. Transfers of Employees

Another measure for adjustment in Japan is that the employees may be re-assigned among different divisions within the same company. Of course, in the event of severity of business fluctuations, if the transfer of this kind within the same company is not found to be feasible and sufficient, then the employees may be sent or leased out to some other companies. It may also happen that the employees may be transferred to some affiliates of the same company.

Here, it should be noted that diversification in Japanese industries is a frequent phenomenon. The commitment to employment to the core labour force of the different industrial units, largely large, at least until the last ditch before bankruptcy, is a strong reason for preferring diversification to retrenchment. Of course, high levels of gearing, bank creditors who could tolerate postponed re-payment, shareholders accustomed to low level of dividends, the taboo on take-over threats may be other factors which provides breathing space for planning diversification to make the long term investment in training, research and market development as well as equipment.

The intra-industry diversification is quite easy; because most firms have tenacious sense of belongings to a particular industry. Again, an Aluminium smelting industry could shift easily its operations towards the manufacture of window frames, but very rarely from spinning to electronic companies. The direction of diversification was also determined by technological expertise. In Japan, diversification used to take place setting up an internal project—from within, gradually accumulating expertise from its own work place. Again, in Japan, diversification is not that easy through acquisitions or mergers or take-over.

10.2.3. Attrition and Stoppage in New Recruitment

Another strategy which the firms use to practise to adopt to reduce the workforce in case of down-turn in business activities is to reduce or even to stop the hiring or intake of mid-career employees in the firms. The firms will also be reluctant to renew contract of future employment with the part-time, seasonal or temporary workers. If situations are acute, the employers may resort to the step of dismissal of these employees. On the contrary, to trim the labour force, the companies are sincerely reluctant to dismiss or dislodge a permanent employee.

10.2.4. Wage Flexibility

This is also an aspect which has helped the employers to adjust to downturn in business activities in Japan without resorting to layoffs. Employee's compensation in Japan generally consists of three components—cash wages scheduled for payment on a monthly basis, which constitutes about 72 per cent of total wage on an average in 1994, bonus payments, 23 per cent and over-time pay, about 5 per cent (OECD Survey, Japan, 1998, pp. 112). Aggregate wages, both in nominal and real terms, have shown more variability in Japan than in other major OECD countries during the last forty years, thus contributing to Japan's low and stable unemployment rate.

Over-time pay is another reason for wage flexibility. Although this is the smallest component of earnings, over-time hours and pay fluctuate during the economic cycle. The use of semi-annual bonuses also contributes to wage flexibility. Bonus payments are reduced when unions agree that bonus is linked to profit payments. By doing so, the personal costs are being adjusted with flexibility.

Changes in pay structures in Japan are more sensitive to firm's performance, as measured by over-all profits-sale ratio and the tightness of labour markets as measured by job-offer to applicants ratio.

The responsiveness of wages to unemployment adjustment which has been the key to preventing the increase in unemployment is substantially higher in Japan than other countries (Layard, Nickali and Jackman, 1991).

10.2.5. Temporary Release of the Working Staff

Under this system of release temporarily, some or all employees are released from work, depending upon the gravity of the situation, for a certain period, of course, without disturbing the employment relationship. As per the Labour

Standard Law, the company is required to pay sixty per cent of the employee's average salary as a temporary release allowance during this period of temporary release.

10.2.6.Voluntary and Compulsory Retirement

There is an emphasis on how to avoid painful decision as much as possible in the process of employment adjustment, because maintenance of employment relationship in Japan is of more crucial importance. If the above measures, 01-05, are found inadequate, another resort is to solicit voluntary resignations, generally, from relatively older expensive employees, a few years before *Teinen* or mandatory retirement, implied in the notion of long-term employment scheme. This is to be 'sweetened' by generous financial settlements (Dore, 1984). When an employer solicits a resignation, he is seen to transgressing the implicit right of a regular employee to work until *Teinen* So the lump-sum severance payment for such resignations carries the price for the breach of trust, in addition to the pro-rated *Teinen* lump-sum to take account of the shortened length of service.

When this has to be done, the first method was to announce the number of persons desired for resignations together with the designations of the desired age -brackets. If a sufficient number came forward by the dead line, that finished the business. If there were not enough volunteers, another round of solicitation was made. The employers sometime approach employees and pat their shoulders to urge an early retirement. If the method failed to generate the desired reduction of employment, specific individuals were picked and asked to volunteer to resign. The way the individuals were chosen for this honour generally suggests that they were actually fired.

10.2.7. Retrenchment and Final Dismissal

Employers in Japan accept an obligation not to dismiss their regular employees. At the same time, the employees feel an obligation not to desert, though are not bound by. The employers completely believe employees to work with reasonable conscientiousness in order to make the firm a success. On the other hand, the employees believe the employers not to play ducks and drakes with their interests (Dore, 1984).

Against this backdrop, dismissal of an employee, the final option of a firm for employment adjustment, is still sparingly used. Of course, the dismissal of an employee in Japan is not an easy job. Employees are legally protected. Employees cannot be dismissed when they are on medical leave, child care leave etc. Practice of discriminatory treatment on the basis of nationality, creed etc. is not encouraged. Employers are required to serve a 30 day-notice on the employee before dismissal, otherwise, he is to pay the wages, averages, for the period of 30 days. On the whole, dismissal without a reasonable factor is tantamount to the abuse of labour and subjected to punishment.

Sometime, because of continuous fall in corporate profits and other reasons, the employers are compelled to go in for dismissal of employees. This kind of dismissal is 'Adjustment Dismissal'. This, in fact, results from employer's convenience

The explanation of sequencing of different steps is as follows.

The decision to freeze hiring mid-career employees is the easiest to make with no adverse effects on the employees. Non-renewal of employment contract may disappoint some of the employees. The reduction of over-time work and some other measures resulting in the reduction of working days may generate lower earnings. The next bundle of measures—transfer and loaning out of employees—would be more onerous to the employees than the reduction of overtime.

Disappointment, frustration and financial losses on the part of the employees would be greater in cases of lay-offs due to temporary slackening or closure of business. Transfer to different plants, temporary lay-offs, voluntary resignations and selective discharges are looked upon as grave threats to employment security by Japanese employees. By far, the most popular measures were hiring freeze and over-time cut backs.

What made the Japanese management to behave in this way? To the Japanese, the maintenance of stable employment relationship is of crucial value. In order to avoid disruption in employment relationship, even the measure like termination of an employment relationship, like voluntary resignations solicited by the employer is generally sweetened by 'generous financial settlement.'

10.3. Managing the Process in Japan

The major impact of the first 'oil shock' followed by Yen appreciation in 1985 on the Japanese economy is the large scale employment adjustment, being carried out by domestic manufacturers. Others are rationalization and streamlining of business firms, spurring of overseas direct investment and the resulting erosion of domestic industrial base, or, de-industrialization has progressed obviously in Japan. In the manufacturing sector, production in consumer-related industries has increased; while, production in machinery related industries which are heavily reliant on exports and in material industries, in steel, non-ferrous and metal industries, among others, has declined conspicuously. By size of manufacturing firms, production has plummeted in big firms. An increasing number of manufacturers have advanced into non-manufacturing fields in the form of establishing subsidiaries and new types of firms,thus actively transferring regular employees between industries and firms.

These trends triggered a variety of employment adjustment measures. The major policy measure for employment adjustment were restriction on overtime work, reduction and suspension of mid-career recruits, transfers and temporary lay-offs and voluntary retirement. The lack of inter-firm mobility resulting from long-term practices in Japan is compensated, to some extent, by mobility within the firms and its affiliated companies, possibly with an objective of qualifying for eligibility for employment adjustment subsidy from the government. The discretion to reassign employees to other jobs helps make it possible for firms to avoid lay-offs during the period of fall in demand for one of its products. Production employees may be transferred, for example, from assembly lines to sales outlets during the down-turn. Companies also attempted to adjust labour forces over the past years through the increased use of early retirement as a supplement to the attrition and across the board wage-cuts.

In Japan, the role of the government in employment adjustment and protection of the unemployed is minimal and indirect. The government tries to protect the interests of the employees mainly through legislations and legal regulations (Rao, 2001).

The two important laws—the Employment Security Law and the Unemployment Insurance Law—were enacted by the Government in 1947, which remained effective till 1973. These two laws acted as the foundation of the employment policy of the Government. 1950 witnessed a period of rapid unemployment in some industries like coal mining. This was caused largely due to changes in technology and energy revolution. Automatically, these industries had to go in for re-structuring. Efforts were made to promote employment of those workers laid off from the coal industry, the declining industries to the newly established growing industries. In this connection, the Labour Standard Law, 1947, was enacted in 1947. This law sets up minimum working conditions and terms of work. It laid down maximum hours, 8 hours per day and 48 hours per week. It also dealt with such matters as unemployment insurance, worker's compensation old age special security programmes. This law has been revised in 1988 to help introduce a shorter 40-hour work per week and to ensure that the employees take all holidays that they are entitled to.

Afterwards, during the sixties and early seventies, the unemployment Insurance Law played important role. A set of new laws relating to employment measures were enacted. All these laws were directed towards the restraining of dismissal and prevention of unemployment. At the same time, a policy for creating employment opportunities started to be implemented in a large measure to arrest unemployment growth.

Another significant law, the Employment Insurance Law was passed in order to prevent unemployment along with the schemes for generation of opportunities for employment in the spring of 1974. This was, of course, a radical refinement of the earlier Unemployment Insurance Law. This law was passed as a part of the Employment Insurance scheme to improve employment. Under the system, employers who need to reduce employment, because of recessions, can receive subsidies from the Government upto one-half, for large firms, or two-thirds, for small and medium-sized firms, of their payments to their temporarily laid-off employees for a maximum of 75 days. Hence, this law provided a very effective policy instrument for preventing or restricting dismissal.

Since 1980, the Government protects the interests of the employees through strict regulation. Even during the decline of the industries, it was not an easy job to dismiss an employee by an employer. Dismissals were used very sparingly, in part, because of legal barriers that boost the costs to a very high level.

Another important feature of the Government policies is the closer linkages of employment policies with vocational ability development policy. Development of occupational skills became an area of increased focus due to increasing technological changes. The Human Resource Development Promotion Law was formulated to take care of this aspect. When employers provide vocational training, particularly, for middle-aged and older employees to gain increasing knowledge and skills for new jobs, grants are provided by the Government to cover two-thirds of the wages during the training period. Under the Policy on Job-Type employment Stability Law, subsidies are extended to employers who take measures to promote employment stability.

In view of redundancy, the Government used to formulate an economic stimulus package, aimed broadly at generating new employment opportunities and employment stability for employees The features of the employment package are:

1. to increase the capacity of work-places as a whole
2. to help workers to improve their employability
3. to bridge the gap in requirements between the demand and supply of labour and
4. to secure a safety net.

In fact, the focus of employment strategies has gradually shifted from the after-the-effect policies to pre-emptive policies with objectives such as preventing unemployment and simultaneously, expanding opportunities for employment.

The range of measures has been generally expanding to include employment maintenance, mis-match matching and job-creation measures.

The Equal Opportunity Law was passed in 1985 in Japan, making it altogether illegal to maintain sex-differentiated policies for employee recruitment, training and promotion. This Law forbids employers to discriminate on the grounds of sex in regard to employee training, recruitment, promotions and benefits and requires employers to endeavour to provide women the same opportunities as men in hiring, job assignment and promotion. It extends maternity leave from 12 weeks as provided for in the Labour Standards Law of 1947 to 14 weeks. So, this Law combines protective provisions for women with promotion of equality between the sexes. 'Of course, this Law embodies no explicit penalties for non-compliance' (Rani, 2003; MIT Dictionary, 2002).

The Government recognizes explicitly the major factors leading to structural and frictional unemployment. They include the expansion of mis-match due to structural changes in labour force supply and demand, mis-match among age-groups expanded after the collapse of the bubble economy, mis-match among the industries, employment directed towards the growing industries, mis-match among regions witnessed after the oil crisis in some areas where manufacturing industries were concentrated, employment worsening largely because of transfer of production bases over-seas, hollowing out of industries etc.. Labour market has been compartmentalized according to occupation-type and industry type.

As to why Japan has reasonably succeeded in achieving structural adjustment in employment without significant frictions, the reasons are in order. The extra-ordinary employment adjustment would have been impossible if workers, either individually or collectively resisted change. The workers and unions are made to appear always adjusting to changes imposed by management and Government. Workers and unions actually appreciated the need for adjustment precisely in the same way as government and management did. Workers individually saw the writings on the walls, so to speak, and exercised ingenuity and initiative in leaving the threatened jobs for new jobs opening up elsewhere. Unions, instead of fighting the change, co-operated by defining the pace of change compatible with industrial peace. To the extent that management's sensitivity, prudence and strategy were in tune with the workers' and unions' capabilities to adopt, it was possible to find an optimum pace and style of employment adjustment. 'Japan's corporate sector works through pervasive consultations among Government agencies, business groups, labour unions and employees' (Dore, 1984).

To help create new jobs and new industries, the Government is consistently extending financial support to different agencies in order to defray expenses for recruitment costs and a part of the wages to small and medium-sized industries which are starting projects. This is particularly meant for those industries in those regions which are affected by hollowing out of industries. The main argument for this kind of policy is that these projects would act as the safety nets for those workers who would have been discharged from the existing declining industries The Government supports. also to create special zones for growth. This depends largely on the initiatives of the local governments and private firms which are better placed for identifying the suitability of the appropriate industries. The zones may also have the potentials to promote the development of clusters of businesses within the zones, such as the production of ethanol from cotton for use as automotive fuel, allowing joint stock companies to run hospitals, open schools etc. in special zones.

In Japan, in order to avoid escalation of opposition of the employees, the employers tend to involve labour unions and address their concerns early in the reform process. It is assured to the labour that their interests are fairly represented and also to assure them that their sacrifices will be balanced More specifically, this involves efforts to: 1. explain the rationale, costs and benefits of reduction; 2. enhance their understanding of the time and method of reduction; and 3. describe the incentives and social safety net measures to be put in place. Precisely, lack of information about the severance payments and other related supported measures tend to create uncertainty. This is what the Japanese believe. Labour unions in Japan are informed not only of job preservation, but also about broader social, environmental and gender impacts of the reforms.

All these help build support for change (Kikeri, 1999).

10.4. Lessons for India from Japanese Experience

Japan is a major force in virtually all fast-growing high technology industries. Its ability to become an important producer and exporter in many of these emerging areas and to do so with apparently a minimum of frictions and unemployment makes Japan a rare example of successful adjustment.

From the above analysis, chief features of Japanese employment and employment adjustment mechanism may be articulated in the following way.

In the first place, unlike the practice of employment followed generally in different countries, the management and the employers in Japan used to lay emphasis more on employment security rather than on job security.

Secondly, companies in Japan have the general tendency to proliferate products in order to respond to changing needs in the market. In order to do this, they clearly recognize the need for developing skills through appropriate training of the employees. Hence, there is a provision of On-the job-training scheme.

Thirdly, enterprise unions in Japan, as we have seen, are organized on the basis of individual enterprises rather than a trade or an industry.

Fourthly, in Japan, under the direction and co-ordination of national organization and individual federations, each enterprise union settles the issues on wage levels and working conditions of the employees in each spring of the year through amicable negotiations with the management.

The right to organize, to bargain and even to strike is provided by Japan's laws for private sector employees. Labour-management relations in Japan are, however, generally are of the nature of co-operation and not of confrontations.

Workers are not treated as hired labour, bought and sold

in the corporate labour market and the company is not generally looked upon as a property of the stock holders to be bought and sold as they wish.

Fifthly, a sense of corporate community on the part of employees is strengthened by the fact that there are no marked differences between blue collar and white collar employees within a company. Employees sense of participation is also enhanced by widespread practices like workers' participation in quality control circles for product improvement, joint labour management consultation system concerning various aspects of work including complaint settlement etc. In all these practices, the Japanese respect for consensus ensures that employees' views are taken into account seriously. At the operational and shop floor level of an enterprise, decision-making tends to be decentralized and organized on the basis of small groups.. It promotes sharing of technical knowledge among workers and helps to cultivate a habit of thinking holistically/ This helps avoid demoralization and alienation of the employees from the mainstream of the company.

Fifthly, in Japan, firms used to take steps to absorb fluctuations in output and reduce costs by adjusting working hours per employee and also through reductions in wages, without resorting to lay-offs.

Sixthly, in order to avoid the dismissal of employees, another measure of significant importance followed in Japan by the employers is the transfer of employees. Employees may be re-assigned among different divisions within the company. Or, in the event of severity of business fluctuations, they may be transferred to some other affiliates or even leased out to some other company. Diversification in Japanese industries is a regular phenomenon.

Finally, the final option of the employer, i.e., dismissal of an employee, is still not very frequently used.

In point of fact, it is interesting to note that the Japanese norm of settlement of disputes or wage fixation etc., is not set by Government or by tripartite council. It is an emergent norm. Before any particular firm or industry gets to serious negotiations about or even formulation of a particular policy, there has been a preceding period of intense public discussion concerning what the economy can afford on an average increase in wage or pay. And out of that discussion, there does emerge a consensus regarding the norm. That consensus has a powerful influence on all who will sit down to bargain. They share the economic sophistication and the data to make the arguments on the line meaningful (Dore, 1986).

Why does the system work? It should be noted that neither Japan's political or social history nor the structure of management and authority in Japanese enterprise gives enterprise union leaders grounds for that underlying sense of diffuse class resentment and secondly, enterprise union leaders in Japan tend to share with the managers a belief in the desirability of careful macro economic management of the economy—a belief that there are criteria of truth and reasonableness and not just political expediency which should be applied to all assertions about the effect of a given level of wage increase. No authoritative norm for wage change is there in Japan. It is an emergent norm arrived at through synchronization.

In Japan, the role of the Government in employment adjustment and protection of the unemployed is also quite significant. It tries to protect the interests of the employees through legislations and active support and involvement as and when required. Apart from different kinds of laws like the Employment Security Law, the Unemployment Insurance Law, the Human Development Promotion Law, the Equal Opportunity Law and the like and regulations enacted to protect the interests of the employees, the Government has developed a closer linkages between the employment policies and the vocational ability development. The Government also used to formulate an economic stimulus package like providing subsidies for creation of employment opportunities, securing safety nets etc. aimed primarily at generating new employment opportunities and employment stability for employees. In fact, the focus of employment strategy is directed more towards the pre-emptive policies rather than the after-the-effect policies.

In Japan, creating jobs through appropriate policy package—rather than preserving jobs in less efficient areas—is the major point of focus of the government policy in order to secure economy-wide gains. They recognize the fact that employee restructuring is often necessary to improve efficiency and competitiveness of weak enterprises. The burdens that loss-making and inefficient enterprises impose on society are simply too large to bear continued Government support at the expense of the society as a whole, diverting resources to subsidize loss-making operations and benefit only a small number of citizens rather than to social sectors that benefit the society and the poor as a whole.

In Japan, there is a belief that concerns that the effects of reduction of excess employees have on the workers are being exacerbated by the lack of information on the mechanism available to reduce the political and social costs of labour adjustment. The steps that are used to adopt are to

a. inform, involve workers and labour unions in the process,
b. ensure that the workers are not deprived of,
c. compensate laid-off workers by providing severance pay and other income support
d. help workers on a selected basis to integrate into the labour market and
e. eliminate obstacles, if any, to job creation.

They also believe that targeted, demand driven re-training support, taking into account the regional market characteristics have better chances of success.

Enterprises are not to be recognized to be designed as a vehicle exclusively for job creation and political patronage.

The extraordinary structural adjustment in employment without significant frictions in Japan would not have been successful if workers, individually or collectively, would have resisted change. Unions, instead of fighting the change, co-operated by defining the pace of change. In order to avoid the escalation of the opposition from any corner, the employers also use to involve employees and the enterprise unions and address their concerns early in the reform process and explain the rationale, costs and benefits of the reductions, enhance their understanding of the time and method of reduction, and also describe the incentives and social safety nets to be in place.

Recognition of common interests among the social partners and the search for consensus that characterizes Japanese society as a whole are the factors that have allowed such changes to take place successfully. Employees and employers feel that they are members of a firm and they show a remarkable propensity to accept both the constraints and the comforts of this group membership. They accept a great deal of wage flexibility and the hardship that comes with adjusting to new jobs and retraining, because the have the confidence that their firm would its best to keep them on the payroll even when the times are hard. This high degree of solidarity is an important factor. In fact, the factors that influenced success in Japan may be attributable not only to the particular policies, but also to the behavioural response of the employers, the employees and the Government.

India can draw lessons from the Japanese experience of frictionless employment adjustment mechanisms and the Government policies. Of course, it is not appropriate to believe that what has led to success in Japan will also be effective in the case of India even though it is true that both the countries, India and Japan, have certain common institutional features like, among others, the well-established legal system, the parliamentary democratic form of Government, the free press, a strong network of financial institutions and the catholicity of the people of both the countries. The traditional forms of employment adjustment, even in Japan followed in the past, may not be that much effective today. And again, the basic characteristics of the two different countries upon which the degree of applicability depends are likely to differ. Two factors are important here; one is culture-specific and hence, nontransferable; the other is culture-free and hence, transferable. The former involves the innate characteristics of the nation concerned—the family spirit, the role of the group, the way the people deal with each other, decision, etc. the later consists of political decision making process, the policies regarding the industrial relations etc.

It should be mentioned here that there are certain policies already used to be practised also in India like Japan. In the public and private sectors in India, there is a practice of employment on a long term basis. An employee is expected to work in that particular company till his retirement, unless he on his own seeks transfer or release from the existing job, or, his services are terminated on some reasonable grounds. It is not that easy to dismiss a permanent employee without some genuine reasons from his employment. In the event of unusual or unreasonable dismissal, there exist different protective measures on the part of the employees for redressal of their grievances.

And again the practices of the rotation and on the job training of the employees are not unique in Japan. Indian companies use to provide facilities for in-service training for the skill formation of the existing employees. This may be done either within the company itself or the employees may be sent abroad for acquisition of skills as and when required. The employees are supposed to be under obligations to serve that particular company. This is precisely valid for the white collar employees. To acquire skills and related knowledge, employees are even required to serve in the affiliates. Of course, this holds good largely for those companies which have subsidiaries. In fact, they are small in number in India.

However, a critical scrutiny of the Japanese practices reveals that the employment adjustment policies followed in India leave much more to be desired. In India, emphasis is on job security of an employee, not the security of employment, as in the case in Japan. So, unlike Japan, when a company faces business downturn, the employers in India tend to fire employees to reduce cost. Employees are hardly able to protect themselves. As we have already mentioned, Japan has also certain methods to reduce costs at the time of recession in the economy through some mechanisms like flexibility in wage structure and working hours. These are conspicuous by their absence in India. Indian employees are found be reluctant to adjust to lowering down in wages or working hours whatsoever. Employees in India do not have in most cases alternative means, employment opportunities or social security measures of any kind, to really fall back upon. Reduction in income to any extent may severely impact upon their low level of living.

The third area of contrast between India and Japan is with regard to trade or enterprise unions. Enterprise unions in

Japan, a non-political entity, are excellent as a mediating force between labour and management. The vertical integration of enterprise unions with centralized national unions and their negotiating style are unique. They are well-positioned to understand both the needs of the employees and also the financial position of the company when conducting collective bargaining. Japanese enterprise unions are effective in matters of direct concerns to workers like wage fixation, job assignment, employees' benefits and even working conditions of the employees. Enterprise unions are expected to take care of the macro-economic details of the company as well as the economy as a whole, while negotiating with the management with regard to wage fixation and other issues.

The role of the unions in Japan are so effective in making the adjustment smooth and without any frictions. Employees are found to respond positively to the changing situations like wage or working hour reductions without any grievances.

In India, we have a parallel trade unions supported by different political parties. The leaders of the union may or may not be a member of the union. Interests were generally confined to the fulfillment of the employees demands without any regard to the macro economic details of the enterprises. Lack of transparency in all matters sometime worsen the situation. Employees ultimately have to bear the brunt of these kind of activities. India has a lot to learn from the practices of enterprise unions in Japan to generate the right kind of mind-set when the unions will be a facilitator in the process of employment adjustment through re-structuring. Unions are required to be a genuine mediator like the Japanese.

Japan has another peculiarity in the form of Shunto system in its employment system. India does not have at the moment this kind of system. It refers to an institutionalized process in each spring of the year during which each enterprise union will negotiate with its management on wage levels, work and leisure, fringe benefits, bonus and training and working conditions etc. The settlement will serve as unofficial guide line for the rest of the economy. Of course, since India has a lot of diversity in respect of size, nature and job specifications in different enterprises, the system may be of small use at the moment. However, with the changes in the nature of the unions, the system may be employed for the fixation of wages, and the determination of other facilities annually in a transparent manner through negotiations between the management and the employees.

As it has been stated that in Japan, in the event of severity of business fluctuations, the enterprises use to transfer employees to reduce costs to their affiliates. Hence, diversification is a strategy. In India, many Indian companies do not survive the threat of competition and they have to move out of the market, resulting in loss of jobs of many employees. Hence, Japanese methods of avoiding closure by way of diversifying production structure in advance may be an effective guide for Indian entrepreneurs.

Another area of concern is with regard to severance payment. India does not have a clear-cut exit policy in the truest sense of the term. Of course, through the setting up of the institutions like BIFR 'the Board of Industrial and Financial Reconstruction', certain arrangements are being made. But even then, the position is not satisfactory. In view of this, employees are very often denied of many of the facilities, even critical minimum. They are laid-off without reasonable amount of compensation. All these call for a re-orientation. Japanese system of severance payment is worth emulating.

The role of the Government in Japan is quite useful for India. The Government does not take care of the sick or loss making enterprises. On the other hand, it is very sincere about how to protect the interests of the employees. So, there are schemes like Unemployment Insurance, Employment Security and generous provisions for severance payment to the employees laid off. The amount is not more than the minimum wages for a very short duration. This implies that the employee need not depend for a long time on the Government assistance. In India, we do not have any scheme for the real rehabilitation of the unemployed; of course, in view of large size of the unemployed, it may not be a feasible proposition like Japan with its small workforce. But there is a need for redesigning the strategy for poverty alleviation. The resources thus mobilized from these schemes may be utilized in this direction. Like the Japanese model, it is better to generate employment opportunities rather than preserve the less efficient employment positions in weak or sick industries.

10.5. Conclusion

In conclusion, certain observations are in order. Developing countries plagued by an evident lack of entrepreneurship, or those in which the indigenous population does not appear to function well in modern industrial organization may find it far more productive to look for solutions, in their own traditionalistic modes of behaviour rather than assuming that the old pattern must be done away with or ignored while industrialization is superimposed. This would mean identifying specific expressive psychological needs fulfilled by traditional behaviour patterns and then consciously attempting to structure the modes of economic organizations and work situation in such a way that these identified psychological needs will also be met, to at least some degree, in the new environment (Hazama, 1978). It is, of course true that the great majority of developing societies including India do not fullfil the condition of 'homogeneity' which is very evident in Japan.

It is not true to say that the Japanese employers have been and are today uninterested in making profits. The point is that the self-interested profit motive has not been acceptable as an overt ethic in Japan. Such ethical incompatibility, with traditional value systems may lie at the root of many of the clashes between tradition and modernity, between development and non-development issues in fact, the course that the labour management relations in Japan has taken implies that the process need not require forsaking its own value system, rather may call for a judicious and conscious retention of the fabric of its own social and ethical values and their incorporation into the structure of development-oriented economic activities. It is argued that if the psychological framework of the members of the society is somehow sustained in the system, then the members are expected to be better equipped to deal effectively with a more technological, urbanized and materially affluent environment (Hazama, 1979). These ideas seem to be relevant even for designing the effective strategy for employment adjustment even in a country like India even though India's social and cultural features of a heterogeneous society might not be identical with those in countries like Japan.

References

Abbeglen, J.C. and George Stalk, Jr. (1985), *Kaisha, The Japanese Corporation*, New York Basic Books.

Abbeglen, J.C. (1958), *Japanese Factory*, Glencoe, Illionois, Free Press.

Aoki, Mashahiko (1988), *Information, Incentives and Bargaining in the Japanese Economy*, Cambridge, Cambridge University Press.

Bronfenbrenner, M. and Yasukichi Yasuba (1987), 'Economic Welfare in The Political Economy of Japan', Vol. 1, *The Domestic Transformation*, ed. By Kozo Yamamura and Yasukichi Yasuba, Stanford University Press.

Business Standard, August 18-20, 2001, Calcutta.

Chandra Sekhar and Jayati Ghose, (2002), *The Market that Failed—A Decade of Neo-liberal Economic Reforms in India*, New Delhi, p. 88.

Clairment, F. and Cavanagh (1994), 'World's Top 200 Mega Corporations', in *Economic and Political Weekly*, February 5, p. 284.

Dore, Ronald (1973), *British Technology-Japanese Factory*, University of California, Berkeley Press.

Dore, Ronald (1987), *Taking Japan Seriously*, Stanford University Press, pp. 70-73.

Dutt, R. and K.P.M. Sundaram (2003), *Indian Economy*, S. Chand Publishers and Co Limited, India.

Genda, Y. (2000), 'Youth Unemployment and Parasite Singles', in *Bulletin of Labour*, Vol. 39, No. 3, Tokyo.

Gerlach, Michael (1987), 'Business Alliance and the Strategy of the Japanese Firm', *California Management Review*, 30, p. 32.

Ghose, Abhik (1995), 'The Catch in Safety Net', in *The Economic Times*, Calcutta, December 4, p. 9.

Goto, J. (1987), 'Keigai Chokusetsu Toshi Tokoyo, Foreign Direct Investment and Employment', in *Rodo Keizeo Tokei Geppo*, Monthly Journal of Statistics on Labour Economics, Ministry of Labour vol. 39, No. 2, February, pp. 12-18.

Government of India, *Economic Survey*, (Different Issues) Planning Commission, New Delhi.

Hazama, H. *et al* (1979), 'Japanese Labour Relations and Uno Riemon', *Journal of Japanese Studies*, Vol. 5, No. 1, Winter, pp. 71-106.

Hsu, Robert C. (1994) *The MIT Encyclopedia of the Japanese Economy*, The MIT Press, Massachusetts.

Ishizumi, Kanji (1988), 'Acquiring Japanese Companies', Yokyo, *Japan Times*.

Japan Business Federation (2003), 'The Current Labour Economy in Japan', *International Labour Policy Review.*

Kesavan, K.V. (ed.) (2001), *Economic Liberalization in India Japanese and Indian Perspectives*, (Different articles) ICSSR and Manak Publishers Private Limited, New Delhi.

Kester, W. Carl (1991), *Japanese Takeaway: The Global Context for Corporate Control*, Boston, Harvard Business School Press.

Khasnobis, Ratan and Sudipta Banerjee (1996), 'Political Economy of Voluntary Retirement Scheme: A Study of Rationalised Workers in Durgapur', in *Economic and Political Weekly*, December 28, p. 71.

Khosla, A., 'The Myth of Japanese Management: Are There Lessons for South Asia', in *Japan's Role in South Asia.*

Kikeri, Sunita (1999), 'Privatization and Labour, What happens to Workers When Government Divests?' *The World Bank, Technical Paper No. 396*, Washington D C.

Layard, Richard, Stephen Nichell and Richard Jackman (1991) *Unemployment, Macroeconomic Performance and the Labour Market*, Oxford University Press

Leibenstein, H. (1984), 'The Management System: A X-efficiency Game Theory Analysis' in *The Economic Analysis of the Japanese Firm* by Masaiko Aoki (Ed.), North Company.

Mani, Sunil (1995), 'Economic Liberalization and the Industrial Sector' in *Economic and Political Weekly*, May 27, p. 45.

McDonald, Jack (1989), 'The Mochiai Effect: The Japanese Corporate Shareholding', *The Journal of Portfolio Management*.

Ministry of Economy, Trade and Industry, Japan (2002), *Trend Survey of Overseas Business Activities*.

Misra and Puri (2004), *Indian Economy* , Himalayan Publishing House, Bombay.

Nakamura, K. and Michio Nitta, (1995), 'Development of Industrial relations in Japan' in *Employment Relations in Changing World Economy* by Richard Locke, MIT Press.

Okabe, Mitsuaki (1995), 'The Japanese Economy in Transition; Introduction and Overview', in *The Structure of the Japanese Economy: Changes in the Domestic and international Fronts* by Mitsuaki Okabe (ed.), Macmillan Press Limited.

Organisation for Economic Co-operation and Development, Paris *Economic Surveys, Japan*, (various issues).

Ozaki, Robert (1991), *Human Capitalism*, New York, Penguin.

Papola, T.S. (1992), 'The Question of Unemployment' in *The Indian Economy: Problems and Prospects*, by Bimal Jalan (ed), New Delhi, p. 309.

Patel, B.B. and Hiraoki Suzuki (1992), 'Safety Net for Workers in India—Counselling, Retraining and Re-Deployment of Displaced Workers under the National Renewal Fund', A Report submitted to the World Bank, Gandhi Labour Institute, Gujarat quoted in S. Kikeri, 1997, p. 7.

Ramaswamy, K.V. (2001), 'Liberalizing, Outsourcing and Industrial Labour Markets in India: Some Preliminary Results', in *Labour Market and Institution in India 1990s and Beyond* by S. Uchikawa (ed.), Manohar, New Delhi, 2003, pp. 155-170.

Rani, Uma (2003), *Women's Employment in the Japanese Economy*, Institute of Developing Economies and Japan External Trade Organisation.

Rao, H. (2001), 'Economic Restructuring and Employment Adjustment: Lessons for India from Japanese Experiences' in *Economic Liberalization in India—Japanese and Indian Perspectives* by K.V. Kesavan (ed) published by ICSSR and Manak Publications Private Limited, New Delhi.

Roy, T. (2003), 'Social Costs of Reforms: A Study of Job Loss with Special Reference to Declining Industries in 1900-1998' in *Labour Market and Institution in India—1990s and Beyond*, edited by Shuji Uchikawa, Manohar, New Delhi, 2003, pp. 121-152.

Takanashi, Anikra *et al.*, (1989), 'Shunto Wage Offensive: A Historical Overview and Prospects', *Japan Institute of Labour*, Tokyo.

Takeshi, Inagami (1988), 'Changing Japanese Style of Employment Practices', *Japan Institute of Labour*, October, Vol. 25, No.10

Veerasekharappa (1994), quoted in Sarath Dawala, 'New Economic Policy and Trade Union Response', in *Economic and Political Weekly*, February 19, p. 407.

Weathers, Charles (1998), 'The Post-war Transformation of Labour Force', in *The Japan Handbook*, Patrick Heenar (ed.) Fitzray Dearborn Publishers, London.

William B. (1984), *Japan's Re-shaping of American Labour Law*, Cambridge, MIT Press.

11

PROTECTION OF LABOUR RIGHTS: AN APPRAISAL OF LABOUR LAWS IN NEPAL

Shyam Bahadur Katuwal

Introduction

The basic aim of the labour laws is to protect the rights and interest of the weaker section of the labour-management relations and to establish a framework within which congenial labour relations can foster. In this regard, government, as an active partner of labour relations, has to harmonize the interests, and control and shape the relationship between employers and employees by using its law making power (Bajrachrya, 1998: 21).

In the recent years, labour laws have not only been considered as an important tool of maintaining harmonious labour relations, industrial peace and economic growth of the country but also ensuring well-being of workers, and socio-economic and political justice and harmony in the country. The labour laws can make positive contribution towards industrial peace and productivity provided they strike balance between the needs and well being of workers, the viability of the industry and the imperatives of development (Thiagarajah, 1987: 24).

To a developing country like Nepal, the issue of labour relations and labour protection is a special significance. In the wake of newly introduced multiparty political system in 1990, government has been enacting, among others, labour laws with a view to protect workers and govern congenial industrial relations in the country. The labour laws can be broadly classified into two groups. The first category deals with condition of employment and management of disputes. The second governs the formation and regulation of trade unions in the country. Major intentions of these laws are to give protection of workers in their jobs, afford them a minimum level of living conditions, protect the workers from unfair labour practices and to preserve their rights of freedom of association. First category of laws includes Labour Act, 1992 and its regulations. The Trade Union Act, 1992 and its regulations fall under the second category of the labour laws. These laws have been found persuaded from the Constitution of the Kingdom of Nepal 1990, ILO standard to which Nepal has ratified, and Labour Policy. Therefore, this article also describes them as a background for the analysis of the labour laws.

Objectives

Labour protection entails a lot of activity ranging from the minimum wage standard, working conditions and environment, health and safety, social security, psychological and secular needs to the protection from anti-union discrimination. These aspects are considered as the rights of the workers. Thus, this paper attempts to throw the light on those provisions in the labour laws, which are relevant for the protection of labour rights and for the maintenance of harmonious labour relations. An attempt has also been made to discuss the practices of these issues in Nepal.

Role of Government

The government plays a crucial role to shape labour-management relations, protect the rights and interests of employees and employers in the country. The role of government in the field of labour relations can be examined from the analysis of the concerned laws that specify the degree of well-being offered to the workers, facilities granted to the management for changing the organizational structure with a view to improve productivity and competitiveness of the enterprises. In this regard, government is a largest employer and wage leader, legislator, and administrator as well. The government has a right to specify the minimum wages for the industrial workers, construction workers, tea plantation workers and other workers in lower wage brackets occupation. The government, through its labour inspection rights can also regulate labour standards in the private enterprises and public enterprise as well.

However, the studies have specified that the government have failed to establish good conditions of employment, labour welfare and the better climate for labour relations in its units. As compared to organized private sector, public enterprises could not show a remarkable progress in these aspects. Furthermore, studies have indicated that there is no uniformity even among the public enterprises with regard to labour welfare and employment conditions (Pant, 2044 BS: 39-40 and Katuwal, 2002).

Another study has found mixed role of government in different terms of employment (IRF, 1998:63). The study of IRF has explained that the quality of work life (QWL) in term of perceived level of average monthly wages, medical facilities, education facilities, insurance, training, job satisfaction and working conditions in terms of sanitation, safety, accommodation facility to workers in public enterprise were better than in the private sector firms. But the QWL in terms of provident founds, pensions, job security union-management relations, level of pollution and drinking water facilities were found better in private sector than in the public sector undertakings.

Labour Issues in the Constitution

The Constitution of the Kingdom of Nepal 1990 is the genesis of all these labour laws. The constitution, among others, guarantees equality before law, equal pay for equal work, prohibits discrimination on grounds of religion, race, caste, sex or place of birth, and also prohibits forced labour and child labour in factories.

Articles 11, 12, 20 and 26 of the Constitution of the Kingdom of Nepal 1990 (MOLJ, 1990) are devoted to the maintenance and promotion of interests of the economically and socially backward groups, including industrial workers in our case. The Constitution has considered the workers as the socio-economic backbone of the country (Article 26.6).

Article 11(2) rules out discrimination based on religion, race, sex, caste, tribe or ideology. Similarly, Article 11(5) guarantees equality in the payment of remuneration between man and woman for the same work. It has also guaranteed the rights to form union and association (Article 12.2c). The Constitution has a provision of protecting the rights of minor child by restricting their employment in factory, mine work and similar hazardous work (Article 20.2). Workers' right to participate in management is also ensured in the Article 26.6 of the constitution.

ILO Standards

As member of the International Labour Organization (ILO) from 1966, Nepal has been trying to include provisions of ILO conventions, recommendations and standards in its constitution, laws, polices and practices. In this connection, Nepal, out of 181 ILO Conventions, has so far ratified following nine conventions of ILO as of February 22, 2006:

List of ILO Conventions Ratified by Nepal as of February 22, 2006

Con. No.	*Yr.*	*Convention*	*Date*
14	1921	Weekly rest (industry)	10:12:1986
29	1930	Forced Labour	03:01:2002
98	1949	Rights to organize and Collective Barging	11:11:1996
100	1951	Equal Remuneration	10:06:1976
111	1958	Discrimination (Employment and Occupation)	19:09:1974
131	1970	Minimum Wage Fixing	19:09:1974
138	1973	Minimum Age of Employment	30:05:1997
144	1976	Tripartite Consultation (International Labour Std.)	21:03:1995
182	1999	Worst Forms of Child Labour	03:01:2002

Source: www.ilo.org/ilolex/English (22 February, 2006).

Labour Policy

Due to lack of specific policy, planning documents were only the source to deal with some policy matter of labour before the announcement of the National Labour Policy in 1999. In the history of Nepalese labour management, Ministry of Labour and Transport Management had announced the first National Labour Policy in 1999 view to fulfilling the lacuna in the labour policy and to show landmark commitment of the government toward the maintenance of harmonious labour relations in the country. The prime objectives of the Labour Policy 1999, among others, were to develop continuous unity between labour and management, to implement labour standards determined by the ILO, to attract Nepalese labour towards the employment in Nepalese enterprises, to encourage the enterprises and entrepreneurs in employing women and handicapped persons and to encourage the activities that promote labour in all respects. It also aimed to carry out labour welfare and social security activities. Besides these, the policy had shown its concern to eradicate bonded and child labour from the country, secure labour standards according to ILO and protect the labour rights through the enactment relative Acts. As of its action plans, the policy had covered almost all aspects of labour-management relations including workers' participation in management, trade unionism and industrial disputes resolution, wage and fringe benefit administration along with the advancement of effective labour administration in the country to make the policy result oriented.

By the execution of this Labour Policy 1999, some positive changes have been felt in the field of labour management in the country. Nepalese labour force found conscious to be organized, some international labour standards are initiated to bring into practices, the labour administration directed towards fostering the culture of bilateral and trilateral dialogue to address the labour problems, every one in the country have started to show their concern for the issues of child labour, bonded labour and the labour in the informal sector and maintenance of harmonious labour relations in the country.

However, the labour policy could not bring substantial changes in the labour and employment condition in the country. Thus, there was demand for more flexible and action-oriented labour policy that could generate income oriented employment opportunities, eradicate different labour problems including unfair labour practices, establish congenial industrial relations and decent work in the changed political scenario and the borderless socio-economic and technological environment.

Consequently, His Majesty's Government of Nepal has announced a Labour and Employment Policy 2006 on February 22, 2006 replacing the previous one. The policy has integrated the labour and employment policy together to make it a composite policy for solving the labour and employment problems in the country. The long-term objectives of the policy are to provide productive, non-discriminating, decent, safe and healthy employment opportunities to the citizens at working age group by creating the investment-friendly environment, and to develop and manage labour market for building national economics capable to compete with international standard.

The working objectives of this policy are directed to facilitate sustainable economic development by creating investment-friendly environment and productive and full employment opportunities to all kinds of manpower; to increase productivity by establishing harmonious industrial relations through the eradication of bonded and forced labour practices and gradual implementation of international labour standards at workplace; to develop social security system even in the informal sector for making the labour market safe, healthy, competitive and flexible and to promote and develop occupational health and safety; to increase the possibilities of employment & self-employment through the process of qualitative and multi-skilled human resources development; to secure equal the approach of women, Dalit, ethnic and displaced groups to the employment; to eradicate child labour; and to make the labour and employment administration active, perfect, capable and effective.

Though the labour policy has adapted various relevant strategies and action plans, enactment of laws, issue of different policies and amendments of the existing laws related to labour and employment are necessary to achieve the objectives of the policy. Similarly, it is also necessary to change the attitudes and behaviour of the workers, trade unionists, government officials and general citizen towards the labour and employment.

Labour Act and Trade Union Act: Milestones of the Labour Laws

Although the existing labour laws are required to amendment according to the context of recently issued labour and employment policy and the demands of trade unions and employers, the Labour Act, 1992 and Trade Union, 1992 and associated regulations are only such laws in Nepal which have tried to cover and regularize most of the essential labour standards and aspects of labour relations required to maintain industrial harmony in the country. Thus, this section of the article is devoted to evaluate whether the labour laws became successful to protect the rights and interests of workers in the country.

Unlike the defunct Factory and Factory Workers Act, 1959, the scope of Labour Act, 1992 has also been expanded to the special types of establishment like tea estates, construction sector, transport, hotel, travel and trekking agencies and resorts. This Act aims at protecting the rights and interests of workers for employment, wages, social security, health and safety, working condition, unfair labour practices and so on. The procedure and methods of settling labour disputes and maintenance of discipline in the enterprises have also been regularized in the Act and the Labour Rules, 1993.

On the other hand, the Trade Union Act, 1992 and the Trade Union Regulations 1993 were promulgated in accordance with the spirit of the Article 12(2c) of the Constitution of the Kingdom of Nepal 1990, which guarantees the right of associations and ILO Convention 98 that confirms the right to organize. The Act protects the rights of the worker for freedom of association and regularizes the process of registration, recognition, operations and management of trade unions in Nepal (LBMC, 1993).

General Perception Towards the Labour Laws

Labour laws in Nepal have been criticized from different sectors. In the academics front, the labour laws are said to be incomprehensive and inadequate when it comes to lay down broader framework of labour relations (Pant, *op. cit.*: 40), vague and inadequate (Gurugharana and Dahal, 1996: 1). However, the Nepalese labour relations are caught up in legislative mesh (Manandhar, 1998a: 32). Furthermore, Manandhar (1998a: 32) writes in his article that management has criticized the Labour Act and Trade Union Act saying that these two laws are drawn singularly with the interest of labour and they are also impractical. The criticism lies in the fact also that the same has trampled the right to hire and fire the workers, although the increased lay-off contradicts with this argument (Gurugharana, 1998: 367).

Despite of some positive trends in the field of labour relations, the labour laws could not remain free from the criticism of concerned group. From side of employees, the General Federation of Nepalese Trade unions (GEFONT) writes in its publication that labour laws are not only incomplete and insufficient but also illusive and unclear (GEFONT and AMRC 1996: 22).

The employers bill the law as pro-workers because the Labour Act, 1992 has failed to introduce the issue of "No Work, No Pay" clause. This leaves employers paying the salary for the period spent under strike and lockouts. Similarly, the analysis of the provisions curtailing the production or services (section 11), lay off and retrenchment of the workers (section 12), firing the workers on disciplinary ground and misconduct (section 53) and call for lockouts (section 77) show that the rights of the management have been curtailed. The management has to take prior permission from the government before taking such actions. However, the workers need not take any prior permission from any one to launch a strike (section 74). They are just obliged to put up a notice announcing the strike (section 76).

In such a condition of criticism, it can be clearly observed that both the parties seem to be unsatisfied from the present provisions in the labour laws calling for reforming labour laws from both sides and call for effective implementation from the side of workers.

There are various lacking in the labour laws. A drawback of the labour law is that the laws do not speak about the large section national labour force that has been working in the agricultural and informal sector. It is the deficiency of the labour laws that makes no difference between the establishment employing ten or more for the application of the major provisions of labour standards. It is obvious that no small establishments can live up to the international standards.

For Tradė Union Act, 1992 and its regulations, workers have been uniting freely under their political banners to protect and protest for their rights and interest. However, backed by political parties in the multiparty political scenario, workers stand divided and inter-union rivalry has come to the fore among them, creating disunity and weakening the strength of trade unions to protect and promote the interests of workers.

Although strong trade unions are essential prerequisites for the effectiveness of industrial relations including collective bargaining and inculcating mutual trust and confidence between management and workers, the Trade Union Act, 1992 has weakened the power of trade unions. The Act facilitates to form more than one union, up to four in a firm and thus, the division among workers has been clearly observed in the country. In the absence of strong trade unions, intervention from government increases only to weaken the bargaining powers of trade unions and it renders the entire bargaining process as mere formality.

Protection of Labour Rights

In the light of the practices, this section of this article attempts to evaluate the provisions of the Labour Act 1992, which were stipulated to protect different rights of the labour and to foster industrial relations in the country.

Issues of Wages

In general, wages is unfortunately low in Nepal though it is the sources of the standard of living of the workers and his family. Because of which workers are forced to live in poverty and most of labour problems also revolve around the wages in Nepal (Pant and Agrawal, 1980:90). Studies have indicated that most of the disputes in Nepal arose due to workers dissatisfaction with wages and fringe benefits. The economic causes including wage were found to be leading causes of industrial disputes in Nepal (RMF, 1982: 116; G.K. Shrestha, 1991 and Katuwal, 2002).

In such a situation, the invention of government in the matter of wages by issuing protective laws is imperative in the situation where the bargaining power of the workers is weak due to inadequate and fragmented trade unions, migrated nature of workers, surplus of unskilled labour and unemployment and low commitment towards industrial way of life of both labour and management. It is also essential due to commitment shown by the government in the Constitution of the Kingdom of Nepal 1990, ratification of ILO Conventions and labour policies adopted by the government.

How Wages are Determined in Nepal?

Government intervention in the determination of minimum basic wage, allowance and benefit is relatively high in Nepal. Government, according to the recommendation of the Minimum Remuneration Fixation Committee (MRFC), a tripartite committee comprising of representatives of workers, employers and government formed under the Labour Act, determines lowest limit of remuneration beyond which the agreement may not be concluded between the General Manger and workers or employees of any establishment.

The Act has also provided legal way of protecting the rights of workers in case of injustice in payment of wages by slapped a ban on deduction from remuneration except in some reasonable causes as fine imposed on him/her, absent from work, loss or damage incurred to the property of the establishment due to negligence of workers and on other disciplinary ground.

In practice though the statutory aim of the fixation of

minimum wages is to protect the workers from the exploitation of employers (Manandhar, 1998b: 243), it is very low than the consumer price index (Upadhya, 1998: 234), cost of basic needs (Shrestha, 1991: 158) and rate of inflation (Dahal, 1995: 10). Because of which workers are not in a position to even purchase the minimum required calories, which has been fixed at 2250 (Mainali 1998: 36). These findings indicate that Nepalese workers have always been in critical position of livelihood and fighting for better wages.

However, because of the over-supply of labour, workers are compelled to accept the wage determined by the employers unilaterally. It is sometime collectively decided but the bargaining power of workers is very weak in Nepal. Similarly, capacity to pay of the factories also determines the wages under the typical situations, and there may be a chance of malpractice in wages distribution in the name of job evaluation. For all practical purposes, what can be safely argued is there is no law governing wage fixation (Shrestha, 1998: 203).

Dearness Allowance

With a view to maintain the living standard even at the rise in the cost of living (inflationary condition), the first amendment of the Labour Act in 1998 has empowered the government to fix the dearness allowance and facilities. Presently, the dearness allowance is of Rs. 860/- per month for adult workers and Rs. 645/- per month for minor workers (MOL, 2003).

Result- oriented Wages

The result-oriented wages payment, though it is considered as the part of incentive scheme in the law, is mostly practiced among others in textile and jute industries and differential piece rate system in the form of production bonus (Shrestha, 1998: 205; Pant, 1998: 211 and Katuwal, 2002:195)

Wage Differentials is Massive in Nepal

Cases of wage differentials in Nepal are massive. The

government itself has also differentiated the wages of workers by skills, industry and age in contravention to the relevant provisions of the Constitution and ILO Convention that prohibit disparity in wage payment for the same type of work. Thus, this section of this article attempts to point out the wage differentials in Nepal based on the minimum wages determined by the government in 2003 and other individual studies.

Differentials by Skill

The wage difference among unskilled, semi-skilled, skilled and highly skilled adult industrial workers within a firm is not very wide. It is only by 50 rupees between un-skilled and semi-skilled, by 110 rupees between semi-skilled and skilled workers and by 190 rupees between skilled and highly skilled workers. The minimum wages for un-skilled adult industrial workers is fixed at Rs. 1700/- per month. The disparity on this is greater between unskilled and highly-skilled worker. It is Rs. 350 per month.

Differentials by Industry and Firm

The study of Pant (1998: 213) reveals that the public sector jute mills workers recorded a higher rate of earning than private sector jute mill. Similarly, another study conducted by Shrestha (1991: 180) indicated that the cigarette factory workers were always highly paid than the jute mill workers. Both these study have got an inter-industry and inter-firm differentials in wages. These study also show that the workers in public sector has always high paid than their counterparts. As per the minimum wages announced by the government in 2003, the inter-industry differential in wages is found only between the tea estate workers and other industrial workers. The tea estate adult workers are paid less than their counterpart in industrial units.

Differentials by Age

According to the minimum wage determined by the government in 2003, minor workers (14-18 years of age) are low paid minimum wage, dearness allowance and daily wages as compared to the adult workers for the same kind of work. The monthly minimum wage for minor workers has been fixed at Rs. 1384/- per month. The same is Rs.73/- for daily wageworkers. Adult un-skilled worker are paid Rs. 90/- per day by an industrial unit. The disparity for daily wages can be observed between the industrial workers and tea estates.

However, in practice, there are various incidents of violation of the governing legal provisions on wage structure, methods of payment and wage differential.

Differentials by Region

Until now, there is no provision of direct geographical or regional variation on the legal minimum wages in Nepal. However, the Labour Act, 1992, section 21(3) has outlined the rights of the government to differentiate in dearness allowance and facilities on regional basis. The study conducted by Shrestha (1991: 185) indicates that the workers of Janakpur were always highly paid than the workers in Biratnagar. The study of Dahal *et al* (1999: 39) also indicated that the workers in the Kathmandu were well paid than the workers in other areas. The same study found all the 252 workers interviewed in Jhapa revealed they were receiving the lowest wages. While their average minimum wage was Rs. 1377 per months, it was Rs. 3263 in the Kathmandu district. The study revealed that the second highest paid workers were in Hetauda followed by Janakpur and Pokhara. The second lowest paid workers were in Biratnagar.

Differentials by Sex

There is no legal ground of wage differential based on sex of workers. However, it is very difficult to implement the concept of equal pay for men and women for equal work and skill in the country like Nepal. Here women are always exploited, among others, by low wages. Hence, they have not been able to pick up skills required to draw higher wages.

Overtime Payment

The Labour Act, 1992, section 19 has stated that the payment of extra remuneration at the rate of 1.5 times of the normal wage for the workers who worked more than the prescribed normal period of work per day. The normal period of working period is not more than 8 hours a day or 48 hours per week (Labour Act, 1992 section 16). The Act has also restricted compulsory overtime work. The same should not be more than 4 hours a day and not more than 20 hours a week (Section 19).

Some of the Nepalese enterprises have kicked off controversy over overtime wages. Some have discouraged it in the name of unfair labour practices. Employers always blame workers of not paying due attention toward their normal work for normal wages. Hence, they consider overtime work as a means of boosting the earnings. It is also true that workers blame employers for not implementing the provision of the labour law regarding the payment of overtime.

Issues of Fringe Benefits

The fringe benefit which is provided for employees in excess to the normal wages or salary compensation for their benefits are maintained by some large industries while it is non-existent in small industries in Nepal.

Labour Welfare: Labour welfare that includes such services, facilities and amenities as may be established in or near undertakings, enables the persons employed therein to perform their work in healthy and congenial surroundings (ILO, 1960). However, the intra-mural or extra-mural welfare amenities (Monappa, 1993: 245), in the form of economic, recreational and facilitative types (Singh, *et al*, 1995: 504), provided in accordance with the legislations (Statutory Welfare Amenities) may be in concurrence with the number of persons engaged.

The Labour Act, 1992 has laid down such provisions to bring uniformity in the amenities available to worker and to counteract the unfair labour practices and labour problems. However, in practice, there is no uniformity among the industries (FNCCI 1997: 31, Katuwal, 2002: 357-359) regarding welfare amenities in Nepal.

Intra-Mural Labour Welfare: The welfare facilities, which are provided inside the work place, is called intra-mural labour welfare. They are discussed below:

Medical Facilities: Medical facilities provided in the work place not only protect the workers from physical injuries and illness but also ensure their fitness to the work and yield increased productivity and reduce absenteeism rate caused by the health problems.

The Act has stressed the need to have health staff, medical treatment center of with a part-time doctor if the establishment has workers between 50 and 1000 and more (Labour Act, 1992: section 39). Likewise, it has a provision for compulsory medical check-ups of workers at least once every year in establishments.

In practice, the researches have indicated the insufficiency of the medical facilities (FNCCI, 1997:23, Katuwal, 2002). Some factories had provided medical allowance (*ex-gratia* payment) and felicitation grant instead of medical treatment facilities. Gautam's study reveals that only 3.45 percent of industries had their own clinic with part time doctor, 17.24 percent industries had arranged First Aid box among which 10.34 percent have no trained persons or 6.9 percent had trained person for first aid treatment (Gautam 1999: 235).

Canteen: The Labour Act, 1992, section 44 specifies that the General Manager of an establishment, where 50 or more workers or employees work simultaneously should provide canteen facilities. In practice, researches have indicated that a few industries have proper managed canteen facilities factory premises (Gautam, 1999:235 and Katuwal, 2002:358).

Crèches: Section 42 of the Labour Act, 1992 has laid down a provision that every establishment employing 50 or more women workers should arrange for a healthy nursery with toys and trained nurse for their babies. However, only small portion of industries were found operating such care centers within the factory premises (FNCCI, 1997: 26, and Gautam 1999: 235).

Rest and Rest Room: For providing rest to the workers and

to utilize the 30 minutes of rest facilities, the Labour Act, 1992 has made a provision of arranging rest room equipped with the minimum necessary facilities for workers of an establishment employing 50 or more workers or employees.

Similarly, the Act also made a provision of one-day weekly paid leave and thirty minutes of rest for a period longer than five hours of continuous work (Section 16 and 15 respectively). The Labour Act, 1992 has prescribed work a maximum of 8 hours in a day or 48 hours in a week.

However, in practice, because of the minimum facility of special rooms to take rest, the workers have to take rest on the ground or corridor of the factory (FNCCI, 1997, and Gautam, 1999: 235).

Facilities of drinking water: According to the Labour Act, 1992, every factory should make arrangement for adequate hygienic drinking water to workers (Section 27.g). However, although water is available in most of the factories, it does not prove its purity and safe. It is revealed in the study of FNCCI (1997: 24 and Gautam, 1999: 234) that the main source of drinking water in industries was tap, tube-well and deep well.

Leaves and holidays: The Labour Act, section 40 has made a provision for leaves and holidays as follows:

- A 13 days of paid Public Holidays in a year
- One day of paid home leave for every 20 days of work.
- A 15 days of half paid sick leave in a year
- A maximum of 13 days full paid mourning leave
- A 52 days paid maternity leave to the women workers before or after her delivery for two times during her entire service period.
- A 30 days of non-paid special leave to the workers who has no leave balance with prior approval from the management.
- A one-day paid leave every week.
- A worker can have a maximum of one year paid accident leave for the treatment of accident.

Extra-Mural Labour Welfare: The welfare facilities, which

are provided outside the work place, is called intra-mural labour welfare. They are discussed below:

Housing: Housing is one of the basic human necessities. It determines the social quality of life and living condition even as it has considerable bearing on the health, efficiency and well being of workers. The Labour Act, 1992, section 41, has made a provision of creating a housing fund by allocating not less than 5 percent of the gross annual profit every. However, not all factories have been providing housing facilities and if is, only for few worker (Gautam, 1999: 235 and Katuwal, 2002:220).

Transport Service: Availability of the best and personal transport services has direct relation with attendance patterns of workers. Though there is no concrete statutory provision on this, the welfare fund can be used for this purpose. On an average Rs. 667 per month for each worker was paid as transportation allowances by large industries in Nepal (FNCCI, 1997: 37). Similarly, 10.34 percent of industries were arranging transportation facilities and 3.45 percent of them had no satisfactory arrangement concerning transport in Nepal (Gautam, 1999: 235).

Recreation Facilities: Though there is no direct provision of the arrangement of recreational facilities to the workers, the labour relations committee, as mentioned in the labour rules 1993 section 14(c), may spend some portion of the welfare fund in order to make necessary arrangement for sports, entertainment, libraries, and clubs and so on for the benefit of workers/employees.

Educational Facilities: Providing educational facilities to workers and their children is as an investment on capital because an educated worker may be more receptive to changes especially those concerned with technological changes. Though the Labour Act, 1992 has made no special statutory provision in educating workers, the Welfare Fund can be used in order to make necessary arrangement for the education of workers or employees or their children (Labour Rules, 1993, Section 14.b).

The studies conducted by FNCCI, (1997: 26) and Katuwal, (2002: 203) found that only small portion of industries, especially large industries and public enterprises located in the industrial districts, were running schools for the children of workers. Likewise, on the whole, it was also found that most of the industries had been paying more than Rs. 100 per worker per month as education allowances (FNCCI, 1997: 37)

Arrangement of welfare funds: In order to provide various types of benefits and facilities to the workers employed in the establishment, the Labour Act, 1992 and Labour Rules, 1993 have made provision to create a Welfare Fund from the 70 percent of the balance left after distributing bonus. The fund according to the laws can be used in providing various facilities to the workers.

Issuses of Social Security

Social Security for Workers: The components of social security, as per Social Security (Minimum Standard) convention No 102 adopted by ILO in 1952, are medical care, sickness benefit, old age benefit, employment benefit, injury benefit, family benefit, maternity benefit, invalidity benefit and survivor's benefit (ILO, 1984: 177-81).

Social security traditionally used by the ILO denotes the protection against economic and social distress caused by the stoppage or fall in income resulting from death, old age, sickness, employment, injury, maternity and temporary unemployment (ILO, 1984).

The social security in Nepal has been introduced because of the changing economic, social, technological and political environment. The social security in Nepal covers the both aspects of social security, which are social assistance and social insurance.

Pension: Although a worker has to get compulsory retirement after the age of 55 years if not extended by the General Manger, statutorily, there is no provision of the pension plan in Nepal for industrial workers. However, according to the Labour Act, the General Manger can extend an additional period of 5 years service of the retired worker.

Gratuity: Gratuity is paid from the Gratuity Fund to the

workers who have been leaving the factory because of the compulsory retirement age, resignation and due to other reasons. The following rate of gratuity is paid to the workers depending on the length of services of the concerned workers with the organization (Labour Rules 1993, Section 24):

(i) For first seven years of services, the half of the monthly salary for each year.

(ii) For seven and fifteen years of services, two-third of monthly salary for each year

(iii) For 15 years and more service, one-month salary for each year

The Act also mentioned that dismissed workers on the ground of certain misconduct have no right to claim gratuity (Labour Rules 1993, Section 23.3).

Provident Fund: The Labour Act, 1992 has provision for the arrangement of a compulsory provident fund in the enterprises for the permanent workers to protect them and their dependent family members from income insecurity after their retirement/death of the concerned workers. In Nepal, deducting 10 percent amount of the monthly remuneration of the permanent worker and adding the same amount from the part of establishment create this fund. The worker can also borrow up to 50 percent of the accumulated amount of the provident fund as a loan (Labour Rules 1993, Section 26).

Accident Compensation and Injury Benefits: According to section 39 of Labour Act, 1992 and Section 15, 16 and 17 of the Labour Rules, 1993, workers are compensated for injury, physical disability and death due to injury or accident caused to them by accidents arising out of and in the course of their employment.

The same section of the Act also provisioned to covers the expenses of the treatment as long as the worker is in hospital for treatment. However, the wages shall be half in case the treatment is being done at home, but not more than for one year.

Disablement Benefit: The physically disabled worker, caused during his work, is entitled to receive the wages up to the period of five years, based on the percentage of the physical disability.

Dependents Benefit: If the worker dies during the discharge of duties due to the injury and accident (but not of natural calamities), a lump sum wages of the three years is paid to his nearest kith and kin (Labour Rules, section 19).

Sickness Benefit: There is no special provision of the payment of periodical sickness benefit other than the half-paid leave for 15 days in a year. It is provided only to the workers who have worked continuously for one year.

Unemployment Benefit: In Nepal, there is no special provision for unemployment benefits. However, the Labour Act 1992, section 12, (3b) has a provision of providing a lump sum amount at the rate of 30 days of salary for every year of service completed if workers lose employment due to retrenchment and lay-off.

Retaining Compensation: The loss of earning of a worker, who had completed one year of uninterrupted services in the establishment, during unemployment due to closure of operation of the seasonal establishment is compensated as the retaining allowance at the rate of at least 25 percent of the remuneration (Labour Act, 1992: Section 13.3).

Non-statutory Measures of Social Security

Although some of the enterprises have been providing a few non-statutory social security benefits to the workers, like insurance scheme, death relief, personal accident insurance, loan and advance, there are no standardized social security and welfare activities in most of the Nepalese industries and most of them have not implemented the entire social security and welfare scheme as mentioned in the Labour Act, 1992. The proportion of industries not having any such scheme is highest among small industries (62 percent), followed by large industries (24. percent) and among 14 percent of medium scale industries (FNCCI, 1997: 22).

Issues of Employment Security

Job Security: Keeping in the mind of the repercussions of job insecurity, the Labour Act, 1992, sections 3 to 15, has made a special provision of job security of the workers in the manufacturing sector as:

- Issuance of appointment letters.
- Permanent job after the 240 days of uninterrupted services.
- Privilege to Nepali citizens for permanency.
- Non-termination of the job due to changes in the ownership of the establishment.
- Non-termination of the job due to changes in the ownership of the establishment.
- Non-termination of the services of permanent worker unless agreed to the provision of Labour Act.
- Requirement of prior permission from HMG/N to keep staff reserve for certain days.

Security for Minor and Women Worker: The job security of the minor and women workers is given special attention in the Labour Act, 1992. According to the Act, employment of children (below than 14 years of age) is strictly prohibited in any establishment (Section, 5.1). However, the minor (14-18 years of age) can be employed, if necessary for the period between 6 am to 6 pm. The section 5 (2) also restricts employing them for more than 6 hours a day and 36 hours a week

In general, the hours of work for women are also same as the minor but the working hours for minor and women can be changed after mutual agreements between the manager and the workers, provided there is appropriate arrangement for security even as the same is informed to the concerned Labour Office of the government (Labour Rules, 1993: Section 3 and 4).

Health and Safety: The health and safety of the workers and their efficiency are directly related to each other. Sound health and safety measure not only result in reduced rate of industrial accidents but also raise the production.

The provision of the accidental insurance is made for the workers engaged in construction work (Labour Act, 1992: Section 46.c), transport (Section 47.d) and trekking, rafting, jungle safari or other adventure enterprises (Section 48.c). In case of industrial workers, compensation is paid as mentioned elsewhere in this study.

Thus, appropriate health and safety-related protection measures have been included in the governing Labour Act, 1992 much in tune with the ILO recommendation number 23 (1919) concerning the prevention of industrial accidents, recommendation number 97 (1953) concerning the protection of workers health and ILO convention number 155 (1981) which is concerned with the occupational safety and health and working environment. The chapter 5 of the Act has outlined a multidimensional measure to ensure good health and safety of the workers as:

(a) Maintenance of neat and clean condition in the establishment.

(b) Provision of adequate ventilation, light and temperature in workroom.

(c) Arrangement for the disposal and distraction of refuse, dirt and filth.

(d) Prevention from inhalation of dust, polluted air and fumes

(e) Arrangement for the protection or reduce the adverse impact of noise produce in the work.

(f) Arrangement of sufficient space for the movement of workers at work place

(g) Arrangement of adequate water for drinking, flushing toxic chemicals and extinguishing fires.

(h) Arrangement of separate toilet for male and female.

(i) Declaring all or any part of establishment as a non-smoking zone based on the nature of establishment.

(j) Arrangement for compulsory medical checkup of workers in the hazardous factory at least once a year.

(k) Arrangement for the protection of the eyes of workers from the bad effect of dust, particulates and radiation.

(l) Arrangement for the protection of the workers from the harmful effects of chemicals and the factory from fire.

(m) Fencing around each part of danger machinery and equipment and timely inspection, lubrication and adjustment by experienced and trained workers.

(n) To prevent from the likely injury the Act has prescribed optimum limit of load to be lifted or moved by the workers based on age and sex. The prescribed loads for adult male is 55 kg, 45 kg for female, 25 kg for minor male and 20 kg for minor female aged between 16 and 18 years. It is 20 kg for the minor male and female of aged between 14 and 16 years.

The Act also has safety provision for the workers who work higher than atmospheric pressure in the production process.

In the absence of adequate and specific study in the sector, it is very difficult to say the exact situation of health and safety provision in Nepalese manufacturing sector. However, many issues raised by workers at the time of their strike indicate that there are few facilities for safety and health in Nepal. The study made by FNCCI (1997: 25) concludes that majority of industries have been fulfilling their health and safety responsibility towards the workers by providing low cost bearing health protecting equipment like masks, gloves, shoes and helmet. In addition, the study also blamed that workers were not found wearing these materials due to negligence and lack of awareness about health hazards associated with their job. However, the heavy and costly instruments like fire extinguisher were not used except in large industries.

Concluding Observations and Implications

Though the Labour Act is said to be progressive in protecting the rights of worker, evidences indicate that provisions of the act have not been uniformly applied in Nepal. The execution part of the law became very weak in the absence of proper monitoring and controlling system. The standard of fringe benefit conceived by the Act was maintained by some large enterprises and it was almost lowest or absence in the small enterprises. Thus, proper follow-up mechanism is to be developed to ensure the workers that their working life is qualitative, secured, and the industrial growth and development in the country is enhanced with the work of satisfied and productive workforce in the country. Employees and employers are not also fully satisfied from the provisions of the labour laws. Thus, a multipartite social dialogue among the stakeholder of the labour laws are to be initiated on the confronting issues in the labour laws.

References

Bajracharya, P. (1998), "Salient Features of the Industrial Relations Dynamics in Nepal", in Pant, P.R. and Mahandahr, N. (eds.), *Industrial Relations in Nepal: A Book of Readings*, Industrial Relations Forum in Collaboration with Friedrich Naumann Foundation, Kathmandu, pp. 21-30.

Dahal, M.K. (1995), *Minimum Wages in Manufactory Sector in Nepal*, A Study Report Submitted by Nepal Foundation for Advanced Studies to Industrial Relations Forum, FNCCI, Kathmandu.

DOLEP (2005), *Labour Administration 2005*, Department of Labour and Employment Promotion, HMG/N, Kathmandu.

FNCCI. (1997), *Survey Report on Wages, Working Condition in Manufacturing Industries in Nepal*, FNCCI, Kathmandu.

Gautam, I.P. (1999), *Study on Employees Welfare and Safety Program in the Industries of Nepal: with Special Reference to Butwal Industrial District*, Ph.D. Thesis (unpublished), Department of Commerce, Deen Dayal Upadhaya Gorakhpur University, India.

GEFONT/AMRC. (1996), *Strengthening Pro-worker Trade Unionism*, GEFONT and Asia Monitor Resource Centre, Kathamandu.

Gurugharana, K.K. (1998), "Labour Market and Industrial Relations in Nepal", in Chanda Ashoka et. al. (eds.), *Labour Employment and Human Development in South Asia*, Institute for Human Development, Institute of Applied Manpower Research and Friedrich Ebert Stiftung, New Delhi, pp. 345-74.

Gurugharana, K.K. and Dahal, N. (1996), *Industrial Relations System in Nepal*, Friedrich Ebert Stiftung, Kathmandu.

ILO. (1960). *Provision of Facilities for Promotion of Workers' Welfare – Second Asian Regional Conference Report II*, ILO, Geneva.

ILO. (1984), *Introduction to Social Security*, ILO, Geneva.

ILO (2006), www.ilo.org/ilolex/English, 22. 2. 2006.

IRF (1998), *Study Report on Social Impact of Industrial Employment of Labour*, Industrial Relations Forum, Kathmandu.

Katuwal, S.B. (2002), *The Workers in the Textile Industry in Nepal: A Study of Industrial Relations*, Ph.D. Thesis (Unpublished), Tribhuvan

University, Faculty of Management, Kathmandu.

LBMC (1993), *Trade Union Act 1992*, The Law Book Management Committee, Kathmandu.

Mainali, U.P. (1998), "Present Sate of the Labour in Nepal", *in* Pant, P.R. and Manandhar, N. (eds.), *Industrial Relations in Nepal: A Book of Readings*, Industrial Relations Forum in Collaboration with Friedrich Naumann Foundation, Kathmandu, pp. 36-41.

Manandhar, N. (1998a), "Scenario of Industrial Relations in Nepal, In Pant, P.R. and Manandhar, N. (eds.), *Industrial Relations in Nepal: A Book of Readings*, Industrial Relations Forum in Collaboration with Friedrich Naumann Foundation, Kathmandu, pp. 31-55.

Manandhar, N. (1998b), "Fixing Minimum Wages, *in* Pant, P.R. and Manandhar, N. (eds.), *Industrial Relations in Nepal: A Book of Readings*, Industrial Relations Forum in Collaboration with Friedrich Naumann Foundation, Kathmandu, pp. 243-45.

MOL (2003), *Nepal Gazette*, Vol. 3 (53), Extra issue 22 (Ka +1), Ministry of Labour and Transport, HMG/N, Kathmandu.

MOLJ. (1990), *The Constitution of the Kingdom of Nepal 1990*, Ministry of Law and Justice, Kathmandu.

MOLTM (1999), Labour Policy 1999, Ministry of Labour and Transport Management, HMG/N, Kathmandu.

MOLTM(2006), Labour and Employment Poli cy 2006, Ministry of Labour and Transport Management, HMG/N, Kathmandu.

Monappa, A. (1993). *Industrial Relations*, Tata McGraw-Hill Publishing Company Limited, New Delhi

Pant, P.R. (1998), "Wage Structure in Jute Industry", *in* Pant, P.R. and Manandhar, N. (eds.), *Industrial Relations in Nepal: A Book of Readings*, Industrial Relations Forum in Collaboration with Friedrich Naumann Foundation, Kathmandu, pp. 209-27.

Pant, P.R. and Agrawal, J.P. (1980). *Industrial Relations in Nepal*, Kirtipur Campus, Institute of Business Administration, Commerce and Public Administration, TU, Kathmandu.

Pant, P.R. (2044 B.S.), "Industrial Relations in Nepal", *Byawasthapan*, Special Issue in Industrial Relations in Nepal, No. 7, pp. 36-48.

RMF. (1982), *Disputes Settlements and Industrial Peace in Nepal: A Study Report*, Research and Management Forum, Kathmandu.

Shrestha, G.K. (1991), *Labour Management in Nepal: A Study of Public Sector Undertakings*, Ph.D. Thesis (Unpublished), Tribhuvan University, Faculty of Management, Kathmandu.

Shrestha, J.B. (1998), "Wages their Structure and Revision in Nepal", in Pant, P.R. and Manandhar, N. (eds.), *Industrial Relations in Nepal: A Book of Readings,* Industrial Relations Forum in Collaboration with Friedrich Naumann Foundation, Kathmandu, pp. 203-08.

Singh, B.P. and et al. (1995), *Personnel Management and Industrial Relations,* Dhanpat Rai & Sons, Delhi

Thiagarajah, R. (1987), "Labour Projection Laws of ASEAN Member Countries, their Enforcement and their Impact on Industrial Peace and Higher Productivity: An Overview", in *Labour Protection and Labour Relations in ASEAN: The Impact of Protective Labour Laws on Labour Relations*, ILO, Geneva.

Upadhya, N.P. (1998), "Minimum Wages in Nepal", *in* Pant, P.R. and Manandhar, N. (eds.), *Industrial Relations in Nepal: A Book of Readings,* Industrial Relations Forum in Collaboration with Friedrich Naumann Foundation, Kathmandu, pp. 228-36.

12

STATE, MIGRANT WORKERS AND ETHNIC POLARISATION: THE CASE OF NORTH-EAST INDIA

Vandana Upadhyay

I. Introduction

Over the past few decades, there has been a distinct shift towards pro-market economic policies in many countries of the world, including the developing countries. With the fall of the socialist block and the erosion of the support base of the left parties in many parts of the world, there has been a systematic weakening of the state-supported welfare measures, and there have been attacks on various labour rights from various stand points. The state-labour relations, consequently, have undergone a fundamental transition in many of the developing countries. With increasing emphasis on the neo-liberal doctrine of market and trade-led growth, the need to bring appropriate changes in labour laws as part of the strategy to attract foreign capital, is being felt by governments through out the world. In many cases it has meant a reversal of the concessions and safe-guards provided to labour after years of struggle. On the other hand, there has been an upsurge in ethnic, linguistic and religious extremism in various parts of the world. Partly such a tendency is linked to the increasing livelihood insecurity in a globalizing world, but in many cases the causes of such conflicts are far more complicated and deeper. Undoubtedly, such a development hinders the growth of labour movements in multi-ethnic societies.

This paper, on the basis of illustrations from India's north eastern states, attempts to argue that in situations of prolonged ethnic conflicts, the space to articulate the demands of labour gets narrowed down. As migration, resulting partly from the process of development itself creates and sharpens insecurities and competitions among ethnic communities, any organized attempt to secure the rights of the workers becomes extremely difficult, and the working poor become vulnerable to various forms of violence by state and non-state forces. The migrant workers and particularly those considered to be illegal and unwanted, suffer most. As the state internalizes the basic logic of ethnic movements and starts differentiating among the workers on the basis of their ethnicity, the workers are denied access to some basic and fundamental rights.

II. Contextualizing Migration

Migration is a complex demographic phenomenon, which confronts serious definitional problems. This is particularly true in the context of the Third World countries, where the labour markets are often fragmented and households adopt a wide range of strategies, including migration, to survive. Another set of problems arise because of the existence of cross-border tribes and ethno-linguistic groups having close cultural and emotional affinities, making the international borders less rigid and viable. Migration may be broadly understood as 'a permanent change in place of residence by the crossing of specified administrative or political boundaries. The persons who fulfill these two criteria are regarded as migrants' (Nabi and Krishnan, 1993). This definition clearly has its limits, as it does not take into account the nomadic or wandering people, seasonal migrants, and movements back and forth of people having more than one residence[1]. The current study particularly tries to understand the linkages between migration, employment and vulnerability in an ethnically polarized region of India.

While economic explanations of migrations induce one to think about ways to reduce economic difference between sending and receiving countries in order to check unwanted international population movements, political explanations for migration induce one to think about ways to resolve political differences among ethnic groups within the sending countries or between a people and their government (Weiner, 1983; 1993). Much of the contemporary literature on international migration focuses on economic conditions as the key determinants of population movements (Bohning, 1984; Borjas, 1990; Adler, 1977), although a few recent studies have also incorporated the impacts of non-economic factors (Myda, 2005).

The question of migration is linked to borders. In the entire third world, where state formation and nation formation have taken different paths, borders have become highly controversial. Most of India's problems with its major neighbours are related to this issue. The border not only fixes the legality or illegality of migration but also plays an important role in determining state responses. Empirical evidence from South Asia suggests that where migrations are politically determined they often diminish the ethnic heterogeneity of the country of origin. On the other hand economic migrations have made the countries of destination more heterogeneous (Weiner, 1992; 1993). Within the scope of cross-national migrations two broad categories of international conflicts may be considered. In the first place, these conflicts can be caused by population pressure upon resources leading to expansionist tendencies (Chandrasekhar, 1954). Secondly, when undesirable population movement affect the demographic balance of the host region as well as the interests of the host population, the host countries are forced to enter into a conflict with the country of origin of the migrants (Weiner, 1985). In the politics surrounding migration and migration policies, factors having religious and ethnonationalist roots are usually the most complex and volatile.

III. Migrant Workers in India's North-East: The Historical Context

The migration of people into North East India[2] is not a recent phenomenon. It is very difficult to say who actually constitute the indigenous population, for almost all groups living in the region have come from different places at different points in time. However, the integration of the entire north eastern region into the British India in the 19th century gave a new direction to the process of immigration. It was only during the colonial rule that material conditions facilitating structural change in the region opened up. Penetration of foreign capital, growth of tea plantations, development of railways and roadways, introduction of English education, emergence of private property in land and common subjection to a highly centralized political authority brought drastic changes in its socio-economic structure. Migration to the region was very much linked with the colonial policies and interests. It was during this period that lakhs of migrants, some representing more advanced nationalities and ethnic groups settled in the region. Five *migratory waves* have been identified during the last hundred years. The *first wave* was associated with the introduction of tea plantation as an industry by European planters in the 19th century. Indentured labourers were brought, mostly tribals from Orissa, Madhya Pradesh, Bihar, Bengal and Madras. During the same time many 'marwaries' also came in search of economic opportunities and settled in trade and business activities. The *second wave* was associated with the saturation of agricultural use of land in East Bengal and the introduction of certain developmental schemes like public education in Assam. Compelled by poverty and over population, lakhs of landless peasants migrated towards the Brahmaputra valley in search of land and livelihoods (Kar, 1980; 1997). These immigrants mostly settled in the present day province of Assam, Tripura and in the Imphal valley of Manipur. By 1931, in Tripura the share of immigrants was higher than that of the indigenous population. The *third wave* comprised the Second World War evacuees from Burma and the Nepali immigrants from Nepal. The Nepalese made a living mainly from animal husbandry and they choose the hill slopes of Assam and Manipur, which were utilized economically. The *fourth wave* occurred during the communal tensions of 1940's and continued in a big way after partition. The majority of the Hindu immigrants are currently engaged in the service sector and small business. The *fifth wave* is associated with the Bangladesh liberation movement and the continuing process thereafter (Kar, 1986).

Besides the above five categories there are also a few lakhs of people from all other states of India, who came to Assam and other north eastern states after independence for employment or business purposes. Finally, there are numerous tribal people who have migrated from bordering states and neighbouring countries, namely Bangladesh and Myanmar for different reasons. These migrations are generally undocumented and irregular.

IV. Extent of Migration

The phenomenon of migration of people from across the borders in North East India has resulted in cultural and demographic crisis which is evidently transforming and reshaping the ethnic, linguistic and religious profile of large parts of the population of the region (Table 1). A variety of factors—political, ethnic, religious, economic and environmental have been responsible for the continuous movement of population from Bangladesh to India. For example, following the partition of India in 1947, in order to escape communal violence, millions of Hindus fled from East Pakistan to India. Again during the liberation war of Bangladesh in 1971, millions of people from the then East Pakistan took refuge in India. During the 1970's and the 1980's thousands of Chakmas fled to India because of ethnic conflicts in the Chittagong Hill Tracts. These were cases of forced migration, which took place in response to particular incidents at a specific point of time. Environmental crisis in the rural areas of Bangladesh has been one of the major causes for uninterrupted and sustained movement of population from Bangladesh to India apart from the religious, ethnic and political causes (Swain, 1996).

In the last fifty years, the population in Bangladesh has increased at a brisk rate. According to the Census, from 42.16 million in 1952 it increased to 129.2 million in 2001, a net addition of 87.04 million people. During 1970-1990 the population of Bangladesh increased at an annual average rate of 2.5 per cent, which declined to 2.3 per cent per annum during 1990-2003 (UNICEF, 2007). Over the last fifty years the countries population has increased three times and has registered an increase in density from 285 to 975 persons per sq. km. Although Bangladesh has registered substantial improvements in reducing population growth, one should consider this increase in population against the background of existing resources. The country represents an environmental pressure point with high population pressure on a limited natural resource base[3]. Scarcity of natural resources causes economic and ecological marginalisation of the poor. Recurring natural disasters in the form of floods, cyclones and riverbank erosion worsens the situation further. The slow urban-industrial economy is not in a position to absorb such a large population. Environmental change causes economic and spatial marginalisation which in turn increases the susceptibility of the poor to shocks and unanticipated shortfalls in income. One of the major consequences of these patterns of interaction has been the migration of people from one region to another within a state or from one state to other neighbouring states as environmental migrants or ecological refugees (Conisbee and Simms 2003; Swain, 1996; Maddock, 1996, de Haan, 1999).

Illegal migration to Assam, from neighbouring countries, particularly Bangladesh, has always been an emotive issue (Weiner, 1983; Baruah, 1986). In popular discussions, the estimates of undocumented and illegal migration to Assam vary widely from 10-14 million to 4-5 million, although a few systematic studies have explored the issue (Bhuyan, 2002; Saikia, Goswami and Goswami, 2003). Some of the important aspects of the demographic changes in the states of the North East India that has been widely discussed in the recent past include the comparatively higher growth rates of population in the region in general and some of the border districts in particular, changes in the religious composition of the population, and the changing concentration of population in the border districts, generally attributed to fresh in-migration of people from Bangladesh. In the context of increasing population pressure on a fragile and depleting resource base, migration has intensified the conflicts over land and other resources.

V. Migration and Ethnic Strife

Studies on the reasons for the relatively high population growth in Assam have identified three major contributory factors: *(i)* high natural rate of increase since 1921; *(ii)* heavy in-migration and *(iii)* the relative absence of mobility of the indigenous people of Assam (Bandopadhyay and Chakraborty, 1999; Goswami and Gogoi, 1984). The large scale influx of people from across porous borders has led to conflicts between migrants and indigenous people over natural resources and employment both in the government and private sectors. Such clashes of interest have directly led to violent tribal insurgencies in many part of the region with guerrilla groups targeting migrant settlers often seeing them as land grabbers. Land is critical to identity formation among agrarian societies in North East India and the core fear about land alienation has generated a sense of insecurity among 'natives'. This, in part, has acted as a contributory factor in the mushrooming of numerous identity movements in the region. The avowed goals of these movements range from protection of the interest of the 'natives' from immigrants to formation of autonomous district-councils and creation of a separate state within India to complete secession from the Indian Union. Towards these ends, the militant outfits resort to all kinds of methods including abduction, killing, extortion and terrorism.

Real and imaginary apprehensions, about loss of identity act as the underlying cause of many of the conflicts and separatist movements in North East India. Migration, land and identity emerge as major rallying points for ethnic conflicts in the region. Exclusionary identity-based polity, however, creates perpetual 'others'. These developments, commentators note, has created a situation where individual, citizenship rights take a back seat in the face of assertions of communities, and other exclusively defined groups. At best, this brand of politics involves psychological prejudice against those labelled as the 'other'. At worst, it leads to population expulsion and ethnic cleansing (Kaldor, 1999).

VI. Nature of the Migrant Labour in North-East India

In the case of North East India, it is clear that migrants who have been entering the region are rarely entering the organized sector, but are being absorbed into what could be called the 'informal' sector. A substantial majority of these migrants are stuck well below the poverty line and can be categorized as the 'working poor'. Migration in the region has not always been voluntary and upwardly mobile, but was in fact seen as a compulsion generated in the context of livelihood insecurity. Since the migrants served as a workers' reserve, it exerted downward pressure on wages and hindered organization of the working class. Migration in the region is of several types. These include; permanent migration, temporary migration, seasonal or circular migration and erratically oscillatory migration. The nature and the causes of migration were quite varied. Migration to large extent is consequential to either pull or push factors. The pull factors can be a positive wage differential or other indicators suggesting upward mobility. Rural poverty, lack of employment opportunities and temporary or permanent loss of entitlements that are vital for peoples' livelihoods are the major push factors forcing out migration. In reality, both push and pull factors seem to work together. 'Mobility Occurs', Srivastava and Sasikumar (2003:5) point out, 'when workers in source areas lack suitable options for employment/ livelihood, and there is some expectation of improvement in circumstances through migration. The improvement sought may be better employment or higher wages/incomes, but also maximisation of family employment or smoothing of employment/income/consumption over the year'.

Within North East India, factors such as disasters on account of floods and earthquakes, landslides, displacement of labour, introduction of new labour displacing technology, social and ethnic conflict, and traditional hierarchy are some other factors, which also have an impact on migration (Hussain, 2000). Each of these reasons structures a pattern of migration that does not necessarily imply upward social mobility. They are meant to be survival strategies for labour (Standing, 1985; Vijay 2002). Kumar and Agarwal (2003), analyzing the census data on migration to Assam report that while males moved to the state mainly for economic reasons, the family related reasons have caused the migration of females. The statewise analysis shows that 'family moved' and 'marriage' were the important reasons for migration from the neighbouring states of Tripura, West Bengal and Meghalaya, economic reasons were prominent for some other states like Bihar, Uttar Pradesh and Rajasthan.

So far as contractual relations of the migrants and their employees are concerned broadly two types of employment patterns can be identified:

(a) *The casual migration arrangement* involves movement of migrant labourers to informal sector employments, mainly, but not only to urban areas, as construction workers, rickshaw-pullers, daily wage labourers etc. Although even in this type of migration, kinship networks and patron-client relationships do play an important role in getting access to employment, but the labour contacts are casual and hence employment insecurity is considerably high.

(b) *The contract migration arrangement* involves tied, personalized contracts, typically involving some credit to the migrants. The migrants are sometimes recruited by middlemen after paying advances in the form of loans. They are then transported to a work site of building, bridge and road construction undertaken by a contractor and are made to work during the period of contracts. This system provides greater certainty of employment than the casual migration system, but may involve coercive contractual obligation. A study on micro-enterprises in Arunachal Pradesh revealed that in the recruitment of labour a majority of the firms relied on ethnic and kinship connections (Upadhyay and Mishra, 2004).

It has been established that the informal economy is specially characterized by a highly segmented labour market which actually puts a constraint on upward social mobility (Rodgers, 1993). This segmentation is also based on non-economic categories of discrimination in the labour market including gender, region and so on. As in other contexts, in north east India too, the informal sector workers face different types of insecurities.

In agriculture a wide range of contractual relations is observed among the migrant workers and their employers—ranging from casual labour contracts to different types of tenurial relations. Studies on Arunachal Pradesh show that in spite of entry restrictions on outside labour, many migrant workers have entered the state as tenants and agricultural labourers (Mishra, 2006).

In respect to the migrant workers of the region another kind of categorization may be useful. Workers coming from outside the north eastern region both from other states of India and from across the borders can be called long distance migrants (LDM). Those coming from within the region may be called short distance migrants (SDM) and those coming from villages of adjacent areas may be categorized as local workers. This categorization suggests not only physical distance but also has relevance in understanding the vulnerability of these categories. Each employment pattern represents a level of security. Although comparing local workers, SDM and LDM, it is generally seen that the local workers have the highest proportion of stable jobs, followed by short distance migrants (Vijay, 2005), in north east India the picture seems to be considerably heterogeneous. There are broadly two different types of migrants to the region at the two different extremes: one, the relatively better educated, skilled and high-earner migrants who come to the services, trade and business; and two, the mass of un-skilled or low-skilled manual workers and petty traders who generally end-up as informal sector workers. Most of the later category workers are LDMs. There is a general pattern of worsening living conditions among the LDMs who end up being discriminated against vis-à-vis locals. It is clear that regional factors play a role in the vulnerability and systematic deprivation among the migrant workers. Access to capabilities and therefore to functioning itself is determined by structures such as ethnic identities, gender and region. Vulnerable groups of workers particularly LDMs end up in insecure employment patterns. This is particularly so in the informal sector (Upadhyay, 2005). The condition of deprivation of these workers in terms of wages and other living conditions itself is seen as a means to discrimination, marginalization and even exclusion (Rodgers, 1993). Seasonal migrants, typically from other Indian states, are also a significant category. Women happen to be the most vulnerable. The condition of the migrant women is generally characterized through oppression at various levels such as: (1) working class, (2) gender, (3) migrant minority group, and (4) acceptance of oppression as their fate (Morokvasic, 1983). Poverty in case of migrant women workers assumes strong gender connotations. However the lack of social security for both men and women workers, is quite conspicuous.

VII. State's Response to Migrant Worker's Problems

The complex interrelationship between the crisis of identity, security and underdevelopment is one of the key aspects of the development process in the entire north east (Madhab, 1999). This multiethnic region is influenced to a great extent by the politics of identity and difference[4]. An important contradiction noticed in the governance of Northeast in general is the strong presence of the Indian state, reflected through the heavy military and financial presence on the one hand, and its relative weakness in safe guarding the basic rights and security of the people in their everyday life (Baruah, 2004). The relative weakness of the state in protecting property rights and enforcing contracts, usually creates a scope for the emergence of ethnic groups to provide private means of securing property rights (Bates, 1998). The progressive wearing down of the state's power in the region as reflected in the government's incapability, or perceived incapability: to safeguard the basic human and property rights; to enforce the ordinary laws of the land; to reward and punish; to collect taxes; to carry out functions of financial management with requisite credibility; to enforce discipline among state employees; and to evoke fear of sanctions has resulted in the erosion of the state government's legitimacy and authority in several parts of the region. This, in turn, has also resulted in the simultaneous acquirement and consolidation of legitimacy and authority by various non-state agencies, including insurgent groups (Sahni and George, 2001).

Both the military and the developmental response to the

unrest in the region[5], by and large, have not been very effective and have resulted in chronic misery for the working class. Firstly, the prominence of the security considerations in the development interventions has often resulted in lopsided development priorities in the region. Secondly, chronic conflicts, long-term military campaigns, and the resultant institutional collapse not only disempowers the civil society, but also results in the denial of basic facilities such as health care and education for a prolonged period. Often, it is the poor; particularly those depending upon wage employment suffer most during such operations. As the recent episodes of targeted violence against the migrant brick kiln workers and milkmen of Upper Assam demonstrates, the immediate result was the disruption of normal work, loss of employment and increased vulnerability. Many of the fleeing workers, news paper reports suggest, could not collect the wages which was due to them.

The development interventions in conflict-prone regions like the north-east, faces additional constraints. Firstly, in situations of widespread breakdown of law and order and institutional collapse, there is complete absence of accountability and transparency. Also the unacceptable risks confronted by local officials executing development projects make the implementation of the project an impossible task. Further, the success of the developmental projects, are being limited by the flight of capital in the region. Militancy and resulting insecurity itself acts as barrier to normal economic activities. Economic activities such as cross border trade and use of forest products, which were very much a part of the life of the indigenous people gets disrupted during insurgencies and violence. The presumption of a clear opposition of interests between militant groupings on one-hand and government agencies on the other is often found to be misplaced. There has been numerous instances where, the insurgents have tried to siphon off a portion of the government funds, through their networks of 'taxes', extortions and transaction fees. Similarly, the bureaucrats and the politicians of the region have entered into collusive contacts with the militant outfits to achieve a range of objectives. The continuation of these arrangements undermines the very right to development of the poor and the marginalized. Apart from these systematic failures of development administration, there are various types of short-run, transient and irregular loss of livelihoods because of the violent conflicts. The workers and cultivators, belonging to both migrant and local population, are sometimes forced to carry loads and do other kind of manual jobs. It is important to note that women as a group face various difficulties and discriminations during such insurgency and counter-insurgency operations. More and more insurgent groups are taking to a form of terrorism that, is signified by attacking soft targets, especially migrant labourers. Ethnic cleansing has become a part of the insurgency cycle and with the state choosing to look the other way, the migrant worker is the first victim. A de-sensitized civil society too has tacitly come to accept the killing of migrant workers as a part of routine killings.

However, it is not just that workers in general and the migrant workers in particular are the only victims of insurgency. Insurgency and militancy has larger implications for the development of the region. Apart from insurgency, there are other factors and forces at work, which creates conditions for the systematic exploitation and marginalization of the migrant workers. Although labour shortage in destination areas plays an important role in inducing migration, Srivastava and Sasikumar in their survey on migration in India observe, 'virtually all available evidence shows that recruitment of immigrants is as much motivated by strategies of labour control and wage cost reduction. ... Migrants are preferred because their labour is easier to control and it is easier to extract labour from them under arduous conditions. Moreover, the supply of labour can be easily increased or decreased with little cost to employers and migrants can work for long and flexible hours. Flexibility of the migrant workforce is reinforced because of the role of contractors and middlemen in recruitment and supervision. The segmentation of the labour market, which also leads to greater control over both migrant and local labour, is another outcome of the process' (Srivastava and Sasikumar, 2003:9). This is true for the north eastern region as well. The operation of entry restriction in some of the states also weakens the bargaining power of migrant workers as most of them do not have the necessary documents and are dependent upon their employer for the entry permits.

The anxieties of the indigenous population regarding the changing demographic composition of the region, has led to a strong articulation of 'son-of-the-soil' demands on many issues. Migration to the region is linked to the very process of development, as apart from the plains of Assam and Manipur, labour is one of the key constraints faced by the economy. While migrant workers, both skilled and unskilled, have played an important role in the economic development of the region, with increasing educated and youth unemployment, the demand for local control over jobs, contracts and other resources of the state has been intensified. Historically, the governments have tried, to some extent, to accommodate these aspirations through constitutional safeguards within the broad parameters of democratic governance, and have also helped in protecting the interests of the local population. However, the politics of affirmative action by the state in the presence of such politicisation of ethnicity and ethnic difference has led to a replacement of civic rules by rules of difference—a process that, according to Sanjib Baruah, has created a 'crisis of citizenship' in the Northeast[6] (Baruah, 2003; 2004a).

In the general framework of politicized ethnicity and ethnic polarization, issues concerning the basic rights of workers, takes a back seat as workers themselves become part of various ethnic groups and fail to press for collective demands. The rhetoric of native-versus-migrant has resulted in a complete collapse of working class solidarity in many parts of the north-eastern region. Even the presence of strong unions in some sectors, such as the tea industry in Assam, has not been able to free itself from the politics of identity and difference[7]. In such a context the bargaining power of the migrant workers vis-à-vis their employers has become virtually non-existent. In fact, the *perceived* identity of the workers as unwanted migrants and/or illegal migrant is in many cases considered to be reasons enough for denial of some fundamental rights to the workers. Apart from the economic exploitation, in terms of low wages, longer working hours and hazardous working conditions, physical and psychological torture in various forms have become parts of the experiences of the migrant workers in many parts of the region.

The response of the state, at the ground level, to such violations of basic rights of the workers, predictably, is not based on any principle of universal rights. It is typically based on the identity of the workers and their employers and their position in the hierarchy of communities in the structure of power at the *local* level. Even when politicians and political parties, try to intervene in favour of some sections of the migrant workers; the entire action is projected as a concession or an action in favour of the *community*, rather than that for the *workers*. When the state differentiates among the workers, and tries to apply different sets of rules for different set of workers, the workers also try to strengthen their bargaining power by forming solidarity networks within the community rather than across the community. This explains, at least partly, the support for ethnic militias among the working classes.

VIII. Conclusion

The experience in the North East show identity driven political and socio-economic processes need not necessarily be progressive or a radical politics of the marginalized communities against the domination of hegemonising forces. More often than not the much claimed struggle against the exploitative all powerful state or indifferent central government ends up as fratricidal conflicts with other communities living in the region. Identity movements draw its strength from prejudices and misconceptions of groups about themselves and others. Feeding on the fear of the 'other' it pits one community against the 'other' and mobilizes the people along divisive lines. In a deeply polarized society, the compulsions of electoral politics compel the state either to look the other way or pursue policies that further consolidate ethnic loyalties and identities. In a scenario of scant respect for constitutional politics and the rule of law, the helpless migrant worker ends up as the canon fodder of identity driven militant groups. In the final analysis, such a scenario weakens the bargaining power of the workers as a group and makes them more vulnerable and marginalized.

Table 1

Growth Rate of Population in the States of North-East India: 1951-2001

State	*Growth Rate of Population*				
	1951-1961	*1961-1971*	*1971-1981*	*1981-1991*	*1991-2001*
Assam	34.98	34.95	23.36**	24.24**	18.85
Arunachal Pradesh*	-	38.91	35.15	36.83	26.21
Manipur	35.04	37.53	32.46	29.29	30.02
Meghalaya	27.03	31.50	32.04	32.86	29.94
Mizoram	35.61	24.93	48.55	39.70	29.18
Nagaland	14.07	39.88	50.05	56.08	64.41
Tripura	78.71	36.28	31.92	34.30	15.74
North East Total	38.04	35.04	26.40	27.46	22.02
India	21.51	24.80	24.69	23.82	21.34

Source: Census of India, various years and Bhuyan, 2002.

Notes:

1. *Census was conducted for the first time in 1961.
2. **Since census was not conducted in Assam in 1981, the rates for 1971-81 and 1981-91 are estimated on the basis of interpolation.

Table 2

In-Migrants in States of North-East India 1991 (Persons born outside the State Classified by Place of Enumeration and Place of Birth)

States	*Total No. Migrants*	*% of Migrants from NE*	*% of Migrants from Rest of India*
Arunachal Pradesh			
Persons	123118	62.38	37.62
Male	74415	57.92	42.08
Female	48703	69.14	30.86
Assam			
Persons	536579	17.93	82.09
Male	308402	6.95	93.05
Female	228177	22.81	77.19

Manipur			
Persons	17381	56.37	43.63
Male	10822	56.00	44.00
Female	6559	57.00	43.00
Meghalaya			
Persons	78895	64.21	35.79
Male	43965	64.48	38.78
Female	34930	69.58	32.02
Mizoram			
Persons	11560	72.38	27.62
Male	7173	67.52	32.48
Female	4387	80.33	19.67
Nagaland			
Persons	49598	58.32	27.62
Male	32396	54.80	32.48
Female	17202	64.97	19.67
Tripura			
Persons	38907	52.40	47.60
Male	18201	41.95	58.05
Female	20706	42.60	37.40

(*Source*: Census of India, 1991, Migration Tables)

Acknowledgements: An earlier version of the paper was presented at the 47th Annual Conference of the Indian Society of Labour Economics at Jawaharlal Nehru University, New Delhi during December 2005. Thanks are due to the participants of the conference and particularly to Prof. Alakh N. Sharma and Dr. A.V. Jose. A slightly abridged version of the paper is forthcoming in World Affairs. The author alone is responsible for the remaining errors.

Endnotes

1. The United Nations' multilingual demographic dictionary suggests that the expressions 'internal migration' and 'international migration' on the one hand and 'move' and 'migration' on the other should be distinguished. While 'internal migration' is a change in the place of residence from one administrative boundary to another within the same country, 'international migration' is a move over a national boundary. Again, while a 'move' is a change of residence within the same political or administrative boundary, 'migration' is a change of residence and also a crossing of the political or administrative boundary' (cited in Nabi and Krishnan, 1993).

2. The 'seven sisters States' of north east India are Assam, Manipur, Meghalay, Arunachal Pradesh, Mizoram, Tripura and Nagaland. Recently Sikkim has also been included in this group. There is however, considerable diversity within and among these states. India's North East region is placed between Bangladesh, Tibet, Myanmar and Bhutan with a thin land corridor linking it with the rest of India—the Siliguri Corridor—connecting mainland India with the outlying border States of the North East.
3. While there are clear adverse implications of population growth in a resource-scarcity environment, the link between population growth and resource scarcity is much more complex, involving issues of distribution and political control. For a discussion on how such simplistic assumptions may lead to a 'miltarisation of environmental policy', see Hartmann (1998).
4. This section draws on our earlier works Mishra and Upadhyay (2004).
5. See Ramesh (2005) on the shifts in central policy towards the north east during the post independence period.
6. Baruah argues that 'the time has come to consider ways of breaking away from the ethnic discourse of the existing protective discrimination regime that, in effect, involves the state forever categorizing groups of people in ethnic terms and making descendents of immigrants into perpetual outsiders' (Baruah, 2003:1626).
7. The term 'tea garden labourer' or 'ex-tea garden labourer' refers to the community of migrant workers. Many of the activities undertaken by the groups speaking on behalf of these communities are primarily attempts at consolidating and articulating the identity in the context of ethnic polarization.

References

Adler, Stephen (1977) *International Migration and Dependence*, Saxon House, Westmead.

Bandopadhyay, S. and D. Chakraborty (1999) 'Migration in the North-Eastern Region of India during 1901-1991: Size, Trends, Reasons and Impact', *Demography India*, Vol. 28, No. 1, pp. 75-97.

Baruah, Sanjib (1986) 'Immigration, Ethnic Conflict and Political Turmoil-Assam, 1979-1985', *Asian Survey*, Vol. 26, No. 11, pp. 1184-1206.

———————(2003) 'Protective Discrimination and Crisis of Citizenship in North-East India', *Economic and Political Weekly*, Vol. 38, No. 17, pp. 1624-1626.

———————(2004a) 'Citizens and Denizens: Ethnicity, homelands and crisis of displacement in North East India', *Social Change and Development*, Vol. 2, No. 1, pp. 105-130.

———————(2004b) 'Historicizing Ethnic Politics in North East India', Keynote Address, Seminar on '*Inter-ethnic Conflict and Ethnic Crisis in North East India*', Department of Political Science, Dibrugarh University, 16-17 Feb, 2004, (unpublished).

Bates, Robert H. (1998) 'Comment on "Structure and Strategy in Ethnic Conflict" by Donald L. Horowitz' in Boris Bleskovic and Joseph E. Stiglitz (eds) *Annual World Bank Conference on Development Economics*, World Bank, Washington, pp. 371-376.

Bhuyan, J.C., (2002) "Illegal Migration from Bangladesh and the Demographic Change in the N.E. Region", *Dialogue Quarterly,*, Vol. 3, No. 3, pp. 71-82.

Bohning, R. Wolf (1984) *Studies in International Labour Migration*, Macmillan, London.

Borjas, J. George (1990) *Friends or Strangers: the Impact of Immigration on the US Economy*, Basic Books, New York.

Chandrasekhar, S. (1954) *Hungry People and Empty Lands: An Essay on Population Problems and International Tensions*, London: George Allen and Unwin, pp. 102-6.

Conisbee, Molly and Andrew Simms (2003) *Environmental Refugees: The Case for Recognition*, New Economics Foundation, London, available at: http://www.neweconomics.org/gen/uploads/lpce0g55xjx5eq55mfjxbb5523102003180040.pdf

de Haan, A. (1999) Livelihoods and Poverty: the Role of Migration. A Critical Review of the Migration, *Journal of Development Studies*, Vol. 36, No. 2, December 1999.

Goswami, Atul and J.K. Gogoi (1984) 'Migration and Demographic Transformation of Assam 1891-1981', in B.L. Abbi (ed.) *Northeast Region: Problems and Prospects of Development*, CRIID, Chandigarh.

Hartmann, Betsy (1998) 'Population, Environment and Security: A New Trinity', *Environment and Urbanization*, Vol. 10, No. 2, pp. 113-128.

Horowitz, I. Donald (1985) '*Ethnic Groups in Conflict*', University of California Press, Berkeley, pp. 185-228.

Hussain, M. (2000) 'State, Identity Movements and Internal Displacement in the North East', *Economic and Political Weekly*, 16 December.

Kaldor, Mary, (1999) *Organized Violence in a Global Era*, Polity Press, Cambridge.

Kar, Biman (1986) 'Socio-Economic Implications of the Migration–Dominated High Population Growth Rates of North Eastern India', in B. Datta Ray, ed., *The Pattern and Problems of Population in North East,* Uppal, New Delhi, pp. 287-88.

Kar, M. (1997) *Muslims in Assam Politics,* Vikas Publishing House, New Delhi.

Kar, M. (1980) 'Muslim Immigration to Assam', *Social Scientist,* Vol. 8, No. 7, pp. 67-75.

Krishniah, M. (1998) 'Regular Farm Labour system in Semi Arid Areas: Emerging Patterns in Andhra Pradesh', *Economic and Political Weekly,* Vol. 33, No. 13.

Kumar, Puspam and S.C. Agarwal (2003) 'An Econometric Analysis of Causes of Migration in Assam', *Demography India,* Vol. 32, No. 1, pp. 107-122.

Maddock, Rowland T., 1996, Environmental Security in M. Jane Davis (ed) *Security Issues in the Post–Cold War World,* Edward Elger, UK.

Madhab, Jayant (1999) 'NorthEast: Crisis of Identity, Security and Underdevelopment', *Economic and Political Weekly,* Vol. 34, No. 6, pp. 320-322.

Mayda, Anna Maria (2005) 'International Migration: A Panel Data Analysis of Economic and Non-Economic Determinants ',IZA Discussion Papers 1590, Institute for the Study of Labor (IZA), Bonn.

Mishra, D. K. (2006) 'Institutional Specificities and Agrarian Transformation in Arunachal Pradesh: Changing Realities and Emerging Challenges', *Indian Journal of Agricultural Economics,* Vol. 61, No. 3, July-September.

Mishra, D.K. and V. Upadhyay (2004) 'Governance and Development in Arunachal Pradesh: The Emerging Challanges', *Dialogue Quarterly,* Vol. 5, No. 4, pp. 73-96.

Morokvasic, Mirjana (1983) 'Women in Migration: Beyond the Reductionist Outlook', in Annie Phizacklea, edited, *One Way Ticket: Migration and Female Labour,* Routledge, London, pp. 13-31.

Nabi Nurun, A.K.M. and P. Krishnan (1993), 'Some Approaches to the Study of Human Migrations', in Kuttan Mahadevan and Parameswara Krishnan, eds., *Methodologies of Population Studies and Development,* New Delhi: Sage, pp. 83-85.

Rodgers, Gerry (1993) 'The Creation of Employment in Segmented Labour Markets: A General Problem and Its Implications in India', *Indian Journal of Labour Economics,* Vol. 36, No. 1.

Sahni, Ajai and J. George, (2001) Security and Development In India's North East: An Alternative Perspective in Gill, K.P.S. (ed.) *Terror and Containment: Perspectives on India's Internal Security*, Gyan Publishing House, New Delhi, pp. 295-318.

Saikia, Anil, Homeswar Goswami and Atul Goswami (2003) *Population Growth in Assam 1951-1991: With Focus on Migration*, Akansha, New Delhi.

Srivastava, Ravi and S.K. Sasikumar (2003) 'An Overview of Migration in India, its Impact and Key Issues', available at http://www.livelihoods.org/hot_topics/docs/Dhaka_CP_2.pdf

Standing, Guy (1985) *Labour Circulation and Labour Process*, ILO, Geneva.

Swain, Ashok (1996) 'Displacing the Conflict: Environmental Destruction in Bangladesh and Ethnic Conflict in India', *Journal of Peace Research*, Vol. 33, No. 2, pp. 189-204.

UNICEF (2006) Statistics available at http://www.unicef.org/infobycountry/bangladesh_bangladesh_statistics.html

Upadhyay, V and D.K. Mishra (2004) 'Micro Enterprises in Hill Economies: A Study on Arunachal Pradesh', *The Indian Journal of Labour Economics*, Vol. 47, No. 4, pp. 1027-38.

Upadhyay, V. (2005) Employment and Earnings in Urban Informal Sector: A Study on Arunachal Pradesh, Project Report submitted to V V Giri National Labour Institute, NOIDA.

Vijay, G. (2002) 'New Industrial Labour: Insecure Employment, Social Conflict and Labour Rights', in G. Saibaba and Srinivas Rao (eds), *Structural Adjustments and its Implications for Human Rights*, Serial Publications, New Delhi.

Vijay, G. (2005) 'Migration, Vulnerability and Insecurity in New Industrial Labour Markets', *Economic and Political Weekly*, May 18, pp. 2304-2312.

Weiner, M. (1983) The Political Demography of Assam's Anti-Immigrant movement', *Population and Development Review*, Vol. 9, No. 2, pp. 279-292.

Weiner, M. (1985) 'On International Migration and International Relations', *Population and Development Review*, Vol. 11, No. 3, pp. 441-455.

Weiner, Myron (1992) 'Peoples and States in a New Ethnic Order?', *Third World Quarterly*, Vol. 13, No. 2, pp. 317-333.

Weiner, Myron (1993) 'Rejected Peoples and Unwanted Migrants in South Asia', *Economic and Political Weekly*, Mumbai, 21 August, pp. 1745-46.

13

SOCIAL SECURITY FOR OLD AGED PEOPLE IN INDIA

Nirmala Kumari

I. Introduction

The prime concern of social security is the conservation of resources into protection and the safeguarding of a sustainable livelihood, rather than the material ownership of assets. Whereas strategies for survival, access and maintenance of access are at the centre of attention in livelihood studies, social security studies are much more oriented towards support, protection, collective and welfare provisions. A social security approach however cannot do without an understanding of strategies of individuals and households and an emphasis on their ways of access to resources. Article 41 of Indian Constitution deals with the State's role in providing social security to the aged. According to this article, "the State shall, within the limits of its economic capacity and development, make effective provision for securing the right to work, to education and to public assistance in case of unemployment, old age, sickness and disablement and in other cases of undeserved want": The Constitution of India (as on 1 June, 1996), Government of India.

In this paper, it will be my endeavour to focus on the kinds of social security systems for the old aged people. In India, old age income security is not well developed. About 85 per cent of the total workforce is in the unorganised sector with little or no formal old age income security. However, the issue of old age security is gaining importance and it is now high on the public policy agenda.

II. Social Sector Policy Initiatives

The Government of India announced a National Policy on Older Persons in January 1999. This policy provides a broad framework for inter-sectoral collaboration and cooperation both within the government as well as between government and non-governmental agencies. In particular, the policy has identified a number of areas of intervention - financial security, healthcare and nutrition, shelter, education, welfare, protection of life and property etc. for the wellbeing of older persons in the country. Amongst others the policy also recognizes the role of the NGO sector in providing user friendly affordable services to complement the endeavours of the State in this direction.

A National Council for Older Persons (NCOP) with 39 members and a seven-member working group has been constituted by the Ministry of Social Justice and Empowerment to operationalise the National Policy on Older Persons. The basic objectives of the NCOP are to:

(1) Advice the Government on policies and programmes for older persons.

(2) Provide feedback to the Government on the implementation of the National Policy on Older Persons as well as on specific programme initiatives for older persons.

(3) Advocate the best interests of older persons.

(4) Provide a nodal point at the national level for redressing the grievances of older persons, which are of an individual nature.

(5) Provide lobby for concessions, rebates and discounts for older persons both with the Government as well as with the corporate sector.

(6) Represent the collective opinion of older persons to the Government.

(7) Suggest steps to make old age productive and interesting.

(8) Suggest measures to enhance the quality of inter-generational relationships.

(9) Undertake any other work or activity in the best interest of older persons.

While recognizing the need for promoting productive ageing, the policy also emphasizes the importance of family in providing vital non formal social security for older persons. To facilitate implementation of the policy, the participation of Panchayati Raj Institutions, State Governments and different Departments of the Government of India has been envisaged with coordinating responsibility resting with the Ministry of Social Justice & Empowerment. The government announced two new initiatives in the social sector in the year 2003-04:

(1) Universal Health Insurance Scheme (UHIS).

(2) Varishtha Pension Bima Yojana (VPBY).

Mandatory welfare schemes though scattered and on a relatively small scale have been provided in the formal sector for long—Central Government Health Scheme (CGHS) providing a health cover for the government employees; Central Government Employees' Group Insurance Scheme providing a life cover for government employees; Employees' State Insurance Scheme (ESIS) providing health and life cover for private employees; and the Employees' Provident Fund and Miscellaneous Provisions Act providing different schemes for provident fund/deposit-linked insurance scheme/pension for private employees (The Employees' Provident Fund Scheme, 1952; Deposit-Linked Insurance Scheme, 1976; Employees' Pension Scheme, 1995).

These mandatory schemes have an aggregate coverage of about 40 million. In addition to the aforesaid, the scattered employer-based schemes in the formal sector have provided varying degrees of social security to about 30 million individuals. In totality, some degree of social security cover has been available to about 110 million people, out of which less than 30 million are the poor from the unorganised sector. In 2002-03, the Government launched the Universal Health Insurance Scheme (UHIS) in the country. UHIS is the first broad-based health social security scheme, having an element of financial contribution from the State.

III. Universal Health Insurance Scheme (UHIS)

In the Union Budget of 2003-04, UHIS was formally launched by the then Prime Minister, Mr. Atal Behari Vajpayee. This scheme principally provides a package of insurance cover for hospital reimbursement of expenses for hospitalisation. The UHIS envisages—imbursement of hospitalization expenses to an individual, a family, specialist nursing expenses and maximum reimbursement for a single illness etc. the aggregate quantum of cover is Rs. 30,000 subject to a sub-cap of Rs. 15,000 for a single illness. The aggregate cover of Rs. 30,000 can be availed of on a floater basis in the case of cover of a family. The scheme also provides personal accident cover/compensation of Rs. 25,000 for the contingency of death in the case of accident and illness for a maximum of 15 (fifteen) days the coverage under this scheme, inter alia excludes all pre-existing diseases, as also some common medical conditions even when contracted after enrolment under the scheme. The insurance becomes substantively effective after the expiry of 30 days from the enrolment of the subscriber. The premium payable for this package of cover under the UHIS is Rs. 365 per annum (i.e. Re. 1 per day) for an individual; Rs. 548 per annum (i.e. Rs. 1.50 per day) for a family having five members (including the first three children; and Rs. 730 per annum (i.e. Rs. 2 per day) for a family of up to seven members (including the first three children and dependent parents). The State provides a contribution of Rs. 100 per family for persons who are below the poverty line (BPL) by way of a subsidy towards the premium of BPL beneficiaries. The policy covers the expenditure incurred during hospitalisation in the listed health services centres i.e. Government Hospitals/ Nursing Homes registered with local authorities and few other hospitals operated by Non Government Organisations (NGOs)/Trusts as well as private parties having the prescribed infrastructure facilities and qualified medical practitioners and other medical assistance.

The UHIS with its proposed premium structure would be a non-starter. In order to have any impact, the government subsidy would have to be substantially increased and that too not limited only to the poorest section. The composition of the subscriber pool would be steeply skewed towards those with very high health risk. Such a composition would make the scheme high-cost and fundamentally non-viable. The core requirement is that govt. subsidise the entire insured pool equally, and that too at a much higher subsidy rate i.e. a rate realistically linked to the actual costs of the scheme. In order to determine the realistic cost of the scheme, first a modest package of health services will have to be delineated. It must be immediately clarified that such a strategy would not result in the subsiding of the economic elite. Even if the UHIS is efficiently run, the scale and quality of services would still remain modest, and anyone who can afford it would be chosen to obtain superior and private health services at personal cost. Thus, there is no reason to believe that this suggestion would result in gross misapplication of the state subsidy.

The scheme as it is shaped today, only covers the risk of hospitalisation. Such schemes are known to be easier to manage. The coverage of primary healthcare i.e. community health measures and ambulatory care requires much greater skills of management and greater organisational strength. Therefore, in the initial stage it is, perhaps, understandable that the promoters test the waters by launching the schemes only covering the risk of hospitalisation.

However, if the scheme is to truly become a universal health scheme, it must include in its package of services, primary healthcare consisting of community health services and ambulatory services. Community health services promote good health through advocacy of healthy practices and reduce morbidity through preventive initiatives. Initiatives in this sector involve advocacy, sensitisation of the target population and influencing the mind-set of citizenry. Such initiatives are low cost in character and have a long-lasting impact on the health scenario. Ambulatory care is also a very cost effective form of health intervention. It is self evident that the introduction of community health services and ambulatory care in the health cover package would reduce the burden of high cost hospitalisation.

Thus the inclusion of primary sector health care component in the UHIS would immensely increase its viability while simultaneously providing much more useful health care services to the subscribers. Today this scheme is only in the nature of a preliminary statement of intent of a possible initiative. It's present form is not adequately fleshed out to successfully implement it across the entire country. Here it is necessary to experiment with the various models of the scheme on a pilot scale. One can make the scheme more palatable by phasing it gently over a longer time span but underestimating the unit cost of the insurance package would be self-defeating. Pilot studies would only be useful if they cover a reasonable package of services at a realistic cost. In this context, the Government may even settle for a slower start to the scheme provided it is fully funded in the areas where it is tried out.

IV. Varishtha Pernsion Bima Yojana

This scheme was also launched by the Government after the Budget 2003-04. This scheme is an old age pension scheme of Life Insurance Corporation (LIC) of India. This scheme provides a minimum pension of Rs. 250 a month and a maximum of Rs. 2000 a month to people over 55 years of age who opt for this scheme.

For the minimum pension, a lump sum payment of Rs. 33,335 has to be made while for the maximum pension of Rs. 2000, a lump sum of Rs. 2, 77,490 has to be made. There is no upper age limit for availing the benefits of the scheme. In the case of death of a pensioner (insured person), this amount would be given to the nominee (dependent). After 15 years, the withdrawal of amount facility is also permitted to the insured person. And, after 3 years, a pension policy-holder can avail of a loan from the LIC of India to the extent of 75% of the premium amount for which the interest rate would be 8.5% per annum for now. This interest rate would be revised periodically.

The main aim of this scheme is to change the social environment in the country because earlier we had families where the aged people and the elderly were looked after by the family members. Today because of economic reasons, this has become difficult and the Government felt the need to step in with the old pension scheme.

Various other insurance schemes viz. New Jeevan Dhara, New Jeevan Akshay, New Jeevan Suraksha and New Bima Nivesh have also been relaunched.

V. The National Social Assistance Scheme (NSAS)

This scheme introduced in 1995, is a centrally funded scheme compromising of National Old Age Pension Scheme (NOAPS), besides the National Family Benefit Scheme (NFBS) and National Maternity Benefit Scheme (NMBS). Here, I will be covering only the NOAPS.

National Old Age Pension Scheme (NOAPS) launched on 15 August 1995, is subjected to the following three conditions:

(1) The person, either male or female, should not be less than 65 years of age to be eligible for this scheme.

(2) The person/applicant must be destitute i.e. those with little or no regular means of subsistence from his or her own source of income or through financial support from family members or other source.

(3) The amount of old age pension for the purpose of claiming central assistance is Rs. 75 per month. State may however contribute further and provide higher benefits as per their financial resources.

The above-mentioned programme is a 100 per cent centrally sponsored programme to insure minimum national standard of social assistance in addition to the benefit from the states. This scheme is implemented in the states and union territories through panchayats and municipalities. Both panchayats and municipalities are encouraged to involve voluntary agencies as much as possible in benefiting the destitute elderly for whom this scheme is intended.

Table 1: Old Age Pension Amounts given by Different States

Name of the State	*Current Amount Pension (Rs. per month)*	*Minimum Age of Eligibility (in years)*
Andhra Pradesh	75	65
Arunachal Pradesh	150	60
Assam	60	65 (males) 60 (females)

Bihar	100	60
Gujarat	200275	60 to 6565 +
Haryana	100	60
Himachal Pradesh	150	60
Jammu & Kashmir	125	60
Karnataka	100	65
Kerala	110	65
Madhya Pradesh	150	60 (males) 50 (females)
Maharashtra	100	65 (males) 60 (females)
Mizoram	100	65 (males) 60 (females)
Orissa	100	65
Punjab	200	65 (males) 60 (females)
Rajasthan	200300	58 (males)55 (females)
Tamil Nadu	150	60
Uttar Pradesh	125	60
West Bengal	300	60
Chandigarh	200	65 (males) 60 (females)
Delhi	200	60

Source: Regional offices of HelpAge India, State offices in Delhi and State government.

There are also few other schemes by the Centre to benefit the older destitute. One of them is the Annapurna Food Security Programme for the older people, launched in March 1999, this scheme entitles below poverty line aged people to get 10 kg of wheat or rice monthly free. This scheme is centrally funded means a tested plan. Initially this scheme was expected to cover a total number of about 6, 60, 000 older destitute in all over the country. However, this programme is still at its infancy and confined to only a limited number of states.

VI. Pension and Family Pension

The revision of pension/family pension approved by the Central Government based on the 5th Pay Commission, is given below:

(1) *Pension:* People who retired from service as on 1-1-96, will get their pension at 50 per cent of their basic

pay. Pension of those who retired before 1-1-96 will be fixed based on 50 per cent of the minimum of the new scale applicable in place of old scale in which he/she retired. Special provision has been made for people retire before completing 10 months of service after 1 January 1999 (before 30 September 1996) and have opted to come over to the revised scales of pay are eligible weightage at 40 per cent on the existing basic pay for arriving at the average pay fixation of pension.

(2) *Family pension:* Family pension of people who retired from service as on 1-1-96 will be fixed at 30 per cent of the pay drawn by the deceased employee based on the new pension formula subject to his having put in 33 years of service. Family pension of people who retired before 1-1-96 will be fixed at 30 per cent of the pay drawn by the deceased employee based on the new pension formula subject to his having put in 33 years service.

For Central Government employees who have been permanently absorbed in public sector undertakings/autonomous bodies, the revision of pension/family pension approved is as follows

(1) *Pension:* Where the Government servants on permanent absorption in public sector undertakings/autonomous bodies continues to draw pension separately from the Government, the pension of such absorbees will be updated in terms of these orders. In cases where the Government servants have drawn one-time lump sum terminal benefits equal to 100 per cent of their pensions and have become entitled to the restoration of one-third commuted portion of pension as per Supreme Court judgment dated 15 December 1995, their cases will not be covered by these orders.

(2) *Family pension:* In cases where, no permanent absorption in public sector undertakings/autonomous bodies, the terms of absorption permit grant of family pension under the CCS (Pension) Rules, 1972 or the corresponding rules applicable to Railway employees/

members of All India Services, the family pension being drawn by family pensioners will be updated in accordance with these orders.

VII. Mobile Medicare Unit Programme

The Mobile Medicare Unit (MMU) Programme is aimed to provide basic essential medicare at the door steps of needy and underprivileged elderly in India. It is being directly implemented by HelpAge India. Presently, HelpAge India has a fleet of 20 directly controlled MMUs (details given at Table 2).

Table 2: Details of Mobile Medicare Unit (MMU)

Location	*Number of MMU*	*Location*	*Number of MMU*
Delhi	2	Lucknow	1
Mumbai	2	Jammu	1
Calcutta	2	Faridabad	1
Chennai	1	Chandigarh	1
Bangalore	1	Bhadohi	1
Hyderabad	1	Bhubaneswar	1
Ahmedabad	1	Paradip	1
Pune	1	Bikaner	1
Nagpur	1		

Three more MMUs at Jaipur, Bhopal and Delhi-III/ Gurgaon are to be launched soon and another at Coimbatore a little later. In addition, HelpAge India has provided about 80 MMUs to grass root NGOs for the similar services.

VIII. Conclusion

In response to the growing changes in the age composition and faster ageing, the centre and state governments in India have for past few years been engaged in drawing a set of policy initiatives to help the older persons. Besides, there have been commitments by the governments at various national and international fora to assimilate the growing number of aged people in the process of development. Internationally, this commitment was practicality more responding in the United Nations Organisation (UNO) sponsored Second World Assembly on ageing in Madrid (Spain) held in April 2002.

The Ministry of Social Justice & Empowerment has also launched a project called "Old Age Social and Income Security (OASIS)". An Expert Committee is constituted under the project. The first report of the Committee and the existing income security instruments available to older persons have been comprehensively examined. The report also contains detailed recommendations for enhancing the coverage, improving the rate of returns and for bringing about a qualitative improvement in the customer service of Public Provident Fund, the Employees Provident Fund, the Annuity Plans of LIC, Unit Trust of India (UTI) etc. further action on the recommendations of the Committee are under consideration. Meanwhile, Phase II of the project is looking at the pension and gratuity schemes of the central government and old age pension provided under National Social Assistance Programme (NSAP). At the core of the second phase of project OASIS, however, lies the designing of a new, fully funded, contributory pension programme for the balance (uncovered) workers including casual/contract workers, self-employed, farmers etc. Overall, these schemes serve to provide opportunities for linking social assistance package to poverty alleviation schemes and provision for the basic needs. These are mostly implemented through panchayats and municipal bodies with provisions to seek assistance from voluntary agencies.

The Government made an attempt to design special and long term deposit schemes for retirement purposes with provision of higher interest earning and finally there is also need to look into the other pillar of social security especially in the public domain. The ceiling on destitute pension needs security. We should also anticipate that the political economy of aging will become operational in the country sooner than later and States may need to evolve a more comprehensive old age pension schemes. Financing of such schemes may be made possible by imposing some form of cess on selected industries including that are health hazard and polluting.

References

Ministry of Social Justice & Empowerment, Government of India *Letter No. 20-32/99-NGO(SD) dated 22nd June, 1999.*

Ministry of Rural Areas and Employment, *NSAP Guidelines for State Governments.*

Ministry of Rural Development with the assistance of Ministry of Food and Civil Supplies.

Government of India, Ministry of Personnel, Public Grievances & Pensions, Department of Pension & Pensioners Welfare, New Delhi *office memo No. 45/86/97-P&PW(A)-Part-II, dated the 27th October, 1997 and F.No. 45/86/97-P&PW(A)-Part-I dated 18-10-99.*

Regional Office of HelpAge India, New Delhi.

Agent Manual-LIC of India.

14

SOCIAL SECURITY FOR THE UNEMPLOYED IN INDIA

Prakash S. Kamble

I. Introduction

Human resource in general and labour in particular is an important productive resource in absence of which economic development is a mere dream. It is the human resource which plays a vital role in the beginning and development of each and every productive activity, whereby rapid and all round economic development of the economy takes place, whatever may be the state of technology. But in an effort to modernize the economy necessary for the rapid and overall development, the rigorous and to the greatest extent possible attempts are being made either to develop advanced technology or import it. It is a fact that advanced technology is a labour saving and employment declining one. This works as a prominent factor in arising as well as intensifying the problem of unemployment. Imports of goods and services in the globaliasing world have helped in promoting further gravity of unemployment. Hence social security for the unemployed has becoming a burning issue. India has made the process of globalisation dynamic particularly since 1991. This shows an urgent need to study the aspect of social security for the unemployed in India. In this background, the present paper endeavors to examine the issue of social security for the unemployed in India in the globalisation era.

II. Social Security

The term social security at present is only related to the employees employed mainly in industry and tertiary sector. This implies that it has not covered the primary sector in general and agriculture in particular till date in the economies like India. Further unemployed people are totally neglected with a few exceptions in the jurisdiction of social security. But it is the need of hour to think of social security with highest priority in the context of unemployed in the globalising world.

Social security implies protection given by the state of government to the workers to offer minimum standard of living in the crisis like accident, sickness, disablement death etc. It is an attempt to give security to the family members during especially bad conditions of the workers. It is an effective measure on labour welfare maximisation

The meaning of the concept social security can better understand with the help of its major and important definitions. The ILO (International Labour Organisation) defines social security as "the security that society furnishes, through appropriate organizations against certain risks to which its members are exposed. These risks are essentially contingencies against which the individual of small means and meager resources cannot effectively provide by his own ability or foresight alone, or even in private combination with his fellows these risks being sickness, maternity, invalidity, old age and death. It is the characteristic of these contingencies that they imperil the ability of the working man to support himself and his dependents in health and decency." According to Lord Beveridge, "social security is an attack on five giants—wants, disease, ignorance, squalor and idleness." Friedlander defines social security, as, " Programme of protection provided by society against these contingencies of modern life—sickness, unemployment, old age, dependency, industrial accidents and invalidism—against which the individual cannot be expected to protect himself and his own ability or foresight." In *The Encyclopedia of Social Work*, social security has been defined as, "the endeavour of the community, as a whole, to afford itself of the almost extent possible to any individual during periods of physical distress inevitable an illness or injury and from the economic distress consequent on reduction or loss of earnings due to illness, disablement, maternity unemployment, old age, or death of the working member".[1]

III. Social Security in India

Social security is the gift of England to the world. India was under the British rule for a long period. Hence we found the introduction and enforcement of social security measures in the pre-independence period. But it is a fact that the scope and importance of social security has been widened significantly in the post independence period. Thus we find that the evolution of social security in India in the systematized methods of social assistance and social insurance as the result of the influence of the west. The following are the various legislative measures adopted by the Government of India which provide protection to the industrial workers in certain contingencies:[2]

1. Workmen's' Compensation Act, 1923.
2. Employees' State Insurance Act, 1948.
3. Coal Mines Provident Fund and Bonus Scheme, 1948.
4. Dock Workers (Regulation and Employment) Act, 1948.
5. Plantations Labour Act, 1951.
6. Employees Provident Fund Act, 1952.
7. Assam Tea Plantation Provident Fund Act, 1955.
8. Maternity Benefit Act, 1961.
9. Family Pension Scheme, 1964.
10. Seaman's Provident Fund Act, 1966.
11. Employees' Family Pension Scheme, 1971.
12. Survivorship Pension Scheme, 1971.
13. Old–Age Pension Scheme, 1971.
14. Payment of Gratuity Act, 1972.
15. Employees' Deposit – Linked Insurance Scheme, 1976.
16. Employee's Pension Scheme, 1995.[3]

The main statutory provision that has been provided so far in the country in the direction of social security is in respect of:[4]

1. Compensation in case of industrial injury and diseases,

2. Maternity benefits to women workers, and
3. The recent schemes of Health Insurance, Provident Funds, Old age and Family pensions, Gratuity, etc.

The social security measures as provided in various legislations in India are narrow in scope and adequate in the extent of assistance. The coverage of measures is restricted to certain industries and to a specified class of workers, leaving quite many industrial workers outside it. Besides, all the risks are not covered, e.g. there is no unemployment insurance. The types of facilities and the rates and magnitude of benefits are inadequate. The finances for their implementation are small. The agencies for their administration are not sufficient and even appropriate. The process of implementation of these schemes is too much time–taking and it suffers from the evils of red-tapism.

IV. Post-Globalization Employment and Unemployment Growth in India

Estimates based on the data available from the most comprehensive official source, namely, National Sample Survey Organization (NSSO), indicated that these occurred a significant deceleration in the growth of employment over the period following the initiation of major economic reforms towards globalisation in the early 1990s.[5]

Using the Current Daily Status (CDS) criterion, employment grew at 2.5 per cent during 1987-88 to 1993-94, but only at 1.07 per cent during 1993-94 to 1999-2000. Corresponding growth rates of GDP for these periods were 5.8 and 6.7 per cent. A faster growth led to a lower employment growth, particularly during the period 1993-94 to 1999-2000. A decline in employment growth is also observed, when employment elasticity declined, sharply from 0.41 during 1987-88 to 1993-94 to 0.16 during 1993-94 to 1999-2000.

A poor employment performance of the growth during the 1990 can primarily be attributed to a virtual stagnation of employment in agriculture which accounted for 60 per cent of total workers and a significant decline in employment in community, social and personal services, which constituted the third largest employer (among the 9 activity sectors) accounting for 11 per cent of workers, in 1993-94. Manufacturing, the second largest sector after agriculture, accounting for over 11 per cent workers in 1993-94, experienced an employment growth of 2.5 per cent per annum during 1994-2000. Other sectors, namely construction, trade, transport and finance also registered employment growth of 5 and 6 per cent per annum. Employment growth has been just over one per cent during the 1990s as compared to around 2 per cent in the earlier decade. If period since 1990 is considered, export oriented industries have shown a much better employment growth than others; employment in them grew at 3.36 per cent per annum, as against 2.67 per cent in import-competing and 3.09 in all industries. Export-oriented industries are also found to have significantly higher employment elasticity (0.48) than the manufacturing sector as a whole (0.33). Recent data available show employment growth of a rate of over 2 per cent per annum during June 2000 to December 2002.[6]

The failure of the Indian economy to generate adequate employment opportunities has been responsible for taking place the problem of unemployment and its growing gravity. According to NSS (National Sample Survey), there were 3.98 million unemployed in India in 1973-74, which increased to 7.49 million in 1993-94 and as much as 9.15 million in 1999-2000. In the mean time, the incidence of employment (defined as the ratio of unemployed persons to the labour force) increased from 1.64 per cent in 1973-74 to 1.96 percent in 1993-94 to 2.25 percent in 1999-2000. Unemployment rate in Urban areas was 8.99 percent in 1972-73, which rose to 10.34 per cent in 1977-78, but slightly declined to 9.36 per cent in 1987-88. The number of educated unemployed rose from 2.44 lakh in 1951, which rose to 68 lakh in 1992. The current Daily Status Unemployment rate for the Rural male workers was 5.64 per cent in 1993-94 as against 4.58 per cent in1987-88. In March 1994, Usual Status unemployment rate for males and females was 1.4 per cent and 0.9 per cent respectively. Farmers cultivating 75 per cent of land remain involuntary unemployed for 4 to 6 months.[7]

V. Need of Social Security for the Unemployed in India

The trends in the growth of employment and unemployment cited above indicate the need for social security for the unemployed in India. Besides social security for employed especially unsatisfactorily, also social protection should be seriously think of for the unemployed in India as well.

Domination of the unorganized sector with irregular and insecure jobs, low productivity and earnings and no social protection, has been a well-known feature of the Indian employment scene. Employment in the temporary, casual and contract, modes of employment by this sector imply exclusion of even those working for enterprises in this sector not only from the job security but also protection net.[8]

So far as the need for social security for the unemployed in India in post-globalisation is concerned, we find a significant deceleration in the growth of employment is observed, which has been consequently increasing the extent of unemployment indicating the urgent need for its coverage. Employment growth registered only 1 to 2 per cent growth rate in the post-globalisation Indian economy. Agriculture is the main occupation of India on various grounds. But it has shown almost stagnation in employment generation. Besides this, Indian farmers as well as agricultural labours have to remain unemployed for about 4 to 6 months in a year. Disguised unemployment in our country is also an important thing of concern in the context of social security. Manufacturing sector an important sector in the context of employment generation has shown about 8.5 per cent fall in employment generation during 1993-94 to 1999-2000 clearly indicates the need for covering the unemployed in the net of social security. In absolute terms, the number of unemployed has been increased substantially by about 2 million in the post-globalisation era must be considered as a signal of the urgency for enforcing social security measures in our economy. Urbanisation is one of the symptoms of economic development, is very slower in India, but urban unemployment has been rose significantly by about more than one per cent during 1972-73 to 1987-88. Literacy is an ingredient of qualitative population. In India about 35 per cent population is illiterate. But educated unemployment is a thing of serious concern, which stood at 68 lakh people in 1992. The nature of unemployment in India reveals that both the males and females are suffering from the problem of unemployment should be part and parcel of social security. Till date, unemployed are totally neglected component of India's social security along with workers from the agricultural sector. In absence of covering the unemployed in India into the net of social protection, they cannot fulfill even the basic necessities of life necessary of just living as citizens of sub-continent country like India. They must also get the basic facilities like education, health, medical, water etc. for which social protection for them is a must.

VI. Policy Implications of Social Security for the Unemployed in India

The above thorough discussions about the various aspects and dimensions of employment and unemployment growth and the need for social security for the unemployed adequately and clearly reveals that, it is the need of hour to introduce and enforce the social security measures for the unemployed in India. The existing all social security measures with their full implementation cannot be a solution for the unemployed social security in our country. But of them, some measures can definitely provide social security facilities to the Indian unemployed. Especially the measures diverted towards insurance, family pension, maternity benefits, old age pension etc. But the social security measures framed based on the following guidelines could be an agenda and a course of action to cover the unemployed into the net of social security system in India.

In absence of an active role assigned to the government, it is rather difficult to get fulfill the goal of social security for the unemployed in India. But at the same time, wherever possible and beneficial private sector of the economy can accompany the government. Like natural calamity fund, the government should create an 'Unemployment Benefit Fund' on the basis of government-private sector participation to provide for employment, basic wants and the necessities like health and medical facilities. Training facilities along with finance should be provided to undertake self-employment activities by the government for the unemployed. Such insurance schemes should be introduced and enforced for the unemployed, without their contribution based on the subscriptions of employed and insurance companies. Attempts should be made to liberalise obstacles and restrictions on the mobility of labours within the country as well as abroad. Union, state and local governments should assign due place to unemployed social security in their annual budgets. Like finance commission, the Unemployment Commission should be appointed after every five years to suggest measures to the government to tackle the problem of unemployment as well as providing social security facilities for the unemployed. The government of India can impose 'Unemployment tax' to mobilize revenue for the unemployed social security measures. It should be made obligatory to government as well as private hospitals to provide free of charge medical facilities in the case of normal sickness and due help of the government for abnormal diseases. On the line of Disinvestments Department, Unemployment Cell should be established at the centre to look at human resource utilization and management, whereby unemployment can be controlled. Family pension benefits should be extended by raising finance from MNCs, IMF, IBRD, and ILO, etc. The World Health organization (WHO) should be given important role in tackling health problems of the unemployed by suggesting measures as well as due assistance. Banks and financial institutions can play a crucial role especially in providing loans & advances whereby employment can be generated for the unemployed through the sources like self-employment and others. The development of export-import oriented industries has potential of generating large employment opportunities on the basis of their post experience. Population control measures and desirable changes in the education system should be brought in the purview of social security measures. Thus, due efforts to generate adequate employment coupled with necessary supply of social security services can be the key of social protection for the unemployed in India.

VII. Conclusion

The problem of unemployment is a major and important problem before the Indian economy having higher and growing intensity. Hence naturally, it is the need of the hour to protect the unemployed socially. Therefore, introduction and enforcement of the social security for the unemployed is inevitable in the modern India. But the same structure of social protection for the employed cannot be accepted for the unemployed. Only social security measures cannot offer due social protection for the unemployed needed for the labour welfare maximization. Due efforts to promote the level of employment along with the social security measures could offer due social protection for the unemployed in India. Social security policy based on the above suggested policy implications could be a definite solution on this burning problem. This paper is a little bit attempts to look at an important issue of the social security for the unemployed in India in the globalisation era. I could not collect necessary and adequate data needed for the through study and writing of the paper.

Endnotes

1. Singh, J.K. (1998): *Labour Economics*, Deep & Deep Publications Pvt. Ltd., New Delhi, p. 115.
2. *Ibid*, p. 415.
3. Misra and Puri (2001): *Indian Economy*, Himalaya Publishing House, Mumbai, p. 664.
4. Dr. Bhagoliwal, T.N. (1976): *Economics of Labour and Social Welfare*, Sahitya Bhawan, Agra, p. 525.
5. Papola, T.S. (2004): 'Globalisation, Employment and Social Protection: Emerging, Perspectives for the Indian Workers', *The Indian Journal of Labour Economics*, Vol. 47, Number 3, July-September, 2004, p. 543.
6. *Ibid.*, p. 545.
7. Kamble, P.S. (2005): *Business Environment (Indian Economic Environment)*, Swaroop Prakashan, Kolhapur (in press).
8. Papola, T.S., above cited, pp. 545-47.

15

SOCIAL SECURITY FOR DOMESTIC WORKERS: A CASE STUDY

Anupama

I. Introduction

The development experience of India has shown that its benefits are unequally distributed among its masses, where the benefits of growth have accrued to the small segment of the society and the millions have been socially excluded. These millions are living a life of persistent sufferings and deprivations (Datta, 2001). In our economy, a big majority of those, who are employed, belongs to the informal sector, which is broadly characterized by these deprivations. About 92 per cent of the total work force in India is working in the informal sector and with the ambitious targets of globalising our economy; this sector had been swelling in size.

The concept of the informal sector is difficult to define precisely. Most often it is defined negatively by pointing out the absence of characteristics that belong to formal activities, viz., security\regularity of work, better earnings, existence of non-wage and long-term benefits, protective legislation and union protection [Papola, 1980; Banerjee, 1985]. Various scholars have pointed out various characteristics of the informal sector while defining this sector. They define it as an easy entry point, particularly for the unskilled workers (Romatet, 1983), they have small scale of operations and lack support and recognition from the government (Sethuraman, 1976 and Weeks, 1975). Moreover, the labour market in the informal sector is mostly unprotected and so, depressed wages prevail in this sector (Mazumdar, 1977). The study group appointed by the National Commission on Labour (2001) has brought out certain general characteristics of enterprises or employment in this sector such as low wages and low earnings, high percentage of employment of women, employment of family labour, child labour and migrant labour, piece-rate payments, home-based work or contractual work, seasonal or intermittent employment, of organisation into trade unions, casual and multiple jobs, existence of debt bondage, existence of cooperatives of self-employed workers, dependence on others for supply of raw material, less access to capital, existence of lack health hazards, etc. With such characteristics, domestic workers fall easily in the category of unorganized informal sector.

The domestic workers may be defined as independent workers as they may not be attached to a single employer and may be serving several households at the same time. They largely belong to the informal sector whose pays and benefits do not conform to existing labour regulations. In many Latin American countries domestic servants are distinguished in the national surveys and together with independent wage-workers are added to the informal sector (Sethuraman, 1998). Very limited data is available on estimates of domestic workers. The *Shramshakti* report of 1989 estimated about 23 lakh domestic workers in the country at that time, out of which 16.8 lakhs were females and about 6.2 lakhs were males (Bhatt, 1989). Then an estimate made by the College of Social Work in Mumbai claims that 80% of domestic workers are women. There are few other localized studies, which discussed about the plight of the domestic workers, particularly, female and child workers. Though quite visible in urban areas, these workers are also engaged in households all over the country even in most distant and intracTable areas. This work does not require any special skill. The persons employed as domestic workers are extremely poor, illiterate and come mostly from rural areas.

As the concept of nuclear family is becoming more prevalent and the number of families is increasing with both the partners going for a job, the concept of hiring a domestic help (full time or part time) is also in vogue. The nature of work of a part time domestic help includes nearly all of the domestic chores like cloth washing, utensil cleaning and house cleanliness services in which the latest is more popular. However, a part time worker does his/her assigned job within an hour or so and leaves for another assignment in another house. A part time worker is generally doing the same work in a number of houses daily, generally from morning to evening without any break. On the other hand a full time worker (resident or non resident) does a variety of works all through the day in a single household. His/her job ranges from that of a part time worker to a child attendant, a cook including the kitchen shopping from the market.

II. A Few Words about the Sample

This paper takes Bathinda city of Punjab as a case to study the economic conditions of the domestic workers. Bathinda city is actually a nouveau riche area. This area in the past was considered among the most backward areas of the state (Punjab) as it has low soil fertility, scanty rainfall and large section of the population was illiterate. So, it was virtually unable to gain from the Green Revolution of the state, which brought prosperity to the state. Much of its growth is attributed to the Thermal Plant, NFL, an engineering college and then some of the industries. All this development invited the workers (skilled and unskilled) from outside the state or from the better off areas of the state. This migration also put pressures on the demand for a quality education. Presently, Bathinda city[2] is far ahead in the field of education, particularly the professional courses like medical and engineering courses. Though there is no medical college in the city, yet the city offers coaching for entrance examination (both for medical and engineering courses- popularly known as PMET and CET) on a wider scale and has a good reputation regarding performance of these coaching centers all through the state. This is clear from the fact that the students from very advanced areas of Ludhiana, Mohali and even from Chandigarh come for the coaching in this city for the respective courses. Now, this fact is very important regarding our study on domestic workers. Due to this migration of the students, a number of households have gainfully adopted the business of running PG Houses (paying guests). On an average a household boards about 7-8 students as paying guests. Assuming an average family of four members, the total number of members becomes 11-12, which means piling up of domestic chores. Thus, a housewife finds it unable to handle all the work by herself alone. So, this has become a major cause of the increase in the demand for full time domestic workers. Since, this is not the sole factor behind the demand for domestic workers as the working women also need a domestic help and even non working women from well off families also employ these workers, we have collected a mixed sample of all of the above categories for this analysis. The objective of this study is to mainly analyze the working conditions, average earnings, job security and social security of the domestic workers, who are virtually unorganised. For this purpose a sample of 400 households is taken randomly among those houses employing domestic help in one way or another. A detailed questionnaire regarding the literacy level, social status, wages, working hours, association with any type of organization or other related issues was framed. A few employers were also interviewed. On the whole, the employers were not much co-operative and seem to over emphasize their help to their domestic servants. On health issues, the results were simply drawn on the basis of the interview of the servants as well as the employers. However, it was felt that, a thorough medical check-up of the servants could give some concrete results regarding the health status of these workers[1]. The extent to which the experience of Bathinda city can be generalized to the rest of the Punjab state or the rest of the country is difficult to predict. The case of metropolitan cities may be different, as the domestic workers have organized themselves in these cities in one way or the other. However, in small cities or the backward areas of the country the situation regarding these workers may nearly be the same as that of the Bathinda city.

III. The Need of Social Security: The Vulnerability Factor

Domestic servants are completely unorganized and unregulated in this city. They have no system of social security to rely upon in the difficult times. For them, a job is the best guarantee for social security right now. They are employed by the middle middle-income group, upper middle-income group and higher income group. Majority of these are women or children. They generally belong to the lower castes. They are illiterate or have very few years of formal education. They live in unhygienic conditions and have very low nutritional standards due to which they generally have to face frequent health problems resulting in loss of earnings and sometimes—even loss of the job. Thus, they also lack the job security as their job depends purely on the will of their emplcyer. In a way they are casual labour. To compensate their low earnings they work for longer hours, virtually working from early morning to late evenings by serving three or four households and some times even more on the same day. Moved by the deplorable working conditions of these workers along with many workers in the informal economy, the social activists have also made attempts to formalize such work. However, with respect to women the larger proportion remains at the bottom of the ladder with very little scope for improvement in pay and work status (Eapen, 2001). The situations are even worse in small cities and towns of the country, which are economically and socially backward. The case of Bathinda city also lies in the same category, as it does not have any organization or a formal group that can raise the voice for the protection of the domestic workers.

Table 1: Distribution of the Households on Basis of Their Activity

Activity status	*Number of the households*
Running a paying guest house for the students	100
Normal households*	300
Total	400

*By normal households we mean those households who are not running any paying guesthouse that is where the employment of labour is not for any type of earning activity.

Above Table shows the distribution of 400 households taken as a sample. Out of these 400 households, 300 are those households, which have employed the domestic help purely for their own domestic chores without earning any thing from their services. However, there are families, especially those who have employed the domestic help for attending their pre-school kids, who have admitted that it would have been impossible for the mothers to work outside without any domestic help to attend their children. Thus, even though these workers have no source of earning for their employer directly, yet they help them to earn their living at least for three years that is up to the time their children start going to the school. On the other hand, for the PG houses (Paying Guest houses), employing a domestic help means a good source of earning. As mentioned above on an average a PG house keeps 8 students and from each student they charge Rs. 3200 per month, which means earnings of Rs. 25600 per month. Out of these, they provide meals, bedding, washed and ironed clothes and their electricity bills (the students do not have any separate electric meters, so their consumption of electricity is included in the owner's electricity bill). Assuming 60 per cent of these earnings to be borne as the cost[5] for above mentioned provisions, this leaves a value addition of Rs. 15360 per month, out of which after payment of Rs 1000 to the domestic help (see Table 3 for average earnings of a full-time worker), this leads to net earnings of Rs. 14360 per month, which would not have been possible without the domestic help (A fact acknowledged by 86.67 per cent of total PG houses). This means that the domestic helps working for the PG houses are highly productive. Moreover, this category of workers is quite different from their counterparts working in the normal households, as the latter do not add to the earning capacity of their employees.

Table 2.1 shows that about 77 per cent of the total domestic workers are the females and only 23 per cent are the males. The females are preferably employed, as they are relatively cheaper, less aggressive and less troublesome than their male counterparts. Nearly 92 per cent of those who have employed full time female workers have voted against employing a male servant. The reasons are nearly common. They avoid employing a male member due to security reasons, due to their younger female children or due to be relatively costly. On the other hand, the female members were much trusted on these grounds. Actually, it was observed on the basis of personal interviews of the employers that the extent, to which an employer sees an employee docile and obedient or less harmful, is also an important criterion in hiring as well as firing. That is why the women and children are more likely to get employment in this particular type of work.

Table 2.1: Distribution of Domestic Workers Age-wise and Sex-wise

Household type	*Adults*		*Children*		*Total*	
	Male	*Female*	*Male*	*Female*	*Male*	*Female*
Running a PG*	15	19	26	40	41	59
	(15)	(19)	(26)	(40)	(41)	(59)
Normal household	24	189	26	61	50	250
	(8)	(63)	(8.67)	(20.33)	(16.67)	(83.33)
Total	39	208	52	101	91	309
	(9.75)	(52)	(13)	(25.25)	(22.75)	(77.25)

PG - Paying Guest House.

Another interesting feature of the above Table is that all of the male domestic workers are the full time workers and none of them was employed for one or two chores such as sweeping or washing clothes. Among the PG Houses it is observed that 41 per cent of the households employ a male domestic help. These are the houses, which have the boy students as paying guests. However, the disturbing feature of the PG Houses is that nearly 66 per cent of the households have employed children, while this percentage is hardly 29 per cent for the normal households. These again shows the degree of exploitation of the children who are low paid, more susceptible to the physical and verbal abuse and are denied their right to education. Further the education status and the social status of the domestic workers covered in the study is given in the following Tables: Table 2.2 and Table 2.3. The Table 2.2 shows that 28 per cent of the workers are totally illiterate and nearly 53 per cent are such that they have education up to the primary level only and only about 18 per cent have education above primary and below the matric. In our sample, hardly 4 workers that is only one per cent of the total number of the domestic workers in the sample have completed their education up to matric. These are the workers who had pursued their studies along with their work and these workers, have showed their interest to further improve their qualification to leave the drudgery of their present job. The Table shows the position of the females regarding their literacy level is worse than their male counterparts. As against 18.6 per cent illiterate male workers, this percentage for the females is 30.7 per cent. None of the female workers has attained education above matric and hardly 10.3 per cent have crossed their primary level of education (whereas this percentage is 46.1 per cent for the males). Thus, the majority of the workers do not have the adequate level of education. Further, the Table 2.3 shows the social status of these domestic workers. The Table shows that majority of them (97 per cent) belong to the backward classes and hardly 3 per cent are from the general category. The gender-wise distribution of the workers on basis of their caste shows that 99 per cent of the females are from the backward classes, while this percentage is 91 for the males. Thus, whereas 9 per cent of the domestic workers come from the general category, only one per cent of the female domestic workers belong to this category. Thus, it is clear that most of the domestic workers are female, belong to lower caste and are illiterate or have a very low level of education, which implies that they belong to the vulnerable group not only economically but also socially.

Table 2.2: Distribution of Domestic Workers on Basis of Their Education Status

Education status	*Number of workers*		
	Males	*Females*	*Total*
No education	17(18.6)	95(30.7)	112(28)
Primary (up to fifth standard)	28(30.7)	183(59)	211(52.75)
Up to matriculation	42(46.1)	31(10.3)	73(18.25)
Matriculation and above	4(4.4)	Nil(0)	4(1)
Total	91(100)	309(100)	400(100)

Figures in bracket show percentages of their respective totals.

Table 2.3: Distribution of the Domestic Workers on Basis of Their Caste

Social status	Number of workers		
	Male	*Female*	*Total*
SC\BC or other reserve categories	83(91)	306(99)	389(97)
General category	8(9)	3(1)	11(3)
Total	91(100)	309(100)	400(100)

Figures in bracket show the percentage values (approx.) of their respective totals.

Table 3: Average Wage Earnings of Various Activities (in Rs. per month)

Activity No.	*Activity*	*Wages (per month)*
1	Cleaning Utensils	200
2	Sweeping	250*
3	Washing Clothes	280#
4	Cooking	500@
1,2	Utensils and Sweeping	450
2,3	Sweeping And Washing Clothes	500
1,2 & 3	Sweeping, Washing Clothes and Cleaning Utensils	650
4	Attending a child	600$
1-4 and many other daily and occasional jobs	Full Time Worker	1000**

* rate for an average household with two bed rooms or total area of 250 sq. yards.

\# the prevailing average rate is Rs. 70 per head. So, with an average family of four members this becomes Rs. 280.

@ rate for cooking two meals a day, with two meals for the cook daily.

** monetary wages only as the full time worker is also entitled to three meals, tea etc.

$ working from morning to evening.

Box 1: Routine Activity Chart of Domestic Workers

Workers doing three activities	*Workers doing less than three activities*	*Full time workers*
Household-1: activity 1, activity 2, activity 3 (approx 3 hours) Household-2: activity 1, activity 2, activity 3 (approx 3 hours), Household-3: activity 1 activity 2, activity 3 (approx 3 hours) Total including the time to commute from one work place to the another work place (approx 1 hr.) = 10 hrs.	Household-1: activity 1 or 2 or 3 or 1&2 or 2&3. Household-1: activity 1 or 2 or 3 or1&2 or 2&3. Household-1: activity 1 or 2 or 3 or 1&2 or 2&3. Household-1: activity 1 or 2 or 3 or 1&2 or 2&3. Household-1: activity 1 or 2 or 3 or 1&2 or 2&3. Total time = approx. 10 hrs.	Activity 1, 2, 3, 4, 5 and many more not enlisted in the above Table. Total time = from early morning to late night for the resident workers and from breakfast to dinner for the non resident workers (in most cases not less than 12 hrs.)

IV. The Wages

The Table 3 shows that for a single activity the wages are below Rs. 300, which means Rs. 10 per day. Assuming that a worker who does a single activity serves about 5 families at the same time, this will mean less than Rs. 50 per day. If a person is performing three jobs at the same time then he\she will be serving not more than three households, which means Rs. 1950 per month or Rs. 65 per day. Taking only money wages in to account, the conditions for the full time workers and those attending a child are worse. These are the workers who are attending a single family and are earning Rs 600 for those who are attending a child and Rs. 1000 for the full time workers. Thus, they are earning respectively, Rs. 20 and Rs. 33.33 per day. The full time workers are doing all of the jobs that is sweeping, washing clothes, cleaning utensils, cooking (Rs. 250+Rs 280[1]+Rs 200+Rs 500=Rs 1230), daily dusting, shopping, bringing children from the school, and even attending the children and several other daily and odd jobs, yet they are paid only Rs. 1000. This payment is even smaller for the children. If we calculate the average earnings of the full time child workers separately, then it is about Rs

825 only. However, since these full time workers are also entitled to three meals and tea, they may be at a better position from part time domestic workers.[3]However, the difference is not much considerable as compared to the workers doing three jobs and serving three families simultaneously. Although, these earnings are little higher than the minimum wages of Rs. 60 per day in the informal sector, yet if we compare the working hours, then the actual wages for the domestic workers are much lower. Taking monthly earnings of Rs. 1950, the daily wages are Rs 65. But these are for 10 hours. If we adjust these wages according to 8 hour working day, then the wages are hardly Rs. 52. Considering the wages of full time workers after including their meals etc. we see that the monthly wages are Rs. 2050 (see note number 4), which means daily wages of Rs. 68.33. But since the full time workers work for more than 12 hours a day their adjusted daily wages come out to be less than Rs. 45.56 only. The National Center for Labour calculated for 1996 that, for a reasonable level of subsistence, a worker would have to earn a daily wage of Rs. 125. At that time the greatest part of the informal sector workers came nowhere near this level of income. Actually, the underpayment in work has forced these workers to work for prolonged hours. In their daily struggle to survive, this vulnerable segment maintains its own reserves—the dependent members of their household. It is usually the weakest and the smallest shoulders that have to bear the heaviest burdens of informalisation (Breman, 2001).

The distribution of the domestic workers in the sample is given in the Table 4, according to their actual monthly earnings. The Table shows that a majority of the workers is earning below Rs. 1500 per month. Hardly, 25 per cent of the males and just 5 per cent of the females are earning above Rs. 1500. On the whole, the average monthly wages are only Rs. 1125 and daily wages of only Rs. 37.5. The monthly wages are even lower for the females. The average monthly wages for the females are Rs. 1057.45 as against Rs. 1299.5 for the males. This means that the women are earning Rs. 35.25 as daily wages as compared to Rs. 43.32 for the males. Thus, the females are earning about 81 per cent of the male earnings in this particular activity. Although, the gender based discrimination regarding wages is common in the informal sector, yet it is more striking in this female dominant occupation. This shows that despite the enactment of the Equal Remuneration Act, 1976 and its subsequent amendment in 1987, the practice of paying lower wages to women for 'same work or work of similar nature' is still rampant. Unni (1999) calculated this discrimination in both the agricultural and non-agricultural sector. It is generally argued that the women are less productive than their male counterparts, particularly in the areas where the skill is not an important factor, so they are paid lower wages than the males. Such comments are highly objectionable, particularly, when we are using the term 'same work or work of similar nature'. Thus, the payment of lower wages to the female workers in this particular occupation should be paid appropriate attention because this area covers those activities, which are most naturally associated to the women in our society. The Shramshakti Report of 1988 deals with this issue. The Report says that specific occupations must be listed out and minimum rates of wages should be notified against these, so that it is possible to verify whether women related occupations are ranked lower in the matter of wages (GOI, 1988).

Table 4: Distribution of Workers According to Their Monthly Earnings (in Rs.)

Monthly Earnings	*Number of workers*		
	Male	*Female*	Total
Less than 500	3	15	18
500-1000	4	105	109
1000-1500	61	175	236
1500-2000	17	12	29
2000 and above	6	2	8
Total	91	309	400
Mean wages	1299.5	1057.45	1125
	(43.32)	(35.25)	(37.5)

Figures in bracket show average daily wages.

V. The Quality of Work and the Nature of Social Security for the Domestic Workers and the Role of the State

The productivity of labour is an essential condition for the prosperity of enterprises and the well being of the workers and their families. While the production facilities at workplace and the remuneration are important, attitudes towards work, and the value placed by the society on dignity of labour are equally important in influencing the productivity of labour (GOI, 2002). One could also count the working conditions and social security attached with the work as an important indicator of the quality of the work. But the domestic workers are not getting their due share neither socially nor economically even though they are highly productive (in case of those working for the PG houses). They are not having good working conditions at their workplace, even when the constitution of India has a number of provisions to protect the interest of its citizens and the reality is that these provisions are not adequately available to the vulnerable groups of the society. Article 39 (a), (b) and (e) of the Constitution requires that the citizens have the right to adequate means of livelihood, that the material sources are so distributed as best to serve the common good, that the health and strength of workers and the tender age of children are not abused, and that citizens are not forced by economic necessity to enter avocations unsuited to their age or strength. Article 41 requires that within the limits of its economic capacity and development, the state shall make effective provision for securing the right to work, to education and to public assistance in case of unemployment, old age, sickness and disablement, and in other cases of undeserved want. Article 42 requires that the State should make provision for securing just and humane conditions of work and maternity relief. Article 43 requires that the state shall endeavor to secure work, a living wage, conditions of work ensuring a decent standard of life and full enjoyment of leisure and social and cultural opportunities. Article 47 requires that the State should regard the raising of the level of nutrition and the standard of living of its people, and improvement of public health, as among its primary duties.

But a look at the Box 1 and Box 2 and then the analysis

of Table 3 and the Table 4 shows that nearly all these rights are denied to the domestic workers. These, problems equally exist for several other workers in the informal sector, for example, the rag pickers (Chikarmane and Narayana, 2000), rickshaw pullers, workers in the dhabhas etc. This points towards the need of government intervention to mitigate the deplorable conditions of these workers. The box 2 shows that the domestic workers are denied every benefit of social security to which a worker in the organized sector is entitled.

Our study shows that the domestic workers do not have any adequate resources of livelihood; they are denied any assistance in case of job loss, disability, sickness and old age. Since they work for longer hours, their working and living conditions are not very decent. The children working as domestic workers are denied the right to education and the women are denied the maternity benefits. During the maternity period, the women have to choose between losing a job or losing the health of their own as well as their newly born children. Nearly, 80 per cent of the women who had undergone delivery had reported that they had to find a new job after the birth of the child. Remaining have reported that they made an alternative arrangement for that period from their own acquaintances on the promise that their household will be given back to them after they are able to come to work. In such cases, most of the women reported that they were back to work within 20 days. However, to save their job this is the mutual understanding of these workers. When these workers make such arrangements, they may be able to save their job, but they may not be able to save their health. The pressure to take extra risk and to perform work under weak physical conditions can and does lead to permanent health damage. The study shows that most of the workers were easy prey to the seasonal diseases. Though, no medical test was conducted upon them, yet by enquiring the workers as well as their employers, it was found that an upset stomach is the most common problem with these workers. Besides, seasonal flues, allergies and diarrhea easily catch them. According to their employers they skip their work mostly on the ground of their own illness or due to the illness of their family members. Again for frequent leaves they have to part with a proportionate amount of their monthly wages or sometimes they have to take advance from the employer to meet these expenses, which were later deducted from their next salary. About 88 per cent of the adult workers and 67 per cent of the child workers reported that a major portion of their monthly wages wears out before the month ends. As discussed before, there is no formal system of social security for these workers and they depend solely on their own resources, theoretically termed as social capital (Nooteboom, 2004). Since, they have relatives and friends of nearly similar economic status, the base of their social capital is also very narrow. The workers were asked the question that to whom they seek for in time of difficulty. Most of them responded that the help by the employer is not generally sufficient, and for most of the times it is on returnable basis. So, either they had to depend upon the local moneylender or their relatives or friends. In case of marriage of the daughter, the employer may help in shape of shagun money, in kind—that is by financing a sewing machine, a fan etc or by giving certain suits to the marrying girl. All these items are non-returnable. But any help beyond these things is deducted from the salary of the worker. Which was not in any case greater than 2500 with exception of only 6 cases where the employers gave Rs. 5000 in time of the marriage of the daughter of the worker, as advance salary. These were the cases where the workers had been serving the same household for at least five years. Thus, this facility could not be available to those workers who had served a household for a lesser time period.

Similarly, in case of illness or any medical expenses the help is provided by the employer in shape of advance salary. Further, there is no concept of old age benefits or disability benefits in case of the domestic workers. Thus, due to insufficiency of timely help from the employer, most of the workers seek the help of their friends or relatives. This help is again on returnable basis. Since there exists no legally established tenable employer-worker relationship between the domestic worker and the employer, they do not come within the purview of any labour legislation that could entitle them to contributory provident fund, insurance, paid leave, bonus, gratuity, old age pension and security of job. This also negatively affects their creditworthiness from the institutional sources (Chikarmane and Narayan, 2000). As a result in time of need they have to depend on debt from the unorganized/ non institutional sources, who charge a very high rate of interest. This further adds to their woes.

Box 2

The social security system for the domestic workers vs the organized sector workers

Workers in the organized sector	*Domestic workers*
*Medical allowance	*No medical allowance
*Paid leaves	*No paid leaves, instead the wages are generally deducted for longer leave period. They do not have even the weekend offs.
*Job security	*No job security as there is no legal binding on the employer for the continuity of the work.
*Old age pension	*No old age security
*Disability benefits	*Loss of job in case of disability
*Regular revision of salary	*wages are stable for a long period of time.
*Working day of 8 hrs and working month not more than 26 days.	*Working day of at least 10 hrs and working month of 30 days.
*Maternity benefits.	*No maternity benefits, instead either the job is lost during this period or the wages are deducted, in case of short leaves. The latter case badly affects the health of the mother and the newly born child.

Such a dismal situation of the domestic workers points towards the need for the state to play an interventionist and affirmative role in the protection and regulation of economic activities of these workers and to provide them a social security network. For these people, work in the informal sector is the only avenue for survival (Bhowmik 2000:1). The informal economy has often been criticized for its poor employment conditions as labour and social welfare laws do not cover the informal sector, wages and working conditions often fail to meet minimal requirements, resulting in long working hours, insecure employment, irregular incomes, lack of access to proper health care and old age or retirement benefits. Moreover, labour often work in unhealthy, unsafe and unprotected working environments. The workers in the informal sector are generally considered the poorest workers in India and most exposed to shocks and stresses threatening their livelihoods (Breman, 1996). For their social welfare they are left to informal arrangements of insurance, mutual help and family assistance. In recent years, however, pressure on the state and civil society has increased and concern and attention is expressed to extend social security to the informal sector. It is widely recognized, however, that covering these workers under social protection and benefits by the state is a difficult and expensive process. So far, the majority of the unorganized workers of the economy remain uncovered. In this respect, it has been argued that the state should not aim to cover all risks and insecurities of the informal sector, but rather promote self regulation and enhance the performance of local systems of social security by enhancing workers' social capital (Conning and Kevane, 2002; Dhanani and Islam, 2002). Although the concept of social capital has gained momentum in the late 1990s and became popular among policy-makers and economists, others have criticized the concept and shown its downsides (Portes 1998; Portes and Landolt 1996) or questioned the validity of these efforts (Nooteboom and Dennis, 2004).

Under such conditions, there is no system of social security on which the domestic workers can depend upon. They work for long hours and do variety of work and sometimes get few hours of undisturbed sleep. In many cases they are not provided with safe and clean places where they can rest or sleep. Since many domestic servants are women and children they run the risk of sexual harassment and exploitation in many houses. There is need to ensure satisfactory conditions of work, humane treatment and acceptable level of social security. The Second National Commission on Labour (GOI, 2001), on the experience of the beedi workers, has recommended the introduction of a system of registration, issue of identity cards and payment of minimum wages to domestic workers. It recommended setting up of a Central Fund from which welfare and social security measures for women workers should be financed. Another recommendation of the Commission was that a separate wing should be set up in the Labour Departments for unorganised workers with adequate number of women employees

The Commission also felt that no solution to the problems of women at work would be complete without taking into account their reproductive functions, which can be effectively tackled through maternity benefit and childcare. Responsibility for this should be borne by all employers, irrespective of whether or not they employed women, through a levy calculated as a percentage of the wage bill. If the employer was not identifiable, the responsibility for providing maternity benefits must lie with the state.

The Commission underlined the need for an integrated perspective on health as most of the health problems that women faced, related to their general life situation, which aggravated the problems they faced as workers such as inadequate nutrition, non-accessibility to healthcare, water, housing, sanitation, maternity benefits and childcare among others.

Much would also depend upon the extent to which the labour movement is able to bring within its fold this section of the unorganized labour force, which had largely been neglected by the trade unions. But, it is also a fact that the neglecting attitude by the trade unions may also be responsible for deprivation of the basic rights of these vulnerable groups. Here it would be quite appropriate to quote Dreze and Sen (1995):

> Successive governments in India have had reason enough to rely on the unending patience of neglected and deprived millions in India who have not risen in fury about illiteracy, hunger, illness or economic insecurity. The stubborn persistence of these deprivations has much to do with that lack of fury.

In this context the voice can be raised by the sufferers' collective action or by the organizations, which fight for their cause, say labour unions. But the fact in case of domestic workers is that, their struggle to improve living conditions is hampered by the weak articulation of collective action. This is further hindered by the lack of security, over-work etc. their state of acute poverty is itself a great hindrance to the collective action (all of the adult workers in the sample have denied any association with any sort of labour union, they even showed ignorance about the existence of any such group in the city that can protect their rights). In such deprived circumstances, they do not have the time, space or reserves necessary to make demands together with those who share their fate (Breman, 2001). Under such conditions the policy of trade union movement to neglect these workers along with many other workers of the informal sector for protecting their rights is really a great blunder. At the same time the policy makers should also devote more attention to the position of such vulnerable groups. For these groups the formulation and implementation of an extensive programme for social security is urgently required. National Domestic Workers' Movement (NDWM), established in 1985, is currently only national body of domestic workers. This body is limited to a few states only. There is an urgent need for a comprehensive coverage of domestic workers by this body, so that greater pressure can be exerted on the government to pay attention towards the genuine and long pending demands of these workers.

Though, some states like Kerala, Tamilnadu and Karnatka have introduced minimum wages for the domestic workers, yet a lot has to be done as far as the uncertainties of the life are concerned. Ironically, the Unorganized Sector Workers' Social Security Bill, 2005 did not pay any attention to this section of workers. Another Bill tabled in Parliament in 1998 regarding the rights of the domestic workers is still unheard and unnoticed. So, instead of having occasional and scattered type efforts by the NGOs and workers' groups, there is a need of collective effort so that at least fair and adequate wages are ensured to these workers. Besides, they should also be entitled to certain securities against their contingencies on lines of the recent recommendations of the National Commission of Enterprises in the Unorganized Sector (NCOEUS).

Thus, to conclude, we can say that the domestic workers are poor and vulnerable. They neither earn adequate income nor they obtain any social security benefits due to absence of definite employer-employee relationship. Plus, they do not have the power to fight discrimination and victimization for protecting their rights to minimal standard of living. So, there should be honest efforts to improve the working conditions of the domestic workers through collective and public action, by means of appropriate legislation by lobbying or by self-organization. According to Dreze and Sen (1995), public action can play a central role in bringing social opportunities within the reach of the masses. At the same time the vigilance and the involvement can play an important role in ensuring an adequate expansion of minimum social security.

Notes

1. This study is not financed by any organization; so, due to lack of funds the thorough medical check up of the workers was not possible.
2. However, regarding the education status, the whole of Bathinda District stands at 13th rank out of 17 districts. The literacy rate for Bathinda district is 61.51 per cent, while that of Punjab state is 69.95 per cent. The female literacy rate for the district is 53.76 per cent as against 63.55 per cent for Punjab.
3. By calculating the three meals at a market rate of Rs. 10 per diet, this amounts to Rs. 30 per day and Rs. 900 per month. By adding monthly wages, this will mean Rs. 1900 per month apart from the tea. If we roughly add Rs. 150 for tea then it will total to Rs. 2050.
4. This amount would be higher for the domestic servants working in a PG house, as the number of heads is higher, but they are paid a lump sum wages only, irrespective of the workload.
5. Though, the employers were reluctant to reveal the actual amount, they earn, yet, it was judged from various other sources that it is not more than 60 per cent in any case.

References

Banerjee, N. (1985): *Women Workers In The Unorganised Sector*, Sangam Books, Hyderabad.

Bhatt, Ela (1989): *Shramshakti,* A Report of the National Commission on Self-employed Women and Women in the Informal Sector.

Bhowmik, S.K. (2000): A Raw Deal, www.india-seminar.com (as retrieved on April 10, 2000)

Breman, J. (1996): *Footloose labour- Working in India's Informal Economy*, University Press, Cambridge.

Breman, Jan (2001): 'An Informalised Labour System-End Of Labour Market Dualism', *Economic And Political Weekly,* December, 29, Vol.36 No. 52.

Conning, J. and M. Kevane (2002); 'Community-Based Targetting Mechanisms for Social Safety Nets: A Critical Review', *World Development*, p. 375-94 vol. 30.

Chikarmane, Poornima and Lakshmi Narayan (2000): 'Formalising Livelihood—Case of waste pickers in Pune', *Economic And Political Weekly*, October, 7, Vol.35 No. 41.

Datta, R.C. (2001), 'Public Action, Social Security and Unorganised sector' in Dev and others (eds): *Social and Economic Security in India*, Institute for Human Development, New Delhi.

Dhanani, S. and I. Islam (2002): 'Poverty, Vulnerability and Social Protection in a Period Of Crisis: The Case Of Indonesia', *World Development*, p. 1211-31 vol. 30.

Dreze, J. and A. Sen (1995): *Indian Economic Development and Social Opportunity*, Oxford University Press, Oxford.

Eapen, Mridul (2001): 'Women In The Informal Sector in Kerala—Need For Re-examination', *Economic and Political Weekly,* June 30, Vol. 36, No. 26.

GOI (1988): *Report of National Commissionon Self-employed Women in the Informal Sector*, Shramshakti, New Delhi.

GOI (2001): *Report of National Commission For Labour*, Ministry of Labour, New Delhi.

GOI(2002): *Draft Tenth Five Year Plan (2002-2007)- Volume Ii*, Planning Commission, Chapter 3.5.

Mazumdar, D. (1977), 'Notes On Urban Informal Sector' in Subbiah Kalpana (ed): *Urban Labour Market Behaviour in Developing Countries,* International Institute of Labour Studies, Geneva.

Nooteboom, Gerben and Weitering Dennis (2004), 'Railway Porters of Mumbai: Social Capital In Practice', *Economic and Political Weekly*, May 29, vol. XXXIX, No. 22.

Papola, T. S. (1980): 'Informal Sector: Concept And Policy', *Economic And Political Weekly*, May 3, Vol. 15.

Portes, A. (1998): 'Social Capital: Its Origins and Applications In Modern Sociology', *Annual Review of Sociology*, Vol. 24.

Portes, A. and P. Landolt (1996): 'The Downsides of Social Capital', *The American Prospect*, vol. 26, 18-21.

Romatet, E. (1983): 'Calcutta's Informal Sector:Theory and Reality', *Economic and Political Weekly*, May 3, Vol. 18.

Sethuraman, S.V. (1976): 'The Urban Informal Sector: Concept, Measurement and Policy', *International Labour Review*, July-August.

Sethuraman, S. V. (1998): 'Gender Informality and Poverty: A Global Review—Gender Bias in Female Informal Employment And Incomes In Developing Countries', October (mimeo).

Unni, Jeemol (1999): 'Women Workers in Agriculture: Some recent trends' in Papola, Sharma and Alakh (eds); *Gender and Employment in India*, Vikas Publications, New Delhi.

Weeks, J. (1975), 'Policies For Expanding Employment In the Informal Urban Sector of Developing Economies', *International Labour Review*, January.

16

STATE AND HOME-WORKERS: A STUDY OF LEGISLATION FOR BEEDI WORKERS IN INDIA

P. Madhavi

Introduction

The general understanding in India is that home-based workers or home workers were recognized quite early through Beedi legislation and the problem if any, is with the invisibility of the workers and the implementation of the law. The opinion of the author is that the legislation itself was never really designed to protect home-workers in a comprehensive way, although it recognizes their existence. Further, there is no provision in the law preventing the shift of beedi rolling from the factories to the homes of the workers. It is possible that when the law was made the proportion of home workers in the industry was far less than what it is today. The law operates just the same, in its original form, without any amendment, even when it is a well known fact that the proportion of home workers (all of who are women, incidentally) has increased manifold.

The paper is organized in the following manner:

1. Profile of Beedi industry.
2. Nature of Beedi work, production process and production relations.
3. Beedi – legislation and the home worker.
4. Specific problems faced by home based Beedi workers.

5. Absence of social protection for Beedi workers.
6. Reduced employment and limited livelihood options for Beedi–Workers.

1. Profile of Beedi Industry

After Agriculture and Handloom industry, Beedi industry employs large number of workers, in India. It is spread in 14 states, namely, Andhra Pradesh, Tamilnadu, Karnataka, Kerala, Maharashtra, Gujrat, Rajasthan, Madhya Pradesh, Uttar Pradesh, Bihar, Orissa, West Bengal, Assam and Tripura. There are 60 Lakh Beedi workers in the country. Beedis are rolled in a leaf called tunikaku or tendu leaf, which is collected from the forests. Around 50 lakh workers are employed in this activity. 40 lac farmers are engaged in cultivating tobacco, which is a basic ingredient in the Beedi. Thus about 1.5 crore persons are directly dependent on the Beedi industry for their livelihood. Nearly ninety percent of Beedi workers are women, most of who are also home workers. Further substantial proportion and are tribals, and dalits, others belong to the backward classes. In addition to the workers who are directly engaged in manufacturing beedi, a few lac persons are engaged in marketing it.

The industry is not only labour-intensive in the sense that it employs large numbers, but also in the sense that, the process is completely manual. The industry may also be described as 'indigenous' as it hardly uses any technology or investment which are foreign. In many parts of the country it is more than a hundred years old. Presently there is crisis in almost every aspect of the working of the industry, all of which have a negative impact on work, conditions of work and livelihoods of those who have been depending on it generations on.

The State of Andhra Pradesh employs around 6 lac workers in the industry. It is spread in the districts of Nizamabad, Karimnagar, Adilabad, Medak, Warangal, Mahaboobnagar, Hyderabad, Nalgonda, Kurnool, Cudapah, Chittoor, Nellore, Prakasam and Guntur. However, districts of the North Telangana region i.e., Nizamabad, Karimnagar, Adilabad and Medak the concentration is very high.

Nizamabad district alone accounts for 3 lakh workers. The present study is made with the backdrop being the Nizamabad district of Andhra Pradesh.

2. Nature of Beedi Work, Production Process and Production Relations

Without going into too much detail, the process of beedi rolling may be described thus: The employer provides the tendu leaf, tobacco and thread to the workers, who rolls them into beedis, ether in the factory premises or in their homes. Each pack contains 1000 beedis of a specific size, (small, medium & big) as required. Workers are paid on the basis of the number of beedi packs they make in a week (generally). Very often the employer delivers the material through a middleman, who exercises varieties of controls over the workers, particularly home-workers. They are at his mercy for getting material regularly. The middlemen decides which of the names he would report to the employer for enrolment and issue of identity cards, which in turn is required for the worker to receive benefits under the ESI Act, 1948 and P.F. contribution by the employer under the EPF Act, 1952. So, enjoying confidence and trust of the middleman becomes a critical factor for the home-workers. The employer has a right to reject the rolled beedis if they do not meet with his specifications.

Production relations in the Beedi industry have always been a matter of controversy. The Beedi and was Cigar Workers (Conditions of) Employment Act was passed in the year 1966. It was implemented in the state of Andhra Pradesh in the year 1968. Owners of Beedi factories contested the law in the High Court where the plea was rejected. The factory owners appealed to the Supreme Court with the argument that beedi workers collect tendu leaf & tobacco, take them home to roll as beedis. They neither use the factory premises and work in specified hours nor does the employer have any control over them. Hence, there is no employer-employee relationship between them, as such they were not bound by the law. The Supreme Court rejected the view and made the law applicable to them, on the ground that they implicitly exercised control over them by rejecting beedis rolled, on various pretexts. Further, employer pays the wages although the workers may be employed through contractors. Even after four decades after the legislation, the conditions of the beedis workers have only deteriorated. Employers found ways and means of avoiding and escaping the implementation of the legislation.

The most convenient and legitimate way was to systematically shift production from factory premises to the homes of the workers. If a few provisions have been implemented it is due to the pressure of unions.

3. The Beedi Legislation and the Home-workers

Beedi workers are covered by two laws specially enacted for them and a few other general labour laws. Beedi and Cigar workers (Conditions of Employment) Act, 1966 to regulate the conditions of service of the beedi workers and Beedi Workers Welfare Fund Act, 1976, to provide welfare schemes for the Beedi workers and their families, in relation to health, education, maternity benefits, group insurance, recreation, housing etc., There are also special schemes to encourage education of the children of Beedi workers, especially for the girl child. Other laws that apply to the Beedi workers are Minimum Wages Act, 1948, ESI, Act 1948, EPF Act, 1952, and Sec.39 of the Industrial Disputes Act, 1947. Social Security is expected to be provided through, Beedi and Cigar workers (Welfare Fund) Act and Beedi and Cigar Workers (CESS) Act, 1976.

Implementation of Beedi workers (Conditions of Employment) Act, 1966 is most crucial, because, it determines whether the rest of the laws are implemented or not. The Act has a total of 44 sections, most of which are not useful for the workers. This is so inspite of fact the preamble to the law clearly says that the Act is for the welfare of labour, and not a law for industries. The true nature and character of the legislation shows that it is for enforcing better conditions of labour amongst those who are engaged in the manufacture of beedi and cigars. The Act clearly states that the provisions are applicable only where beedi rolling is performed in a factory premises, and not else where, for instance at the homes of the workers.

The Act defines home-workers, recognizes and acknowledges their presence. However, home workers are covered only if their employer is covered by the legislation. An employer is covered only if he is registered under the Act and has a license to operate the factory. The law makers visualized the possibility of work shifting to the homes of the workers and have implicitly consented to it.

Some of the provisions in the Act deal with issuing licenses and their renewal to the factory owners. The truth is that, licenses have been issued even when formalities for issue of licenses were not fulfilled. Some provisions deal with construction standards of the buildings housing Beedi factories. Sections 8-13 deal with specifications regarding ventilation, cleanliness and hygene, toilet and other facilities to be provided, facilities for drinking water, first-aid etc. to be specific, Sec 8-13 deal with provisions relating to physical surroundings in which Beedi-work is performed. Sec.14 provides for crèches for children below 6 years, where 30 or more women are employed. It prescribes facilities and standards of cleanliness, light, ventilation adequate accommodation and the employment of a trained woman to take care of the children. Sec.16 requires that maintenance of a canteen where not less than two hundred and fifty employees are ordinarily employed. These provisions are meaningful (even assuming that they are implemented seriously), only when beedi work takes place in the factory premises. Where 90 percent or more of the work has been systematically shifted out of the factories, it has hardly any relevance. The homes of the Beedi-workers are so small and congested and work is performed in very unhygienic conditions. Children of the workers live and some times work in such conditions. Even where a small percent of the beedi workers are employed in factories, there is not a single instance of creches being maintained.

The Act has specific provisions relating to hours of work, rest intervals, wages, holidays, over time wages and annual leave with wages, for workers working in an industrial premises. These facilities and benefits are not available to home workers. Home-workers may work for many hours beyond 8 hours a day. They receive no overtime as they are piece-rated workers. Further, there is no record of the time them work. Even where women/men work in factories, conditions required under the Act, do not prevail. Women beedi rollers, whether working in factories or as home-workers are entitled to maternity benefits i.e. maternity leave with wages. This is not implemented in any Beedi factory in Andhra Pradesh. According to the Act in 1966, beedi workers are entitled to the credit of one paid leave for every 20 working days, and a paid holiday for every week (7 days). These provisions are implemented only in case of workers with Identity cards and those who are also covered under provident fund regulation. Since majority of the workers are home workers, and not covered by PF, these provisions are not implemented. Beedi workers work with tobacco and are exposed and are prone to ill health. Casual and sick leave facilities are essential for their well-being.

In the Telangana region women start rolling beedis at a very young age. After 30-40 years, they still roll beedis without substantial improvement in their levels of earnings. In this process of they do not acquire any other skills. Employment insecurity leads to all other insecurities like income, health old age etc., It also leads indignities. With the exception of a few places in Nizamabad and Karimnagar, in rest of the Telagana region beedi rolling is through contractors. The industry employs rollers, packers, carriers, roasters, tray fillers, clerical staff, cashiers, supervisors, branch managers etc. Except for rollers men are employed for all the other jobs.

Employers were required to revise wages every once in two years. They hardly ever do that. Not only that, the Government itself has revised the DA, under the Minimum Wages Act, 1948 in 2004, 5 years after it was due, which is yet to be implemented.

The Act prohibits the dismissal of any worker with more then 6 months work experience, without sufficient reason. A worker who has been removed may appeal to the Deputy Labour Commissioner within 30 days, whose decision is final and is also binding on both the parties. This clause has not prevented employers from dismissing workers. Decisions on the appeal take any where from a few months to a few years. Employers have not implemented the Award given by the appellate authority. An employer is punishable with a fine of Rs. 250/-, if he violates the Award. The worker may have to seek the assistance of Labour Court or High Court for the implementation of the Award.

Under the Payment of Wages Act, 1936, monthly wages have to paid before the expiry of the tenth of the succeeding month. Very often wages remain unpaid for 3-6 months after earned. The Act does not provide for any compensation for the delay.

Beedi workers are covered by the Minimum Wages Act, 1948. Not only minimum wages are different in different states, but in many states, wages are paid in different ways. Where unions are strong, wages are dependent on agreements reached with unions, which could be different from minimum wages. A third category wages are paid to the non-unionised workers, which is far lower than both the above. This does not include paid leaves, holidays, bonus or deductions for P.F. Where the agreement is for Rs. 49.50 per 1000 beedies. What is actually paid is Rs. 25.30. This amounts to workers being deprived of Rs. 100–150 crores p.a.

Manufacturing beedi without license or registration, is 'illegal'. In the State of Andhra Pradesh it is called 'Vardi' beedi. Employers who produce vardi beedi tend to exploit the workers more. The only way in which this can be stopped is by making inspection more rigorous. The problem of 'Vardi' beedi is more prevalent in those districts in Telangana, like Hyderabad and Nalgonda, where unionization is low. Manufacture of 'Vardi' beedi is going unchecked and is on the increase. Labour Department has a responsibility to stop this process if employment and livelihoods of the beedi workers have to be protected.

4. Specific Problems Faced by Beedi Workers

Problem of the Leaf (Tunikaku): This is a serious problem faced by beedi workers all over the country. Workers often lose the wage battles they have won through unions as the employer has the opportunity to exploit them through this method. 'Tunikaku' is supplied by the employer (or a contractor) in which beedi is rolled. 'Tunikaku' grows in the forests which is picked by, generally, by the forest dwellers most of who are tribals, as a non-timber forest produce. It is available in various sizes, dimensions, and ranges of quality. The quantity of the leaf required to roll 1000 beedis depends on all the above factors. Employers are expected to supply sufficient quantity of the leaf to roll 1000 beedis. Irrespective of the quantity of the leaf supplied, they expect to get back 1000 beedis of a specified quality, and size. For want of sufficient quantity, size or poor quality of the leaf, if 1000 beedis cannot be made, the shortage has to be made up by the worker herself, by purchasing the leaf in the market at her own expense. In some places the employer may supply the worker with the shortfall, but deduct equivalent amount from the wages to be paid. This type of exploitation is prevalent in all parts of the country. On an average there is a loss of 100 gms – 200 gms of raw material per 1000 Beedis, resulting in loss of Rs.6-12 per worker per day, Rs. 60 – Rs.120 a month. Can we call this as an authorized deduction under the Payment of Wages Act, 1936? Even when the Labour Department (State Government) is aware of this practice, there is no recommendation that the law be amended requiring the employer to provide tunikaku of a specified quality. Where he is not able to do so, he himself should bear the loss. Such a loss cannot be legitimately passed on to the workers. There is no other industry where the worker pays for the poor quality raw material.

Beedi workers are covered by Sec. 39 of the Industrial Disputes Act, 1947. Matters relating to poor quality raw material and shortfall raw material can be raised as a dispute by the union under the provision. The labour department directs the employers to supply required quantities of the leaf. Employees have appealed to appellate authorities that the employees have not implemented the awards. Workers and their unions can ill afford frequent visits to the Labour Department. In many villages, there are no labour officers. Traveling long distances at the cost of employment is not possible for the workers. The possible solution is to examine and cut the tunikaku at every factory/branch/office of the beedi manufacturers and issue required quantities, which may vary on a day to day basis. An amendment to this effect could reduce the conflict between employers, workers and unions in this regard.

Occupational Diseases: Women working with beedi are affected but continuous exposure to the tobacco dust, contract diseases related to lungs like T.B., Cancer and also backache due to postural problems. Very few are covered by ESI or any other medical facility.

Unions of beedi workers: Unions working in the region for the past five decades nearly have been able to positively influence the wages. However not all women workers in the beedi industry are members of the union. Resistance comes from not only the employers but the family as well. Women workers themselves have been threatened repeatedly by the contractors and employers, with dire consequences for organizing. Some of them have lost their employment as well. Unions have been asking for protection of the beedi workers in their present employment rather than identify alternatives. This could also be a measure of protecting their own existence and identity.

Regulating beedi work: The beedi industry does not systematically employ workers for 8 hours every day. Employers have no compulsion to provide daily employment also. Number of hours of work, number of days for which employment is available also varies between factories. Quantum of work available may vary from one month to another. All these are decided as per the convenience of the employer. Some workers get chance to roll thousand beedis, others 800 or 500. Some factories are able to provide 1500 – 2000 beedi work in a day also. Workers are provided with cards denoting the quantity of work available. Quantum of work, at times, varies with changes in the market conditions. But not always so. Employers do it just to keep the workers in their control, as a threatening device. Where workers appear to be organizing and gaining consciousness, employers use it to counteract union influence over the workers. Variations in work, for whatever reasons, creates upheavals in their lives. According to unions, the Beedi Act should be amended to provide 8 hours/1000 beedi work every day, for 26 days in a month, and paid holidays. The employer should be made to compensate for reduction in work.

All beedi factories in the region are not licenced. The unlicenced factories manufacture illegal or 'vardi' beedi. Such factories do not pay even minimum wages. Wages paid for 'Vardi' beedi workers are as low as Rs. 25 – Rs. 30 per 1000 beedis, whereas those working for licensed factories may be paid around Rs. 45. Problem of unlicensed factories is prevalent in Nalgonda and Hyderabad Districts of the region in a big way and in all pockets to some extent or the other. This phenomenon is on the increase in the Telagana Region. Union claims that annually, there is a loss to the beedi workers to the extent of Rs. 100 to 150 crores in the process.

5. Absence of Social Protection

If the definition of social protection were to be widened as proposed key Unni (2005), it covers three dimensions: (i) Basic security, (ii) Economic security, and (iii) Social security. Basic security covers a decent standard is living, food, health, education and shelter. Economic security covers access to productive income generating work with core labour standards applied to all forms of work. Such security will enable the workers to cope with shocks that are due to structural factors. Social security covers core contingencies that affect problems such as old age, death, unemployment, illness, disability, property loss etc.

If this is the standard against which we would be studying the extent of social protection available to the beedi workers, there is in no protection at all.

6. Reduced Employment and Limited Livelihood Options for Beedi Workers

ILO took up a pilot action project for developing alternate livelihoods for beedi workers. In the Telangana region women are not thinking in terms of alternate livelihoods at present. A small proportion of beedi-workers are educating their girls children and discouraging them from taking up beedirolling. But most of them do not have enough per capita income to give their children sufficient education or training and skill for sustainable livelihoods, middle aged women are not willing to take up alternate occupations as they are used to home based work. Young girls have no training in beedi rolling, but neither have skills nor opportunities for alternate livelihoods. Unions seems to think that making laws to protect the home worker and ensure their effective implementation, providing employment for 26 days in a months, social security, medical and health protection and old age pensions would be far more useful than planning for alternate livelihood opportunities. This proposition requires further probing.

The ILO has conducted studies in various regions manufacturing beedi and has identified some alternative sources of livelihood, like diary farming, tailoring and embroidery, domestic work, working as agriculture labour etc. Studies also showed that in the past ten years there is an increase in the number of branches of beedi units, numbers of workers, increasing involvement of children, number of companies in the unorganized sector and increase in the number of contractors. Contrary situation appears in the Telengana Region. In the Nizamabad District owners of the beedi Factories themselves acknowledge that they are not able to employ same number of workers they used to earlier because of reducing market for beedis, problems of shortage of supply of raw materials, reduced profits, which also means that they are not in a position to provide the benefits demanded by the unions.

One ironical factor is that, in absolute terms even in Telagana Region the problem is not as much reduction in employment as shifts in employment from registered beedi factories to unregistered beedi factors. This is not an accident. It is done on purpose to reduce the bargaining capacity of the workers and keep them at their mercy. There does not seem to be any law against this.

It may be true in relatively developed regions of Dakshina Kannada region (as reported by the ILO) various alternatives are available. In the Telagana region which is highly backward similar or even other alternatives are not available. In the Nizambad District, some work is available seasonally on sugarcane farms. In the remaining districts like Karimnagar,

Medak and Warangal which are drought prone districts even this is not available. So it is necessary to study viable alternative livelihoods to suit the peculiarities of the region. It is the contention of the researcher that there is no single solution that suits beedi workers in different regions. Regions specific studies should be made to identify alternatives. For instance, women workers in Kerala have promoted Kerala Dinesh Beedi Workers Cooperative Society employing 32,000 workers as an alternative to home working. It is also the contention of the researcher that home workers are no longer invisible. The Labour Department could easily come out with actual figures not just estimates if it wished to do so.

Conclusion

In conclusion it may be said that beedi industry, where about 90% of those employed are women, should be protected, if the welfare of women has to be protected, particularly in regions like Telagana where lacs are employed in the industry. One of the major factors is ensuring continued employment of the women. This should not be left to the discretion of the factory owners and traders. The state should try to address problems like shortage of raw material, exploitation by the middlemen, competition from mini cigarettes and other tobacco substitutes.

If the women in the region who are extensively dependent on beedi rolling have to live with dignity and contribute meaningfully to their families and the society, protecting their livelihoods is essential.

It also raises the question of whether the role of the state is complete by enacting laws and implementing them. Between the time when Beedi Workers (Conditions of Employment) Act 1966 was enacted and now the conditions of the beedi workers have deteriorated largely particularly in the back ward region like the Telagana. In case of home based beedi workers it will not be just a matter of overcoming legislative apathy, but rising to a crisis where the very livelihood is no longer available to them.

References

Unni, Jemol (2005) Economic Security for unemployed and home based workers, paper presented at International Conference On Employment And Income Security in India, IHD, New Delhi.

Beedi Workers (Conditions of Employment) Act 1966.

17

STATE ACTIVISM IN 'LABOUR' MARKET: A STUDY OF GUJARAT, MAHARASHTRA AND KERALA

Arti Nanavati

State activism in 'labour' market encompasses its role from formation of quality human 'resource' to the various stages from entry to exit in employment/gainful work of labour, which gets operationalized mainly through the agency of 'government'. Government impacts labour market directly through three main channels, *a)* as an employer, creator, facilitator and enhancer of human capabilities for generating 'human resource', *b)* through its budgetary resource allocation in social sector in general and labour in particular, and *c)* through various legislation, policies, programmes etc. The indirect activism is realized through its involvement in the process of economic development as a facilitator and regulator of 'market' and also as an active partner. In India the employment scenario in the post reform period has been characterized by relatively low/falling employment elasticity with respect to output, growing informalization and gradual withdrawal of state as an employment generator. All these necessitate proactive role of government in a Welfare State, in terms of, human capital formation, welfare of labour and protecting especially the informal sector workers through socio-economic security measures. (Sundaram, 2001; Sreenivas, 2004; Papola and Sharma, 2004; Tendulkar, 2004; Bhattacharya and Sakthivel, 2005; Vaidyanathan, 2005 among others).

Further with the increasing role of market a fear is often expressed that the principle of, 'Economic Darwinism' may lead to widening and deepening of inter-state disparity in 'human development'. Hence at state level, social sector expenditure needs analysis, as it is one of the major components of a State activism in the labour market. This is more so due to the fact that a major portion of social sector expenditure, which directly impacts labour market, falls within the purview of state governments. The present paper therefore focuses on the social sector expenditure scenario at state level and correlates this to the employment characteristics of the states. It also attempts to identify the potential areas where State activism is revealed through the secondary data sources. The significance of such an analysis is also due to the fact that though the relationship between government expenditure on economic sector and economic development is well documented, the same is not true between expenditure on social sector and its consequent impact on the process of economic and human development. (Wilson, 2001: Roy, 2005). The paper also intends to contribute in this endeavour.

For a detailed state level analysis, the paper concentrates on three states, Gujarat, Kerala and Maharashtra. Gujarat and Maharashtra due to their economic progressiveness and Kerala due to its social progressiveness. The paper confines to few aspects of State activism in terms of, *i)* structure and composition of government expenditure, *ii)* state specific employment and human capital characteristics, and *iii)* perception of potential 'women' labour regarding the role of government, as a characteristic which cuts across all the states was 'women' being bypassed in the process of growth. The paper is divided in three sections. Section I analyses the relative expenditure on different social services and using the UNDP guidelines on social sector expenditure examines the appropriateness of the resource allocation in the states of Gujarat, Kerala and Maharashtra. Section II using the 50th (1993-94), 55th (1999-2000) and 59th rounds (2002-2003) of NSSO comments on State activism based on the employment characteristics of these States in terms of activity status, industry/sector wise distribution and women's perception regarding the role of government. III concludes the paper.

I

One of the major indicators of State activism in labour market is government expenditure on social sector in general and labour in particular. The expenditure pattern of the states needs to be contextualized in the backdrop of declining shares of states in total plan outlay over the various plan periods, which came down from 50% in IV, V, VI Plans to 40% in the Xth Plan (Sarma, 2005). Secondly for sustaining the expenditure across different sectors, the 'development' component should form a large proportion of total expenditure. Social sector falls mainly within the per view of state governments. UNDP has prescribed guidelines in the form of various desirable expenditure ratios, which could gauge the adequacy of social sector allocation. Further two main components of social sector, which indicate State activism in 'labour' market, are expenditure on human capital formation for 'quality human resource' and on 'labour its welfare and security' which need analysis so as to link it to the employment scenario of the states. These aspects of expenditure pattern are discussed below with respect to Gujarat, Maharashtra and Kerala.

Structure of Government Expendiure

Across the three states, the per capita expenditure on both economic and social services is highest in case of Gujarat. As per the Budget estimates, (State Finances, 2003) per capita expenditure on social services in 2002-03, of Gujarat was Rs. 1726, Maharashtra Rs. 1427, Kerala Rs. 1622, and average India was Rs. 1175. On economic services, respectively for the states the per capita expenditure was Rs, 1413, Rs. 476 and Rs. 953 respectively. The national average was Rs. 686. Per capita expenditure indicates the average macro/regional scenario, the structure and composition of expenditure across different heads and subheads of expenditure discussed below indicate the nature and direction of State activism in the three states under consideration.

It can be seen from Table-1 that in Gujarat the share of development expenditure in total expenditure was 68% in

1991-92, which with some fluctuations remained around 68% till 1999-00 and then increased to 74% in 2001-02. The share of social services in total development expenditure remained around 42% to 45% during 1991-92-1998-99. Thereafter the increase to 59% in 2001-02 was mainly due to natural calamities. The corresponding share of economic services during 1991-92 to 2001-02 decreased from 58% to 41%.

In case of Maharashtra, the share of development expenditure in total expenditure was 64% in 1991-92, which with fluctuation declined to 50% in 2001-02. In total development expenditure the share of social and economic services was respectively 63% and 37% in 2003-04, which was 47% and 53% respectively in 1991-92. Thus the relative share of social services has increased. The proportionate share on Social services was 4% points higher than Gujarat.

The development expenditure of Kerala was 56% of total expenditure in 1991-92, which declined to 55% in 2001-02. The share of social services in total development expenditure was around 61% in 1991-92 and that of economic services 39%. Almost the same relative shares one finds in 2001-02 with some fluctuations in the intervening years. Though the expenditure was 2% points lower in social services as compared to Maharashtra, the important difference is that the expenditure on social services has remained almost consistently higher in Kerala as compared to Gujarat and Maharashtra. Thus among the three states Kerala has been the most active and Gujarat the least active in social sector.

Considering the period 1991-92—2003-04, one can observe that the deterioration in the various ratios across states started from 1996-97/1997-98 onwards. Thus the period of roughly fifteen years can be divided in two periods, one till 1996-97 and the period thereafter. Among the three states the share of development expenditure in total expenditure turns out to be highest of Gujarat and lowest of Maharashtra. The share of social services in total development expenditure turns out to lowest in Gujarat (highest in economic services) and highest in Maharashtra (lowest in economic services) closely followed by Kerala. One thing which is common among the states is that percentage share of social services expenditure exceeds expenditure on economic services. However from the point of view of sustaining the growth the performance of both Maharashtra and Kerala are dismal as development expenditure as proportion of total expenditure is almost continuously falling over the years. Thus despite increasing share of social service expenditure the impact on the labour market may not be fully realized since the expenditure on economic services may not be able to sustain employability of people.

Composition of Social Services Expenditure

The changing share of various sub-heads of social services in total social services expenditure is shown in Tables 2, Table 3, and Table 4 respectively for the states, Gujarat, Maharashtra and Kerala.

It can be seen from Table 2 that the highest expenditure in Gujarat throughout the period of 1991-92 to 2003-04 is on education, sports, arts and culture. However the percentage share, which was 54% in 1991-92 and 58% in 1996-97, is declining there after and in the year 2003-04 was expected to be 38%. Medical and public health gets second priority. The expenditure, which was 15% during 1991-92-1994-95, fell to 12% during 1995-96- 1999-00 and then to 8% from 2000-01 onwards. In the last few years there is a sizable increase in expenditure on natural calamities, the percentage share, which was 0.91 in 1997-98, increased to 6.39 in 1999-2000 and to 39% in 2001-02. This adversely affected expenditure on other heads of social sector. In 2003-04, expenditure on human capital formation (education and health) was 46% and on labour and social security was around 3.55% of total social sector expenditure.

In case of Maharashtra, (Table 3), one finds the largest item of expenditure is on Education etc. The percentage share was 57% in 1991-92, which declined to 55% in 1998-99 and with some increase declined to 56% in 2003-04. The next largest item of expenditure is medical and public health whose share was 15% in 1991-92 and it declined to around 12% in 1995-96 and continued to remain the same till 2003-04 with some minor fluctuations.

In case of Kerala, (Table 4) education etc. receives the highest percentage allocation. The State allocated around 62%of social sector expenditure on this item in 2003-04, which was higher than Gujarat and Maharashtra. The next major item is medical and family welfare with 12.28% share comparable to Maharashtra but higher than Gujarat. Expenditure on labour and social security was around 6% in 2003-04, which was higher than both Maharashtra and Gujarat.

In order to examine the relative expenditure of human capital formation to labour and social security, the percentage ratios were calculated which are shown in Table 5. It can be seen from the Table that between 1991-92 to 2003-04, the ratio of expenditure on labour and social security to education and health increased from 5% to nearly 8% in case of Gujarat. In 1991-92 the same ratio was 7% for Maharashtra and 9% for Kerala. The ratio remained almost the same in case of Maharashtra where as in Kerala; it increased to around 11% in 2000-01 and decreased to 8% in 2003-04. Thus among these three states the relative expenditure on 'labour' was much higher in Kerala as compared to Gujarat and Maharashtra. Between these two states in case of Gujarat, the ratio continued to remain around 5% till 1997-98 and then increased to 8% in 2003-04 where as in case of Maharashtra, it continued to remain around 7% with a declining trend since 1997-98. Thus among the three states State activism in 'labour' is highest in case of Kerala and lowest in Gujarat.

Social Development Expenditure Ratios

The efficacy of expenditure on social sector was expressed in terms of various ratios suggested by UNDP. Table 6 gives information about the same for Gujarat, Maharashtra and Kerala.

It can be seen from the Table that except Gujarat, public expenditure ratio (PAR= public expenditure as a % of Net state domestic product) is lower in both Maharashtra and Kerala. In Gujarat the ratio exceeded the prescribed minimum of 25% only in 2000-01, in the earlier period the ratio was much lower than that. Between Maharashtra and Kerala, in the former the ratio increased to 18% in 1990-00 from around 16% in the period before that, and in case of the later it remained around 21%. Thus only in Gujarat, one finds an increase in the ratio. Thus the overall activism of Maharashtra and Kerala is low with respect to level and growth of public expenditure, which is not be a welcome sign for sustaining human development.

The Social Allocation Ratio (SAR= Social services expenditure as % of public expenditure) was lower in all the three states as compared to UNDP prescribed percentage of 40%. It was 33% in Gujarat and 25% each in Maharashtra and Kerala in 2003-04. If one takes the period 1991-92—2003-04, one finds that in case of Gujarat and Maharashtra the ratio remained around 30-32% and in case of Kerala between 32-36%. The ratio exceeded prescribed ratio of 40% in case of Gujarat in 2001-02 mainly due to earthquake. Thus in none of the states the prescribed UNDP norm is attained and thus there is a need to increase State activism in social sector.

The expenditure on social priority (education etc., medical & public health, family welfare and nutrition) is expected to be 50% and more as per UNDP norms. On Social priorities, the expenditure ratio was higher in all the three states as compared to the prescribed norm. In Gujarat the ratio was almost the same as the prescribed ratio of minimum 50%, in 2003-04. It is to be noted that except Kerala, where the ratio increased from 74% to 81% during 1991-92 to 2003-04, in Gujarat it declined from 73% to 50% and in Maharashtra it declined from 88% to 79% during the same period. This shows that the decline in expenditure on human priorities is much faster in Gujarat than in case of Maharashtra. In terms of level also the expenditure is lowest in Gujarat as compared to the other two states. Thus the state activism in expenditure on social priorities is much higher in Maharashtra and Kerala than Gujarat.

As far as human expenditure ratio is concerned except Kerala, which exceeds UNDP prescribed norm, the ratio was almost the same in Gujarat and Maharashtra as the prescribed norm of 5%. Analyzing the four ratios together, one can deduce that with the declining public expenditure ratio, a relatively lesser amount of resources are available for social and economic services. Since social allocation ratio is lower than the UNDP prescribed ratio, there is a need to increase relative expenditure on social services so that the ratio reaches the prescribed one. Since expenditure on social priority is much higher than prescribed ratio in Maharashtra and Kerala than in Gujarat, there is a need to examine the composition of social sector expenditure of these states. The declining trend in social allocation ratio in Gujarat coupled with declining social priority ratio impacts social sector much more adversely as compared to Maharashtra and Kerala. These states are having low social allocation ratio, (which is less than UNDP prescribed norm) but their social priority ratio is higher than UNDP prescribed norm and that of Gujarat. Thus Gujarat is spending less on social priorities than these two states in relative terms. This is not a healthy social sector development scenario of the state. However the overall fiscal situation of Gujarat is better than Maharashtra and Kerala where the public expenditure ratio is low and not showing an increase. Thus Gujarat has the potential to raise allocation to social sector (to attain UNDP prescribed norm) and within it on social priorities. Maharashtra and Kerala need to raise their social allocation ratio and reexamine their social priority ratios.

II

The above analysis indicates that the State activism in social sector is far less than it should be. Further the relatively low/declining labour and social security to human capital expenditure ratio indicates that especially Gujarat and Maharashtra, are relatively less oriented directly towards, 'labour' and their welfare as compared to Kerala. Though there could be several reasons for such a State activism, it could be of interest to examine the nature of their employment structure and level of human capital, which correlates with such an expenditure pattern. This would also help identify the potential areas of desired State activism.

In this Section therefore the employment characteristics of the states are examined using various rounds of NSSO including the latest 59th – 2003 round, with respect to, *i)* usual activity status, *ii)* non-agriculture sector workers across different enterprise tsypes, relative distribution of workers in different sectors, *iii)* human capital characteristics and, *iv)* role perceived of government by potential 'women' entrants in labour market since it represented to some extent the 'demand' for State activism.

Usual Activity Status Employment Scenario

Table 7 gives the percentage distribution of persons engaged in broad usual activity. The Table shows that in Gujarat, the extent of self-employment in rural male is highest and in casual labour it is lowest. Between Maharashtra and Kerala, self-employment is higher in Maharashtra and casual labour is higher in Kerala—it is highest among all the three states. In case of rural female, self-employment is highest in Gujarat. Casual rural female labour is highest in Maharashtra followed by Gujarat and Kerala. Regular wage and salaried labour is highest in Kerala both in case of rural male and rural female. Urban Male self-employment is highest in Gujarat. Regular wage and salary labour is highest in Maharashtra and proportion of casual labour is highest in Kerala and its differential with Gujarat and Maharashtra is substantial. In case of urban female labour the self-employment was highest in Kerala followed by in Gujarat and Maharashtra. Regular wage and salary labour was almost the same in Maharashtra and Kerala (about 7%) but in Gujarat the percentage was only 3. Casual labour was highest in Kerala. Overall urban female labour was highest in Kerala 20% and almost the same in Gujarat (14%) and in Maharashtra (15%).

The employment structure which emerges of the three states is dominance of self employment in Gujarat in all the categories except urban male where regular wage and salary percentage is higher than self employment, (though across states, Gujarat had highest percentage of self employed urban male). In Maharashtra self-employment and casual labour are almost equally important in rural category and in case of urban male and female it is regular wage and salary labour, which is dominant, followed by self-employment. In Kerala, casual labour is predominant for rural males, and self-employment for rural females. Self-employment is dominant in case of both urban male and female, however the extent of casual labour is much higher in urban male whereas in urban female it is regular wage and salary. The only phenomena which is common in all the three states is the extent of female labour which is much lower than male and the gender differentials are much higher in urban than rural areas.

The disturbing scenario, which emerges is that of Kerala, where there is predominance of casual labour both in rural and urban areas and relatively a higher percentage of women are not in the labour force mainly due to their being engaged in domestic duties. Thus despite a much favourable financial resources allocation, the quality of employment is not favourable due to predominance of casual labour and marginalization of women in employment market. In urban Gujarat, a high proportion of women are engaged in domestic activities as compared to Maharashtra and Kerala. In Maharashtra a much higher percentage of rural women are employed as compared to Gujarat, however urban female percentage is not very encouraging and a relatively high percentage 'as students' is not a sufficient reason for their low economic participation.

Thus orientation of the policies/resource allocation in Gujarat could be towards self-employment in rural areas (mainly with respect to primary sector), which will address both male and female issues. With respect to urban employment scenario the policy orientation could be with respect to regular wage and salaried and self-employed male. In case of Maharashtra, the policies should be oriented towards both self employed and casual male and female labour in rural areas and in urban areas mainly for wage and salaried. For Kerala, it could be both for self employed and casual male and female labour and for urban areas for all the three main categories, i.e., self-employed, wage and salaried and casual male labour. As far as women are concerned the issue is much more towards facilitate and empower them enter the employment market. It would be therefore of interest to examine how much resources go in human capital formation of 'women' and what are the constraints from demand and supply side to mainstream them. The prevailing State activism with respect to policies and programmes pertaining self-employed and wage and salaried thus get geared towards male labour. Since casual labour in practice most of the time escapes government activism, both male and female labour suffer. Across the states, it is likely that the dominance of self-employed in Gujarat might be a factor for relatively less State activism of the state directly for 'labour and its welfare'. This is an issue, which needs further exploration.

Non-Agriculture Sector Workers

Another approach to examine the areas of relative State activism is the employment characteristics of non-agriculture workers across different types of enterprises. In order to do this the ratio of non agriculture workers in public sector to proprietor and partnership enterprise was calculated based on 55 Round of NSSO. (1999-2000). The Table 9, below shows that the ratios of public sector non agriculture workers to workers in proprietorship and partnership are very low in rural Kerala as compared to Gujarat and Maharashtra. In case of rural male the ratio was highest in Maharashtra and in case of rural female the ratio was highest in Gujarat. In Gujarat it is almost nearing 40%. In case of urban labour the differentials across states is not glaring. It is again lowest in Kerala. Maharashtra has the highest ratio in terms of urban male and Gujarat has the highest ratio in case of urban female. This implies that the State activism focusing on public sector workers need to be high in Gujarat and Maharashtra whereas in Kerala it should focus on private sector enterprises and should be gender sensitive.

Sector-wise Distribution of Workers

The distribution of labour across different sectors of the economy shown in the Table 10 indicates that Kerala has to focus in relative terms more on primary sector labour as compared to Gujarat and Maharashtra. Between Gujarat and Maharashtra, it is the former, which has to address in relative terms issues pertaining primary sector labour. In case of rural male and female labour, Maharashtra has to focus more on secondary and tertiary sectors, as compared to Gujarat and Kerala. Tertiary sector dominates for both male and female labour in all the three states. However Maharashtra in relative terms has to focus more on urban male and female labour in primary sector as compared to Gujarat and Kerala.

Perception of Potential 'Women' Labour Regarding Government's Role

Incidence of low female- male employment is a common employment characteristics in all the three states irrespective of their economic and social progressiveness. The main reason of low women participation is a high incidence of women being engaged in domestic duties. This proportion is much higher in urban than rural areas. Hence in order to examine the state activism needed which could raise their economic status, the NSSO Reports on, 'Participation of Indian Women in household work and specified activities (50th and 55 rounds) were referred. The Table 11 shows the type of assistance envisaged by women who are willing to accept work in these three states.

It can be seen from the Table that initial finance was considered to be the main assistance required by the women in all the states in 1993-94 both in urban and rural areas. In all the states its importance declined in 2000 except in rural Kerala. Next in importance was working finance (in Gujarat and Kerala). Training was considered important in all the three states however in Maharashtra the percentage was highest. The importance of 'assured market' also emerged as an important factor. In Maharashtra and in Kerala the importance of initial finance is replaced by training and assured market. In all the three states 'training' and facilitating women to market their produce are the areas, which need focus from government. This implies that the State to be active in both monetary and social sectors. However in relative terms the State activism for providing finance needs to be higher in Gujarat and Kerala and in terms of providing 'training' in Maharashtra and in urban Gujarat and Kerala.

Another important feature of women employment, which emerges from the 50th and 55th Rounds is that only about a slightly higher than one fifth to one third of women are willing to take up economically gainful work. In Gujarat the no. of women willing to accept work is lower in 1999-2000 as compared to in 1993-04. Between Maharashrtra and Kerala, the relative willingness is much higher among Kerala women than Maharashtra women. Thus the resources, policies etc., should not only be geared to facilitate women to make some earnings but also to generate awareness in them attain independent economic status.

Government's Activism in Education

In order to identify the levels of education where state activism should be directed, the information contained in 59th Round (2003) of NSSO Survey was used. It can be seen from the Table 12 that the percentage of non-literate is still very high in Gujarat and Maharashtra. In rural areas 'above secondary' the proportionate distribution is low both for male and female. Across the states, the relative female education is lower than male education at all the levels. In this respect Kerala's performance is much better than Gujarat and Maharashtra. Thus in Gujarat and Maharashtra there is a need to consider all the three stages of education as equally important, i.e., primary, secondary and tertiary whereas in Kerala the focus should be more on higher education. A proactive role of State in case of Gujarat and Maharashtra is envisaged to be much higher in forming quality human resource as compared to Kerala, which already has made significant strides in primary and secondary education. The employment and human capital scenario situated in the context of budgetary allocation to social sector reflect that a state like Gujarat, which in relative terms is more inclined towards self-employment, needs a different State activism especially in terms of appropriate financial and skill formation, as compared to Maharashtra and Kerala. Maharashtra where all the three, i.e., primary, secondary and tertiary sectors are almost equally important from the point of view of employment, employment structure tilted towards casual and wage and salaried labour and human capital base is low need a policy orientation geared to these features. Kerala despite high human capital base and relatively higher expenditure on 'labour', has not been able to increase employment potential of the state both in terms of quantity and quality as reflected in higher unemployment ratio, higher percentage of women engaged in domestic duties and a relatively high incidence of casual labour as compared to Gujarat and Kerala. This calls for State activism to be raised more in economic sector so that employment potentials could be increased. State Policy framework should be a pro woman and atleast 30% of budgetary allocation should be for them.

III

Conclusion

i) The overall public expenditure scenario is not sustainable in all the three states except Gujarat. Across the states, Kerala is the most active in social sector in general and 'labour' in particular, Gujarat the least.

ii) The employment structure of the three states in terms of activity status, rural urban break up, public v/s other business types is diverse and call for appropriate State activism.

iii) In states like Gujarat and Maharashtra all the three levels of education is important from the point of view of State activism whereas in Kerala the bias can be for tertiary education.

iv) A common area of State activism, which emerges is education and participation rate of 'women' in paid labour market. Gujarat needs to do much more in comparison to Maharashtra and Kerala in this regard.

v) Finally a sizable amount, nearly 40% of total plan outlay on social sector is in the domain of central government thus 'State' activism should be 'state' activism in 'labour' so as to have 'state specific' 'State activism'.

Table 1

Percentage Share of Various Expenditure Heads to Corresponding Total 1991-2004: Gujarat, Maharashtra and Kerala

Description	*1991-92*	*1992-93*	*1993-94*	*1994-95*	*1995-96*	*1996-97*	*1997-98*	*1998-99*	*1999-00*	*2000-01*	*2001-02*	*2002-03*	*2003-04*
Gujarat													
1 Dev. Exp/ Total Exp.	68.16	65.12	66.29	64.92	68.21	66.56	67.76	68.05	66.99	69.69	73.92		
2 Social Service/ Total Exp.	28.82	26.47	29.44	29.81	29.91	28.42	29.47	30.70	31.96	34.19	43.40	17.43	32.80
3 Eco. Service/ Total Exp.	39.34	38.66	36.85	35.11	38.30	36.81	38.29	37.34	35.03	35.50	30.52	21.85	29.94
4 Social Service/ Total Dev. Exp.	42.28	40.64	44.41	45.92	43.85	42.70	43.49	45.12	47.71	49.06	58.71		
5 Eco. Service/ Total Dev. Exp.	57.72	59.36	55.59	54.08	56.15	55.31	56.51	54.88	52.29	50.94	41.29		
6 Non-Dev. Exp./ Total Exp.	21.04	22.31	23.29	24.27	24.17	26.46	24.47	25.03	26.94	23.14	22.66		
Maharashtra													
1 Dev. Exp/ Total Exp.	64.49	74.56	66.65	68.56	66.42	66.99	65.46	59.34	52.62	59.01	49.85		
2 Social Service/ Total Exp.	30.44	29.95	29.58	27.01	31.32	30.35	31.83	32.02	29.71	31.44	31.63	25.38	24.61

3 Eco. Service/ Total Exp.	34.05	35.52	37.02	41.55	35.10	36.64	33.63	27.33	22.91	27.57	18.22	19.42	15.75
4 Social Service/ Total Dev. Exp.	7.20 4	40.17	44.39	39.39	47.15	45.31	48.63	53.95	56.46	53.28	63.46		
5Eco. Service/ Total Dev. Exp.	52.80	47.64	55.55	60.61	52.85	54.69	51.37	46.05	43.53	46.72	36.54		
6 Non-Dev. Exp./ Total Exp.	26.57	26.35	25.62	24.13	26.32	26.91	28.36	35.26	32.98	34.54	44.22		
Kerala													
1 Dev. Exp/ Total Exp.	56.16	58.42	57.19	57.85	57.10	58.40	58.22	58.80	55.12	56.78	54.78		
2 Social Service/ Total Exp.24.79	34.54	33.93	35.50	35.69	34.38	34.93	32.21	32.32	33.12	32.93	33.53	20.74	
3 Eco. Service/ Total Exp	21.63	24.49	21.69	22.16	22.72	23.47	26.01	26.48	22.00	23.85	21.24	15.35	19.51
4 Social Service/ Total Dev. Exp.	61.49	58.08	62.08	61.70	60.21	59.82	55.33	54.97	60.08	58.00	61.21		
5 Eco. Service/ Total Dev. Exp.	38.51	41.92	37.92	38.30	39.79	40.18	44.67	45.03	39.92	42.00	38.78		
6 Non-Dev. Exp./ Total Exp.	30.62	30.84	32.27	33.56	34.13	33.44	31.93	33.84	38.95	37.23	39.06		

Source: All the Tables unless specified are based on the data provided in CMIE, Public Finance statistics.

Table 2
Percentage Share of Various Social Services to Total Social Service Expenditure of Gujarat

Description	*1991-92*	*1992-93*	*1993-94*	*1994-95*	*1995-96*	*1996-97*	*1997-98*	*1998-99*	*1999-00*	*2000-01*	*2001-02*	*2002-03*	*2003-04*
1 Education, Sports, Arts & Culture	54.17	54.19	55.69	55.51	58.35	57.67	51.68	53.36	49.73	37.25	26.87	43.41	38.20
2 Medical & Public Health	14.32	14.97	14.46	14.64	12.21	12.51	12.16	12.81	12.07	8.06	5.48	8.78	7.79
3 Family Welfare	0.00	0.00	0.00	0.00	2.36	2.13	2.20	2.09	1.79	1.57	0.99	1.68	1.20
4 Water Supply & Sanitation	5.55	6.46	6.38	8.94	4.80	5.36	6.51	8.60	9.77	11.21	2.98	6.81	5.78
5 Housing	3.66	5.13	3.78	3.55	3.48	3.22	3.51	3.94	3.91	3.91	2.84	4.46	6.11
6 Urban Development	2.25	1.70	2.02	1.52	2.37	2.42	2.87	3.24	3.65	2.69	2.17	3.78	4.01
7 Welfare of SC, ST & OBC	6.88	7.98	7.53	6.65	6.93	7.10	6.58	6.18	6.22	5.14	3.28	5.20	5.14
8 Labour & 2.09 Labour Welfare	0.00	2.15	1.98	1.98	2.03	1.75	1.65	1.58	1.39	0.90	1.41	1.83	
9 Social Security & Welfare	1.49	2.13	1.64	1.48	1.47	1.52	1.66	1.77	1.81	1.52	1.02	3.11	1.72
10 Nutrition	4.53	4.95	4.70	4.53	4.17	3.66	3.52	2.71	2.47	2.25	1.49	2.29	2.60
11 Relief on A/c of Natural Calamities	3.90	-0.99	0.74	0.44	1.02	1.50	6.78	2.92	6.38	24.47	39.02	11.27	11.05
12 Others	1.12	1.08	0.92	0.77	0.88	0.89	0.77	0.73	0.60	0.55	12.96	-	-

Table 3
Percentage Share of Various Social Services to Total Social Service Expenditure of Maharashtra

Description	*1991-92*	*1992-93*	*1993-94*	*1994-95*	*1995-96*	*1996-97*	*1997-98*	*1998-99*	*1999-00*	*2000-01*	*2001-02*	*2002-03*	*2003-04*
1 Education, Sports, Arts & Culture	57.40	56.54	57.31	56.74	55.34	56.04	55.70	55.18	64.27	62.95	61.34	57.15	55.93
2 Medical & Public Health	14.89	15.14	15.26	14.29	11.56	11.85	11.35	11.23	11.32	10.60	11.00	10.36	12.05
3 Family Welfare	0.00	0.00	0.00	0.00	1.96	1.67	1.37	0.98	0.94	1.38	1.89	1.87	1.14
4 Water Supply & Sanitation	5.69	5.70	5.05	5.2	4.96	6.01	7.86	7.37	6.3	5.89	6.15	8.24	7.68
5 Housing	3.16	3.09	3.18	2.75	2.78	2.23	2.27	3.94	2.18	3.22	3.63	3.56	3.79
6 Urban Development	3.13	3.76	3.74	2.40	4.05	2.81	3.26	2.76	2.78	3.02	2.62	3.79	3.67
7 Welfare of SC, ST & OBC	5.14	5.15	5.63	5.42	4.39	5.27	6.25	5.87	5.84	5.62	5.02	5.76	7.51
8 Labour & Labour Welfare	1.85	1.60	1.65	1.93	2.05	1.93	2.24	1.96	2.13	1.56	1.52	1.46	1.76
9 Social Security & Welfare	3.41	3.69	3.69	3.48	3.20	3.00	2.65	2.80	2.61	3.72	3.25	4.82	3.42
10 Nutrition	1.58	1.77	1.42	2.20	2.53	2.16	2.60	2.91	0.53	1.15	1.86	1.46	1.76
11 Relief on A/c of Natural Calamities	2.98	2.40	2.51	4.91	5.04	6.18	3.85	4.39	0.55	0.41	1.26	1.23	1.18
12 Others	0.76	0.74	0.68	0.64	0.61	0.64	0.57	0.59	0.54	0.46	0.44	0.47	0.54

Table 4

Percentage Share of Various Social Services to Total Social Service Expenditure of Kerala

Description	*1991-92*	*1992-93*	*1993-94*	*1994-95*	*1995-96*	*1996-97*	*1997-98*	*1998-99*	*1999-00*	*2000-01*	*2001-02*	*2002-03*	*2003-04*
1 Education, Sports, Arts & Culture	61.73	63.13	64.21	64.55	61.26	59.21	56.56	57.89	61.46	60.78	62.16	64.05	61.85
2 Medical & 16.75 Public Health	16.16	16.36	16.77	14.96	13.93	13.86	14.41	14.17	13.90	14.10	10.85	12.28	
3 Family Welfare	0.00	0.00	0.00	0.00	2.58	2.40	2.28	2.36	2.48	1.27	1.18	1.80	1.60
4 Water Supply & Sanitation	5.01	4.81	4.56	4.15	4.29	3.79	4.59	4.36	4.30	4.57	3.81	4.78	5.03
5 Housing	0.85	0.79	1.29	1.38	1.85	1.47	1.66	1.38	1.21	1.18	1.14	1.35	1.47
6 Urban Development	0.72	0.52	0.50	0.57	0.57	3.01	3.71	4.30	3.44	3.70	3.78	4.30	5.27
7 Welfare of SC, ST & OBC	4.50	3.78	3.49	3.41	3.67	7.97	6.18	6.43	5.00	5.06	4.63	5.17	5.30
8 Labour & Labour Welfare	2.34	1.51	2.05	2.15	2.20	1.96	3.34	1.69	2.06	2.88	2.55	2.14	2.77
9 Social Security & Welfare	4.68	4.42	4.59	4.47	4.08	4.29	4.71	4.70	3.75	4.62	4.62	4.27	3.12
10 Nutrition	0.46	0.41	0.43	0.47	0.45	0.42	0.33	0.14	0.09	0.09	0.06	0.017	0.03
11 Relief on A/c of Natural Calamities	2.24	3.75	1.74	1.57	3.51	1.04	2.29	1.83	1.53	1.43	1.45	1.27	1.25
12 Others	0.42	0.43	0.52	0.51	0.58	0.50	0.49	0.49	0.50	0.51	0.54	-	-

Table 5
Ratio of Labour & Social Security Expenditure to Education and Health Expenditure (in %)

Year	*Gujarat*	*Maharashtra*	*Kerala*
1991-92	5.22	7.28	8.95
1994-95	4.94	7.60	8.14
1997-98	5.35	7.30	11.44
2000-01	6.41	7.19	10.99
2003-04	7.73	6.97	7.96

Table 7: Percentage Distribution of Persons by Broad Usual Activity (Principal and Subsidiary) 2003

Status	*Gujarat*	*Maharashtra*	*Kerala*	*Gujarat*	*Maharashtra*	*Kerala*
		Rural Male			*Rural Female*	
Self-Empl.	30.9	29.0	20.9	26.4	22.6	11.7
Regular Wage/ Salaried	6.1	5.6	7.3	1.5	0.8	4.2
Casual Labour	18.4	24.1	29.9	11.7	21.8	6.8
All	55.4	58.8	58.1	39.5	45.1	22.7
Unemployed	0.4	0.6	2.6	0.1	0.2	2.0
Not in Labour Force						
Students	25.9	25.0	24.9	20.3	22.0	21.4
In Domestic Duties	0.3	0.2	0.7	24.3	17.0	40.2
All	44.2	40.6	39.3	60.4	54.7	75.3
		Urban Male			*Urban Female*	
Self Empl.	22.2	19.5	19.9	7.3	4.9	8.7
Regular Wage/ Salaried	27.7	29.6	14.5	3.3	6.8	6.5
Casual Labour	7.7	6.1	17.3	3.1	3.3	4.8
All	57.6	55.2	51.7	13.7	15.0	20.0
Unemployed	2.5	2.5	3.5	0.1	0.6	2.0
Not in Labour Force						
Students	25.2	25.4	27.6	21.1	25.2	21.1
In Domestic Duties	0.3	0.3	0.6	52.7	44.0	41.9
All	40.0	42.3	44.8	86.3	84.4	78.0

Source: Calculated from the raw data of, Household Consumer Expenditure and Employment and Unemployment Situation in India- 2003.

Table 6: Social Development Expenditure Ratio 1991-2004 (in %)

Description	*1991-92*	*1992-93*	*1993-94*	*1994-95*	*1995-96*	*1996-97*	*1997-98*	*1998-99*	*1999-00*	*2000-01*	*2001-02*	*2002-03*	*2003-04*
Gujarat													
1 Public Exp. Ratio	-	-	20	17	18	17	20	22	24	30	-	-	-
2 Social Allocation Ratio	29	26	29	30	30	28	29	31	32	34	43	17	33
3 Social Priority Ratio	73	74	75	75	77	76	70	71	66	49	33	56	49
4 Human Exp. Ratio	-	-	4	4	4	4	4	5	5	5	-	-	-
Maharashtra													
1 Public Exp. Ratio	-	-	16	17	15	16	16	16	18	-	-	-	-
2 Social Allocation Ratio	30	30	30	27	31	30	32	32	30	31	32	25	25
3 Social Priority Ratio	88	90	89	88	89	89	86	80	85	82	75	83	79
4 Human Exp. Ratio			4	4	4	4	4	4	5	-	-	-	-
Kerala													
1 Public Exp. Ratio	-	-	22	21	20	20	22	21	22	21	-	-	-
2 Social Allocation Ratio	35	34	36	36	34	35	32	32	33	33	34	21	25
3 Social Priority Ratio	74	75	76	78	75	72	68	68	72	68	67	88	81
4 Human Exp. Ratio	-	-	6	6	5	5	5	5	5	5	-	-	-

Note: Public Expenditure Ratio = Public Expenditure/Net State Domestic Product at 1993-94 price. (25%); Social Allocation Ratio = Social Services Expenditure/Public Expenditure (40%); Social Priority Ratio = Expenditure on Social Priority/Social Services Expenditure (50%); Human Expenditure Ratio = Expenditure on Social Priority/Net State Domestic Product at 1993-94 price. (5%); Social Priority = Expenditure on Education etc.+ Medical and public health + Family welfare + Nutrition

Figures in bracket are UNDP norms.

Table 8
Relative Dominant Usual Status Employment Scenario-2003

	Gujarat	*Maharashtra*	*Kerala*
Rural Male	Self Employment	Self Employment+ Casual Labour	Casual Labour
Rural Female	Self Employment	Self Employment+ Casual Labour	Self Employment
Urban Male	Regular Wage Salary+Self Employment	Regular Wage Salary	Self Employment+ Regular wage salary+ Casual Labour
Urban Female	Self Employment	Regular Wage Salary	Self Employment+ Regular Wage Salary

Table 9
Ratio of Non Agriculture Workers in Public Sector (including Semi Public) to Proprietorship and Partnership Enterprise, According to Usual Activity Status (PS+SS) – 1999-2000

Category	*Gujarat*	*Maharashtra*	*Kerala*
Rural Male	0.21	0.33	0.08
Rural Female	0.36	0.27	0.13
Urban Male	0.21	0.27	0.20
Urban Female	0.26	0.24	0.21

Source: Calculated from the raw data of 55 Round NSSO, Non Agriculture Workers in Informal Sector based on Employment – Unemployment Survey' 1999-2000.

Table 10: Percentage Distribution of Usually Working Persons by Broad Group of Industry, 2003

	Gujarat			*Maharashtra*			*Kerala*		
Category	*Pri.*	*Sec.*	*Ter.*	*Pri.*	*Sec.*	*Ter.*	*Pri.*	*Sec.*	*Ter.*
Rural Male	68.8	14.7	16.5	44.6	23.5	31.9	74.2	11.9	13.9
Rural Female	88.7	6.2	5.1	64.8	16.5	18.7	92.8	3.5	3.6
Urban Male	4.4	45.3	50.3	14.6	30.0	55.5	3.8	36.3	59.9
Urban Female	15.8	32.0	52.2	29.1	23.0	47.8	12.4	31.2	56.5

Source- Calculated from the raw data of, Household Consumer Expenditure and Employment and Unemployment Situation in India- 2003.

Note:. Pri=Primary; Sec.= Secondary; Ter.=Tertiary

Table 12: Percentage Distribution of Persons of Age 7 yrs and above by Level of Education, 2003

	Gujarat		*Maharashtra*		*Kerala*	
Education Level	*R. M.*	*R.F.*	*R. M.*	*R.F.*	*R. M.*	*R.F.*
Not Literate	22.2	44.2	20.3	42.7	6.0	12.8
Primary	21.4	16.6	20.7	17.6	19.5	20.2
Middle	20.9	16.2	24.8	18.9	35.8	30.9
Secondary	10.9	5.3	11.4	5.2	14.8	13.7
Higher Secondary	2.8	1.5	4.6	1.7	4.4	4.4
Diploma/Certificate	0.5	0.1	1.0	0.2	3.5	2.9
Graduate	1.6	0.3	2.4	0.7	2.5	3.0
Post Graduate	0.3	0.2	0.5	0.3	0.9	0.6
	U.M	*U.F*	*U.M*	*U.F*	*U.M*	*U.F*
Not Literate	6.2	24.2	8.4	21.0	3.1	8.9
Primary	17.1	17.6	15.8	16.2	5.8	16.0
Middle	27.8	17.5	24.8	21.9	31.0	26.8
Secondary	19.3	14.0	17.9	14.8	16.7	17.3
Higher Secondary	5.4	7.7	8.8	6.5	7.5	9.3
Diploma/Certificate	2.1	0.6	1.8	0.9	3.9	3.1
Graduate	7.8	5.6	8.3	7.3	9.6	6.6
Post Graduate	2.3	1.6	2.8	1.3	3.2	3.0

Source: Calculated from the raw data of, Household Consumer Expenditure and Employment and Unemployment Situation in India- 2003.

Note: RM= Rural Male, RF= Rural Female; UM= Urban Male, UF=Urban Female.

Table 11: Percentage Distribution of Women Age 15 Years and above Usually Engaged in Domestic Duties and willing to accept work at the household by Type of Assistance required (1993-94 and 1999-2000)

	Gujarat				*Maharashtra*				*Kerala*			
	Rural		*Urban*		*Rural*		*Urban*		*Rural*		*Urban*	
	93-94	*99-00*	*93-94*	*99-00*	*93-94*	*99-00*	*93-94*	*99-00*	*93-94*	*99-00*	*93-94*	*99-00*
No Assistance	3.2	4.5	3.7	4.0	3.0	4.8	6.2	8.2	2.6	3.7	2.7	3.0
Initial Finance	62.1	49.8	52.6	32.7	68.5	51.6	46.4	34.0	54.4	60.1	57.6	54.1
Working Finance	9.5	9.6	6.5	19.0	9.5	8.1	9.0	7.2	8.3	14.0	10.8	12.0
Raw Material	4.1	2.2	4.8	5.1	1.6	1.2	2.9	3.2	4.5	3.2	4.7	1.1
Assured Market	2.5	6.1	4.8	8.3	0.7	5.4	4.7	8.6	1.0	4.7	2.1	2.9
Training	9.0	17.6	20.1	19.6	11.7	19.7	18.7	27.3	8.6	7.6	8.8	14.1
Accommodation	0.3	0.3	0.9	0.6	0.6	0.7	3.5	2.3	-	0.1	1.0	2.6
Others	9.2	10.0	6.7	10.1	4.4	7.1	8.6	7.6	12.2	9.6	4.4	7.1
No. of Women Willing to Accept work per '000	273	246	284	276	249	317	268	317	248	352	237	335

Source: Participation of Indian Women in Household Work and Specified Activities, NSSO, 50th Round, July 1993-94 and 55th Round, July 1999-2000.

References

Bhattacharya, B.B. and Sakthivel, S. (2005) Employment, "Wage and Output Relationships in India: A Comparison of Pre and Post Reform Behaviour", *The Indian Journal of Labour Economics*, Vol. 48, No.2

Government of India (2003) *State Finances.*

National Sample Survey Organization (2001) Report on Non Agriculture Workers in Informal Sector based on Employment—Unemployment Survey, 1999-2000.

——————(2003) Report on Employment and Unemployment in India 1999-2000, Key Results NSS 55th Round July 1999-June 2000 December.

——————(2003) Household Consumer Expenditure and Employment and Unemployment Situation in India

—————— Participation of Indian Women in Household Work and Specified Activities, 50th Round July 1993-June 1994 and 55th Round- July 1999-June 2000.

Papola, T.S., and Sharma Alakh (2004) "Labour: Down and Out" (www.india-seminar.com)

Sarma, E.A.S. (2005) "Social Sector Allocations", *Economic and Political Weekly*, April 2.

Sreenivas, M.A. (2003-04) "Employment Projections for the Tenth Five Year Plan: How Realistic Are They?", *The Indian Economic Journal*, April-June.

Roy, Indrajit (2005) "Good Governance and the Dilemma of Development: What Lies Beneath?", *Socio-Economic Review 3.*

Sundaram, K. (2001) "Employment – Unemployment Situation in the Nineties—Some Results from NSS 55th Round Survey", *Economic and Political Weekly*, March 17.

Tendulkar, Suresh (2004) "Organized Labour Market in India Pre and Post Reform", Conference on Anti-Poverty and Social Policy in India, Mac Arthur Research Network on Inequality and Economic Performance, Alwar, Rajasthan, Jan 2-4. (unpublished paper).

Vaidyanathan, A. (2005), "Employment Guarantee and Decentralization", *Economic and Political Weekly*, April 16.

Wilson, James (2001) "An Institutionalist Take on State Activism in Economic Development: A Theoretical Framework", http://askew.fsu.edu

18

STATE AND UNORGANISED LABOUR: THE ORISSA SCENARIO

D.V. Giri and P.C. Das

I. Introduction

In recent years, there has been a growing interest among researchers to study various dimensions of the unorganised labour in India. The notable studies are the ones undertaken by Venkata Ratnam (2000), Kurien (2000) and Sankaran (2000). Empirical in nature, these studies have not only provided conceptual clarity about the unorganised sector, but also identified potential areas of research in this sector. Further, these studies have provided suggestions that have implications for policy formulation by the state.

In this paper, it is attempted to make a critical analysis of the state's role in respect of the unorganised labour in Orissa. The data for this study were collected mainly from the State Labour Institute, Orissa and a cross-section of the officials of the Labour Directorate, Orissa, employers and workers in the unorganised sector, and trade union leaders active in this sector.

II. The Unorganised Sector of Orissa

The unorganised sector of Orissa accounts for about 95 per cent of the total labour force of 14.8 million in the state (V. V. Giri National Labour Institute: 2004). Within this sector, agriculture alone accounts for three-fourths of the total employment, employing about 10.4 million workers. The non-agricultural sector, which employs 3.6 million workers, includes workers engaged in the livestock, forestry, fishing, hunting and plantations, orchards and allied activities. The building and other construction workers, migrant labour, child labour, and workers engaged in stone breaking and stone crushing are the other categories of workers, who are predominantly engaged in the state's unorganised sector.

The following Acts are applicable to the unorganised sector workers in the state.

1. Minimum Wages Act, 1948
   (However, workers engaged in fishing are not covered under this Act)
2. Contract Labour (Regulation and Abolition) Act, 1970
   (Applicable to workers engaged in the construction industry)
3. Equal Remuneration Act, 1976
4. Inter-state Migrant Workmen's Act, 1979
5. Payment of Wages Act, 1936
6. Beedi and Cigar Workers Act, 1966
7. Workmen's Compensation Act, 1923
   (Not applicable to agricultural labour)
8. Payment of Bonus Act, 1965
   (Applicable only to the Kendu leaf workers)
9. Child Labour (Regulation and Prohibition) Act, 1986

III. Administrative Arrangements for Enforcement of Legal Provisions

The Government of Orissa sanctioned 65 Rural Labour Inspector posts in the year 1986-87 to ensure effective implementation of the Minimum Wages Act, 1948 in the following segments of the unorganised sector: agriculture, beedi and cigar establishments, forestry, construction, and salt pans. However, the Government had initially appointed 38 RLIs, and out of this, 32 posts have fallen vacant due to promotions and retirements of the RLIs. Thus, at present only 6 RLIs are manning the job of inspection under the Minimum' Wages Act in the above mentioned segments, which account for 85 per cent of the total workforce in the unorganised sector of the state.

For the enforcement of (i) the Minimum Wages Act in other segments of the unorganised sector, and (ii) other legislations, the Government appointed 65 Assistant Labour Officers. Due to promotions, 17 posts of ALO have fallen vacant. The Government has not yet taken any initiative to fill these vacancies.

IV. Social Security Measures for Unorganised Workers

All the workers in the unorganised sector of the state, except agricultural labour, are entitled to the workmen's compensation payable under the Workmen's Compensation Act, 1923. All the Additional District Magistrates, Assistant Labour Commissioners and Deputy Labour Commissioners in the state are declared as commissioners under this Act.

Our interviews with a cross-section of employers and unorganised workers revealed that hardly any employer observes the provisions of this Act. The workers in general are not aware of the existence of this Act. However, in some establishments the employers pay the insurance premiums for workers (as groups) under the Group Insurance Scheme.

Unorganised Sector Workers Social Security Scheme, 2004

Introduced by the Central Government, this scheme has provision for health insurance and old age pension to the unorganised sector workers. The scheme was initially launched in 50 districts in the country, including two districts of Orissa: Khurda, and Kalahandi. Anybody, above 18 years and below 50 years of age drawing up to Rs. 6500 a month as wage is eligible to join the scheme. Under this scheme the per month contribution of the workers is Rs. 50 for those in the age group of 18-35 years and it is Rs. 100 for those in the age group of 36-50 years. The employer's contribution in case of both the age groups is Rs. 100 per worker per month. The per month contribution of the Central Government is Rs. 250 per worker.

Under this scheme the workers or their dependents are entitled to the following benefits: (a) payment of lump sum in the event of (i) permanent disablement, and (ii) accidental death; (b) hospitalisation—medical benefit for self/spouse/children; and (c) payment of pension: (i) to the worker on attaining 60 years of age, (ii) to the widow on member's death while in service or after retirement; and (iii) to the worker in the event of his/her total disablement.

Despite various attractive features of the scheme, the Government of Orissa has not facilitated the implementation of the same in the districts of Khurda and Kalahandi for unknown reasons.

V. Wages

The Minimum Wages Act, 1948 is applicable to all the workers in the state's unorganised sector, except those engaged in fishing. However, we have come across quite a few cases, where the employers are not paying the minimum wages, and in many cases the workers have no idea about the minimum wages to which they are entitled.

A large number of beedi workers, who are entitled to Rs. 45 for rolling 1000 beedies, reported that they are being paid less than the minimum rate. On the contrary, the Kendu leaf workers, whose number is very high in the unorganised sector, are getting the minimum wages due to the efforts of their unions (affiliated to the BMS, HMS, and INTUC). These workers are also getting the minimum bonus of 8.33 per cent under the Payment of Bonus Act, 1965.

While the stone-crushing workers are paid the minimum wages, the stone-breaking workers are not paid the same. Reportedly, employers of the stone-crushing units pay the minimum wages, as they are always apprehensive of the implementation officials making visits to their units anytime because of the location of these units near the National Highway-5. However, the employers of the stone-breaking workers do not have any such apprehensions as the stone breaking operations take place far away from the National Highway.

VI. Welfare Fund for the Construction and Building Workers: A Myth?

The Government of Orissa prepared the Orissa Building and other Construction Workers Rules, 2002 having a provision for collection of welfare fund cess from the principal employer -one percent out of the total cost of the work undertaken. However, these Rules have remained only in paper, as the same are not being implemented by the Government.

The joint efforts of the key leaders of the building and other construction workers' unions—both independent unions and those affiliated to the AITUC, CITU and INTUC, could not evoke any positive response from the Government. Reportedly, these leaders had recently harangued and pelted stones at the Labour Commissioner's office to express their ire and displeasure.

VII. Migrant Labour: Role of Government

The Government's failure to provide employment forced thousands of workers to migrate from Orissa to other parts of the country. Most of these workers belong to socially and economically backward areas in the districts of Bolangir, Ganjam, Kalahandi, Khurda, Nuapada and Puri. These workers are mostly engaged in unskilled operations in the brick-making industry and construction works (roads, canals, dams and buildings), often for less than the minimum wages prevailing in the respective states where they work. Most of those engaged in hazardous jobs are not even provided the minimum safety equipment (Giri & Das: 2003; p. 767).

Leading a lonely life, some of the young workers, both married and unmarried, who have migrated to Mumbai, reportedly seek paid sex. Because of ignorance, they often do not take protective measures against HIV/AIDS, which most of the sex workers at Mumbai carry. When they subsequently return to their villages, they infect their wives or sexual partners and thus expose others to risk.

There are also reports that young women belonging to Kalahandi district are willing even to go to far off places like Mumbai with middlemen for manual jobs. After reaching their destinations, they are finally enrolled as daily wage workers in the brick-kilns located in interior places and are often sexually abused by their employers. Once in the clutches of these employers, they find it very difficult to escape and continue to be exploited sexually.

While the Government is yet to succeed in tackling/ regulating the problem of inter-state migration of workers, it had done hardly anything concrete to: (i) check the abuse of the young women workers, (ii) ensure payment of minimum wages, safety measures and other benefits to the migrant workers, (iii) prevent migrant workers from contracting HIV/AIDS, and (iv) rehabilitate the thousands of workers carrying the virus and their families.

VIII. Child Labour

The problem of child labour persists in the unorganised sector of Orissa. According to a survey conducted by the State Government in 1997 covering 2,54,711 establishments/work sites, as many as 1,74,811 of the establishments engaged child labour (female: 1,21,526 and male: 93,696) both in hazardous and non-hazardous jobs.

Due to the national policy on child labour and the Labour Ministry's project based plan of action, announced in 1987, 18 National Child Labour Projects are operating in 18 districts of Orissa with the financial support from the Central Government. However, the State Government, especially the Labour Directorate, is mainly responsible for the ineffective functioning of these projects. Reportedly, although there have been some instances of improper utilisation of the funds by the project personnel, the government's machinery has been somewhat lenient in its approach while inspecting these projects. Further, although the state gets financial support to the tune of Rs. 20 crore every year, the same is not fully utilised. The National Child Labour Project situated at Malkangiri is virtually in a state of moribund since the last several months. These facts indicate that the personnel heading these projects—Project Directors, DRDA (Panchayat Raj) and District Project Coordinators (Education Department) probably lack time to fully concentrate on the day-to-day functioning of the NCLPs. In this connection, it may be suggested that the State Labour Department, the Review Committee (headed by the Chief Secretary, Government of Orissa) concerned with the functioning of the NCLPs, and the District Collectors, who are the Chairmen of the District Level Child Labour Societies need to work in a well-coordinated manner. It may also be suggested that instead of appointing the Project Directors of District Rural Development Authorities and District Project Coordinators of the State's Education Department, the Government should appoint full-time Project Directors to oversee the functioning of the NCLPs.

Employment of Children as Domestic Helps

There is no regulation in the state regarding the prohibition of employment of children as domestic helps. Nevertheless, the Government had issued an administrative order in the year 2000 prohibiting the employment of children as domestic helps by the civil servants. Despite this, reportedly, the bureaucrats are engaging child labour in their homes. Thus, the administrative order has not served the purpose for which it is meant. Surprisingly, the Government has not brought out any administrative order regarding the prohibition of employment of child labour as domestic helps by others.

Thus, the Government and the bureaucrats tend to pay a lukewarm attitude to the problem of child labour in the state.

IX. Scheme for Organising the Unorganised Labour

In 1986-87, the Government of India identified 80 socially and economically backward blocks in Orissa for educating the rural unorganised labour about their rights and privileges, and organising trade unions and cooperatives. Accordingly, the Government of Orissa appointed 80 Honorary Organisers with an honorarium of Rs. 250 per organiser per month. But the scheme was abruptly abolished by the State Government in March 1997. Strangely, the government has neither made a review of the progress of the scheme, nor has it specified the reason for the abolition of the scheme suddenly.

X. Conclusion

The unorganised sector in Orissa has been expanding steadily over the years, adding further misery to the lives of the labour in this sector. Given the kind of attitude of the Government, both as a policy maker and as a protector of the rights of the unorganised labour, it is Utopian to expect that these workers will be assured of their rights in the near future.

A weak trade union movement in the state, apathy of the bureaucrats in general to the issues concerning the unorganised labour, inadequate media coverage on the problems of labour in the unorganised sector, and lack of efforts by the NGOs to educate the unorganised labour about their rights are some of the factors that perpetuate the misery of the unorganised labour in the state. Given this scenario, one cannot take a sanguine view about the work life and non-work life of the millions of the unorganised workers in Orissa.

It is time that the Government in Orissa drew a few lessons from the Kerala experience with regard to the state's role in the unorganised sector.[1]

Notes

1. In Kerala the following legislations and schemes are in operation for the unorganised labour.
   i. Old Age Pension Scheme for Agricultural Workers, 1982;
   ii. Kerala Artisans and Skilled Workers' Benefit Scheme, 1991;
   iii. Agricultural Workers Act;
   iv. Maternity Benefit Scheme for Landless Agriculture Women Workers;
   v. Scheme for Financial Assistance to Destitute Widows for marriage of their daughters, 1976;
   vi. Kerala Akbari Workers' Welfare Fund Act, 1989;
   vii. Kerala Headload Workers Act, 1978;
   viii. Kerala Cashew Workers' Relief and Welfare Fund Act, 1979;
   ix. Kerala Construction Worker's Welfare Fund Act, 1989;
   x. Kerala Handloom Worker's Welfare Fund Act, 1989;
   xi. Kerala Labour Welfare Fund Act, 1975;
   xii. Kerala Motor Transport Workers' Welfare Fund Act, 1985;
   xiii. Kerala Agricultural Workers' Welfare Fund Scheme, 1990;

xiv. Kerala Autorikshaw Workers' Welfare Fund Scheme, 1991;
xv. Kerala Beedi and Cigar Workers' Welfare Fund Act, 1995;
xvi. Kerala Tailoring Workers' Welfare Fund Act, 1994, and Kerala Tailoring Workers' Welfare Scheme, 1995;
xvii. Kerala Bamboo, Kattuvalli, Thaza Workers' Welfare Fund Act, 1998

For more details about the role of the state in the unorganised sector of Kerala, see Kurien (2000) and Sankaran (2000).

References

Giri, D.V. and Das, P.C. (2003); "Industrial Relations in Orissa: Emerging Scenario", *Indian Journal of Labour Economics,* Vol. 46, No.4, pp. 765-781.

Kurien, P.H. (2000), "Labour Welfare Schemes of Kerala for Unorganised Labour" in Oberai, A.S., Sivananthiran, A., and Venkata Ratnam, C.S. (eds.), *Perspectives on Unorganised Labour,* SAAT, ILO and Indian Industrial Relations Association, New Delhi.

Sankaran, T.S. (2000), "Social Security in India in the Unorganised Sector" in Oberoi, A.S., Sivananthiran, A., and Venkata Ratnam, C.S. (eds.), *Perspectives on Unorganised Labour, op. cit.*

V. V. Giri National Labour Institute (2004), *Unorganised Sector in Orissa: Overview, Issues and Concerns.*

Venkata Ratnam, C.S. (2000), "Trade Unions and the Unorganised Sector" in Oberai, A.S., Sivananthiran, A., and Venkata Ratnam, C.S. (eds.), *Perspectives on Unorganised Labour, op. cit.*

19

CHILD LABOUR (PROHIBITION AND REGULATION) ACT, 1986—ITS OBJECTIVES AND OUTCOMES

Mini Goyal & Pratibha Goyal

The future of a nation is linked, up to a great extent, with the status of children. It is the foremost duty of a society to bring them up well. If they are neglected, the nation gets deprived of potential human resource. Despite these realizations millions of children in India are subjected to work at a very tender age. Actually child labour is not a recent phenomenon. Children of poor have been working since ages. In ancient times they gave helping hand to their parents in household chores and in family occupations. But in modern times the origin of the problem lies in the process of industrial revolution. The need for more production at cheaper costs, motive to earn more and more resulted in using the helping hands as working hands (Chandra, 1997).

India has been concerned about the well being of children since ancient times. But the necessity to enact laws to protect child labour was felt when child labour was ruthlessly exploited in the post industrial revolution period. Many cases of long working hours, poor working conditions and sheer exploitation of child labour were discussed in the British Parliament. Literature written in this period brought to limelight the problem of child labour. It was felt that it robs the child of his childhood and denies him the opportunity to education, play, rest, physical and mental growth. Moreover the establishment of International Labour Organization in 1919 started a crusade in this direction. Due to all these reasons the government of British India became conscious of the problem. The earliest law that contained any provision to regulate the employment of children was the Factories Act, 1881. Its main provisions prescribed a minimum age of 7 years for employment of children and regulated the working hours to a maximum of 9 hours a day. But the Act was operative only on establishments employing over 100 workers and using mechanized power.

The Royal Commission on Labour in India, which was established in 1929, enquired into the conditions of labour in industrial undertakings and plantations in British India and reported about pathetic conditions of child labour in some industries. It recommended prohibition of child labour in some industries, curbing pledging of children and raising of the minimum age for employment of children. These recommendations led to the passing of two important enactments i.e. the Children (Pledging of Labour) Act, 1933 and Employment of Children Act, 1938.

It was followed by other enactments like the Factories Act 1948, The Plantation Act 1951, The Mines Act, 1952, The Merchant Shipping Act, 1958, The Apprentices Act, 1961, The Motor Transport Act, 1961, Bidi and Cigar Workers (Conditions and Employment) Act, 1966, The Bonded Labour System (Abolition) Act, 1966.

In spite of so many laws it was felt that though there are a number of Acts which prohibit the employment of children below 14 years or 15 years in certain specified employments yet there is no precedent laid down in law for deciding employments, occupations or processes in which the employment of children should be banned and there is also no law to regulate the working conditions of children in most of the employments where they are not prohibited from working and are working under exploitative conditions.

Therefore, the Child Labour (Prohibition & Regulation) Act was passed in 1986 with the following objectives.

— Ban on employment of children i.e. those who have not completed their fourteen years on specified occupations and processes.

— Lay down a procedure to decide modifications to the schedule of banned occupations and processes.

— Regulate the conditions of work of children engaged in forms of employment in which they are permitted to work.

— Prescribe enhanced penalties for employment of children in violation of the provisions of this Act and other Acts that forbid employment of children.

— Establish uniformity in the definition of child in laws concerning them.

A detailed study of the enactment in view of the problem of child labour in India reveals that the Child Labour (Prohibition and Regulation) Act, 1986 suffers from a number of drawbacks.

The Act prohibits employment of children only in certain processes and occupations (Sec 3 Part A and B of the Schedule). These occupations and processes are those, which are ostensibly arduous in nature (Mishra, 2000). The list of banded occupations and processes is virtually identical to that of the 1938 Act. Researches have shown that in a span of more than fifty five years some processes and occupations need to be added and perhaps some to be deleted from the list (Burra, 1998).

Hazardous work is defined as the one which exposes the children to physical psychological or sexual abuse, work at underground, underwater, at dangerous heights or confined places with the dangerous machinery or tools which involve heavy tools, work in unhealthy environment and work under particularly difficult conditions such as long hours during nights or where the child is confined to premises of employer (Mehandale, 2002). In other words, the work, which hampers the physical and mental development of the worker, is hazardous in nature.

There are some occupations and processes that may appear to be apparently harmless but undertaking them may be fraught with risks. For example, agriculture, which till recently was considered a light work, has today been accepted as one of the most hazardous sectors. Agricultural workers, especially child workers are faced with great risk of endemic and parasite diseases of the respiratory tract (Menalievich, 1979 and Singh and Verma, 1979). In some industrialized countries agricultural sector accounts for the largest number of occupational fatalities of those under 18 (ILO, 2002). In a sample survey fifty per cent of the agricultural child labour was reported to be having minor cuts in hands or feet, headache problem and other mishaps like dog bites, skin burns, asthma and anemia. Wheat harvesting, potato digging, fodder cutting, and stubble harvesting causes wounds in hands. Paddy transplantation by bending in water filled fields at a temperature of about 40 or above causes severe headache, skin burns among children. In Punjab children are engaged in pea-plucking in severe winter in the months of December and January. Plucking pea in open fields in thick fog and severe cold causes cough and cold and lack of medical facilities leads, sometimes, to asthmatic problems to child labour (Goyal, 2001). Watching crops and grazing cattle for long hours not only cause skin problems but also fatigue the children at tender age. When they return home, they are weary and exhausted. By that time formal school hours are over and they are already so tired that the question of their attending even a non-formal school in the evening seems a remote possibility (Mishra 2000). So even those employments which are considered non-hazardous may hamper physical and mental development of children. Children engaged in these activities grow up as underdeveloped human resource of the nation. So the question arises that if child labour is prohibited in hazardous forms of work should it be permitted on non-hazardous or less-hazardous employment. That too when we are well aware of the fact that a child worker cannot devote time to education and ultimately remains deprived of it and ends up as an illiterate workers of the society. Right place for a child is not a factory or a field. He belongs to school (Swamy, 2000). Therefore, child labour is undesirable in all forms of occupations and processes be they hazardous or non-hazardous. The policy makers should take note of it as employment of child labour, in any form, blasts the present and future of the whole nation and plays havoc with the human resource. Therefore, the scope of the Act needs to be extended to all forms of employment of child labour.

The Child Labour (Prohibition and Regulation) Act, 1986 Act prohibits employment of child labour in certain occupations and processes carried out in factories. Sec. 3 of the Act states that it does not prohibit employment of child labour in any workshop wherein any process is carried on by the occupier with the aid of his family or to any school established by or receiving assistance or recognition from government. The Act does not cover household child labour therefore in those hazardous works which are performed at home, child labour can work. For example child labour is prohibited in carpet weaving and manufacturing of sports goods involving exposure to synthetic materials, chemicals and leather. But in these industries raw material is supplied to the households where large number of children also participate in the work. A survey in the sports goods industry of Jalandhar revealed that child labour constitutes 9.6 per cent of the total labour engaged in football manufacturing. In case of such industries in Punjab contractors deliver the kits at the residence of the workers. Payments are made to them on piece rate basis. Family is interested in producing more and more so that the income increases. To increase the family income, children also start trying their hand at the work. Slowly they pick up the skill but lag behind in studies. Poor quality schools, poor standard of living, lack of family orientation towards studies and desire to earn more, all these factors slowly pull the children away from education and finally they drop out to be full time labour. Therefore, the problems of educational drop outs and child labour become interlinked (Goyal, 2005).

In the dark and dingy houses they keep working with speed without putting any light on because they think that switching on the light will increase their electricity bills. Side by side the whole day they keep watching television, putting extra burden on their eyesight. In this way due to outsourcing:

— Employer becomes free from the responsibility for working conditions

— Employer does not take care of the health, safety and welfare of the workers, which otherwise he has to do if the worker comes to his factory premises to perform the work.

— Children start helping their parents and soon become full time child labour.

The beedi industry with its rolling, labeling and packing operations is a hazardous occupation. The continuous bending causes backache, continuous inhalation of tobacco is harmful to the respiratory system and none of these problems is minimized because the operations are carried out at home. Similarly carpet weaving industry in Punjab employs family child labour (Goyal, 2005). But the nature of hazardous occupation does not change merely because it is performed at home or in any part of the residential premises with the help of family members.

The problem of child labour in these industries can be solved up to a great extent if the work place is shifted from home to factory or if household child labour is also brought under the scope of law.

Moreover Article 39 of the Constitution of India provides that the state shall, the particular, direct its policy towards securing the health and strength of workers, men and women, and ensure that the tender age of children is not abused and that citizens are not forced by economic necessity to enter a vocation unsuited to their age or strength. Article 45 provides for free and compulsory education for children. These aims under our Constitution can be fulfilled only if the scope of the Child Labour (Prohibition and Regulation) Act is extended to all occupations and processes and to all forms of child labour. Government should see that all children of the nation are given opportunities and facilities to develop in a healthy manner and in conditions of freedom, dignity and that childhood is actually protected against exploitation. Legislations at present cover only 15 per cent of the child labour force that are in the formal industrial sector in occupations identified as hazardous (Vora *et al* 1997). The existing legislations do not cover the majority of child labour in unorganized urban sector, where they work as domestic servants, workers in hotels, restaurants, canteens, way side shops, rag pickers, newspaper sellers, paddlers coolies, shoe-shine boys, vendors or helpers in repair shops (Sharma and Mittar 1990) in unorganized rural sector of agriculture and allied activities. The children of marginal farmers and landless labourers usually participate in agricultural occupations from their infancy. Law concerning the employment in agriculture and domestic service are almost non-existent. The agricultural sector, which employs the majority of the child labour, has remained a sector of neglect for the policy makers and law making machinery.

The law regulating the employment of the children suffers from the loopholes, which are generally exploited by their employers to their end. Problems have been faced in regard to determination of age to the child. Generally declaration of parents or the age revealed by the employer in the register is the only proof of age. Parents compelled by their poverty often betray their children to achieve their entry into a vocation, which is detrimental to their growth and strength. In case of dispute over the age of child the case is referred to the medical authority. It is well known in India that rich factory owners can manage such certificates very easily.

This Act does not provide any clue about the wages of child labour. The Minimum Wages Act, 1948, aims at fixing, reviewing, revising and enforcing minimum rates of wages relating to scheduled employment, different classes of work in the same scheduled employment for adults, adolescents, children and apprentices. But under this Act minimum wages are rarely fixed for the child labour working in those occupations and processes where they are not prohibited from working. In the absence of the minimum wages fixation for child labour they are given arbitrary payments suitable to the employer and thus the meager wages are exploitative in nature.

The Child Labour (Prohibition and Regulation) Act also aims at regulating the conditions of work of child labour in those establishments where they are not prohibited from working. But researches indicate that in spite of the provisions regulating working hours, rest intervals, holidays and health and safety as given under the Act, child labour continues to work for as long as ten hours or even more under unhealthy and unsafe working conditions (Goyal and Goyal, 2001). Literature is full of such instances where we find that the regulatory provisions are not being implemented and enforced vigorously. Therefore, there is a great need to review the implementation machinery of the Act.

Conclusions

The Child Labour (Prohibition and Regulation) Act, 1986 protects only a small section of child labour in India. Rest of the children goes unprotected by the law. This half-hearted approach of banning child labour in few establishments and regulating it in a few others and that too with inefficient implementation machinery without adopting a holistic or integrated approach will not solve the problem. Therefore, the policy makers need to review and revise the Child Labour (Prohibition and Regulation) Act, 1986 in the light of findings of the present day researches.

References

Burra, Neera (1998), *Born to Work*, Oxford University Press, New Delhi: 11-193.

Chandra, K. Suman (1997), Problems and Issues on Child Labour in India, *Social Change*, September-December, 27 (3-4): 38.

Goyal, Mini (2004), *Child Labour in Agriculture and Allied Activities in Punjab* (Unpublished), Guru Nanak Dev University, Amritsar.

Goyal, Pratibha (2005), *Little Wards that Work—Child Labour in Punjab*, PBG Publications, Ludhiana.

Goyal, Pratibha and Mini Goyal (2001), A Study of Child Labour in Small Scale Units in Ludhiana, Indian Economic Panorama, 10 (4): 30-34.

ILO (2002), *Future without Child Labour—Report of the Director General of ILO*, 90th Session, International Labour Conference, Geneva.

Mendalievich, Elias (1979) *Children at Work*, International Labour Office, Geneva.

Mishra, Lakshmidhar (2000), *Child Labour in India*, Oxford University Press, New Delhi.

Sharma, B. K. and Vishwa Mittar (1990), *Child Labour and Urban Informal Sector*, Deep and Deep Publications, New Delhi: 9.

Singh, Surendra and R.B.S. Verma (1979), *Problems and Social Service Needs of Child Labour in Agriculture in U.P.* (Unpublished), Department of Social Work, University of Lucknow, Lucknow.

Swamy, Subramanian (2000), *India's Labour Standards and the WTO Framework*, Konark Publishers Pvt. Ltd., New Delhi.

20

LABOUR STANDARDS IN THE TIMES OF GLOBALISATON: A CASE OF IMPLEMENTING MINIMUM WAGES

Manali Chakrabarti[1] *& Rahul Varman*

Introduction

In the present order that is supposedly governed by the twin gods of profits and market forces, issue of minimum wages has been the text book case of the consequences of going against the orthodoxy (Champlin & Noedler, 2002). In standard theory there is no level below which the wages cannot fall; and the 'neoclassicalists' as well as the World Bank have for decades now been making a 'convincing' case of how having minimum wages is not good for the welfare of the workers themselves! Protective labour regimes, of which the minimum wage laws have invariably been a basic constituent, are said to be the relics of the primitive past. And yet, minimum wage policy has remained in contention, with economists and policy makers aligned on both the sides of the debate (Card and Krueger, 1994; Levin-Waldman, 2004; Neumark & Wascher, 2000; Waltman, 2000). In spite of several progressive labour related legislations already in place in most countries because of the legacy of the global labour movement, at present, these laws are largely ignored or blatantly flouted. Further, increasingly the state has also been forced to formally retract several of these laws under the onslaught of the globalisation of capital. This has resulted in a precipitous drop of wages for workers, especially in the so-called 'unorganised sector'—

the section of the workforce in the lowest rung of skill and economic hierarchy in the present world order. As a response, several movements for 'living wages', 'fair wages', 'minimum wages' have emerged in the last couple of decades, in both the developing as well as the developed regions of the world (ACORN 2001).

The present note is an attempt to capture the process and consequences of institutionalisation of payment of minimum wages in a public sector academic institute situated in an industrial city in North India[2]. In keeping with the ground reality of the whole country including that of the city, almost no contractor in the Institute campus pay the stipulated Minimum Wages, at least for unskilled and semi-skilled work. In fact market conditions in and around the campus are such that men and women are ready to work at even half the existing rates of the minimum wages. The note[3] describes and analyses the role of a concerned group of middle-class individuals within the campus community, who with the support of the existing labour laws, have tried to use official means to make a dent in the contractor-administration nexus and work towards ensuring 'fair' wages within the campus. The writing starts with a historical backdrop and then describes the chronological unfolding of events over a span of five years from December 2000 to December 2005. And finally the whole process has been summarised and then analysed to bring out its implications for any initiative on issues similar to the one dealt in this writing (the implementation of minimum wages).

The Context

The city is an old industrial centre in North Central India which flourished in cotton textiles, leather and leather products, woollen textiles, engineering products, etc. In the recent times though, the city has been in the news only for its rapid industrial decline, fast deteriorating socio-economic order and very high unemployment and crime rate. It had a militant working class movement, but as the capital has moved out of the city and the mills have closed down, the trade unions are in shambles and the working class movement has virtually collapsed.

The present case is situated in a premiere technological institute of the country; the Institute[4] was set up in one of the most important industrial centres of the country in the late 1950s with collaboration of the US as part of the Nehruvian post-colonial nation building project. The Institute accords fair amount of autonomy to the faculty and functions on the principles of parliamentary democracy. In the early years, probably because of being part of the first generation in the phase of post-colonial nation building, some of the members of the faculty brought in notions of social concerns to this fully residential campus (mainly for teaching staff and students and partly for non-teaching staff as well). Some of them were able to find academic as well as practical expressions for their social concerns within the campus, given the liberal environment and a degree of academic freedom. The liberal culture of the campus was further enhanced by a vibrant employees' union, which came up in the early 1970s.

Employees at the lower levels were mostly from the nearby places, while faculty and students had fair representation from different parts of the country. Efforts at unionisation of the temporary workforce in the Institute began in the late 1960s with participation of the academic community. The general socio-political environment of the region, country and probably the whole world in the 1960s and 1970s affected and furthered the movement in the Institute too. This resulted in a strong trade union, and eventually, a permanent work force within a few years. But by the 1990s, with the onset of the economic reforms, the industrial relations in the Institute too, as across the whole country, entered a new phase. Many of the labour and union rights have receded, as permanent work and workers are being rapidly replaced by contingent workforce.

In the past decade, sub-contracting of work by the Institute has multiplied manifold, and therefore, the contingent workforce has also commensurately increased. Many kinds of jobs have been completely taken over by the contingent workers—construction and civil maintenance, security, sanitation, horticulture, and even research assistance and office help; though the last category is not the focus in the present work. There has also been a tremendous rise in the infrastructural facilities within the Institute, primarily because of monetary contributions from the alumni (mostly from those who have been successful abroad), which have been pouring in, in the wake of liberalisation. Though we do not have the formal figures, yet by an informed estimate, at present the strength of the permanent work force is probably matched by the contract and temporary workers and would be around two thousand each. The discussion here is limited to the so-called 'unskilled'/'semi-skilled' manual work, where minimum wage is an issue.

Demand for Minimum Wages

The MWs became an issue in the campus in the early 1990s. An informal group called the *Vivekanand Samiti* (VS)[5] began a literacy drive amongst the migrant[6] *Chattisgarhi*[7] workers employed on some of the construction sites in the campus. Initially the effort concentrated in getting the children of the workers to attend a temporary school[8]. Through interactions with the children the volunteers of VS gradually got to know about the miserable wages being paid to the workers in the campus (which was less than even half of the stipulated minimum wages), and they decided to take up the issue with the Institute authorities. Legally the primary responsibility for ensuring the payment of minimum wages lies with the 'principal employer', the Institute in this case. In actual practice the contract workers have little job security and no employment rights. No formal rolls are maintained by the contractors, and since these workers have no organisation to mediate with the employers, they literally work at the mercy of the employers' will and live with the constant fear of loosing their employment. Hence all these organising efforts by the VS had to be done surreptitiously. But, in the process a few workers did loose their jobs and were blacklisted by the whole set of contractors working for the Institute. Some of these workers formed the core of the later efforts at organising that led to the formation of a workers' cooperative in the campus.

The simplicity of the issue, the absolutely unambiguous position of the law of the land on the minimum wages, and the overall irony of the context of an elite institution with no apparent dearth of funds and resources not paying the MWs to the lowest rung of workers, caught the imagination of many amongst the academic community, at least for a while in the beginning. Several faculty members and students supported the cause and the Institute found itself in an indefensible position as to the reasons for non-payment of minimum wages, but for some practical difficulties in implementing the same given the market forces, etc. Though the administration could not wish away the issue of MWs it could not implement it either as the body of contractors unitedly opposed it by adopting several deterring tactics like firing the protesting workers, threatening to stop work, etc. Under these circumstances the Institute formed a committee of a few concerned faculty members to deal with the issue. But given the political economy of MWs, the committee could not make much headway and failed to ensure the payment of minimum wages as a norm within the campus[9].

The core group of agitating workers and the initiated middle class supporters came up with an ingenuous solution to the problem. They decided to form a workers' cooperative that would bid on behalf of the workers and take up contracts so that the workers would have the freedom to pay themselves the MWs without the interference of the contractors. Thus a workers cooperative, Samiti, was formed in 1992, though in its early phase it faced significant resistance from the administration. The Institute administration even refused to give tender forms to Samiti, and when the fledgeling cooperative did manage to bid, they would reject it on some ground or another. But Samiti survived and over the years, has grown to a size of around 200 members at present, and is widely acknowledged as the only contracting organisation on the campus, which pays the MWs. But this is not the place to relate Samiti's tale. We have attempted to capture some of the organisational features of Samiti in another work (Varman & Chakrabarti, 2004). We will touch upon Samiti in the final section to make certain observations regarding the labour markets.

After its inception as an economic entity, Samiti and its members have largely abstained from militant activism, and have primarily worked towards making their organisation economically viable. Though Samiti's existence could not force other contractors to pay the MWs, it did affect them, and probably for this reason, the wages paid within the campus were higher than those paid outside. Moreover, Samiti, including its members and sympathisers, have been taking up several cases of gross violation of MWs and bringing them to the attention of the larger community and the authorities. But for all practical purposes except for Samiti market forces largely decided the norm for the wages in the campus, irrespective of the stipulated MWs. But as the economic crisis deepened in the post-liberalisation decade and has continued to through this millennium, there has been a gradual realisation, at least among some of the friends of Samiti, that the cooperative will not be able to survive the onslaught of the market forces. For Samiti to continue as a MW paying employer, payment of minimum wages would have to be established as a norm, because if other contractors paid less then they would be able to outbid Samiti on the contracts[10].

Besides the global phenomena of recession of worker rights the situation in the campus was aggravated over the 1990s, probably because of a spurt in construction activity aided by huge sums of alumni money, where large numbers of workers (many of them migrants from distant places) were employed at wages which were only 50-60% of the statutory minimum wages. Concerned members of the Institute community have been regularly voicing their concerns at several formal and informal forums on the issue; some of the instances are as follows.

- At least two reports on non-payment of minimum wages in the campus were prepared by students as part of their course work—one comparing the state of construction workers vis-à-vis the Minimum Wages Act, which made a grim reading on the conditions of the workers in the campus. The second report compared the state of other contract workers on cleaning work with those of Samiti and brought out how the latter was an exception in paying MWs. The *faculty forum*[11] convener forwarded both the reports along with a letter signed by a set of faculty members expressing their concern 'about the blatant flouting of minimum wage laws for contract jobs', to the higher authorities seeking their response.

- Several individual workers risked their jobs to register grievances about non-payment of minimum-wages. Many of these grievances were channelled either through the concerned members of the academic community, Samiti or *Valmiki Samaj,* a local chapter of an all India organisation of the *Valmiki* caste, who are involved in most of the cleaning work in the campus.

Probably because of all these sustained efforts, in November 2000 the administration decided to constitute a committee for monitoring minimum wages in the campus—Monitoring Committee - Wages (MCW). The following is the account of the journey of MCW from its inception in December 2000 to December 2005. An important aspect of the Committee and its functioning which should be mentioned at the outset, has been the sustained support it received from a large informal group consisting of members of the faculty, students, staff and other members/residents of the campus community. The MCW had to tread uncertain and often extremely contestable territories, with almost no previous experience or precedence to go by. Under these circumstances the informal group acted as a sounding board both for new ideas as well as for delicate decisions. On situations of impasse with the authorities as well as with the contractors and the administration, the informal group has also formally supported the MCW, including by being part of official delegation on behalf of the Committee. Though it is difficult to adequately capture the significance of this informal group within the scope of the present note, one can only assert that such a group has been continually an integral part of the Committee's efforts in various ways. In the following section we will attempt to capture various phases of the Committee and volunteers' work in brief.

Dynamics of Wage Monitoring Committee

I. Proceduralising Wage Disbursement

The constitution of the first Committee in December 2000

appears to be an interesting balancing act by the administration. A senior faculty member, who had been involved in the signature campaigns and meetings with administration on the issue of MWs, was asked to head the Committee, while three persons from three different administrative units constituted the other members of the Committee; some of them had a reputation of not being sympathetic to the workers' cause. As the chairperson was going on a semester leave immediately after the appointment of the committee (there were no prior consultations regarding the constitution of the committee including even the availability of the members, it was unilaterally decided by the administration and as the sympathisers to the cause were keen to take it up, the chairperson accepted it in spite of her prior commitments), she asked for co-opting another faculty member in the Committee, and thus it became a five member committee. Even the appointment letter of the Committee was all of one line which indicated that probably no serious thought had been given to the functioning and role of the committee and it could at best be considered an official acknowledgement of all the criticism levelled on the issue of MWs. All that the office-order said was:

> The committee shall oversee the disbursement of wages to Daily Wage Workers engaged in various units of the Institute and deal with the related disputes.

The Chairperson was abroad for the first 6 months and MCW took a while to begin its formal activities. Of course the administration did not seek any progress report either; another indication that the administration would have been quite happy if this particular committee did little or no work! The Committee began its work in earnest only in June 2001. Its first concern was to try to understand and appreciate the views of all the concerned parties on the issue and work in a 'non-confrontationist' style. It began by meeting the Superintending Engineer (SE), the head of the Works Department (WD). The Institute has an exclusive WD to oversee the construction and the civil maintenance work; off late, even sanitation, horticulture and estate offices have also begun to report to the SE. By all accounts, and by the very nature of the activities of the WD, the lines of nexus between the contractors and administration are likely to pass through the WD. Therefore the SE, as the all-powerful boss of the WD, was one authority whom the MCW had to be regularly contended with. Through the SE the Committee met a set of contractors as well. In a written note prior to the meeting to all the contractors, the MCW clarified that it had nothing against them as a group and were concerned for their profits too, but the payment of MWs was non-negotiable.

In the meeting all the contractors accepted that none of them (but for Samiti) paid MWs, but they also voiced certain difficulties from their side in paying the MWs. Meanwhile the Committee received its first formal complaint by a set of workers (cleaners) for non-payment of MWs in July 2001. Around this time the MCW began to monitor some of the contractors' actual wage payments. Members of the Committee soon realised that the system for payment of wages was not amenable to external monitoring as there were no proper record of workers on rolls, attendance records, advance payments, wage payment, etc. The first task of the committee therefore became to design a system amenable to monitoring and subsequently implementing them across the several contracting organisations. Only then was it possible for the committee to embark on monitoring proper at any scale. For the purpose the Committee sought the cooperation from those of its own members who also happened to be administrative heads and the preliminary monitoring was performed in their departments. On the basis of their initial understandings of the wage disbursement processes the MCW sent its first set of recommendations to the Director, the head of the Institute. The recommendations in brief were as follows:

1. Need for an appropriate and formal format for recording attendance, advance payment, and monthly wage payment; it also recommended a format for implementation.
2. Need for regular monitoring of wages and payment in the presence of the Institute representative (this was in fact legally mandatory on the Institute as per the Contract Labour Act, 1970).
3. A system for eliciting grievances in case of non-

payment of MWs.

4. Finally to make it mandatory to mention the minimum person hours in notice inviting tenders, at least in those kind of work that had a large labour component, so that a base bid can be set, below which the bid would be deemed invalid.

This set the stage for the actual monitoring of wage payments by the MCW. Probably the first confrontation that the Committee faced was triggered by a complaint filed by 9 workers employed by a contractor handling horticulture work in the Institute. The workers complained that they were getting only about 2/3rd of the MWs as they were not aware of the stipulated MWs. Interestingly the administrative head of this unit was part of the MCW! There was pressure on him from the Committee members to initiate monitoring in his unit. While this process was going on, the contractor dismissed two workers immediately after he saw them talking to the Chairperson of the MCW. In spite of the persistent efforts of the Committee they could not get those workers back in the job. Actually when the contractor was pressurised, he did take them back, but gave them impossible targets and then threw them out on the pretext of poor quality work—it was the same old story of identified 'trouble makers' turning overnight into 'bad workers'! Finally, three months after the complaint was lodged with the MCW, three of the nine workers including the two who were seen talking, were laid off. During the monitoring, the Committee found that all the workers were being paid the MWs; but the sums when added up left no profit margin for the contractor. See Appendix for a variety of contracts and issues around contract workers and minimum wages.

In September 2001 the Committee submitted an interim report to the Director. The report began by emphasising the significance of MWs followed by a background of the work done till then. The report asserted: 'It is apparent from conversations with all the three groups (administrators, contractors, workers) that minimum wages are not paid as a rule but there is no formal procedure to ascertain it'. The Committee also emphasised on the significance of its consultative approach and attempts to build 'consensus' to which the Director noted, "This is a very positive approach". The MCW had the following recommendations to make:

1. To make it mandatory for all wage and attendance records to be kept in prescribed format issued by the Institute. (As a follow up, the SE issued a circular to all executive officers to ensure that the contractors under them start maintaining attendance on the format provided by the Committee.)
2. The Committee sought more time to resolve the issue of contradiction between the practice of awarding the contracts to the lowest bid, which often did not even add up to the minimum wages of the labour employed, making it practically impossible to pay MWs.
3. Since the Committee's term was about to end, it also made suggestions regarding constitution of future committees and recommended a two-year term for it, given the complexities of issues involved. (The Director in principle appeared to be in agreement and he extended the term of the then Committee to two years).

II. Monitoring Wages

Meanwhile, in October 2001, the first of the two incidents involving Earthline[12] occurred, where a set of 53 workers from Central Bihar lodged a complaint with the MCW to settle their claim of Rs. 2,28,170/, which according to them was due as outstanding wages for the months of July to October for the work done on the construction site of a new hostel. All these workers belonged to one subcontractor[13] of Earthline, the main contractor for the project.

The workers lodged the complaint to the MCW through a labour lawyer, who was earlier associated with Samiti. But, once the complaint was made by the workers, the contractor dismissed all of them from work summarily. Since these workers lived in temporary shelters on space provided by the contractor at the construction site, the contractor also threatened them of eviction. Faced with the prospect of loosing everything including their due outstanding wages, jobs, as well as the shelter, the workers would come daily to the WD office, and petition to the officials, but to no avail. They were repeatedly told that the company's *sahib* would come from Delhi and do their *hisaab* (clear their dues). Finally the chairperson of the MCW had to seek intervention of the newly appointed Director and some settlement was arrived at. But again the main difficulty was that there were practically no verifiable and credible records, and what workers finally got was through lengthy negotiations including acrimonious claims and counter claims. Typically in any such situation, migrant workers, with no local social moorings to sustain a prolong stay without work; settle for any compensation, usually much less than their dues.

Soon after this incident it was decided by the Committee to make a presentation to the new Director and apprise him of the developments. Based on the analysis of six representative cases, the presentation emphasised that as a norm the minimum wages were not being paid in the Institute, and reiterated the need to develop a system that could be monitored. It also stressed on the need for decreeing some punishments for the defaulters and developing a 'confidential grievance cell' for all the concerned parties, especially the workers.

As the monitoring picked up momentum in the early months of 2002, an interesting development was observed during disbursement of the wages. The Committee and the volunteers noticed that though the correct wages seem to be given on paper, the actual money disbursed was significantly lower as there were large amounts of advance payments registered against every worker. By the consistency of this practice across several contractors it was surmised that this was most likely a tactic devised for not paying the minimum wages and yet maintaining proper records. There were no proper records maintained for the advance payments claimed to be made; but, in spite of the observers' repeated reassurances, none of the workers were willing to testify that advances were actually not paid to him/her. The committee at a later point tried to get around this tactics of the contractors by pressurising them to pay wages at a greater frequency, may be fortnightly or even weekly so that the workers would not need advances. But, this measure could not be enforced because of the opposition of the contractors and the indifference of the authorities. Unofficially observers were told that generally the contractors organised a meeting with the workers before every payment and threatened them of dire consequences if they spoke up against the contractors. In September the Committee in a curt letter, communicated its frustration regarding lack of proper records by contractors regarding workers and the indifference of the administration on the issue, to the concerned authorities.

The Second Earthline Case

In November 2002 there was another showdown of the Committee with the Institute authorities on the issue of non-payment of due wages to a set of 36 construction workers working for a subcontractor of M/s Earthline, on one of the hostel construction sites in the campus (see endnote 14). These 36 workers and their subcontractor belonged to the same village in Chattisgarh. The workers complained that they had not been paid their dues for the previous four months. The usual practice followed by petty contractors is to give some advance to the workers every month and settle the dues of the workers only once they get the payment from the 'company', the original contractor (M/s Earthline in this case). The subcontractor bids for specific work for certain amount of money (and usually they operate on very low margins given the extremely competitive market for the supply of unskilled labour) but there is always a chance of such estimates going wrong because of miscalculations or mismanagement or a combination of both. Now in this case, the petty contractor claimed that *'humko ghata hua hai'* (he had suffered losses) and hence he could not pay his workers. The issue went through several claims and counter claims amongst the three parties—M/s Earthline, sub-contractor and the workers. The 'Company' claimed that they had cleared all the dues, while the petty contractor claimed otherwise—and there probably was truth on both sides as the initial claims of the sub-contractor was so low that it was most likely impossible to do the work in that amount and the fact remained that the workers were not paid their due wages. The Institute felt the issue was beyond their purview since it had cleared the main contractor's wages, Earthline after pocketing a huge profit was still 'legally' correct for having settled the petty contractor's due, and the petty contractor would have also cleared himself of any liability towards the workers if the workers had let him go. But the workers held on to their claims and since the petty contractor belonged to the same locality and his economic means were only marginally above the workers themselves, he was stuck with them. To further complicate matters it was very difficult to determine how much was due to the workers, as there were no attendance records with anybody, so it was reduced to an issue of whose claims one was ready to trust and to what extent.

But the matters took a different turn from here. These workers did not get any dues for weeks and in the process other actors like Samiti got involved on behalf of the workers. Meanwhile in spite of repeated reminders to the Institute by the MCW to take some action when nothing happened, the Chairperson of the MCW decided to talk personally to the SE. The SE in response went on a personal diatribe against the chairperson on the phone itself. Though the general body of faculty had been generally uninvolved on the issue of minimum wages, this 'misbehaviour' of the SE with a colleague invoked a collective outrage. In a signed letter to the Faculty Forum 16 faculty members asked for a GBM to discuss the issues of relationship between the administration and a committee duly appointed by the Institute, participatory governance system and the role of the community. The meeting began with a presentation by the MCW where they emphasised that the WD had not shown any commitment in implementing the formal system of wage monitoring on the construction sites and that has led to the present deadlock. The house recommended that the MCW should be a standing committee with a two-year term and that the administration should extend all help to the Committee. An interesting observation made by one of the members present succinctly summed up the mood of the house:

> Though monitoring contractors is works department's (WD) job, it often appears that WD and contractors

are on the same side and they are in contradiction with the Committee.

III. Administering in the Wage Office

In January 2003 the MCW was reconstituted for another two years. The three members, including two faculty members and an official from the accounts department, who were relatively more active and more sympathetic to the workers' cause remained in the Committee, while the other two officials representing the administration were replaced by higher level officials; the Chairperson remained the same. The term of reference of the Committee remained as loosely defined as the previous one.

Right in the beginning of its second term the Committee decided to direct its energy first in implementing a 'monitorable' formal system across various sites of contract workers. In this regard, MCW designed and printed sheets for formal record keeping (attendance, etc.) and distributed it to a number of units with instructions to the officer in charge to oversee the implementation. This was accompanied by a detailed instruction sheet as to how to fill up the forms and maintain appropriate records. The Committee also decided to focus on construction sites (which employed a very large number of the contract workers) and asked the administrators to facilitate monitoring of wage payment by scheduling them conveniently.

Gradually through the persistent efforts of the Chairperson, individual group members as well as the informal group, the Committee was able to gain some authority. In July 2003 the sanitary inspector on his own initiative sent a report to the Committee about the payment record of the three contractors within his charge and specifically made a note on one of them who refused to make the payments in his presence. In a related development the executive engineer of works department (who was also a member of the MCW) sent a schedule of wage payments of four contractors so that the Committee could monitor. The Committee also made posters for the information of workers in the campus on minimum wages and got them pasted on all public spaces across the Institute. Around this time the Committee also sent a report to the higher authorities on a contractor Krishna Housekeeping, (the Appendix carries a note on this contractor as an example for understanding the issues regarding MW in perennial contracts for cleaning), who had been a regular defaulter for payment of minimum wages, and recommended that punitive action be taken against him to deter such practices.

In the months of August, September and October 2003 the Committee attempted to do as many monitoring as possible and did more than 20 of them across various kinds of contracts—sanitation, horticulture, civil maintenance, electrical, etc. Based on the continuing monitoring the Committee decided to meet the Deputy Director to apprise him of its work and make specific recommendations. One of the important recommendations made was to seek a specific location to be assigned for the disbursement of wages and for the authorities to ensure that all the wage payments be conducted there. This was to tackle the high incidence of 'advance' payment in the civil maintenance contracts (mentioned earlier). The Committee had observed that the proportion of advance had a high correlation with the difference between the statutory minimum wages and the actual wages paid. As the contractors claimed that they had to give advance because the workers could not meet their requirements through monthly payments, the Committee suggested that wages be paid at a shorter interval, fortnightly or even weekly. The idea behind a specific location for wage payment was that this location would be open for a few pre-specified hours daily, and would have some volunteers representing the Committee present during that period, so that the contractors have the flexibility to make payments (of all kinds) on any day of the month, but in the presence of a monitoring authority. After pursuing for months the proposal was formally approved by the higher authorities in February 2004. An office order was issued to the effect that the contractors would have to make all payments only in the wage office and only after they had received a payment slip from the office certifying their payment, would they be eligible to receive their payment from the Institute. The

Committee, with the help of the informal group, gradually started the implementation of the proposal by the end of March 2004.

Since monitoring began in the wage office in February 2004, volunteers have opened the wage office for two hours or more every single working day and all the Saturdays, sometimes even on a holiday. Approximately 15-20 faculty members, some of the senior institute functionaries, a few students and other residents of the campus have volunteered to take up various roles and though some older members have dropped out but new ones have also been added over the months. At the beginning of every month a duty schedule is prepared, though volunteers may adjust and replace each other sometimes depending upon the contingencies. There have been differences of opinion amongst the volunteers as well as differences in their commitment for the issue, yet the wage office has been opened every single working day for more than a year now. Volunteers meet every month to take up emerging issues. In the terminal report to the administration in February 2005, based on one year of monitoring in the wage office, the Committee identified the following major problems:

1. The attendance records are usually manipulated to avoid paying workers for all the days that they have worked.
2. Workers are paid in the wage office, but are compelled to return a part of the money later.
3. Some individuals, shown as supervisors/managers etc., are paid substantially higher than the minimum wages and are usually identifiable as part of the contractor's management. In the absence of any records regarding the contract, which have not been provided to the Committee in spite of repeated requests, it is impossible to determine whether these payments are as per the contract or not.
4. Contractors work with lesser number of workers than what is stipulated in the contract. To get around this discrepancy, sometimes the same worker is paid multiple times under different names (and even for

different contracts under the same contractor), who then returns the excess amount to the contractor. This is hard for the volunteers to identify since workers do not carry any identity card.

5. Workers who complain are either threatened or removed from the employment rolls.
6. Functionaries of the Institute, whose cooperation is necessary for the committee, have been consistently uncooperative. In spite of multiple requests, copies of the contracts have not been provided to the committee.
7. The most important impediment for the effectiveness of the Committee has been the fact that no real action has been taken against defaulters. Contractors, against whom complaints are outstanding, have been given new contracts indicating that the feedback of the Committee has been ignored.

In the closing months of 2005 the volunteers have attempted to deepen their work by focusing on the following:

1. Target a few but persistently erring contractors against whom complaints have been registered regularly.
2. Insist on receiving a copy of all contracts that contain a labour component so that the wage record of every contractor can be cross checked.
3. Gradually pass on the responsibility of maintaining attendance records to the user sections/departments, which would be then sent to the Committee, so that a more effective check can be kept on the contractor's records.
4. Ensure that payments are made to the contractors by the Institute only when a receipt is produced from the wage office.
5. Insist that recommendations or complaints of the Committee regarding malpractices be taken into account when awarding/renewing contract and in cases of repeated infringements the contractor(s) should be blacklisted.

6. Set up a tripartite standing committee to handle all disputes and grievances and also to ensure protection of workers from victimisation in cases of pending disputes.
7. Make efforts for issuance of identity cards to the workers to facilitate the wage payment to the right person.

Recently the Committee voluntarily expanded its role by giving a written recommendation against the reappointment of a top ranking official of the Institute administration. The Committee opined that "he acted as a hindrance to the activities of the Committee". Though no formal acknowledgement was made of the recommendation, as a matter of fact, the official did not get another term.

As the Committee's and the voluntary group's understanding of the complexity of minimum wages have deepened over these five years there has been a general consensus for focussing the limited energy of the group on contracts which are most amenable to monitoring. The idea was to set examples and send the correct signal to the all concerned. Therefore in the recent past, the Committee has attempted to focus more on the contracts pertaining to hostels where student volunteers can play an important role by exercising their rights as users to judge the performance of the contractors; helping to mobilise the workers as well as protecting them; and even monitoring the contractors by cross checking their attendance records, etc. This phase has just begun and hence, hence this story has to be told later.

Summarising the MCW Experience over Five Years

In summarising the experience of the struggle for minimum wages in the Institute over the last five years in which the MCW has been in existence, one may simply say that even today minimum wages are not paid as a norm in almost all the contract jobs in the campus. The workers usually work longer hours than the legal limit of eight hours, and are paid lower than their due wages. There have hardly been any official punitive measures taken against any of the erring contractors even in cases where there have been repeated written complaints. And yet the existence of the Committee has definitely pushed the cause for implementation of minimum wages some way:

1. The wages paid within the campus have been rising and are significantly higher than those paid outside the campus in several kinds of work where wages are being monitored regularly.
2. The Committee has gradually gained strength—some officially proffered and some just taken voluntarily by pushing the ambiguous boundaries of its role, and now has risen in significance vis-à-vis the Institute authorities.
3. A small but committed group of faculty members have veered around the issue which has made monitoring on a daily basis possible. The group has been able to successfully involve members of other sections of the campus community including student, staff, the larger community and even some officials of the administration.
4. There appears to be an increasing awareness amongst contract workers regarding their rights of minimum wages and working hours which also seems to be leading to situations of conflicts and disagreements between workers and contractors as well as complaints regarding wages.
5. The formation of the Committee for minimum wages and its efforts (with the help of the informal group) in the five years of its existence have elevated 'minimum wages' to the status of a 'right' for workers at least among the official circles. All the involved parties to the issue in the campus—the administration, the contractors, the authorities, the involved users (students, faculty and staff) as well as the workers have to formally acknowledge that minimum wages are not paid in the campus. At some places where the committee received the support of the administrative heads it also met with partial success in protecting the dissenting workers. Further, even if

for the sake of mere 'lip service', in all formal forums the involved parties have to assert that this situation ought to be corrected.

Implications

The understanding from the above micro but long drawn and evolving experience of institutionalising of minimum wages in the Institute over the years can be generalised at three levels.

1. Political Economy of Wages and Policy with Regard to Minimum Wages

The debate regarding minimum wages and contract labour has been rife in the policy circles. Neo-liberals have been insisting that market forces must reign and the Contract Labour Act has been a target of our chambers of commerce for some time now. Our experience from the case described above suggests that if the market forces were given a free hand, wages would go for a free fall. Without the accountability of the principal employer along with legal provisions for minimum wages, no check on the wages could have been enforced. In a recent survey by a group of student volunteers in one of the hall messes, it was found that the contractor takes money back from *all* the mess employee after paying them *full* amount under intense scrutiny in the wage office, but the amount that is taken back differs depending upon where the concerned worker is situated in the political economy of the wage market. The deduction is close to 55 percent for women who come from villages around the city to cut vegetables, it is around 45 percent from the migrant workers who have come from Bihar and who stay in the space provided by the contractor, and it is 30-35 percent from those workers who belong to neighbourhood; though all of them are actually made to work anywhere from 12–14 hours a day. As the pressure from the wage volunteers increased over time, the mess contractor has tried to reduce the local workers and replace them with women and migrant workers. Whereas, the same contractor hires workers en-masse from *the locality* to run a mess all the way in Mumbai (discussed in the Appendix).

The existence of Samiti, the workers' cooperative, provided the initial impetus in pulling the wages up in the campus and later the pressure from the wage monitoring committee appears to have bolstered the upward pull. The change from the status quo was brought about initially by Samiti and subsequently; the Committee's efforts have forced the contractors to adhere to some minimum rules or at least to formally acknowledge them. It has made a difference to the distribution of the surplus by making some dent in the profits of the contractors and also probably stopped some of the impossible L1[14] biddings of the earlier years. But none of these actors, Samiti or the concerned group of individuals, would have been able to make any headway in the absence of the existing unequivocal laws on minimum wages and contract workers. Thus the point that comes out clearly from our experience is that, contrary to what the mainstream labour economists recommend, a legal framework is imperative for mediating worker-management relations, more so as we move to the lower end of the market, where workers are at a greater disadvantage due to lack of access to the establishment as well as absence of their own organisations. Even in the case of industrialised economies, some labour economists have argued against the market model and made a case for the regulatory institutions (Dickens et al, 1999; Pischke, 2005).

Another important understanding which emerges from the above experience is regarding the vital role which public sector can still play in institutionalising norms for minimum wage payment. The whole effort, especially the official sanction it has been able to garner, however reluctantly, would have been largely impossible in the private sector. And yet, an example set in the public sector is likely to influence the general practice on the issue including in the private sector. Thus in spite of their receding presence public sector organisations still act as a deterrence to the downward pull on wages as dictated by the free market. Perhaps the experiment, in hindsight, was possible also because of the specific situation of the Institute in the global economy as a supplier of work force to the silicon valleys of US and India. Due to the global linkages, the Institute is flush with resources and at least needs to uphold certain 'standards' on paper and the wage volunteers have regularly made use of such rhetoric and the contradictions inherent in it to push the cause.

2. *The Limited Role of the Middle Class Public Action*

The case also brings out the significance as well as the limitations of the role of the middle classes. It is obvious that whatever has been achieved above has indeed been primarily because of the initiative of the middle classes, barring the role of Samiti, the workers' cooperative. In spite of the fact that the laws regarding minimum wages have been in place for several decades, the actual wages paid even in this public Institute ranged from 1/3rd to half of the legally stipulated due. The attitude of the elite was (and to a large extent is) that the workers should neither be seen nor heard and should be used as an extremely dispensable and contingent resource. For instance, when the Institute run mess for the hostel is closed during the summer vacations, even those workers who have been working for the Institute for several years are not paid any wages. Similarly if a worker is injured during work, it is left to be dealt with by the contractor and his employee(s), with no intervention from the Institute. Even the health care facility of the Institute is largely inaccessible to the contingent workers. This general indifference of the Institute towards its contingent workforce indicates that only because of the persistent efforts of the pressure group could the minimum wages laws be upheld to some extent. Yet the case also starkly brings out the limitations of the middle class action. Three kinds of tendencies are observed here:

i. There has been a continuous attempt to bring in more and more procedures and standards through which the contractors can be monitored and held accountable. The MCW began with the attendance procedure, to procedures for advance payment, wage payment slip, the wage payment records in the wage office, to its present endeavour to have the identity cards, bank accounts and grievance redressal procedures.

ii. The modes of enforcing MWs have been confined to petitioning to the higher authorities and reasoning it out with them. The most intense debate within the group has been essentially limited to whether to involve students, the alumni, the judiciary, the press, etc., again very much within the middle class domain. Though it is acknowledged to some extent by the members of the group, that all their efforts are likely to be circumvented by the contractors, unless the workers themselves are able to hold them to adhere to minimum wages laws, middle-class participants find it very difficult to establish any kind of working relationship with the working classes.

iii. And lastly, but not surprisingly given the context, there have been enormous enthusiasm for using technological measures to check the contractors by deploying surveillance measures, like smart cards, devices for marking attendance, automating the records, etc.

Thus in the absence of a groundswell among the working class to ensure their rights, middle class participation has got confined to increasing methods of policing through rules, regulations and technology.

3. *Need for Working Class Collective Action*

The most conspicuous aspect in this whole account is the absence of the working class actors and their voices, especially collective voices, with the significant exception of Samiti. The whole initiative has not yet succeeded to catch the collective imagination of the contract workers in the campus in all these years. Many workers have voiced dissent under heroic circumstances, and yet no organising attempt has reached anywhere under the combined onslaught of market forces and the complete absence of any institutional support. Without a minimum assurance of job security, it is almost impossible for migrant and contract workers to organise over a sustained basis; and we think that probably it is more likely to happen only if a fresh institutional framework can be put in place, which would be one of the most optimistic of the possible fallouts of the present initiative.

But if one does not treat the working class (in the Institute) as an undifferentiated entity and analyses at some depth the peculiarities of the several sections which constitute it, one gets a better understanding of the situation. Workers with social moorings in the immediate vicinity of the Institute generally get higher wages than the migrant workers. Taking the case of cleaning workers as an example, most of whom belong to the *Valmiki* caste and stay in an adjoining area to the campus; they are paid higher wages than almost all other categories of workers. The fact that most of the workers of Samiti also belong to this category further substantiates the understanding, that any kind of organising initiative is more likely to be successful among workers with local linkages. In the case of Samiti, besides a strong organisational initiative (through the workers' cooperative) the other important factor for its success has been the presence of a dynamic social organisation at their living place—the *Valmiki Samaj*. This caste based organisation helped in fostering a strong sense of identification among the members and also acted as a social arbitrator on several contentious issues. Thus a combination of factors like entry barriers in the labour market (due to caste biases), organisation at the work place as well as at the living place buttressed by a strong middle class support and a relatively liberal corporate environment of the public sector Institute have helped in pushing up the wages for these workers and have also facilitated in sustaining an effort like Samiti. Significantly the Institute authorities have recently been voicing their concern for what they claim to be "too much money being spent in sanitation work", (it is actually a small fraction of massive expenditures of the institute), and are contemplating to "use technology" to *curtail* the costs. This development suggests that, wherever workers achieve even a semblance of associational power, in this case through Samiti and *Valmiki Samaj*, there is an endeavour to break it, as in this case through a 'technological fix' (Silver, 2003).

To conclude, the case signifies that progressive labour policies are imperative to ensure fair wages to the contingent work force. And yet only having a formal policy is not enough under the offensive of present neo-liberal order given the political reality at the ground level. The civil society must also intervene at the grassroots and be committed for a long haul. And even then, any tangible change will come only if middle class action is combined with a vibrant working class movement. Only if economic struggles are combined with political movements will they reach anywhere, where it can potentially give meaning to a progressive policy framework. The point that has to be noted here is that the policy framework (like the present Minimum Wages Act and Contract Labour Act) is a relic of another era and the challenge is to find innovative ways to make it practical for the present context instead of working only for progressive policies on paper. For instance, in the US, the relatively more unionised states have significantly higher minimum wages than the federal indicating that minimum wages and its implementation above all is a matter of politics (Johnson, 2002; Levin-Waldman, 1998). Discerning readers will realise that we have not even raised the most fundamental issue, that of cultural aspects, like democratic relations between the working and the middle classes and nature of collective consciousness, etc. But in spite of these shortcomings this present attempt based on a daily practice of concerned middle class individuals to make democracy 'un-extraordinary' (Lachelier, 2002) is probably worth the narrative. In the final analysis whether they would be able to achieve any success in institutionalising the issues or would end up being co-opted into the larger administrative framework still remains a question (Selznick, 1966).

APPENDIX

Nature of Contracts and Contractors and Variety of Issues Involved in Monitoring Minimum Wages

The Institute has several types of contract work in the campus and they can be broadly classified as: cleaning, messing, security, civil maintenance & painting, horticulture (gardening), and construction. Of these the first three are perennial contracts and the rest except for construction are partly perennial and partly need based and each of them present different sets of complications with respect to monitoring of wages. Wage monitoring is the most difficult in construction as these workers are confined to their site or their living quarters, which are usually outside the campus (see the description below). The perennial contracts are relatively easier to keep track of, as the work is well defined and there is constant user interface and contacts are for at least one year. To start with the Committee has been concentrating on ensuring minimum wages in these contracts. A brief description of the complexities of some of the contracts is brought out through specific examples below.

Krishna Housekeeping

This contractor has many cleaning related contracts in the campus, like garbage disposal and hostel cleaning, etc. The first contract was for garbage disposal and in fact he bagged this contract from the Samiti in 1999, who were doing it since 1992. All the workers employed by him belong to the *Valmiki* caste, who live in the neighbouring locality. Also, many of them are related to the workers of Samiti. Because of this connections with the earlier agitating workers as well as a semblance of job security because of the caste dynamics (as no other caste will take up the 'dirty' work of cleaning!), the workers have been persistent with their complaints. He was the first contractor monitored by the MCW and, over the five years since the Committee was formed, several complaints have been filed against him. Initially he showed the 'extra' amount (the difference between actual wages and those disbursed) as advance paid. Later when he had to pay even advance in the wage office, he started taking money back by threatening the workers. But the workers also persisted with their complaints, including there have been incidents of dismissal when workers have refused to pay back. The Committee has accumulated a massive record of complaints against him and has been demanding strict action against the contractor. Though fresh contracts have been given to him, yet in some ways he symbolises the distance that the committee has travelled. When the monitoring began, informal reports suggested that he used to deduct Rs. 20-30/ from a wage rate of Rs. 70/ per day; today when the minimum wage for the cleaning work is Rs. 85/ he is able to take back only about Rs. 10-12/. From all accounts workers face less repression at work also, as they keep threatening him with complaints to the committee. But all this 'progress' remains tenuous given the deterioration in local labour markets – it is simple to find cleaning workers for Rs. 40/ to 50/ a day. The last we heard is that he is attempting to reduce the local workers and bring workers from 'outside'.

Food Supply Co.

Several messes in the hostels have been privatised in the last five years and Food Supply Co. this contractor has bagged many contracts for messing. It has also been another persistent target of the Committee due to the never-ending number of complaints against him. This contractor operates at multiple locations in the country and has got his workers from far off towns. Interestingly for a mess contract in Mumbai, he has booked virtually a whole compartment and taken around 50 young men from the neighbourhood, while consistently refusing to employ any local youth for the Institute messes! He has rented an accommodation and keeps all his migrant workers there. The workers report to work at 7.00 am and stay there practically for the whole day and are let off only after dinner around 11.00 pm (there are short breaks in between two meals). This is the routine for all the days of the week and they get unpaid leave to go home only during the lean period when the hostel strength is less due to the vacations, etc. The contract specifies number of workers for every kind of work—cooking, serving, cleaning, coupons, supervision, etc and the contractor is supposed to maintain the workforce irrespective of the volume of work all through the year. His payments, though, are made on the basis of number of students dining. The contractor provides the workers with food in the mess itself. In spite of having such tight control over his workers, there have been persistent complaints by them against the contractor. The first dispute happened over a procedural matter on the very first occasion he came to the wage office. The volunteer present objected to the policy of deducting almost 1/3rd of the wages for the food provided pointing out that it was against the law. Then there were complaints that though he showed full amount, actually he showed less attendance and/or took money back later. But when he showed less attendance the volunteers cross-checked his claims by calculating the man days as specified in the contract and when they were found to be significantly lower (approx. 1000 against 1400 in the contract), his payments from the Institute were deducted proportionately for the month. In anther case reported against him it was alleged that when a worker refused to give the money back, he was beaten up badly and the committee asked the Institute to setup an inquiry committee. In spite of an unfavourable report, he got another mess contract, but the workers have kept complaining and the Committee has tried to find ways of checking the malpractices. In the latest move the wardens have agreed to a proposal of the MCW wherein the volunteers can talk to the workers on minimum wages, make surprise checks of attendance records and even keep parallel attendance records. Further the contractor has been asked to provide ID cards to all his workers, and make available a duty roster of his workers to the Committee.

Construction Work

As mentioned in the Earthline case above there are layers of contractors in such work for the workers and most of the time these are migrant workers. Here is a part description of workers of a subcontractor on a hostel construction site by a MW volunteer in 2004:

Most of the contractors belong to the same place from where

they get the workers. For instance we were told about the petty contractor from Malda. He takes charge of his workers right from the moment they step out of their village—travelling, food, etc. He gets them for 50 days and pays them any amount ranging from Rs. 3000 to 4000. He even gets a maharaj for cooking meals. But the people apparently have to work for 14 hours everyday for 50 days to get their money. Even their food is served at the work site. The 50 days are nonnegotiable; even if somebody is unwell he is expected to go for work. It is reported that one old man died recently because he had to keep working in spite of being unwell.

Endnotes

1. The names of the two authors are only in an alphabetical order. The real authors of the story are all the volunteers of the minimum wage group, who over the years, have kept trying under difficult circumstances. Of course, the story is being written only because the contingent workers in the campus have continued to voice their concerns while working against tremendous odds. The purpose of this piece is to acknowledge their extra-ordinary efforts. Finally, we must clarify that the case does not, in our opinion, reflects negatively on the Institute in isolation. If anything, the case relates how at least a section of the campus residents and authorities have attempted at improving the matters as will be evident to the readers of this piece. In fact we would like to see such attempts and better in various other campuses and establishments.
2. In a country like India where the majority of the population do not have access to even the basic requirements of health, nutrition and education and have no effective state sponsored social security system either, the effect of free market has been particularly devastating. The unorganised workforce, which constitutes over 90 percent of the total working population of the country, is very vulnerable in terms of security of their employment and working conditions. In a labour surplus economy the contract workers are largely non-unionised and do not have access to any of the benefits available to the organised sector. They often have to settle for meagre wages, long hours of work and harsh work conditions. At present there is a statutorily prescribed minimum wage (MW) for a variety of work in the unorganised sector as per the Minimum Wages Act 1948. The government regularly (every six months) revises it according to the fluctuations of the price index. MW in the government gazette is based upon the nature of job—skilled, semi-skilled, and unskilled; the setting—rural, urban; or the type of job—agriculture, construction, factory, etc.

3. The present note is based on our participant observation, as both of us stay in the campus and have been involved with the minimum wage issue almost since the beginning of the account narrated here. Though both of us have been part of the group of volunteers, and one of us teaches in the Institute, yet neither of us has been involved either with the Institute or the minimum wage issue in any official capacity.
4. For the present study it will be referred to as the Institute.
5. Formed in the name of an important 19th century religious and social reformer by some of the campus residents—students, faculty members and their family members.
6. The migrant workers of India are some of the most exploited sections of the population. Most of them come from rural areas and constitute the large proportions of landless workers of the economy. During the four months of the monsoon they find some employment in the local context but the rest of the year the workers, sometimes the whole family, go to far flung areas in search of subsistence. The most destitute of the lot are often kept as bonded labour by the contractor. Some slightly better off are able to scrape some savings which goes primarily to repay a debt back 'home', or under extremely fortuitous circumstances, maybe even to buy a piece of land.
7. An even less economically developed area of the neighbouring state of Madhya Pradesh, now a separate state of Chattisgarh.
8. The children of construction workers often do not have access to any formal education partly because most sites do not offer any schooling facilities and also because of the temporary nature of their parents' jobs wherein they have to keep moving from one construction site to another in quest of employment.
9. The Contract Labour Act, 1970 requires that the wages be paid in presence of a representative of the principal employer to ensure fair practices, but in reality this was not the case. Therefore though records showed that fair wages were being paid, it was only on paper, but it was very hard to find formal evidence for the malpractice. Contractors would pay the full wages in front of the committee representatives, but take the 'surplus' back from the workers later, or worse, threaten to strike work when pushed further. Of course the Institute's priorities were quite clear – no 'trouble' was permitted which hampered 'work'.
10. Earlier the Institute used to issue the approximate number of man-days required for each job put out on a contract. This ensured some kind of a baseline approximation of the cost of the project. In several instances Samiti had been able to ward off unfair competition by campaigning for

disqualification of all bids whose value amounted to less than the value arrived at by simply MWs multiplied by the specified number of man-days. Samiti with lesser overheads could often bag contracts by bidding the lowest of all valid bids and still be able to pay the MWs. But later the Institute refused to specify estimated number of man-days even in labour intensive jobs like sanitation and cleaning. An example of the kind of absurd situation it led to is what happened in 1999 when a contractor could outbid Samiti on the Institute Garbage Cleaning contract (the mainstay of Samiti at the time) by a bid which was practically half of the previous year's (Samiti had the contract at that time) while the specified work had actually doubled. When asked how such a contractor could pay MWs, the concerned authority retorted "who knows, he may pay from his pocket, let's give him a chance (!)".

11. An association of faculty members.
12. Names of the actors have been disguised to maintain anonymity and the cases are used merely as illustrations of general practice.
13. Generally the practice for such large contract like this building is that the Institute awards the contract to one 'big' contractor. But what actually happens is that the main contractor in turn carves out 'petty' contracts for small-local contractors who bring their own set of labour; at times there may be multiple layers in the process. This process streamlines the dealings of the Institute but often at the cost of the worker. The Institute actually has to shell out a much larger sum of money for the same work as the charges of the big contractors like the Earthline are much higher than smaller operators, while often only fractions of the stipulated wages reach the workers. The blame of non-payment of minimum wages get pinned down to the last layer of sub-contractor above the workers who most of the times are very small operators with resources barely above the workers themselves.
14. The policy of awarding the contract to the lowest quote irrespective of the feasibility of such a quote, if minimum wages and other labour laws were enforced.

References

Association of Community Organisations for Reform Now (ACORN) 2001, Living Wage Success: A compilation of living wage policies on the books. <*http://www.livingwagecampaign.org*>

Card, David & Krueger, Alan B. 1994, Minimum Wages and Employment: A case study of the fast-food industry in New Jersey and Pennsylvania. *The American Economic Review*, 84, 4, 772–793.

Champlin, Dell P. & Knoedler, Janet T. 2002, Wages in Public Interest: Insights from Thorstein Veblen and J. M. Clark. *Journal of Economic Issues*, 36, 4, 877–891.

Dickens, Richard, Machin, Stephen & Manning, Alan 1999, The Effects of Minimum Wages on Employment: Theory and evidence. *Journal of Labor Economics*, 17, 1, 1–22.

Johnson, Colleen F. 2002, The Politics of Minimum Wage Legislation in the Western United States: Lessons in policy and power. *Journal of Economic Issues*, 36, 2, 331–337.

Lachelier, Paul 2002, Making History, Making Democracy Un-extraordinary: Harvard students make history. *Center for Critical Education, Inc.*

Levin-Waldman, Oren M. 2004, Policy Orthodoxies, the Minimum Wage, and the Challenge of Social Science. *Journal of Economic Issues*, 38, 1, 139–154.

Levin-Waldman, Oren M. 1998, Exploring the Politics of Minimum Wage. *Journal of Economic Issues*, 32, 3, 773–802.

Neumark, David & Wascher, William 2000, Minimum Wages and Employment: A case study of the fast-food industry in New Jersey and Pennsylvania: Comment. *The American Economic Review*, 90, 5, 1362–1396.

Pischke, Jorn-Steffen 2005, Laour Market Institutions, Wages, and Investment: Review and implications. *CESifo Economic Studies*, 51, 1, 47–75.

Selznick, Philip 1966, *TVA and the Grassroots*. New York: Harper & Row.

Silver, Beverly J. 2003, *Forces of Labor: Workers' Movements and Globalization since 1870*. Cambridge: Cambridge University Press.

Varman, R. & Chakrabarti, M. 2004, Contradictions of Democracy in a Workers' Cooperative. *Organization Studies*, 25, 2, 183-208.

Waltman, Jerold 2000, *The Politics of the Minimum Wage*. Urbana, Ill.: University of Illinois Press.

21

LABOUR EMPLOYMENT IN PUNJAB AGRICULTURE AND THE STATE POLICIES

M.S. Toor, S.S. Chahal and H.S. Kingra

I. Introduction

The transformation of agriculture in Punjab through increase in area under irrigation and high yielding varieties, application of fertilizers along with effective price policy, particularly for wheat and rice crops, was accompanied by increase in employment in agriculture up to early eighties. The simultaneous and massive use of labour saving techniques like mechanization of farm operations, use of herbicides and harvesting combines coupled with slow down in productivity of two major crops wheat and rice since mid 1980s, gradually overpowered the growth in agricultural employment (Oberai and Ahmed, 1981). Consequently, the demand for human labour in the crop sector in the state had decreased significantly since late 1980s (Sidhu and Grewal, 1991). Various Rounds of NSS data for the country as a whole also revealed the decline in rural employment, along with informalization, casualization and feminization of rural employment (NSSO 2000, Chadha, 2001 and Biradar and Bagalhoti, 2001). The growth rate of rural employment in Punjab during 1983-94 was negative (-2 per cent) which improved to 1.5 per cent during 1994-2000. This improvement in growth rate of rural employment in Punjab during 1994-2000 was mainly due to the growth of labour intensive dairy sector, which fully compensated the fall in demand for labour in crop sector. In case of small and marginal farmers, the dairy accounted for about two-third and four-fifth of their utilized family labour respectively.

After cultivators, agricultural labour is the largest rural worker category accounting for 30.5% of total rural workers, slightly lower than that for India as a whole (31.8%). Agricultural labour accounts for as much as 88.4% of the total rural labour in the state, with the rest being mainly brick kiln workers (10.8%). Further, about 25% of the agricultural labour is migrant, and 2/3rd casual. Major reasons behind casualization of farm labour in the state have been mechanization of major farm operations, inflow of migrant labour, slow down of agricultural growth, and non-viability of small and marginal holdings (Singh, 2003).

It is also evident that there was a moderate shift of rural workers from agriculture to non-agriculture until late 1980s and virtual stagnation in early 1990s. Even this growth of non-agriculture employment was being growth led or distress induced is still inconclusive (Parathasarthy, 1998 and Biradar and Bagalhoti, 2001). This shifting pattern of rural employment should be viewed in the light of decline in proportion of small and marginal holdings during nineties in Punjab as many of these small holdings found it difficult to survive and disappeared by leasing out their land to medium and large size categories. Due to unfavorable nature and structure of industrial sector in the state, these cultivators were not absorbed outside agriculture. It is due to the above facts about unfavorable facets and dimensions of rural employment in Punjab since 1980s on one hand and the annual growth rate of labour force of 2.5 per cent on the other have become the central theme for research and debate at various levels to generate gainful employment in agriculture. Various studies have shown that well organized and integrated farming system with crops and other labour intensive enterprises like dairy, poultry, vegetable, fruits, mushrooms, etc. can significantly increase the income and employment of farm families particularly small and marginal farmers having surplus family labour (Pasha 1991, Saleth 1997, Singh and Sharma 1988, Bhalla 2004). The introduction of these enterprises is not possible without the proper guidance and help from the government sector. The role the state lies in creating proper infrastructure and a set of policies conducive for employment generation. This study has been undertaken with a view to examine the employment scenario on the one hand and role of state policies on the other.

II. Result and Discussion

i) Shifting of Rural Workforce

In an agrarian economy like Punjab, farming and related activities constitute the basic fabric of rural setups, thus contributing significantly towards income, employment and the quality of life. However, the significance of agriculture in terms of its capacity to absorb labour force in adequate number has been declining. In other words, it could not keep pace with the ever-increasing labour force. This does not lessen the potential role of farming in the rural development of Punjab, but the contribution of alternative economic activities in the non-farm sector, which may offer durable prospects of income, employment and economic progress, should also be considered.

Table 1: Classification of Workers and Non-workers in Punjab, 1991 and 2001

(Per cent)

Particulars	*Rural*		*Urban*		*Total*	
	1991	*2001*	*1991*	*2001*	*1991*	*2001*
Workers	71.23	69.82	28.77	30.18	30.87	37.58
Non-workers	70.10	63.77	29.90	36.23	69.13	62.42
Total population	70.45	66.04	29.55	33.96	100.00	100.00

Source: Census of India, 1991 and 2001.

Although, a substantial decrease was witnessed in the share of rural population in Punjab during the last decade, yet it continues to be a predominantly rural state as 66.04 per cent of its population still lives in the rural areas (Table 1). As such, the share of rural population declined from 70.45 per cent in 1991 to 66.04 percent in 2001. The share of workers was 30.87 per cent in 1991, which increased to 37.58 per cent in 2001. In spite of this increase of working population on the whole, the share of rural workers has registered a decline of 1.41 per cent points in 2001 over 1991. On the other hand, the share of urban workers increased from 28.77 per cent in 1991 to 30.18 percent in 2001. This indicated a shift of rural workers to urban areas (1.41 per cent), albeit, not as significant as the shift in population from rural to urban areas (4.41 per cent).

ii) Composition of Workers

The composition of workers showed that there was a decline in the proportion of agricultural workers in Punjab (Table 2). It has declined from 55.26 per cent (31.44 per cent cultivators and 23.82 per cent agricultural labourers) in 1991 to 39.36 per cent (22.96 per cent cultivators and 16.40 per cent agricultural labourers) in 2001. The results further revealed that the proportion of non-agricultural workers increased from 44.74 per cent (1.33 per cent household industry workers and 43.41 per cent other workers) in 1991 to 60.64 per cent (3.36 per cent household industry workers and 57.28 per cent other workers) in 2001. This indicated a shift of 15.90 per cent workers (8.48 per cent cultivators and 7.42 per cent agricultural labourers) from agricultural to non-agricultural sector from 1991 to 2001. This shift was more discernible in the rural areas as compared to urban areas and was constituted jointly by cultivators and agricultural labourers. The respective figures were 11.30 and 8.75 per cent for rural workers while 2.36 and 2.96 per cent for urban workers.

Table 2: Composition of Workers in Punjab, 1991 and 2001

(Per cent)

Particulars	*Rural*		*Urban*		*Total*	
	1991	*2001*	*1991*	*2001*	*1991*	*2001*
Cultivators	42.81	31.51	4.18	1.82	31.44	22.96
Agricultural labourers	30.75	22.00	7.23	4.27	23.82	16.40
Household industry workers	1.17	3.13	1.72	8.55	1.33	3.36
Other workers	25.27	43.36	86.87	85.36	43.41	57.28
Total workers	100.00	100.00	100.00	100.00	100.00	100.00

Source: Census of India, 1991 and 2001.

iii) Change in Literacy Rate

The relevance of education for the progress of the rural society in general, for bridging the rural urban gap and for strengthening the grass root development of the economy, needs hardly to be questioned. Education would be an extremely important input for economy of the future; it just cannot be sustained by the army of the present-day illiterate rural workers (Chadha, 2003). Education, as interpreted in a proper sense, produces better economic men, responsible citizens and sensible negotiators. Further, the per worker productivity is invariably higher, in all fields of economic activities, among the educated group of workers than among the illiterates or low-educated ones, is hardly a disputed fact. Moreover, the increasing level of literacy over time has been creating awareness among the rural population to go in for alternative employment activities either in allied agricultural sector or in the non-farm sector. Consequently, the considerable increment in rural work force seems to have been absorbed in diverse non-farm occupations (Eapen, 1994, Kashyap and Desai, 1990, Bhat *et al* 1996 and Chahal *et al* 1996,). In this backdrop, the role of government in providing education and its impact on employment in rural Punjab can be viewed.

The information relating to literacy rate in Punjab (Table 3) showed that during the period of 1961 to 2001, a significant change has been noticed as for as the education of rural and urban areas is concerned. In case of rural areas 219.3 percent increase was calculated during the above-mentioned period whereas this change was about 65.5 per cent relating to urban areas.

Table 3: Literacy Rate in Punjab by Sex and Area, 1961 - 2001

(Per cent)

Year	*Rural*			*Urban*			*Total*		
	Male	*Female*	*Total*	*Male*	*Female*	*Total*	*Male*	*Female*	*Total*
1961	28.12	11.51	20.41	56.09	37.07	47.82	34.70	17.41	26.74
1971	34.69	19.87	27.81	58.55	45.41	52.49	40.40	25.90	33.67
1981	50.54	33.32	42.58	72.95	60.28	67.10	56.81	40.87	49.38
1991	60.71	43.85	52.77	77.26	66.12	72.08	65.66	50.41	58.50

2001	71.70	57.91	65.16	82.97	74.63	79.13	75.63	63.55	69.95
% Increase (1961-2001)	154.9	403.1	219.3	47.9	97.9	65.5	117.9	265.0	161.6

Source: Census of India, 1991 and 2001.

However, this increase in literacy rate was 161.6 per cent in case of Punjab state as a whole. Further, the change is more in case of education of females as compared to males in both rural as well as in urban areas. This seems to be due to the fact that during 1961 very little attention has been paid to the education of females in comparison to their male counterparts as compared to the year 2001.

iv) Distribution of Gross State Domestic Product

The performance of various sectors of the economy can be viewed from the share of these sectors in the gross state domestic product. The share of different sectors at 1993-94 prices in Punjab economy is presented in table 4. It is evident from the table that the share of agriculture and livestock remained at the top. It ranges from 45.80 per cent in 1993-94 to 37.24 percent in 2002-03. Agriculture and livestock are responsible for making primary sector as the major contributor towards gross state domestic product. Further, the share of secondary sector remained almost stagnate at 21.77 per cent in 1993-94 and 23.16 per cent in 2002-03 in Punjab State. The share of territory sector showed some growth from 32.10 per cent in 1993-94 to 39.01 percent in 2002-03. As agriculture and livestock remained major contributors, emphasis should be given to the proper development of this sector in the coming years to sustain the growth of state domestic product in the state.

Table: 4 Distribution of Gross State Domestic Product by Economic Activity at 1993-94 prices in Punjab (1993-94 to 2002-03) (percentage)

Economic activity	*1993-94*	*1997-98*	*1999-00*	*2000-01*	*2001-02*	*2002-03*
Agriculture and Livestock	45.82	40.16	39.74	39.22	38.90	37.24
Agriculture	33.06	26.69	26.98	26.76	26.42	24.43
b) Livestock	12.76	13.47	12.76	12.46	12.48	12.81
Forestry and Logging	0.13	0.13	0.14	0.14	0.13	0.13

Fishing	0.19	0.31	0.36	0.38	0.42	0.46
Mining and Quarrying	0.01	0.00	0.00	0.00	0.00	0.00
Sub total of Primary Sec.	46.15	40.60	40.24	39.74	39.45	37.83
Secondary Sector	21.73	23.85	23.48	23.49	22.96	23.16
Tertiary Sector	32.12	35.55	36.28	36.77	37.59	39.01

Source: Economic Survey of Punjab, 2004.

v) Distribution of Land Holdings

The distribution of land holdings is very important as farm incomes along with the level of technological adoption depends on the size of the farm. Over time, size of the farm is going down in Punjab state as well as at national level. This change has been occurred due ever increasing population. The distribution in case of Punjab State has been given in table 5.

It is revealed from the table that 1,22,760 holdings falling in the size group up to 1 hectare out of the total 9,97,372 holdings comprising 12.31 per cent. Further, it is also observed from the table that 62.57 percent of the holdings are below 4 hectares of land. Again only 37.43 per cent of the land holdings having farm size more than four hectares. The share of holdings of area more than 20 hectares is only 1.17 per cent. This showed that the distribution of land holdings is not equitable in nature as for as different size categories are concerned.

Table: 5 Distribution of operational holdings in Punjab, 2000-01

Size (ha)	*No. of holdings*	*% to total*	*Cumulative no. of holdings*	*Cumulative percentage*
Up to 0.5	42055	4.22	42055	4.22
0.5-1.00	80705	8.09	122760	12.31
1.00-2.00	173071	17.35	295831	29.66
2.00-3.00	214765	21.53	510596	51.19
3.00-4.00	113466	11.38	624062	62.57
4.00-5.00	127770	12.81	751832	75.38
5.00-7.50	118043	11.84	869875	87.22
7.50-10.00	55141	5.53	925016	92.75
10.00-20.00	60660	6.08	985676	98.83

>20	11696	1.17	997372	100.00
Total	997372	100.00	–	

Source: Department of Agriculture, Punjab Chandigarh.

vi) Declining Crop-wise Labour Employment

It is observed that human labour employment on different crop enterprises declined over time due to higher use of machinery and other chemical inputs. To examine this change, the use of various inputs has been reviewed by analyzing the data from 1981-82 to 2000-01. The information relating to wheat, paddy and cotton crop and changing pattern of input use is given in table 6. It can be seen from the table that the per hectare use of human labour on wheat, paddy and cotton declined by 29.44, 50.38 and 6.45 per cent respectively during the study period. The bullock labour has been almost vanished in case of all these crops over the study period. Further, in case of machine use, an upward shift was calculated to the tune of 58.28, 118.81 and 215.83 per cent relating to wheat, paddy and cotton crop respectively. The use of chemical input also increased by 843.71, 115.69 and 808.90 per cent for these three crops respectively. The yield level of wheat crop showed an upward trend of 48.39 per cent whereas the increase in yield was observed to the extent of 36.08 per cent in case of cotton crop during 1981-82 to 2000-01. However, in case of paddy crop, the yield level remains almost stagnant. It is concluded from this analysis that over time, human labour had been replaced by intensive use of machinery and chemical inputs.

vii) Agricultural Diversification and Labour

Crop diversification plan adopted by the Punjab government becomes the basis of agricultural diversification policy in the state during the last decade. Contract farming being used to bring about diversification, is practiced in vegetable, fruits and cereals crops by both multinational companies and local firms. The contracts specify quantity, quality, acreage, timing, marketing channel and price of the produce to be grown by the participating farmers. The contracting companies also provide seedlings on part credit basis and specify production practices and inputs to be used

Table 6

Changing Pattern of Labour and Other Input Use on Traditional Crop in Punjab

(1981-82 to 2000-01)

Input	*Wheat*				*Rice*				*Cotton (cleaned)*			
	81-82	*91-92*	*2000-01*	*% Change over 81-82*	*81-82*	*91-92*	*2000-01*	*% Change over 81-82*	*81-82*	*91-92*	*2000-01*	*% Change over 81-82*
Human labour days	47.99	40.36	33.86	-29.44	107.19	73.13	53.19	-50.38	97.32	107.74	91.04	-6.45
Bullock labour days	3.93	1.04	0.44	-88.80	4.56	0.91	0.05	-98.90	4.96	1.29	0.48	-90.32
Machinery (Rupees)	474.24	526.0	750.62	58.28	310.21	445.16	678.76	118.81	216.67	379.20	684.30	215.83
Chemical use (Rupees)	22.51	92.27	212.43	843.7	119.36	155.49	257.45	115.69	144.44	527.29	1312.82	808.90
Yield Qt./hect.	30.75	38.34	45.63	48.39	29.57	32.57	35.06	18.57	3.16	5.88	4.30	36.08

Source: Various CACP reports and cost of cultivation.

on the particular crop. The participating farmers benefited by assured marketing and the firms benefited on account of assured quantity and quality of the major input. Further this contracting plan has led to more and better employment opportunities for labour, especially the women in rural areas. The labour use intensity of tomato, potato and other vegetable crops is much higher than that of the traditional crops, as farm operations are not much mechanized due to easy availability of cheap labour. The labour intensity was 640 hours per hectare for potato, and 3600-4000 hours per hectare for tomato, as against only 740 hours per hectare for paddy. Thus, employment in vegetable crops like tomato is 5 times higher than that of in paddy crop. This has come as a big employment boom in contract production pockets of the state as the mechanisation of sowing and harvesting operations of paddy and wheat crops had reduced manual work to negligible (Singh, 2003).

viii) Contract Farming Plan of Punjab Government

The Punjab government has made a plan of area to be diverted from paddy-wheat rotation to other crops for the period ranging from 2003 to 2007. In the first year four lakh acres were proposed to be diverted to the high value crops and up to 2007, total area planned will be twenty-five lakh acres (Table- 7). Punjab Agro Food grains Corporation Ltd. is implementing agency of Crop Diversification Programmes through Contract Farming Programmes. The Programme was taken during Rabi-2002 with new and other identified crops viz. Hyola (hybrid rapeseed mustard), Barley (high malt content), Winter Maize, Spring Maize, Sunflower and winter vegetables. An area of 22312 acres was brought under these crops. During Kharif 2003-04 the crops identified were Basmati paddy, Maize, Guar, Moong and Castor and an area of 1.27 lakh acres were brought under these crops. Again in Rabi 2003-04 another crop Durum wheat was grown on 0.60 lakh acres of land.

Table: 7 Contract Farming Plan of Punjab Government for Period 2003-2007

Target Plan in acres

Sr. No.	*Crop*	*2003*	*2004*	*2005*	*2006*	*2007*
1.	Hyola	75000	200000	300000	400000	500000
2.	Barley	5000	15000	25000	40000	70000
3.	Winter Maize	3000	5000	11000	12500	15000
44.	Durum Wheat	100000	200000	300000	400000	500000
55.	Sunflower	12500	40000	100000	150000	225000
6.	Spring Com	5000	15000	15000	40000	80000
7.	Basmati	25000	50000	70000	100000	150000
8.	Kharif Corn	150000	300000	400000	500000	700000
9.	Guar Gum	5000	6000	7500	10000	14500
10.	Castor/Jastropha	5000	10000	20000	40000	50000
11.	Groundnut	1000	1500	15000	20000	25000
12.	Organic Basmati	1000	3000	5000	7000	15000
13.	Vegetables	2000	4000	6000	10000	20000
14.	Others	10500	50500	25500	70500	135500
15.	Total	400000	900000	1300000	1800000	2500000

Source: Deptt. of Agriculture, Punjab.

During Kharif season of 2004-05 an area of 0.86 lakh acres has been allocated to new crops and during Rabi an area of 1.53 lakh acres is expected to be brought under the diversification Programme through Contract Farming Programme.

III. Summary and Conclusions

The present study brought out that the share of agriculture sector in gross state domestic product has declined. The significance of agriculture in terms of its capacity to absorb labour force in adequate number has been declining. In other words, it could not keep pace with the ever-increasing labour force. The interesting feature noticed was casualization of agricultural labour in case of both male and female work force. Major reasons behind casualization of farm labour in the state have been mechanization of major farm operations, inflow of migrant labour, slow down of agricultural growth, and non-viability of small and marginal holdings. Further, the use of human labour in the production of wheat, paddy and cotton crops has been declined over a period of time. This decline is attributed to higher use of machinery and chemical inputs on these crops. There was a moderate shift of rural workers from agriculture to non-agriculture but due to unfavorable nature and structure of industrial sector in the state, these cultivators were not absorbed outside agriculture. It is concluded that the well organized and integrated farming system with crops and other labour intensive enterprises like dairy, poultry, vegetable, fruits, mushrooms, etc. can significantly increase the income and employment of farm families particularly small and marginal farmers having surplus family labour. As agriculture and livestock remained major contributors in state gross domestic product, emphasis should be given to the proper development of this sector in the coming years to sustain the growth of state domestic product. As the introduction of these enterprises is not possible without the proper guidance and help from the government sector, role of the state lies in creating proper infrastructure and a set of policies conducive for employment generation. Crop diversification policy of the state government is a good effort on this account during the last decade. This has led to better employment opportunities for agricultural labour, especially women in the rural areas. The policy of creating Rural Business Hubs will also be helpful in creating gainful employment in rural areas. Under this scheme, the government and the private sector would extend assistance in creating proper business environment along with marketing of the produce. These policy measures will be helpful for generating employment opportunities and improving the economic conditions of the rural economy of the state.

References

Bhalla, Kushal (2004), An Economic Analysis of Different Farming Systems in Ludhiana District of Punjab State, Unpublished *M. Sc. Thesis*, Punjab Agricultural University, Ludhiana.

Bhat, K.S., Nirmala, V. and Joseph, A. (1996), Socio-economic and Political Determinants of Shifting of Workers from Primary Sector to Non-primary Sector in Indian States, *Indian Journal of Labour Economics*, 39: 879.

Biradar, R.R. and S.T. Bagalhoti (2001), Changing Facets of Employment in Rural India: Emerging Issues and Challenges, *Indian Journal of Agricultural Economics*, 56 (3): 538-52.

Chadha, C.K. (2001), Impact of economic reforms on rural employment: No Smooth Sailing Anticipated, Keynote Paper, *Indian Journal of Agricultural Economics*, 56 (3): 492-525.

Chadha, G.K. (2003), Indian Agriculture in the New Millennium: Human Response to Technology Challenges, *Indian Journal of Agricultural Economics*, 58:1-31.

Chahal, S.S., Dhawan, K.C. and Kumar, R. (1996), Non-farm employment and wage pattern in Rural Punjab: A Case Study, *Manpower Journal*, 32: 33-40.

Eapen, M. (1994), Rural Non-agricultural Employment in Kerala: Some Emerging Tendencies, *Economic and Political Weekly*, 29: 1285-96.

Kashyap, S.P. and Desai, R. (1990), *Employment Scenario: A Sub-zonal View*, Agro-climate Regional Planning Unit, Planning Commission, Ahmedabad.

NSSO (2000), Report on employment and unemployment in India, 1999-2000: Key results. SS 55th Round July 1999- June 2000, *Report* No.455 (55/60) December, New Delhi.

Oberai, A.S. and Iftikhar Ahmed (1981), Labour use in Dynamic Agriculture –Evidence from Punjab, *Economic and Political Weekly*, 16(3): AI-A4.

Parthasarthy, G. Shameem and B. Sambi Reddy (1981), Determinants of Rural non-Agricultural Employment: The India Case, *Indian Journal of Agricultural Economics*, 53 (2).

Pasha, S.A. (1991), Sustainability and Viability of Small and Marginal Farmers, *Economic and Political Weekly*, 26, A-27-30.

Saleth, R.M. (1997), Diversification strategy for small farmers and landless: Some Evidence from Tamil Nadu. *Indian Journal of Agricultural Economics*, 52: 73-86.

Sidhu, R.S. and S.S. Grewal (1991), Demand for human labour in Punjab agriculture: An Econometric Analysis. *Indian Journal of Agricultural Economics*, 46 (2).

Singh, J.S. and A.K. Sharma (1988), Income and employment increasing possibilities under different farming systems on small farms in mid-western region of U.P. *Agricultural Situation in India*, 43: 17-23.

Singh, S. (2003), Reaching the Rural Poor under Globalization and Structural Adjustment Regimes in India: The Institutional Dimensions" in *Indian Economic Association Conference (86th) Volume of the Millennium*, IEA, Calcutta, 741-748.

22

EFFECTIVE LABOUR MANAGEMENT RELATIONS IN A PUBLIC SECTOR GIANT

*A. Jagan Mohan Reddy**

Introduction

With the attainment of independence and with the launching of planning era, serious and earnest efforts have been made towards rapid economic development of India. India has made an ambitious and critically important effort to raise the living standards of her people by an integrated, industrial and economic development plan. Due to rapid and planned industrial development the size of industrial labour in India has increased remarkably. The increase in industrial labour led to the formation and development of trade unions and various social groups.

It has been recognized that management without labour would be sterile and labour without management would be disorganized, ill equipped and ineffective. Further, it has also been realized that the concrete co-operation between labour and management is highly essential to fulfill the individual, organization and national goals. The First Five Year Plan has clearly demonstrated the fact that, "an economy organized for planned production and distribution, aiming at the realization of social justice and the welfare of masses can function effectively only in an atmosphere of industrial peace"[1].

All these necessitate the maintenance of harmonious industrial relations so as to maintain higher productivity to fulfill the goals of the Five Year Plans in India. The investment in and the scope of industries in India have been growing plan after plan. Much of the success or failure of Indian Five Year Plans would be dependent on the maintenance of harmonious employee-employer relations. Frequent industrial conflicts not only affect the management and labour but also tend to impoverish the community as a whole. They lead to wastage, foment class hatred, embitter mutual relations and inflict damages on the progress of the nation. They affect production and national income in an adverse manner. They also clog the progress and development of the nation.

Need for Industrial Peace

The objective of maintenance of industrial peace is not only to find out ways and means to solve conflicts or to settle differences but also to secure the unreserved cooperation of and goodwill among different groups in industry with a view to drive their energies and interest towards economically viable, commercially feasible, financially profitable and socially desirable channels. It also aims at the development of a sense of mutual confidence, dependence and respect and at the same time encouraging them to come closer to each other for removing misunderstandings, redressing grievances, if any, in a peaceful atmosphere and with open mind and fostering industrial pursuits for mutual benefits and social progress. But the maintenance of congenial industrial relations, particularly in a democratic society like ours is not only a significant task but also a complicated one.

The case of Singareni Collieries Company Ltd (SCCL) is a turnaround story of a Colliery. Paradoxically all those forces and factors that led to the sickness of the unit transformed it into a success story. As we all know, coal continues to occupy the centre stage of India's energy scenario, considering the limited reserve potentiality of petroleum and natural gas, eco-conservation restriction on hydel projects and geo-political perception of nuclear power. In the light of this, it is worth looking into the turnaround strategy of SCCL and the role of industrial relations in putting the company back on the path to progress.

SCCL: A Brief Profile

Singereni Collieries which commenced coal-mining operations in 1889 at Yellandu in Khamman district of Andhra Pradesh (Earlier known as "Hyderabad Deccan Company Ltd), came under State control in 1949 and became a government company under Companies Act of 1956. Now it is jointly owned by the Government of Andhra Pradesh and the Government of India with equity participation in the ratio of 51:49.

In view of the growing energy requirements and in pursuance of the socialistic policies of the government the emphasis was more on enhancing coal production rather than project viability. But frequent strikes, law and order problems, low productivity, apart from the un-remunerative coal price vis-à-vis cost of production during the period 1989-1990 to 1991-92 affected the financial health of the company.

Package Approved in March, 1994

- Equity contribution of Rs.487 crores by Govt. of AP and Rs. 402 by Govt. of India
- Waiver of outstanding and penal interest
- Adhoc coal price increase of Rs. 30 per tonne

Restructuring of operations with a liberal financial package from the government (see the box) and reduction in production cost, due to a series of progressive reforms saved the company from the brink of a possible closure.

However, the company faced rough weather due to several factors such as non-revision of coal prices after June 1994, major strikes by workmen in 1995-96 etc. As a result the company was not able to generate adequate internal resources to meet capital investment requirement of its mines and became sick and on finalization of its accounts for the year 1995–96 was again referred to BISR.

Let's have a look at the status of SCCL as on 31st March, 1997:

Manpower		1, 13, 823
No. of mines		71
a. Underground	60	
b. Open cast	11	
Production per annum		28.73 millions tons
Output per manshift (OMS)		0.98 tonnes
Turnaround		Rs. 1796 crores
Accumulated losses		Rs. 1296 crores

So during 1996-97 the SCCL was experiencing a stormy weather with its financial performance-hitting rock bottom with accumulated losses of over Rs. 1200 crores. Its other maladies included low quality of coal, no customer focus, old and obsolete technology etc.

One of the important reforms introduced by Singareni Collieries was in the area of industrial relations, which were strained and hindered the growth of the company. The large number of trade unions and frequent strikes badly affected production and led to confrontations.

Before we have a look at the strategy adopted, *of which maintenance of sound and cordial industrial relations formed an important part,* initiatives taken which resulted in *a spectacular turnaround of this company* let's consider the industrial relations climate prevailing in the pre-turn around period. Because the frequent IR problems in the pre-1997 period adversely affected machine utilization resulting in increase in the cost of production which impacted the bottom lines of the company.

Industrial Relations at SCCL in the Pre-Reform/Pre-turnaournd Period

Though the coal mining activity started in SCCL in the year 1889 organized labour movement started at a later date. Due to illiteracy and ignorance of workers, repressive methods were adopted by the labour contractors and the then Government of Hyderabad. As a result workers organized strikes during 1921, 1922 and 1935. But the real movement of trade unionism started with the establishment of AITUC under the name of SC Workers Union in 1945 at Kothagudem as its Head office. The Tandur Coal Mines Labour Union (presently SCML Union) started at Bellampalli in 1949 under the influence of INTUC Leaders.

After 1950 trade union movement grew by leaps and bounds and the figure touched 90 by February, 2003 out of which 65 were graft unions/associations. But by and large industrial relations (IR) scenario was satisfactory prior to 1976-77. Because there were less number of craft associations/ splinter trade unions and less inter-union rivalry. Further, law and order in coal belt areas was peaceful, like in other parts of the state, with almost no extremist activities in coal belt areas. There was no whipping of sentiments and emotions of workmen by external forces and the general tendency on the part of workmen was to obey the instructions of the management.

Year	*No. of mines*	*Manpower strikes*	*No. of*	*Man days lost*	*Production lost*
1976-77	44	53,741	12	35,387	44,791
1977-78	47	58,503	73	1,71,131	1,97,283
1978-79	49	62,160	185	8,37,687	7,74,204
1979-80	50	64,870	376	6,41,251	7,02,757
1980-81	51	68,031	360	6,26,874	6,82,036
1981-82	51	76,587	212	6,97,636	7,79,181
1982-83	53	83,109	453	12,45,129	14,91,635
1983-84	57	87,570	460	14,24,072	14,09,796

Source: Personnel Department - SCCL.

Industrial Relations During 1976-77 to 1983-84

Industrial Relations during the period 1976-77 to 1983-84 (details are given below) were not satisfactory and characterized by a number of illegal and cat call strikes. The reasons for unsatisfactory industrial relations are proliferation of craft associations/splinter trade unions, emergence of new unions affiliated to BMS, HMS, IFTU and inter-union rivalry. Further, there was a tendency to give strike calls on sectarian demands by craft association and extremist organizations started influencing the trade unions and workmen. Majority of the workmen chose to go by the trade unions, good or bad and didn't give credence to the management views/ versions.

The Eighth Plan period (1992 to 1997) witnessed one of the worst phases in the history of SCCL. There was a spurt in activities of militant trade unions especially during the period 1989 to 1993.

Industrial Relations in SCCL

1985-86	225
1989-90	450
1990-91	440
1991-92	475
1992-93	425
1993-94	240
1996-97	310

Source: Personnel Department, SCCL.

The number of strikes reached a peak of 475 nos in 1991-92. There were multiple trade unions and the management had no details of actual patronage of workers. The average no. of strikes during 1989 to 1993 was 447 with a production loss of 1.83 million tonnes per year. This had contributed to gross indiscipline and deterioration in work norms in the company. As a result the mine management was constantly engaged in industrial relation issues and could not concentrate on mine planning and improvement of production and productivity.

Further, efforts made by the management to enforce work norms were stoutly opposed by the trade unions. Poor communication with workmen and their lack of awareness about the financial position of the company helped the trade unions to mislead the work force and organize catcall strikes. In other words, management of SCCL failed to communicate the significance of change in the work culture and as such faced a strong opposition to the introduction of technological innovations. Some of the major reasons that could be attributed to more no. of strikes and consequent unsatisfactory IR's which impacted the performance of the company adversely pushing it to the brink of closure, are as under:

- Proliferation of craft associations/splinter trade unions numbering about 77.
- Acute inter-union rivalry and one upmanship attitude on the part of the trade union leaders.
- Absence of specific well laid down IR and personnel policies.
- Workmen being excessively conscious about non-existing rights and lack of sense of belongingness towards the organization.

In a nutshell SCCL's IR problems during the pre-reform period were as under:

- There were nearly 100 trade unions vying with each other for supremacy and catcall/illegal strikes were a common feature.
- Spurt in activities of militant trade unions like SIKASA (A banned outfit of people's war group) especially during the period from 1989-90 to 1992-93.
- Competition and one-upmanship attitude among multiple trade unions resulting in more no. of strikes.

So frequent strikes, law and order problems and high cost of production during the period 1989-90 to 1991-92 affected badly the financial health of the company. Further, the low literacy levels, extreme hardships in working conditions, strong opposition to innovation and change-worsened workforce–management relationship.

Industrial Relations SCCL in Post–Reform Period

When the going gets tough,
The tough gets going

As we all know, troubles for companies, much like for individual and countries, come not as a spy or two but in battalions. But successful and resilient companies, like great individuals and nations of character, emerge stronger from testing times. Singareni Collieries Company Ltd emerged stronger and victorious. The reforms story of SCCL has many marvelous facets but most significantly reforms were humane, logical and transparent. The traditional perceptions of role of management, labour, technology etc. were redefined and made allies in the building and growth of the company. Let's look at the success story.

As the company's accumulated losses rose to Rs.1296 crores, as on 31-3-1997, and the performance had hit rock bottom (the worst ever in its history of over 100 years) the need for urgent remedial action was realized. The management identified the areas for introducing the reforms, articulated the needed change and brought about a phenomenal turnaround. Further, the introspection and open brainstorming sessions made the problems clear and the lateral approach to finding solutions strengthened the plan of comeback. The table below gives in nutshell about the problems identified, historic errors committed and the new approach adopted by the SCCL's management for revamping its operations in order to put the company back on the growth track.

SCCL's innovative and Changed perceptions at a Glance

Problems identified	*Historic errors*	*New approach*
Industrial unrest through multiplicity of trade unions	Succumbing or reacting to wild catcalls/strikes	Unifying trade unions through path breaking elections
Low literacy and awareness among workforce	Neglecting the issue	A high pitch communication drive harnessing media, launching literacy programs
Poor quality of life for workers	Lip service or ignore issue	Focused multi-faceted workers' welfare programme
Inefficient and high cost of over burden removal operations	Persisting with status quo	Establishing outsourcing of non-core and ancillary activities through public-private partnerships
Management inacc-essible to labour force at large	Oblivious to issue, maintaining distant management style	Innovative programs launched like Dial-your-GM, field visits, interactions, follow-ups
Huge interest payments	Accumulating losses, banked on Govern-ment's write-offs or support	Used innovative financial instruments like debt swaps

Little customer care or quality consciousness	Oblivious to issue. Bank on regulatory industry status	Fuel supply agreements, technology infusion for quality testing, work force visits to client's sites
Lack of clear corporate blue print for growth	Sporadic moves	Focus on safety, environment protection, labour welfare.

As can be seen from the above, the company decided to take on the problems head on and because of the innovative/ creature turnaround strategy (*of which effective labour-management relations was an important one*) adopted by the company, which was more humane, logical and transparent eventually the entire work force including the trade unions and leaders also backed the plan and *made the comeback possible*. Now let's look at some of the key elements of turnaround / reform strategy adopted by the company.

Turnaround Strategy of SCCL

1. *Trade Union Elections:* For the first time in the history of the coal industry in India. Trade union elections were held in September, 1998 in SCCL Further, elections were held under secret ballot system to elect one recognized union at the company level and one representative union at the area level. This put in place a mechanism that enabled mine managers to concentrate more on production and productivity matters. The company successfully conducted trade union elections in 1998, 2001 and 2003. As a result the following benefits accrued:
   - No wild catcall strikes
   - Negotiations became easy
   - The move provided foundation for the greater shift in thrust from a protected environ to a fiercely competitive market condition and from employee–management confrontation state to one of partnership

- The management harnessed the first step towards consolidating industrial relations.

2. *Financial Reconstructing Package:* Government of India approved a package in 1999, which included infusion of fresh equity of Rs. 268 crores by Government of Andhra Pradesh, Rs.257 crores by Government of India, ten-year interest free moratorium on overdue interest, rescheduling of central loans etc.
3. *Financial Re-Engineering:* This included discharging of high-interest bearing central loans (17 & 16%), liquidating receivables through which company saved Rs. 61 crores in a 4 year period.
4. *Cost cutting measures:* The company undertook several cost-cutting measures such as:
   - Rationalization/right sizing of manpower through the introduction of voluntary retirement scheme.
   - Energy conservation in mines/townships and reducing power pilferage in colonies.
   - Inventory reduction by adopting rate contracts for spares and fast moving items.
5. *Use of IT:* Underground Mine management system was introduced for the first time in the Indian coal industry at Kothagudem.
6. *Customer–centric measures:* Customer meets have been arranged for getting first hand details of their grievances. Further, automotive samplers and electronic weigh bridges were installed to avoid quality and quantity disputes.

Since industrial relations is major factor in ensuring positive work atmosphere let's have a look at the specific HR and welfare strategy with in the overall turnaround strategy, adopted by the company.

Human Resource Strategy

The management grasped the potential risk of lack of strong internal communication and work force reach out programs. Further, there has also been a growing perception among the work force that the management is isolated, distant and insensitive to the needs of the workmen. Therefore, the management realized that an effective two-way communication is necessary to achieve understanding and co-operation at all the levels.

Most of the difficulties in the communication process in SCCL were due to its labour intensive nature of the industry with majority of the work force being illiterate and unaware of conventional rules and procedures and the directions in which the company should be moving. Apart from this, another important barrier was the geographical distance between employees of the organization in terms of location of miner spread cover 350 km in 4 districts.

With a view to bring about awareness among the workmen, maintain transparency in administration etc company took several initiatives some of which are as under:

A. Communication cells: The Company opened communication cells, which used TV as a medium for bringing home the key issues facing the company. The company also disseminated information to its employees through in-house magazine "Singereni Vaarthalu". Further, apart from conducting pro-active press meets, posters and pamphlets too were used to educate workmen on various issues.

B. Multi-Departmental Teams: Multi-departmental teams, comprising of members drawn from various disciplines, visited mines and departments to high light the performance of the company and the issues concerning production, safety, welfare etc. These teams used local language, dialect and visual aids to communicate effectively. Further, suggestions were invited and implemented wherever possible.

C. Literacy drive: To achieve total literacy among employees, a scheme called, "Telugu in 7 days" was launched with the help of a NRI and many employees are participating in this campaign.

D. Education: Apart from the 2 colleges and 22 schools being managed (providing education to 13386 students) by "The Singereni Collieries Education Society", established by SCCL, the company has provided land/

infrastructure to private schools on a nominal rent basis.

In addition to the above the welfare measures taken by the company include:

- Providing (47, 250 quarters) housing to employees
- Amenities like recreation clubs (33) stadia (11), and community halls (10)
- Supplying drinking water to its colonies and surrounding habitat
- Medical and health facilities— 7 hospitals with 1006 beds, 43 dispensaries.

Results of Turnaround

The process of turning around a sick company—which commenced in 1997-98, reached its logical conclusion when SCCL totally wiped out its accumulated losses and entered the financial year 2003-2004 with a net profit of Rs.80.45 crore.

Comparative Performance

	Pre- 1997 (1996-97)	*Post – 1997 (2004- 05)*
Man power	1,14,486	91,097
Coal production pa	28.73 million tonnes	35.30 million tonnes
Output per manshift (ons)	0.98	1.62 tonnes
No. of strikes	310	14
Turn over	Rs.2114 crores	Rs. 3413.73 crores
Net profit	(-) 1219 crores	Rs. 361.26 crores

Source: Personnel Department, SCCL.

The results of turnaround can be seen when we have a look at the comparative performance of the company during the pre-1997 and post 1997 period i.e., pre and post reform periods. The paradigm shift from strike culture to work culture at SCCL was made possible because of the innovative and bold initiatives taken by the company which made even the workers and their trade unions to reason out and a partnership culture slowly ushered in a much turbulent and disturbed terrain.

Challenges Ahead

Singereni Colleries completed the turnaround from a loss making PSU into a profitable one. With huge coal deposits and growing demands from the energy sector in particular, the company is gearing up for highest production challenges.

The emerging challenges for the company could be:

- Possible reduction in import duty of coal
- Rationalization of railway freight rates
- Tightening environmental stipulations
- Discovery of gas reserves in Krishna-Godavari Basin in AP and consequent impact on SCCL market share.

Conclusion

The establishment of good industrial relations depends on the constructive attitude on the part of both management and the union. The constructive attitude in its turn depends on all the basic policies and procedures laid down in any organization for the promotion of healthy industrial relations. It depends on the ability of the employers and trade union to deal with their mutual problems freely independently with responsibility. The case of SCCL demonstrates the vitality of maintaining cordial relations between the labour and management in setting aside a situation of mutual acrimony and distrust into an atmosphere of partnering and caring. This case can be picked up by other organizations passing through similar phases and try to emulate its practices to tide over tough times. SCCL is now looking to reinvent itself backed by smart management, motivated workforce and responsible leadership of workforce. This public sector giant in the coal industry is keen on providing investing opportunities, competing in a more market-oriented scenario and preparing itself for further possible changes in the future.

CONTRIBUTORS

1. Dr. L. Mishra is Former Union Labour Secretary, Former Senior Adviser, ILO, ROAP, Bangkok, Hony Professor, IMI, Delhi.
2. Dr. A.Venkateswarlu is Fellow, at Centre for Economic and Social Studies, Hyderabad.
3. Dr. Dipa Mukherjee Lecturer, Narasinha Dutt College, Howrah, West Bengal.
3. Dr. Rajarshi Majumder is Lecturer, Department of Economics, University of Burdwan, West Bengal.
4. Dr. K. Alamar is Reader & Head Department of Economics (Centre for Research) Arul Anandar College (Autonomous), Karumathur.
4. Dr. N. Murali is Reader, Department of Economics (Centre for Research) Arul Anandar College (Autonomous), Karumathur.
5. Dr. S.V. Hariharan is Professor of International Economics, School of Economics, Madurai Kamaraj University, Madurai – 625 021.
6. Dr. Errol D Souza is Professor, Economics Area, Indian Institute of Management, Ahmedabad – 380 015.
7. Dr. Maniklal Adhikary is Professor, Department of Economics, University of Burdwan Golapbag, Burdwan, West Bengal, PIN 713104.
7. Dr. Ritwik Mazumder is LecturerDepartment of Economics, Assam University, Silchar, Assam PIN 788011.
8. Dr. Golak Bihari Nath is Principal, Gandhi Mahavidyalay, Deogaon, Rourkela, Dist. Sundargarh, Orissa, PIN – 769 004.
9. Dr. L. J. Perry is Faculty Member at School of Finance and Economics, University of Technology, Sydney. PO Box 123, Broadway NSW.

10. Dr. Sib Ranjan Misra is Professor of Economics & Politics, Visva-Bharati, Santiniketan, Dist. Birbhum, West Bengal.
11. Dr. Shyam Bahadur Katuwal is Lecturer, Faculty of Management, Tribhuban University Post Graduate Campus, Biratnagar, Nepal.
12. Dr. Vandana Upadhyay is Senior Lecturer, Department of Economics, Rajiv Gandhi University, Itanagar, Arunachal Pradesh.
13. Dr (Mrs.) Nirmala Kumari is Lecturer, University Department of Industrial Relations and Personnel Management, T.M. Bhagalpur University, Bhagalpur, Bihar, PIN – 812 002
14. Dr. Prakash S. Kamble is Faculty at Venutai Chavan College, KARAD, Dist. Satara, PIN - 415 124, Maharashtra.
15. Dr Anupama, Lecturer, Department of Economics, Punjabi University Regional Center, Bathinda, Punjab.
16. Dr. P. Madhavi is Reader, Department of Commerce, Kasthurba Ghandhi Degree & P. G. College for Women, West Marredpally, Secunderabad – 500 026.
17. Dr. Arti Nanavati is Professor of Economics, Department of Economics, M.S. University of Baroda, Vadodara.
18. Dr. D. V. Giri, is Professor, Department of Industrial Relations and Personnel Management, Berhampur University, Berhampur-760 007, Orissa.
18. Dr. P. C. Das is Director, State Labour Institute, Bhubaneswar, Orissa.
19. Dr. Mini Goyal, Associate Professor of Economics, Punjab Agricultural University, Ludhiana.
19. Dr. Pratibha Goyal, Associate Professor of Business Management, Punjab Agricultural University, Ludhiana.
20. Dr. Manali Chakrabarti is with Institute of Development Studies, Kolkata.
20. Dr. Rahul Varman is with Indian Institute of Technology, Kanpur.
21. Dr. M. S. Toor, Associate Professor, Department of Economics, Punjab Agricultural University, Ludhiana-141 004.
21. Dr. S. S. Chahal, Senior Economist (Marketing), Department of Economics, Punjab Agricultural University, Ludhiana-141 004.
21. H. S. Kingra is Assistant Farm Economist, Department of Economics, Punjab Agricultural University, Ludhiana-141 004.
22. Dr. A. Jagan Mohan Reddy is Associate Professor (HR), Osmania University Campus, Hyderabad – 500 007.

INDEX